CENTRAL AMERICA SINCE INDEPENDENCE

The following titles drawn from
The Cambridge History of Latin America edited by Leslie Bethell
are available in hardcover and paperback:

Colonial Spanish America

Colonial Brazil

The Independence of Latin America

Spanish America after Independence, *c.* 1820 – *c.* 1870

Brazil: Empire and Republic, 1822–1930

Latin America: Economy and Society, 1870–1930

Mexico since Independence

Central America since Independence

CENTRAL AMERICA
SINCE
INDEPENDENCE

edited by
LESLIE BETHELL
Professor of Latin American History
University of London

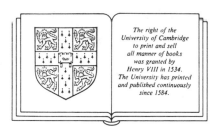

CAMBRIDGE UNIVERSITY PRESS
Cambridge
New York   Port Chester   Melbourne   Sydney

Published by the Press Syndicate of the University of Cambridge
The Pitt Building, Trumpington Street, Cambridge CB2 1RP
40 West 20th Street, New York, NY 10011, USA
10 Stamford Road, Oakleigh, Melbourne 3166, Australia

The contents of this book were previously published as parts of volumes III, V and VII of *The Cambridge History of Latin America*, copyright © Cambridge University Press, 1985, 1986, 1990.

© Cambridge University Press 1991

First published 1991

Printed in the United States of America

Library of Congress Cataloging-in-Publication Data

Central America since Independence / edited by Leslie Bethell.

p.   cm.

"The contents of this book were previously published as parts of
volumes III, V, and VII of The Cambridge history of Latin America
. . . 1985, 1986, 1990" – T.p. verso.

Includes bibliographical references (p.   ) and index.

ISBN 0-521-41307-9 (hardback). – ISBN 0-521-42373-2 (paperback)

1. Central America – History – 1821–1951.   2. Central America –
History – 1951–   I. Bethell, Leslie.   II. Title: Cambridge history
of Latin America.

F1438.C3824   1991

972.805 – dc20   91-9093

British Library Cataloguing in Publication Data

Central America since independence. – (The Cambridge history
of Latin America).

1. Central America, history

I. Bethell, Leslie

972.804

ISBN 0–521–41307–9 hardback
ISBN 0–521–42373–2 paperback

CONTENTS

MAPS

PREFACE

The Cambridge History of Latin America is a large scale, collaborative, multi-volume history of Latin America during the five centuries from the first contacts between Europeans and the native peoples of the Americas in the late fifteenth and early sixteenth centuries to the present.

Central America since Independence brings together chapters from Volumes III, V, and VII of *The Cambridge History* to provide in a single volume an economic, social, and political history of Central America since independence from Spain (and Mexico) in 1821–3. There are general chapters on Central America covering the periods 1821–1870, 1870–1930, and 1930 to the present, followed by chapters on each of the five Central American republics – Guatemala, El Salvador, Honduras, Nicaragua, and Costa Rica – since 1930. This, it is hoped, will be useful for both teachers and students of Latin American history and of contemporary Latin America. Each chapter is accompanied by a bibliographical essay.

1

THE AFTERMATH OF INDEPENDENCE, 1821 − c. 1870

The first half century of national independence was an unhappy time for the provinces formerly comprising the kingdom of Guatemala: Guatemala, El Salvador, Honduras, Nicaragua and Costa Rica.[1] Tensions in the economic and social structures of the late colonial period led to bitter political struggles and civil war, and the high expectations expressed by Central American leaders at the beginning of the period were soon dashed on the hard rock of reality. Economic stagnation, class antagonism, political tyranny and anarchy replaced the relative tranquillity and stability of the Hispanic era. Instead of a united and prosperous independent isthmian nation, a fragmented and feuding cluster of city states calling themselves 'republics' had emerged by 1870. Nevertheless, however disappointing the rate of economic and social change, some important and necessary steps had been taken in the transition from colonialism to modern capitalist dependency.

Historians of Latin America often pass rapidly over Central American independence with the suggestion that it came about merely as a natural consequence of Mexican independence. It is true that Central America was spared the bloody wars that characterized the struggles for independence in Mexico and Spanish South America. Central American creoles did not seize control of the government following Napoleon's invasion of Spain in 1808. Peninsular rule continued in Guatemala City until 1821. And independence when it came was the result of an act of an assembly of notables who on 15 September 1821 accepted the *fait accompli* of Agustín de Iturbide's Plan of Iguala. However, during the first two decades of the nineteenth century the kingdom of Guatemala had experienced severe

---

[1] Chiapas, a province of the kingdom of Guatemala, joined Mexico at independence. Panama was a province of the viceroyalty of New Granada and became part of the republic of Gran Colombia.

economic stress and social dislocation, and significant political activity. The conflicts of the years immediately preceding independence bear directly on the issues that disrupted the Central American union during the half century after 1821.

The period 1810–14, in particular, witnessed the beginnings of the political struggles in Central America that were to last for decades. There were creole conspiracies and rebellions in El Salvador, Nicaragua and Honduras as early as 1811 and 1812 and, towards the end of 1813, in the capital itself, but the strong and efficient government of José de Bustamante y Guerra, captain general and president of the *audiencia* of Guatemala (1811–18), denied success to these movements. Meanwhile, the Cortes of Cádiz and the Constitution that it promulgated in 1812 provided political definition and substance for the emerging creole liberals who had already begun to articulate economic and social griev-ances. The Constitution of 1812 established freedom of the press, elections not only for city councils but new provincial bodies (*diputaciones provinciales*) and colonial representation in Spain; it pointed the way towards more representative government and more democratic proce-dures; it encouraged freer trade and threatened traditional *fueros* and monopolies. The political foundation of the Liberal Party in Central America and of much of its programme for the remainder of the century was laid.[2] Bustamante abhorred the Cádiz Constitution and did his best to prevent or delay its implementation. Finally, the restoration of Ferdinand VII in 1814 justified Bustamante's authoritarian dictatorship and his repression of the liberals. But his successor in 1818, Carlos Urrutia y Montoya, feeble with age and illness, first relaxed the strong-arm rule and then accepted the re-establishment of the 1812 Constitution following the Revolution of 1820 in Spain.

The 1812 Constitution had not only encouraged and strengthened liberal political arguments in Central America, but also emphasized the function of local and provincial governments in making decisions for themselves and in standing up against the traditional domination of the metropoli – Spain, Mexico or Guatemala. This regional resentment and the emergence of separatism in Central America can be documented in all of the provinces, but nowhere was it so obvious as in El Salvador. Long an integral part of the province of Guatemala, El Salvador had grown in importance in the eighteenth century as the principal producer of indigo, the kingdom's leading export. Following the destruction of Santiago de

[2] Mario Rodríguez, *The Cádiz experiment in Central America, 1808–1826* (Berkeley, 1978).

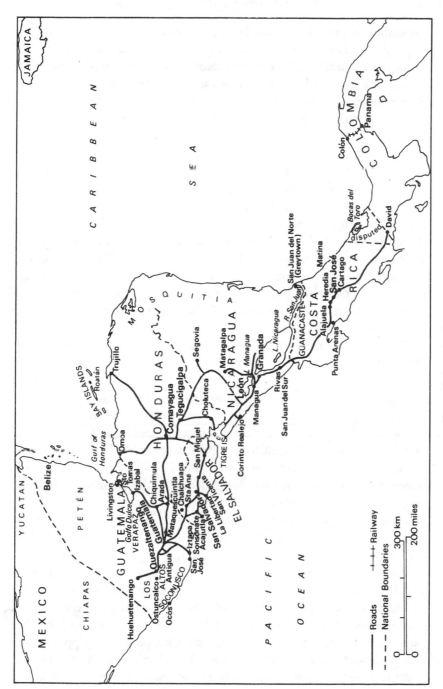

Central America in 1855

Guatemala in 1773 and its move to a new site about 40 kilometres away in 1776, San Salvador became the largest city in Central America and remained so until well after the establishment of independence. The creation of an intendancy in San Salvador in 1786 provided a degree of administrative autonomy for the first time and can be seen as the first step toward Salvadoran nationalism. Calls for ecclesiastical autonomy followed, as Salvadorans demanded their own bishop and separation from the diocese of Guatemala. The Cádiz reforms offered the Salvadoran creoles an opportunity for self-rule, and, understandably, San Salvador became a hotbed of liberal thought and action.

The resentment Salvadoran liberals felt towards what they termed the 'aristocracy' in Guatemala City, the conservative families (mostly creole) who controlled the land, the *consulado* and the *ayuntamiento*, was echoed in other provincial centres from Chiapas to Costa Rica. The restoration of the 1812 Constitution and the call for elections for the *ayuntamientos* and *diputaciones provinciales* in 1820 stimulated an increase in the level of political activity and a renewal of the political debate of 1811–14 throughout Central America.

Within the capital itself, the dialogue was between liberals and moderates and it was made public in the pages of two newspapers. *El Editor Constitucional,* directed by the fiery Pedro Molina, a physician of illegitimate parentage, without close ties to the principal families and representing the creole *letrados*, now for the first time challenged traditional institutions and the continuation of Spanish rule. Answering him was *El Amigo de la Patria,* edited by José Cecilio del Valle, who had come to the capital from a Honduran ranching family for an education and stayed to become one of the colony's leading intellectuals and a prominent attorney, widely respected among the creole elite. He had risen in position and importance during the Bustamante years as a loyal servant of that government, and his government connections caused him to counsel moderation and caution regarding independence. The leading creole families, led by the Aycinena clan, however, supported Molina's rabble-rousers, for they were now uneasy with the threats to their positions of prestige and monopoly that the return to power of the Spanish liberals promised. José del Valle, on the other hand, had the support of the colonial government, the Europeans, the opponents of free trade and the less wealthy creoles. The elections at the end of 1820 were not decisive, although Valle himself won election as *alcalde* of Guatemala City.

In February 1821 Iturbide began his rebellion in Mexico and news of his Plan of Iguala in favour of an independent monarchy spread southward. The new emphasis on local decision-making came into play, as the *ayuntamientos* in each city took it upon themselves to decide how they should react to events in Mexico. In Chiapas, the *ayuntamientos* of Comitán, Ciudad Real and Tuxtla each declared separately for the Plan respectively on 28 August and 3 and 5 September 1821 and joined independent Mexico. In Guatemala the acting Captain General, Gabino Gaínza, agreed on 14 September to the Diputación Provincial's request for a general meeting of the representatives of the principal institutions. In a stormy session the next day, creole and peninsular leaders debated the issues while a crowd outside clamoured for independence. In the end, the delegates, including most of the moderates led by José del Valle, voted in favour of independence. Virtually nothing else changed. The Spanish bureaucracy, headed by Gaínza, remained. The Guatemalan aristocracy were left in control of the government and the economy. Having escaped from the Spanish liberal regime, the creole elite no longer needed its alliance with Molina and the more radical of the local liberals; the Conservative Party was born.

It was intended that the decision taken in Guatemala City in favour of independence should apply to the entire kingdom, but the idea of local participation was now so powerful that each municipality voted separately as news travelled southward. All accepted independence from Spain, but there were variations in their approaches to the future. In San Salvador on 29 September a junta under the liberal leadership of Father José Matías Delgado proclaimed the independence of El Salvador and forced those who favoured union with Guatemala or Mexico to leave the city. Other Salvadoran towns responded differently and trouble broke out. Meanwhile, in Honduras Tegucigalpa accepted Guatemalan leadership while Comayagua insisted on independence from Guatemala as well as from Spain. Similarly, in Nicaragua conservative Granada promised to support the central government in Guatemala while León declared independence from Spain and Guatemala, although it was apparently willing to unite with Mexico! Costa Rica, remote and generally aloof from activities in the captaincy general, seceded from Spain on 27 October, leaving its position with respect to Guatemala and Mexico ambiguous while it established a provisional government completely independent of that in Nicaragua. But almost immediately its four major towns began to quarrel, as San José, Heredia and Alajuela vied for equality with Cartago, the colonial seat of power. As the national period opened, then, Central America was politically fragmented and caught up in a wave of regional and local acts of separation.

Annexation to Mexico became the first real issue clearly dividing conservatives and liberals. In general, conservatives all across Central America endorsed annexation, while liberals called for an independent republican federation. Because they controlled the apparatus of government in Guatemala and most of the other states, the conservatives succeeded in thwarting liberal efforts to resist annexation. Iturbide's dispatch of a Mexican army at the end of November furthered the annexationist cause. Violence flared in Guatemala and Nicaragua, but only in El Salvador did the republicans gain the upper hand. By the end of December 1821, 115 (104 unconditionally and 11 with certain stipulations) *ayuntamientos* had declared for incorporation into the Mexican empire. Another 32 left the matter to the provisional government while 21 declared that only a general congress could decide the issue. Only two *ayuntamientos* had opposed union absolutely, while 67 remained to be heard from. Also on the side of annexation was the powerful influence of Archbishop Ramón Casáus, who had only reluctantly accepted independence. On 5 January 1822 the provisional government declared that annexation was the overwhelming will of the country – as expressed through the *ayuntamientos* – and a few days later Gaínza, who remained titular head of state, prohibited further opposition to the decision. The provisional junta dissolved itself and Gaínza supervised a speedy election of delegates to the new congress in Mexico.

Only San Salvador and Granada rejected annexation outright, although division on the question continued in Costa Rica, where there was also sentiment for union with Colombia, and in Honduras, where the rivalry between Comayagua and Tegucigalpa continued. Led by Delgado, San Salvador turned to arms to maintain its position. Its forces, under the command of Manuel José de Arce, defeated Gaínza's Guatemalan army near Sonsonate, touching off a bloody war which was to continue intermittently for decades and was to poison chances for a successful Central American union. The arrival of a new captain-general, Vicente Filísola, with 600 Mexican troops proved decisive. Filísola took office on 22 June 1822 and immediately sought to reach a negotiated settlement. San Salvador entered into these talks apparently to buy time, for by November it was clear that the city would not submit peaceably to Mexican rule. Late that month Filísola invaded El Salvador with a force of two thousand. Frantically San Salvador sought a way out of its predicament, including a declaration of annexation to the United States. All failed, and the city capitulated on 10 February 1823. In the meantime, however, Granada continued to hold out against the annexationists in Nicaragua and in April in Costa Rica anti-Mexican troops from San José and Alajuela subdued the pro-imperial forces in Cartago.

Iturbide's empire, of course, was already doomed. While Filísola had subdued the liberals in El Salvador, liberals in Mexico had pronounced against the empire with the Plan of Casa Mata. After news arrived of the emperor's abdication, Filísola told the Guatemalan Diputación Provincial on 29 March that Mexico was in a state of anarchy. The provinces responded enthusiastically to his call for a Central American congress in accordance with the plan of 15 September 1821. Elections followed and the body which began its sessions on 24 June 1823 represented all of the states except Chiapas, which chose to remain with Mexico. Perhaps the most representative ever assembled by a Central American authority, this congress was decidedly more liberal than the previous government. Many of the conservatives were still in Mexico, and they had in any case been discredited by the collapse of the monarchy. Under the presidency of Father Delgado of El Salvador, on 1 July 1823 congress declared Central America free and independent and adopted the name *Provincias Unidas del Centro de América*, 'The United Provinces of the Centre of America'. The next day the congress became a National Constituent Assembly and set to work writing a republican constitution. Mexico recognized the United Provinces in August as Filísola and his army withdrew.

The new Central American republic began with rather naive expressions of unity and optimism for the future after nearly two years of disunion and chaos which were now blamed on Spain, Mexico and their 'servile supporters'. Despite the sudden turn of political events in favour of the liberals, the real situation in Central America was not conducive to the success of the sort of modern, progressive nation that the framers of the 1824 Constitution envisioned. Serious economic and social problems and divisions stood in the way.

The United Provinces, even with the loss of Chiapas and excluding Belize, had a population of more than a million persons.[3] (See Table 1)

---

[3] Contemporary estimates of the population vary widely and are of doubtful reliability. The estimates in Table 1 reflect an analysis of these estimates together with colonial and late nineteenth-century demographic data and an estimated growth rate of about 1.3% during the first fifty years of independence, taking into consideration some variations caused by local disasters, epidemics and other circumstances.

Table 1   *Estimated Population of Central America, 1820–70*
(Thousands of inhabitants)

State	1820	1830	1840	1850	1860	1870
Costa Rica	63	72	86	101	115	137
El Salvador	248	271	315	366	424	493
Guatemala	595	670	751	847	951	1080
Honduras	135	152	178	203	230	265
Nicaragua	186	220	242	274	278	337
Central America	1227	1385	1572	1791	1998	2312

Most were illiterate peasants or peons with little voice in the future of the country. About 65 per cent of the population of Central America were Indian, 31 per cent *ladino* (*mestizo* and mulatto) and only about 4 per cent white. Individual states varied considerably from these estimates, of course. Guatemala had a larger percentage of Indians than any other state, while Costa Rica's tiny population was predominantly white. El Salvador, Nicaragua and Honduras had substantial *ladino* populations. There were some blacks, principally along the Honduran and Nicaraguan coasts, but they were for the most part outside Central American society.[4]

The economy of Central America had experienced considerable change in the two decades prior to independence, which placed additional burdens on the new republic. Briefly, in the late eighteenth century the kingdom of Guatemala had become an important exporter of Salvadoran and Guatemalan indigo. Exports beyond the isthmus from the other provinces were not very great, but Honduras and Nicaragua, and to a lesser extent Costa Rica, were important suppliers of livestock and agricultural foodstuffs to the indigo-producing regions and administrative centre of the kingdom. Growing evidence suggests that the late colonial economy was, therefore, very much tied to the international

[4] Reliable statistics on the racial composition of the population do not exist, but for the whole region, see the estimates of Severo Martínez Peláez, *La patria del criollo, ensayo de interpretación de la realidad colonial guatemalteca* (Guatemala, 1971), 397–8. Martínez Peláez says that Nicaragua was 84% *ladino* at the close of the colonial period. Alejandro Marroquín, *Apreciación sociológica de la independencia* (San Salvador, 1964), 25–8, has calculated the following percentages for El Salvador in 1807 (not including Sonsonate and Ahuachapán, which were still part of Guatemala): Spaniards 0.86%; creoles 2%; *ladinos* 53.07%; negroes and mulattos 0.1%; Indians 43.07%. It is probable that the racial composition of the Central American population did not greatly change during the period, although the process of *mestizaje* certainly continued. It is also probable that, owing to European immigration, the percentage of whites in Central America very slightly increased during the period 1821–70.

economy and that there was significant integration of the economy within the kingdom.[5]

The rapid decline of Salvadoran indigo production during the first two decades of the nineteenth century, however, brought serious economic dislocation throughout Central America. Locust plagues, attacks on Spanish shipping and competition from other indigo-producing areas with better access to European markets contributed to this significant reduction of exports and forced planters in Salvador and Guatemala to shift to producing foodstuffs, in turn cutting back purchases of livestock and grain from Honduras, Nicaragua and Costa Rica. Thus, as the colonial period closed, the kingdom was becoming less interdependent and less tied to the international market. This meant reduced living standards at a time when heavy taxes and loan demands by the Spanish government during the Napoleonic Wars were additional burdens on the Central American elites.[6]

The Guatemalan aristocracy, understandably, looked towards expanding trade, the removal of economic restrictions and new exports, notably of cochineal, as a means out of their difficult straits. Some had already turned to contraband trade, principally through British Honduras, compounding their difficulties with the Bustamante regime. At the same time they opposed economic advancement for other elements of the society and after independence the basic conservatism of the dominant class became manifest. Opposing them, especially in the provinces, were representatives of the professions and middle sectors and government bureaucrats who saw in liberalism the opportunity for greater advancement and economic opportunity. Both factions represented only a tiny percentage of the total population; the mass of Indians and *ladinos* were outside the political debates. But the economic hard times were felt not only by the elites. Indeed, the spread of poverty among the urban poor increased social tensions at the time of independence and helped to provide soldiers for the armies of both sides in the conflicts that followed.

The issues that divided liberals from conservatives at the outset of the national period were not very different from those which divided

---

[5] See Alberto Lanuza Matamoros, 'Estructuras socioeconómicas, poder y estado en Nicaragua (1821–1875)', (unpublished thesis, University of Costa Rica at San José, 1976), 83–9.

[6] R. L. Woodward, Jr, *Class privilege and economic development: the Consulado de Comercio of Guatemala, 1793–1871* (Chapel Hill, N.C., 1966), 39–41; R. S. Smith, 'Indigo production and trade in colonial Guatemala', *Hispanic American Historical Review*, 39/2 (1959), 183; Miles Wortman, 'Government revenue and economic trends in Central America, 1787–1819', *loc. cit.*, 55/2 (1975), 262–4.

Spaniards at the same time, and they had largely been delineated in debates over the Cádiz Constitution of 1812. Conservatives felt more secure with a monarchy while the liberals were republican. The Spanish Bourbons had not endeared themselves to either group sufficiently to allow monarchy to remain an institution long cherished by the conservatives, but even after the issue of monarchy *versus* republic was apparently settled in 1824, Central American conservatives retained serious scepticism about the ability of any but the educated and propertied to govern. A more important institution in the liberal–conservative struggle was the Church. The liberals sought to disestablish it and remove it from political and economic power, while the conservatives cherished it as a defender of their privileges and a vital element in both controlling and securing the support of the masses. Liberals sought to destroy monopolistic control of the economy and to eliminate the *fueros* of the conservatives – ecclesiastical, commercial, university, etc. Education was an issue closely related to the Church controversy, for the liberals favoured secular education with mass education as the ultimate goal, while conservatives defended an elitist educational system under the supervision of the Church. Leaders in both parties recognized the need for modernization and a rational approach to economic problems, as the utilitarian influence of Jeremy Bentham on both sides illustrates. Although the leading families of Central America were connected across the region by ties of family and marriage, differing economic and political circumstances at the local level tended to divide them along conservative or liberal lines. At the outset, there was considerable political manoeuvring, but the bitter struggles that wracked Central America after independence removed much of the middle ground and crystallized the two parties into warring camps that would characterize Central American politics for the remainder of the century.

After the declaration of independence from Mexico (1 July 1823) the liberals at first dominated the National Constituent Assembly. They moved quickly to remove class privileges. On 23 July all titles of distinction, royalty or nobility, including even the use of 'don', were abolished. The same decree included anticlerical reforms; bishops and archbishops, for example, were stripped of any title except 'padre'.[7]

---

[7] Colonial terminology was also rejected: *audiencias* and *ayuntamientos* became, respectively, *cortes territoriales* and *municipalidades*. Later, other ceremonial forms, symbols and aristocratic vestiges were abolished (21 August 1823). 'Dios, Union, Libertad', replaced 'Dios guarde a Ud. muchos

Annulment of all acts of the imperial Mexican government and peremptory dismissal of Spanish and Mexican officials soon contributed to resentment against the liberals. The first violence flared in mid-September, when Captain Rafael Ariza y Torres led a revolt, ostensibly demanding backpay for the military. It resulted in a reshuffling of the government towards more conservative interests, but then liberal troops from El Salvador arrived to support the government. Civil war was averted, but Guatemalan residents resented strongly the presence of the Salvadorans and ill-feeling persisted even after the troops left. This uprising – and a pro-Spanish revolt which the army also quicky suppressed – revealed the unsettled conditions in Guatemala and the growing hostility to the liberal assembly. Inevitably, therefore, the balance of power in the assembly began to shift as debate over the proposed constitution continued. The document that finally emerged in November 1824 was a compromise between radicals and conservatives, and José del Valle played an important part in its formulation. It blended elements of the Spanish Constitution of 1812 with the U.S. Constitution of 1789. Dedicated to the protection of 'liberty, equality, security and property' (art. 2), the 1824 Constitution guaranteed Roman Catholicism as the religion of the state 'to the exclusion of the public exercise of any other' (art. 11), outlawed slavery (art. 13), and provided extensive guarantees of individual liberties (arts. 152–76). A complex system of indirect election provided for a unicameral federal congress (arts. 23–54). All legislation had to be approved by a senate composed of two senators from each state, no more than one of whom could be an ecclesiastic (art. 92), although the congress could override senate vetoes with a two-thirds vote, except in cases concerning taxation, which required a three-fourths majority (arts. 76–86). The president had no veto and was required to execute the law once it had passed the senate (arts. 87–8). The president, who also was commander-in-chief of the armed forces, and vice president were indirectly elected for four-year terms. A supreme court, also elected indirectly, had from five to seven justices serving two-year, staggered terms (arts. 132–40). The Constitution provided for a federation of five autonomous states with state assemblies, state executives and state judicial officers, whose first duty would be to form state

años' as the official compliment closing all correspondence (4 August 1823). Alejandro Marure, *Efemérides de los hechos notables acaecidos en la República de Centro-América desde el año de 1821 hasta el de 1842* (2nd edn, Guatemala, 1895), 11–12; Isidro Menéndez, comp., *Recopilación de las leyes del Salvador en Centro América* (2nd edn, San Salvador, 1956), I, 20, 126.

constitutions consistent with the federal charter. Each state was also to have a representative council, analogous to the federal senate, to approve legislative acts and advise state governors (arts. 177–95). The Constitution went into effect immediately, even before it was ratified by the first elected congress in August 1825.[8]

The first national elections were dominated by a spirited campaign between Salvadoran liberal Manuel José de Arce and moderate José del Valle, both members of the interim governing junta. Violence erupted in several places, and the government threatened those who opposed the new constitutional system with death. When the new congress convened in February 1825, presided over by Guatemalan Dr Mariano Gálvez, liberals appeared to have triumphed, yet the election for president in April favoured the more moderate José del Valle. Receiving 41 of the 79 electoral votes actually cast, he nevertheless lacked by one vote a majority of the 82 votes authorized, and thus the election was thrown into the Congress. Arce intrigued not only to win the presidency, but also to form a broadly-based coalition which, he believed, would allow the federal government to govern successfully. To this end he gained support from conservative members with assurances that he would not insist on a separate bishop for El Salvador. The congress elected Arce by a vote of 22–5. Valle refused to accept the vice-presidency, as did the liberal radical, José Francisco Barrundia, the position finally going to the Guatemalan conservative Mariano Beltranena. The new republic began its existence, therefore, under the cloud of suspicion of betrayal of the wishes of the electorate and with the extreme liberals (the Barrundia faction) already disenchanted with the liberal president, who they believed had sold out to the hated '*serviles*' (conservatives).

President Arce's government never really had effective control of any of the five states which made up the federation. Each continued to go its own way. State governments organized themselves in accordance with the Constitution, but in several there was serious disagreement between liberal and conservative factions. Arce had personally led the troops in pacifying Nicaragua early in 1825, but the peace he established there was but a brief interlude in the struggle between Granada and León. Costa Rica, under the firm hand of Juan Mora, remained aloof from the federal government and achieved a degree of order and progress. Serious trouble loomed in El Salvador, where the installation of Father Delgado

---

[8] 'Constitución Federal de 1824' in Ricardo Gallardo, *Las constituciones de la República Federal de Centro-América* (Madrid, 1958), II, 103–38.

as bishop faced opposition from Archbishop Casáus and Arce's coalition federal government in Guatemala City. This was a symbolic issue, representing the powerful Salvadoran urge for independence from Guatemala. The most urgent problem faced by Arce, however, was the Guatemalan state government, dominated by the liberal '*Fiebres*' and led by Juan Barrundia. That government proceeded along radical lines, repeatedly offending the more conservative elements in the federal government with whom Arce had allied. During Arce's first year in office the rift between the two governments widened. In April 1826 Arce deposed Barrundia and in September he placed him under arrest. The remainder of the Guatemalan state government, under Lieut. Governor Cirilio Flores, fled first to San Martín Jilotepeque and later to Quezaltenango, where the state legislature enacted inflamatory liberal laws, declaring children of the clergy legal inheritors of Church property, abolishing the merchant guild (*Consulado*), and cutting the *diezmo* in half. These laws were unenforceable, but they served as a basis for much liberal legislation after 1829. The liberals' tenure in Quezaltenango was short-lived, for in October a mob attacked Flores, tearing him literally limb from limb, and the liberal government collapsed.

A new Guatemalan state government under the conservative Mariano Aycinena now co-operated with President Arce in driving the remaining liberals from the state. But Salvadoran liberals now rose to challenge the pro-Arce government in San Salvador, touching off a bloody three-year civil war. Arce commanded the federal forces, but his government depended so heavily on the state of Guatemala that Aycinena soon supplanted him in importance. Bitterness and atrocities characterized both sides in this vicious struggle that spread over much of Guatemala, El Salvador and Honduras. In the latter state, Francisco Morazán rallied the liberals and, following his defeat of federal forces at La Trinidad, Honduras (10 November 1827), emerged as the leading liberal military figure. Arce now sought conciliation, and when that failed he resigned the presidency in February 1828. Vice-President Beltranena took over, but in reality Aycinena became the principal leader against the liberals. His government drew heavily on forced loans from the clergy and local wealthy citizens, including foreign merchants, causing the latter to welcome a liberal victory. Federal troops won a bloody and costly victory in March 1828 at Chalcuapa, but thereafter the tide turned in favour of General Morazán. Completing his reconquest of Honduras and El Salvador by the end of 1828, he invaded Guatemala early in 1829, laying siege to the capital in February, when the liberals re-established a state government at Antigua. Morazán's victory at Las Charcas on 15 March was decisive, although Aycinena did not finally capitulate until 12 April.

The immediate fruits of the civil war (1826–9) were a vindictive policy toward conservative leaders and the enactment of radical liberal legislation. José F. Barrundia presided over the republic until September 1830 when elections elevated Morazán to the presidency. Morazán defeated José del Valle who, unassociated with the Arce–Aycinena government in Guatemala, was now able to return to politics, although unable to stem the liberal landslide. Juan Barrundia was reinstated briefly as governor of Guatemala, but in 1831 Mariano Gálvez won election there. Although clearly in the liberal camp, Dr Gálvez was less radical than the Barrundias, and eventually a serious split would surface between them. Morazán also had allies in office in the three central states and liberals had the upper hand in Costa Rica, but opposition in all of these states soon began to limit their effectiveness. Difficulties within El Salvador contributed to Morazán's decision to move the national capital to San Salvador in 1834.

The presidential election of 1834 reflected widespread dissatisfaction with Morazán and his programme, and José del Valle successfully challenged his bid for re-election. Unfortunately for the moderate cause, however, Valle died before taking office, and Morazán, with the second highest number of votes, constitutionally remained as president. With José del Valle, it appears, died the last hope for a moderate course. Morazán's victory under these terms left widespread bitterness and resentment among moderates and conservatives. Their frustration turned to hatred as grievances against the liberals mounted.

The case of Guatemala state best illustrates the nature of the conflicts of the 1830s and their results. Gálvez shared Morazán's belief that Central America could become a modern, progressive republic through enlightened social and economic legislation. With the leading conservatives in exile, a period of peace and order seemed assured, as, armed with extraordinary powers to deal with opposition, the Gálvez government became the pilot for Morazán's liberal programme. Convinced that Spanish colonialism was at the root of their underdevelopment, they sought to destroy Hispanic institutions and to replace them by emulating the apparent success of the United States. In practice, however, although Gálvez gained substantial acceptance of his programme among the elite, he failed to overcome widespread opposition among the lower classes of the country.

The sources of opposition were several. Liberal trade policy had damaged seriously the native weaving industry, and Gálvez's tariff modifications were too late to protect it. More serious was a new direct head tax of two pesos per capita which contributed to peasant restlessness generally. In El Salvador such a tax resulted in widespread popular rebellion in 1833, forcing suspension of the levy there, but Gálvez maintained the tax in Guatemala. Heavy demands for forced labour to build roads and other public works intensified the resentment.

Another unpopular aspect of the liberal economic programme was the policy of promoting private acquisition of public or communal lands as a means of increasing production and exports. Cochineal expansion began to increase the demand for the land and labour of Indians and *ladinos* in central and eastern Guatemala. Moreover, a number of large grants to foreigners caused considerable unrest. British commercial activity at Belize had intensified the traditional suspicion of foreigners. Spanish colonial administrations had dealt vigorously with foreign interlopers, but since independence liberal policy had welcomed them, causing apprehension among those who believed themselves to be victims of foreign competition. Foreign influence was evident in many aspects of the Gálvez programme, but the concessions made to mahogany loggers and the projects to populate the northern and eastern areas of the country with English colonists caused residents of those regions to regard the liberals as favouring foreign rather than national interests. Between March and August 1834 the Guatemalan government ceded nearly all of its public land to foreign colonization companies. As the British hold on Belize, the Miskito Shore and the Bay Islands tightened, and as Anglo-American colonizers in Texas threw off Mexican rule, many Guatemalans began to doubt the wisdom of Gálvez's colonization schemes. Ignoring or suppressing petitions from residents against the colonization contracts, however, Gálvez rejected the idea that the liberals were betraying their country to Europeans. Revolts which broke out in Chiquimula and other eastern towns in the autumn of 1835 were possibly linked to an uprising in El Salvador against Morazán. Troops suppressed the rebellion, but the inhabitants remained resentful, especially after the arrival of the first shipload of British colonists in the middle of 1836.

Another part of the liberal programme which proved offensive to the rural masses was the attack on the clergy. Anticlericalism ran especially high since the Church had backed the conservative regime of Mariano Aycinena from 1826 to 1829. Morazán's federal government exiled many anti-liberal clergy, beginning with Archbishop Casáus. Following the suppression of the regular orders and the establishment of religious liberty, the federal government prevailed on state governments to continue the assault on the traditional power and privilege of the clergy. Between 1829 and 1831 Guatemala censored ecclesiastical correspondence, seized church funds and confiscated the property of religious houses. In 1832 Gálvez stopped the collection of the tithe, ended many religious holidays, confiscated more church property, decreed the right of the clergy to write their wills as they pleased and legitimized the inheritance of parents' property by children of the clergy. Later, the Guatemalan legislature authorized civil marriage, legalized divorce and removed education from church supervision. In Indian and *ladino* villages where parishioners were already chafing at Gálvez's policies on other grounds, the priests railed against a government that challenged their authority and attacked their sacred institutions, brought Protestant foreigners into the country and threatened the very foundations of society. These rural priests were in the vanguard of the uprisings that rocked Guatemala in 1837.

Further opposition to Liberal government was provoked by the new judicial system. Persuaded that the Hispanic system of private *fueros* and multiple courts was unjust and antiquated, the liberals adopted the Edward Livingston Codes, which went into effect on 1 January 1837. José F. Barrundia promoted these codes, written for Louisiana in 1824, as a modern replacement for the system they had been abolishing piecemeal. Trial by jury was the central feature of the new system, and almost immediately problems arose in the countryside, where illiteracy was general and the deeply entrenched class structure made trial by jury impracticable. The mass of the population identified the Codes more with centralized rule from Guatemala City, with foreign influence and with anti-clericalism than with social justice. Moreover, the authoritarian manner in which the liberals introduced these and other reforms did little to improve relations between government and people. Military repression in Central America had been escalating ever since the strong-armed rule of Bustamante, but the insensitivity of both the federal and state governments in their efforts to develop the export economy, in the regulation of the morality of the inhabitants, in suppressing criticism of their own policies and in persecuting their political enemies through exile and confiscatory measures added to their unpopularity, as did the conduct of government troops.

The cholera epidemic which entered the country from Belize in 1837 turned the threatened and real grievances of the peasants in eastern Guatemala into open rebellion. In March 1837 the government quarantined infected areas and pursued other sanitary measures, undoubtedly justified but poorly understood. The peasants, already alienated from the Gálvez government, feared the vaccines and believed the priests who told them that the medicine which health officials put into the water was poison. Panic and violence resulted. Although the first major insurgency of 1837 took place at San Juan Ostuncalco, in Los Altos, where natives rioted against officials charged with effecting the Livingston Codes, the greatest trouble was in the Montaña region of eastern Guatemala. A natural leader, José Rafael Carrera, emerged who was to organize and lead the peasants to victory, and to determine the destiny of Guatemala for the next twenty-five years, until his death in 1865. Born in the capital in 1814, Carrera, a *ladino*, had served as a drummer in the conservative army during the 1826–9 civil war and later drifted into the Montaña. There he became a swineherd and gained some property after a village curate arranged a marriage with a woman of Mataquescuintla. Carrera initially commanded a patrol charged with enforcing the cholera quarantine, but he turned against the government and took his troops to the aid of peasants who were resisting a government force at Santa Rosa. Carrera's leadership turned their defeat into victory there and soon he commanded a guerrilla band that controlled much of eastern Guatemala. The cholera epidemic limited the government's ability to raise troops, but Carrera's partisans increased in numbers and effectiveness. In late June he listed his demands in a manifesto that reflected the conservative influence of the priests who advised him: 1. abolition of the Livingston Codes; 2. protection of life and property; 3. return of the archbishop and restoration of the religious orders; 4. repeal of the head tax; 5. amnesty for all exiles since 1829; and 6. respect for Carrera's orders under pain of death to violators.

Faced with popular insurgency, Gálvez formed a coalition of national unity with the conservatives, reminiscent of Arce's earlier action. He thus drove the more radical liberals led by J. F. Barrundia and Pedro Molina into an opposition faction. The divisions among the elite in the capital played into the hands of Carrera, whose ragged army extended the area of its control and terrorized the propertied classes, commerce and foreign travellers. Efforts to patch up the rift among the liberals ended in Gálvez's resignation in favour of Lieutenant Governor Pedro Valenzuela, who was more acceptable to Barrundia. But it failed to prevent Carrera's horde from over-running Guatemala City on 31 January 1838. He soon withdrew his forces from the capital and returned to his home district of Mita, but not before the beginnings of an alliance with the conservatives was born.

The economic power of the creole aristocratic class – large landowners and merchants – had been damaged but not broken by the liberal rulers. In fact, some had acquired confiscated church property and actually expanded their holdings during the 1830s. Although some members of the class remained in the liberal camp, most now supported the conservative cause. In 1833 the conservatives made a strong resurgence in the Guatemalan legislature and courted 'General' Carrera by attempting to satisfy some of his demands. The Church regained its former status; liberal military commanders were relieved of their posts; there was a move toward return to constitutional rule that allowed conservatives to gain election to office; the Livingston Codes were repealed in March. These acts reflected the popular will as voiced by the guerrilla caudillo. The preamble to a decree of 12 March, 1838, terminating all non-elected officeholders, illustrated the attention the legislature paid to this will when it acknowledged that 'a great majority of the population of the State have armed themselves to resist the administration that violated their guarantees and the fundamental pact', and justified the revolution against Gálvez, 'directed to establishing law and liberty . . . in self preservation against tyranny, [as] not only legitimate but consecrated by reason and justice'.[9]

Carrera, impatient with the slow progress of the legislature in dismantling the liberal reforms, resumed his guerrilla attacks and threatened to invade the capital once more. At the same time, conservative electoral gains and the new representative council headed by the conservative Mariano Rivera Paz put the Barrundia faction in an untenable position. In the end, Barrundia fell back on his liberal ally, Morazán, who rallied to his aid in mid-March with a thousand Salvadoran troops. Valenzuela's government had cautioned the federal caudillo against invading Guatemala, warning that it would upset the understanding with Carrera who had returned to Mita in peace. But when Carrera returned to the offensive, it forced the state to look to the federal government for help.

[9] *Boletín Oficial* (Guatemala), no. 11 (17 March 1838), 474–7.

Morazán launched an all-out campaign to track down and destroy Carrera's forces, while arresting the conservative direction of the Guatemalan government. The guerrillas responded with new ferocity. Atrocities multiplied on both sides. And by this time the federal government also faced conservative opposition in Nicaragua, Honduras and within El Salvador as well as Guatemala, while Costa Rica, now under the mildly conservative rule of Braulio Carrillo, was effectively ignoring the federation. The British consul, Frederick Chatfield, who formerly had supported Morazán, now regarded the federal cause as hopeless and sought to develop close British ties with the emerging conservative rulers. When the federal congress, recognizing and feeling these pressures, declared on 7 July 1838 that the states were 'sovereign, free and independent political bodies', Morazán returned to San Salvador to reassert his authority there.[10] He had by this time greatly weakened Carrera's influence, but had not eliminated the threat altogether.

Thus, by mid-1838 the battle lines were drawn. Carrera was the champion of the conservative cause for autonomy against Morazán and the liberals for federation. In other states the conservatives consolidated their strength and organization in alliance with the emerging popular caudillos. Thus, conservatism became closely related to local autonomy and the breakup of the Central American federation. With Morazán in San Salvador the conservatives in Guatemala quickly regained power, and on 22 July Valenzuela turned over the executive power to Rivera Paz. The new government resumed the dismantling of the liberal programme. In the country Carrera once more controlled a large area. A sudden counter-offensive in September by liberal General Carlos Salazar, however, forced Carrera to retreat into la Montaña, and when Morazán rejoined the chase, Carrera bought time by agreeing on 23 December to lay down his arms and recognize the government at Guatemala City in return for restoration of his military command in the district of Mita.

Encouraged by the apparent collapse of Carrera's guerrillas, Morazán on 30 January 1839 deposed Rivera Paz and replaced him with General Salazar. In the meantime, however, conservatives had gained power in Honduras and Nicaragua and joined forces against the liberals in El Salvador. The new liberal thrust had convinced Carrera that there could be no peace until Morazán was eliminated. On 24 March 1839 in a *pronunciamiento* from Mataquescuintla, he accused Morazán of cruelty

---

[10] Manuel Pineda de Mont (comp.), *Recopilación de las leyes de Guatemala* (Guatemala, 1869), I, 69.

toward the clergy and other Guatemalans, of destroying commerce, of confiscating private property and of spreading terror throughout the land. Swearing to restore Rivera Paz, he joined in alliance with the Honduran and Nicaraguan conservatives against Morazán. Within a month Rivera Paz and the conservatives once more ruled Guatemala. Carrera spent the remainder of the year mopping up in El Salvador and Honduras. Then, in January 1840, he swept into Los Altos, which in 1838 had seceded from Guatemala, and crushed the liberals there.

The inevitable showdown between Carrera and Morazán came in March 1840, when Carrera's forces routed the liberal army at Guatemala City. Morazán and a few of his officers escaped and eventually reached David in Panama, but the federation was finished. Two years later Morazán returned, reorganized his army in El Salvador with less support than he anticipated and then invaded Costa Rica, where he toppled Braulio Carrillo. Morazán's dreams of revitalizing the federation fell almost immediately before a popular insurgency that rose against him. Following a quick trial, he was executed by firing squad on 15 September 1842.

The defeat of Morazán and liberalism reflected both popular and elite disenchantment with liberal policy and a nostalgic search for a restoration of the supposed tranquillity of the Hispanic era. Also discernible is a pro-Hispanic xenophobia vaguely related to the birth of nationalism in each of the five states. The trend was most obvious in Guatemala, traditional seat of Spanish authority and tradition. However, while the conservatives had clearly strengthened their position, they were not yet dominant. In a period characterized by civil war within and between the states, the immediate masters of Central America in the 1840s were local caudillos of whom Carrera was the greatest. Carrera tried to maintain his dominance in Guatemala by playing off liberal and conservative members of the elite against each other, removing governments whenever they failed to be submissive to his bidding. The Church was the major beneficiary and his leading institutional supporter and the Jesuits and other religious orders returned to Central America. However, the liberals found that Carrera was a potential ally against the conservatives, and they were largely responsible for his accession to the presidency for the first time in 1844. Some checks on clerical privilege followed, but Carrera would never condone a full return to liberal policies, so it was inevitable that the liberals should eventually try to oust him.

New uprisings in eastern Guatemala combined with liberal opposition to force Carrera from office in 1848. The liberals were in control of Congress and Carrera's failure to end the uprising in the Montaña led him in January to offer his resignation. The conservatives persuaded him to withdraw it, but as matters worsened, he decided to accede to liberal demands for a new constituent assembly which he convened on 15 August. Addressing its opening session, he reviewed his efforts to bring peace in Guatemala, the economic growth that had occurred and his establishment of absolute Guatemalan independence in 1847. He then announced his resignation and headed for exile in Mexico, initiating at the same time the crisis that would lead to his triumphant return.

Chaos followed as Carrera watched from Chiapas. None of the series of short-term governments that followed were able to restore order or provide unified government. In mid September the conservatives regained temporary control of the Guatemalan Congress, declared Carrera a national hero and confirmed his 1847 declaration of Guatemalan independence. The liberals faced a united conservative opposition divided among themselves, as so often in this period. On 1 January 1849 Colonel Mariano Paredes took office in Guatemala City as a compromise chief of state. Closely advised by conservative statesman Luis Batres, Paredes publicly opposed Carrera's return, but privately condoned it. On 24 January Carrera announced his decision to restore peace and order in Guatemala. Liberal forces attempted to deny his return, but the Paredes government undermined their effectiveness and Carrera took Quezaltenango in April. Soon after, the government reached a peace agreement with the caudillo. Paredes remained as president, but Carrera, recommissioned a lieutenant-general, became commander-in-chief of the armed forces. Restoring order, he dealt vindictively with the liberal leaders who had opposed him. The threat of death faced those who did not flee. Thus, the liberals ceased to play a major role in Guatemalan politics for twenty years, although a few remained in the Congress and in minor offices.

After crushing rebellion in la Montaña and marching into El Salvador to assist the conservatives there (see below), Carrera once more became president of Guatemala (6 November 1851), and from 1854 president for life, a virtual monarch, with authority to designate his successor. Until his death in 1865, closely allied to the Church and the conservative aristocracy, he remained one of the most powerful caudillos in the hemisphere. He maintained friendly governments in Honduras and El

Salvador by force and also influenced the politics of Nicaragua and Costa Rica.

No Central American state escaped domination by conservative caudillos during the mid-nineteenth century, although only Guatemala had one of such durability as Carrera. In El Salvador, Honduras and Nicaragua, the turmoil among rival caudillos was especially devastating. With the liberals in disarray, some caudillos, notably Trinidad Muñoz of Nicaragua and Francisco Dueñas of El Salvador, switched parties in order to take advantage of local opportunities and circumstances.

Despite continued liberal strength in El Salvador, no leader professing Morazanista views could long escape Guatemalan intervention. Following Morazán's defeat in 1840, Carrera had placed one of his own officers, Francisco Malespín, in power. The latter's command of the military made him the dominant caudillo in El Salvador and a political force in Nicaragua and Honduras until his assassination in 1846. In addition to his ties to Carrera and the Guatemalan conservatives, Malespín worked closely with the politically active bishop of San Salvador, Jorge Viteri, and the British consul, Frederick Chatfield, so that while liberals might continue to hold political and legislative offices, conservative interests prevailed. The strength of liberalism in El Salvador, however, caused Malespín to co-operate with and use liberals (as did Carrera himself in the 1840s), which at times gave him problems with his conservative allies.

Meanwhile, Carrera's ally in Honduras, Francisco Ferrera, worked to establish conservative rule there, and he co-operated with Malespín in neutralizing the liberals in El Salvador and Nicaragua as well. Like Carrera, Ferrera came from a lower class *ladino* background and was unconnected with the leading families. As with Carrera, too, the clergy had a very great influence on his rise to power and on his way of thinking. A bitter foe of the Morazanistas, Ferrera, who had first ruled his state in 1833–5, became its first 'president' in January 1841. Although he was the leading caudillo in the country until his death in 1848, the liberals kept Honduras in a state of war much of the time. Ferrera and Malespín checked the liberals regularly. On 22 May 1845 a *coup* in Comayagua briefly gave the liberal leader, Trinidad Cabañas, control of the government for forty days. Soon back in control, Ferrera declined the presidency in 1847, but continued as minister of war under Juan Lindo, one of the more enlightened caudillos of the period and one not easily classified as liberal or conservative.

Lindo had served as first president of El Salvador (1841–2) under the protection of Malespín, where he had opposed restoration of Morazán's federation. Returning to his native Honduras he gained Ferrera's protection, although he was disliked by some of the more militaristic conservatives. Among his memorable acts as president of Honduras was his declaration of war against the United States in July 1847, in support of Mexico. In 1848 he convened a constituent assembly which established a more conservative constitution. Lindo's enlightened conservatism provided Honduras with its first real peace since independence. That peace was broken, however, when his foreign minister, General Santos Guardiola, attempted to oust him in 1850. The intervention of Trinidad Cabañas with Salvadoran liberal troops and the promise of Nicaraguan aid saved Lindo, whose conservatism was nearer that of José del Valle than that of Guardiola or Carrea. This event decidedly moved him into the liberal camp, and Lindo joined Cabañas in El Salvador in an effort to defeat Carrera in 1851. Carrera, however, won a decisive victory at San José la Arada, near Chiquimula, on 27 February 1851. In 1852 Lindo declined a third term as president and allowed the congress to elect Cabañas to succeed him. The more blatant liberalism of Cabañas and his renewed efforts to establish the Central American federation led almost immediately to an invasion from Guatemala by Guardiola, supported by Carrera, and resulted in Cabañas' defeat on 6 July 1855. Following a brief struggle for the presidency, Guardiola took possession of the office in February 1856 and held it until 1862. His unenlightened conservative rule brought some order but little progress to Honduras.

In Costa Rica, after the execution of Morazán in 1842, conservative interests generally prevailed, although the state remained politically unsettled until the strong-armed but enlightened conservative, J. Rafael Mora, seized power in 1849 and held it for a decade. By contrast Nicaragua suffered more than any of the other states from the mid-nineteenth-century civil wars between liberals and conservatives. Here the opportunistic struggles between local caudillos were more pronounced than elsewhere and the continual meddling, especially by the liberals, in the affairs of El Salvador and Honduras led to bloody and costly conflict. As conservatives consolidated their position in and around Granada, they, too, sought alliances abroad to check the persistent liberal strength of León. Nicaraguan conservatives even showed some willingness to consider reunification as a solution to the constant disorder they had experienced since independence. Fruto Chamorro, illegitimate son of an immigrant from Guatemala at the close of the colonial era, emerged as the leading conservative caudillo and established one of the most important Nicaraguan conservative clans. Liberal control of León was dealt a severe blow when José Trinidad Muñoz, renouncing his former liberal allies and supporting conservative J. L. Sandoval, took over in 1845. Sandoval and several conservative successors were almost continually besieged by liberal caudillos supported from El Salvador. In 1847 Bishop Viteri was transferred to Nicaragua where the political climate was far more favourable to him than in liberal San Salvador, and soon after Nicaragua reached a new concordat with the pope. When Muñoz returned to the liberal camp and rebelled against the government in 1851, Chamorro's forces defeated him and exiled him to El Salvador. The rise of Managua as a compromise capital between León and Granada began about this time, as several chieftains, including Chamorro in 1852, established temporary headquarters there. The conservatives generally held the upper hand during the early 1850s and followed the pattern elsewhere in Central America of emphasizing state sovereignty. They designated Nicaragua a 'republic' in 1854, changed the supreme director's title to 'president', and symbolically replaced the top stripe in the blue-white-blue liberal tricolour with a yellow stripe. Similarly symbolic was the motto of the republic's new seal: 'Liberty, Order, Labour'. A conservative constitution replaced the 1838 liberal charter. Yet the liberals refused to give up and by 1855 liberals invading from El Salvador gained control of the western part of the country and established a rival government again in León. It was at this point, as we shall see, that the filibustering expedition of William Walker arrived to play a decisive part in the conflict between liberals and conservatives in Nicaragua.

Since the independence of Central America commercial interests in North America and Europe had viewed the isthmus in terms of an interoceanic transit route. Both federal and state governments had encouraged canal schemes, but British, Dutch, American and French efforts during the first two decades after independence were ill conceived and undercapitalized. They had little effect beyond fuelling high expectations. Great Britain and the United States, however, pursued an active diplomacy designed both to insure their respective rights in any interoceanic route and to protect the interests of their subjects.

United States economic interests on the isthmus before 1850 were negligible, yet a series of U.S. agents did a remarkably good job of protecting the few Americans there, and, perhaps more importantly, they were direct carriers of the 'Jacksonian revolution' to Central America. (The French representatives had a similar ideological impact and were important noticeably in the Guatemalan revolution of 1848.)

Britain's economic and territorial interests were more substantial. British settlements at Belize and along the Miskito Shore from the Bay Islands to Costa Rica had secured for Britain a major share of Central American trade even before the close of the colonial era.[11] During the early years of independence Belize became the principal entrepot for Central American trade, while London financial houses supplied credit and loans for development to both state and federal governments. Soon after independence the English government sent George Alexander Thompson to investigate trade and canal possibilities, especially in Nicaragua. He initiated close relationships between British diplomats and Central American leaders, particularly those of the conservative party. In 1837–8 an English designer, John Baily, surveyed a canal route for the Nicaraguan government which, combined with the detailed report on canal potentials prepared by United States agent, John Lloyd Stephens, soon after, stimulated much foreign interest in the project. From 1834 to 1852 Frederick Chatfield represented the British government in Central America and worked deliberately to foster and protect British economic interests as well as trying to involve his government in more ambitious imperial schemes. Although he did not actively disrupt the Central American union, his sympathies ultimately lay with the conservatives and he became an important element in the intrigue and political manoeuvring of the 1840s as he sought guarantees for British bondholders and called in the Royal Navy when necessary to force concessions. In league with leading Guatemalan and Costa Rican conservatives, he played a significant role in the emergence of strong conservative governments in those states. Chatfield's personal secretary was Manuel F. Pavón, one of Carrera's leading advisers. Thus, as the middle states sought to restore the liberal federation, Chatfield worked to counter it with a conservative league or separate conservative sovereign states.[12]

From the outset British pretensions along the eastern coast of Central America had troubled the liberals. The Belize settlement, the ill-fated

[11] Troy S. Floyd, *The Anglo-Spanish struggle for Mosquitia* (Albuquerque, N.M., 1967).
[12] See Mario Rodríguez, *A Palmerstonian diplomat in Central America: Frederick Chatfield, Esq.* (Tucson, Ariz., 1964).

Poyais colonization adventure of Gregor MacGregor on the Honduran coast in 1823–4 and British trading posts along the Miskito coast of Nicaragua served the expansion of commerce, but they also challenged Central American sovereignty. British pursuit of fugitive slaves from Belize into Guatemalan territory was a further irritation to the liberals, who had abolished slavery immediately following independence.

In 1839 a British warship ejected Central American troops from the Bay Islands, and two years later Lord Palmerston declared that the islands were British territory, and that the British subjects who had settled there should be given some protection. This latest example of gunboat diplomacy provoked a storm of protest across Central America. The mid-century conservative governments proved more successful at resisting most British territorial ambitions and defending national independence than their liberal predecessors.

Meanwhile, close trading relations had developed between Britain and the isthmus. The Belize commercial firm headed by Marshal Bennet and John Wright took advantage of Belize's role as the principal port for Central America's exports and imports. Lacking protected deep-water ports of their own, Central Americans turned after independence to the Belize merchants to get their products to market as well as to supply them with manufactured goods. British merchants did not generally establish themselves in Central America to the extent they did in several Latin American states, but there were a few notable exceptions. Of these the most important was Bennet, who established the Guatemalan house of William Hall and Carlos Meany as a branch of his Belize firm in the 1820s. In the same decade George Skinner and Charles Klee established mercantile houses which continue to be important to the present day. Among others who served British mercantile interests during the first thirty years of independence were Thomas Manning, John Foster, Jonas Glenton and Walter Bridge in Nicaragua; William Barchard, Richard McNally, Frederick Lesperance, William Kilgour and Robert Parker, who operated with less permanent success in El Salvador; and Peter and Samuel Shepherd on the Miskito coast. The Shepherds received a massive land grant from the Miskito king in return for a few cases of whiskey and bolts of cotton chintz.

Central American imports reflected the close ties to British commerce. By 1840 nearly 60 per cent of Guatemalan imports came via the Belize settlement, while another 20 per cent came directly from Britain. Of the remaining 20 per cent, three-quarters came from Spain. The expansion of the British textile industry was important in providing markets for Salvadoran and Guatemalan indigo and cochineal. And from 1825 Britain had steadily reduced her duties on nearly all Central America's principal exports: cochineal, indigo, dyewoods, mahogany and other fine woods, hides and tortoise shells. By 1846 all Central American produce except coffee entered Britain duty free. Coffee, which had become more important than tobacco in Costa Rica after the collapse of Cuban coffee exports in the mid-1830s, soon received preferential treatment as well. Tables 2, 3 and 4 reflect the extent and expansion of British commerce during the first thirty years of independence.[13]

Belize remained the only Caribbean port of any importance, despite repeated Central American efforts to develop their own stations. Such ports as the Central Americans did maintain – Izabal, Omoa, Trujillo, San Juan del Norte, Matina – seldom harboured ships trading directly with the outside world. They served simply as transfer wharfs for the small skiffs and schooners that sailed between Belize and the Central American coast. Efforts to provide a second British entrepot at San Juan del Norte (Greytown) to serve Nicaragua and Costa Rica generally failed during the first half of the century. Most Nicaraguan and Costa Rican produce was shipped from the Pacific ports of Corinto, which gradually replaced the colonial port of Realejo in importance, or Puntarenas. Only after the completion of the Panama railway in 1855 did Central American commerce in general shift dramatically to the Pacific.

Loans added a bond of debt to that of commerce between Britain and Central America. The fiasco of the Barclay, Herring and Richardson loan of 1825 restrained investors from rushing in to Central America. Nevertheless a series of loans from British firms to the Central American states created a maze of debt problems which was not unravelled until the twentieth century. The liberals encouraged such arrangements, and

---

[13] Tables 2, 3 and 4 are based on data compiled from Customs records in the Public Record Office, London, by Robert A. Naylor, 'Tables of Commercial Statistics, 1821–1851', 'British commercial relations with Central America, 1821–1851' (unpublished Ph.D. thesis, Tulane University, New Orleans, 1958), 310–69. The tables are based on 'official values'. Naylor's tables in many cases also provide 'declared values' (generally lower) and volumes in tons, pounds or other units of measure as appropriate to the commodity. Tables 2, 3 and 4, of course, indicate only exports and imports between Central America and Great Britain and include produce of Belize and other British-held territory on the Central American east coast. Ciro F. S. Cardoso and Héctor Pérez Brignoli, *Centro-América y la economía occidental (1520–1930)* (San José, Costa Rica, 1977), 324–5, have compiled two statistical tables based on Naylor's data showing annual imports and exports between Britain and Central America. Unfortunately, there are some serious errors in their tables, especially in the one dealing with British exports to Central America, where Cardoso and Pérez have mistakenly included all British exports of foreign and English colonial goods to Jamaica as Central American imports. In addition, there are some mathematical or typographical errors in their totals.

Table 2 *Central American Imports from Great Britain and Jamaica,*
1821–50
(in thousands of £)

Years	British Exports directly to Central America	British Exports to Belize	Jamaican Exports to Central America	Totals
1821–25	6.7	1,455.9	0.0	1,462.6
1826–30	12.6	2,805.6	0.0	2,818.2
1831–35	112.3	2,937.6	74.0	3,123.9
1836–40	40.3	6,328.9	61.2	6,430.4
1841–45	76.0	4,578.1	56.4	4,710.5
1846–50	2,376.4	3,961.5	85.4	6,423.3

Table 3 *Central American Exports to Great Britain and Jamaica,*
1821–50, directly and via Belize, Peru and Chile
(in thousands of £)

Years	British Imports from Central America			Jamaican Imports from C. America	Totals
	Directly from C. America	via Belize	via Peru & Chile		
1821–25	12.8	395.9	3.3	0.0	412.0
1826–30	23.9	402.7	14.2	0.0	440.8
1831–35	105.3	1,214.5	51.0	44.9	1,415.7
1836–40	368.7	2,719.8	129.7	41.4	3,259.6
1841–45	308.1	4,133.7	435.2	6.9	4,883.9
1846–50	2,631.7	5,526.7	73.0	2.7	8,234.1

Table 4 *Principal Central American Exports to Great Britain, 1821–50*
(As percentages of total Central American exports to Great Britain)[a]

Years	Woods[b] %	Cochineal %	Indigo %	Coffee %
1821–25	73.9	7.7	15.5	0.0
1826–30	66.9	21.6	8.4	0.0
1831–35	46.3	42.6	4.2	0.3
1836–40	30.7	63.6	4.3	0.5
1841–45	18.5	67.3	1.6	12.2
1846–50	20.9	61.2	0.9	18.8

[a] Total Central American exports to Great Britain based on Table 3.
[b] Mahogany, Nicaragua wood, Brazil wood, logwood, cedar, lignum vitae, fustic. Other forest products not included. Most of these woods were imported to Britain from Belize or the Miskito Shore and thus are not a major part of the trade with the Central American republics.

although conservative governments were more wary, these transactions did not end altogether. The Carrera government, for example, in negotiating a loan with the London firm of Isaac and Samuel in 1856 to pay off its earlier debt, had to pledge 50 per cent of Guatemala's customs receipts to service the debt.

As has already been mentioned, the liberals had also encouraged English colonization efforts. From Guatemala to Panama, governments designed projects to attract European immigrants. The results were disappointing. A trickle of Englishmen came, but most of them either died, returned home or drifted into urban centres. Notable were the Gálvez government's projects in Guatemala.[14] Small grants to individual foreigners were followed by a massive concession to the Eastern Coast of Central America Commercial and Agricultural Company, a group whose origins were suspiciously linked to Gregor MacGregor's Poyais enterprise. The company agreed to develop the entire eastern part of the state from Izabal and the Verapaz into the Petén. Unfortunately, the English were more interested in exploiting mahogany stands than in agricultural colonization. In the end, the project only heightened anti-British sentiment among residents of eastern Guatemala. A similar arrangement with a Belgian company to develop the port and region of Santo Tomás eventually superseded the English grant. Carrera and the conservatives had grave doubts about the wisdom of that concession, but, through bribery and intimidation, the government approved the Belgian contract and did its best to ensure its success. It had, however, collapsed by 1852 and the lowland region remained undeveloped. One by-product of these colonization projects was the improvement in shipping service from the Caribbean coast. The English company's steamer, the *Vera Paz*, linked the Golfo Dulce with Belize, thereby increasing the commercial dependence of Guatemala on the British port. The Belgian company later provided service with Belgium on an irregular basis. By 1850 there was regular, if sometimes unreliable, steamship service to Europe from the Caribbean coast.

If the British involvement in the isthmus was greater and by 1850, thanks to Chatfield, identified with the conservative cause, the United States was becoming increasingly involved in the middle of the century and usually in support of the liberals. This became more obvious after the appointment in 1849 of E. G. Squier as American envoy to Central

---

[14] William J. Griffith, *Empires in the wilderness: foreign colonization and development in Guatemala, 1834–1844* (Chapel Hill, N.C., 1965), treats this subject in detail.

America. Anglo-American rivalry intensified and came to a head over the question of control of the transit route across the isthmus. The discovery of gold in California in 1848 greatly accelerated United States interest in the isthmus. As Americans streamed across Nicaragua via a route developed by Cornelius Vanderbilt they discovered that the British had taken control of territory on both sides of the isthmus, at San Juan del Norte (Greytown) and Tigre Island in the Bay of Fonseca. War was averted when cooler heads agreed, by the Clayton–Bulwer Treaty of 1850, to bilateral control and protection of any isthmian canal; Britain and the United States pledged themselves not to 'occupy, or fortify, or colonize, or assume or exercise any dominion over . . . any part of Central America'. While the treaty lessened the hostile atmosphere created by Chatfield and Squier, it hardly ended Anglo-American rivalry in Nicaragua at the very time when the liberal–conservative showdown was occurring there.

Among those who crossed the isthmus in 1850, probably at Panama rather than Nicaragua, was William Walker, the son of an austere family steeped in Protestant frontier religion and Jacksonian Democratic principles. Walker was a prodigious student; he had studied medicine at the universities of Nashville (later Vanderbilt), Pennsylvania, Edinburgh and Heidelberg before abandoning medicine for law in New Orleans at the University of Louisiana (later Tulane). Almost immediately, however, he turned to journalism and became editor of the liberal and controversial New Orleans *Crescent*. The untimely death of his fiancée, however, led to his abandonment of New Orleans for a fresh start in California. There he once more took up journalism, but failed either to prosper or to satisfy his restless spirit. Through associates he involved himself first in an abortive filibustering expedition into Mexico and then agreed to organize an expedition to support the hard-pressed Nicaraguan liberals.

Walker's band of 58 men landed near Realejo on 16 June 1855 and had remarkable success in assisting the liberals to several key victories. Yet the liberals also suffered reverses in the campaign, and the death – through battle or disease – of several liberal leaders enabled Walker quickly to become the dominant liberal military chieftain in Nicaragua. Granada fell to his forces in a fierce battle, following which Walker attempted to bring peace through the formation of a coalition with conservative collaborationists. He assured the Church that he had no ill will toward it and offered high office to several conservatives, including

Patricio Rivas who became president of the Republic. Some liberals, dismayed, now broke with Walker, while many conservatives refused to join the coalition. The struggle thus became one between Walker's 'democrats' and the 'legitimists'. The other Central American governments, now all under conservative rule, sent aid to the Nicaraguans opposed to Walker. Rafael Mora in Costa Rica took the lead in organizing this 'national campaign' against him. Rivas, realizing his untenable position, eventually resigned, and Walker himself succeeded him in the presidency. North Americans, mostly Mexican War veterans from the lower Mississippi Valley who had been promised land and other concessions, poured into Nicaragua to join Walker. *El Nicaragüense*, a bilingual newspaper more English than Spanish, proclaimed the liberal revolution and the establishment of a democratic regime.

The Nicaraguans and their allies – Mora's Costa Ricans, Guatemalans commanded by Mariano Paredes, Salvadorans under Gerardo Barrios and Guardiola's Hondurans – soon outnumbered Walker's forces. They first contained and then pushed back the North Americans and their remaining liberal cohorts, who suffered a cholera epidemic as well as battlefield losses. For their part the British supplied arms and other supplies to the allies through Costa Rica. The government in Washington vacillated; it never recognized Walker's regime (although the U.S. minister in Nicaragua had done so), but it was slow to take action against him. Finally a U.S. naval force arrived, in effect to rescue Walker and the few survivors of the expedition. The end came on 1 May 1857 when Walker surrendered. Returned on board a U.S. naval vessel, he received a hero's welcome in New Orleans and soon gained support for a new filibustering venture. Thwarted several times by U.S. officials, Walker finally succeeded in launching an expedition in collaboration with disgruntled British residents on Roatán who opposed Honduran sovereignty over the Bay Islands, to which Britain had agreed in 1859. Walker hoped to use Roatán as a base for a new invasion of Central America and was in touch with Trinidad Cabañas, still struggling against Guardiola in Honduras. When Walker reached Roatán, however, the British had not yet evacuated, so Walker struck directly at Trujillo. After a brief success he was captured as a result of British naval intervention, and handed over to the Honduran authorities. Following a brief trial, Walker fell before a firing squad on 12 September 1860.

The Walker episode had long-term results for Central America. The residue of anti-American and anti-British feeling remained long after to create suspicion and distrust in international relations and to encourage the xenophobia that the Conservatives had already nourished. Alliance with Walker further discredited liberals throughout Central America and allowed the conservatives to gain a stronger hold everywhere, but especially in Nicaragua. By 1860 the liberals continued to represent a serious threat only in El Salvador. Central America, although now definitively divided into five sovereign states, was solidly conservative.

In general, of course, the conservatives had better relations with Britain and Spain than with the United States or France. Spanish recognition of the Central American states and new concordats with Rome were positive achievements of conservative foreign policy. Old difficulties with the British were generally worked out amicably. The debt question was resolved through apportioning a part of it to each state, although only Costa Rica, with the smallest share, ever completed full payment. Guatemala reached apparent settlement of the Belize question in 1859, when by the Aycinena-Wyke Treaty Guatemala recognized British sovereignty there in exchange for British construction of a cart road from Guatemala City to the Caribbean. British failure to build the road eventually led to the abrogation of the treaty, as later liberal governments were unwilling to renegotiate a settlement. Honduras also settled its territorial disputes with the British by 1860, and Nicaragua made progress in the same direction, although final renunciation of British responsibility for protection of the Miskito Indians would not come until the end of the century.

Conservative domination of Central America arrested somewhat the emphasis on expanding exports and developing the country along capitalist lines which had been a feature of the liberal period. The cultural and political tone of conservative rule reflected traditional Hispanic-Catholic values, and there was a return to subsistence agriculture and a greater concern to protect Indian and *ladino* communal lands. The cities grew little, if at all, during the first half-century of independence and life remained predominantly rural. Yet the return to order after the civil wars was inevitably accompanied by an increase in agricultural production, and conservative governments could not resist the lure of increased revenue from foreign trade. Exports grew rapidly after 1840 except in Honduras which exported only livestock and foodstuffs to El Salvador and Guatemala. The dependence on natural dyestuffs of the late colonial and immediate post-independent period continued, with El Salvador and

Nicaragua the leading indigo producers and exporters. Guatemala also expanded its indigo production slightly, but depended principally on its cochineal exports. By 1845 Costa Rica's early success with coffee had begun to stimulate producers elsewhere in Central America. This became more intense after the discovery of coal-tar dyes in 1856 jeopardized the indigo and cochineal industries and eventually led to their ruin. Although dye exports continued to be the mainstay of the Salvadoran and Guatemalan export economies, coffee became increasingly important, especially in the Guatemalan highlands. By 1871, when the conservative regime finally ended there, coffee already accounted for 50 per cent of Guatemalan exports. The Civil War in the United States (1861–5) had allowed Central America to gain a larger share of the international cotton market, but only temporarily. Reliable statistics are not available for all of the states, but Tables 5, 6 and 7 (see below) illustrate the growth that occurred between 1850 and 1870.[15]

Britain remained the most important supplier of imports after 1850, even though the importance of Belize declined enormously with the development of Pacific trade after 1855. From 1850 to 1870, imports into Guatemala, as valued by customs, came from abroad in the percentages indicated in Table 8 (see below). As Table 8 also reflects, there was little trade between the Central American states. The roads were built from the capitals and producing regions to the ports, while interstate routes remained impassable. The economic interdependence that had begun to develop at the close of the colonial period was finally gone by 1870. The states were becoming more separate. Finally, while foreign involvement on the isthmus was limited when compared to other regions of Latin America, it was nevertheless highly significant from the point of view of the Central American states themselves and prepared the way for more substantial foreign domination once the liberals returned to power.

The restoration of order in most of Central America by 1860 and the emergence of coffee as a major export coincided with the resurgence of liberal efforts to control most of the Central American states. There was a restlessness among younger members of the elites, especially those

---

[15] Only fragmentary and often unreliable trade statistics have yet been compiled for most of this period in Central America. A guide to some of this material may be found in Thomas Schoonover, 'Central American commerce and maritime activity in the nineteenth century: sources for a quantitative approach', *Latin American Research Review*, 13/2 (1978), 157–69.

Table 5 *Leading Guatemalan Exports as Percentages of Total Exports,*
1851–70

Years	Value of Exports (Millons of US$)	Cochineal %	Cotton %	Coffee %
1851–55	6.2	78.4	0.0	0.0
1856–60	7.8	81.1	0.0	0.3
1861–65	7.4	56.4	8.3	11.3
1866–70	10.8	46.6	2.0	32.4

Source: R. L. Woodward, *Class privilege and economic development: the Consulado de Comercio of Guatemala, 1793–1871* (Chapel Hill, N.C., 1966), 58–63.

Table 6 *Leading Nicaraguan Exports as Percentages of Total Exports,*
1841–71

Years	Value of Exports (Thousands of US$)	Indigo %	Precious Metals %	Hides %	Cotton %	Rubber %	Woods %	Coffee %
1841	167.8	83.1	0.0	14.8	0.0	0.0	1.5	0.4
1851	1,010.0	7.9	39.6	1.2	0.0	0.0	15.8	3.0
1864	1,112.4	8.6	9.1	17.2	47.9	8.8	2.0	1.2
1865	1,155.0	16.9	12.3	8.9	47.1	4.6	2.5	2.6
1867	893.9	44.8	11.4	9.5	9.4	12.6	2.7	4.9
1870	930.3	27.0	17.9	18.0	1.7	15.7	9.7	5.4
1871	1,424.7	26.6	13.0	7.1	5.0	18.3	8.1	8.7

Source: A. Lanuza Matamoros, 'Estructuras socioeconómicas, poder y estado en Nicaragua (1821–1875)' (unpublished thesis, University of Costa Rica, 1976), 126–204.

Table 7 *Leading Salvadoran Exports, 1864–74*
(Millions of US$)

Years	Value of Total Exports	Indigo Value	Indigo % of Total Exports	Coffee Value	Coffee % of Total Exports
1864	1.7	1.13	67.4	0.08	4.8
1866	2.4	1.59	65.1	0.20	8.1
1870	?	2.62	?	0.66	?
1874	3.8	1.70	44.8	1.33	35.0

Sources: Mario Flores Macal, *Orígenes de las formas de dominación en El Salvador* (San José, 1977), 147–63; David Browning, *El Salvador. Landscape and Society* (Oxford, 1971), 162.

Table 8 *Origins of Guatemalan Imports,*
1850–70[16]
(percentage of total)

Great Britain	61
Belize	6
France	17
Germany	5
Spain & Cuba	4
U.S.A.	3
Belgium	2
Others	2
	100

connected to coffee production, and a growing general awareness that, despite modest increases in exports and economic growth, Central America lagged far behind the rapidly expanding economies of western Europe and the United States. This liberal resurgence occurred first in El Salvador. Gerardo Barrios, originally a Morazanista, had served conservative governments and co-operated with Carrera and Mora against Walker, but after he gained power in El Salvador in 1859 his liberal sentiments once more surfaced, as he symbolically ordered the remains of Morazán to be brought to San Salvador for burial with state honours. Economic, political and educational reforms followed, while he carefully avoided attacking the Church and diplomatically assured Carrera in Guatemala of his continued friendship. Carrera watched suspiciously and assembled an army on the frontier. When the inevitable anticlericalism surfaced in 1863 Carrera invaded, but Barrios repulsed him at Coatepeque. Barrios then turned against Nicaragua in an effort to end Conservative domination there, but was himself defeated. A second Carrera invasion of El Salvador in October 1863 ended Barrios's regime; he was replaced by the more reliable conservative, Francisco Dueñas. An attempt by Barrios to return two years later failed, but even under Dueñas many of the liberal reforms remained.

Carrera's death in 1865 brought new hope to the liberals throughout the region. Vicente Cerna continued conservative rule in Guatemala until the *reforma* of Miguel García Granados and Justo Rufino Barrios brought him down in 1871. In the meantime, liberals in Honduras ended Conservative rule there and co-operated with Salvadoran liberals to oust Dueñas in the same year. In Nicaragua conservatives held on to

[16] Compiled from data published in the *Gaceta de Guatemala*, 1851–71.

power until 1893, but a trend toward liberal economic policy nevertheless began soon after 1860. Costa Rica's transition to Liberal rule was
somewhat more orderly, but the pattern was not significantly different.
Mora was overthrown in 1859 and there followed a decade of domination by the Montealegre family, moderates who had been very important in the development of coffee cultivation. Although politically
conservative, certain liberal tendencies began to appear during the 1860s
in their educational, ecclesiastical and economic policies. More clearly
bringing the liberal *reforma* to Costa Rica, however, was General Tomás
Guardia, who established a liberal dictatorship in Costa Rica in 1870.

The liberal *reforma* of the 1860s in Central America challenged the
creole elites who had established neo-Hispanic regimes. After destructive civil wars and political experimentation, the leading families of the
late colonial period had largely succeeded in restoring their economic
and social hegemony. At the same time, collaboration with popular
caudillos had hastened the process of *ladino* participation in government,
so that by 1870 the white elites no longer held a monopoly of high
government office in Central America. Moreover, conservative rule had
failed to provide the progress and expansion of the export-oriented
economies at levels that significant portions of both elite and middle
sectors demanded. Despite the restoration of much of the institutional
framework of the colonial era, two new developments of the period were
caudillismo and state sovereignty, both of which would survive in Central
America long after the conservative party had ceased to be a force.

2

THE LIBERAL ERA, *c.* 1870 – 1930

The six decades from 1870 to 1930 witnessed the somewhat late full integration of Central America into the capitalist world market through the expansion of its export economies. They also saw the formation of several relatively viable states and, therefore, the strengthening of the division of the United Provinces of Central America established after independence into five republics, even though there were some attempts to restore the lost union. Central American scholars were, and still are inclined to see the history of the isthmus (with the exception of Panama, which only became an independent state in 1903) as a unity. They preserved a somewhat vague, even romantic aspiration that the five *patrias chicas* ('small homelands') should eventually merge again in a *patria grande* (that is to say, a united Central America). Up to a point, there are grounds for such an ambition. In this period, for instance, some of the central features of economic life – for example, the production and export of coffee and bananas – were shared by most Central American countries; as, in politics, they shared the upheavals of Liberal reforms and then the hardships of Liberal dictatorships, as well as a common and very strong dependence on the United States. But much more striking in such a small region are the strong differences which existed between the five Republics. In this chapter we shall frequently be contrasting the evolution of Costa Rica with that of the other countries in the isthmus. Costa Rica, Guatemala and El Salvador, from 1870 to 1930, may be seen as more advanced countries economically and politically than Honduras and, to a lesser degree, Nicaragua. Because of the very divergent previous structures, the expansion of coffee and the spread of banana plantations did not always create the same structures or have the same consequences in all Central American Republics. So although approaching the area as a whole some of its most important historical contrasts will be examined.

ECONOMY

Population

Table 1 presents population data for each Central American country and for the region as a whole during the period 1870–1930. As we can see, there was great disparity between the five countries in terms of their populations, rates of population growth and population densities. For example, the so-called 'demographic revolution' was evident in Costa Rica as early as the 1860s, whereas in Guatemala it only began around 1920. El Salvador was already an unusual case, with a population density much higher than was found elsewhere in Latin America.

A common feature of the five countries was the failure of all the endeavours of both Conservative and Liberal governments to foster European or North American rural colonization schemes with the aim of establishing a white peasantry in Central America. A limited number of immigrants did come from Europe and the United States; however, most of them already possessed some capital, and they became influential members of the local upper classes. Towards the end of the nineteenth century, West Indian and Chinese immigrants arrived at the almost deserted Caribbean lowlands of the isthmus, to work in railway construction and later in the banana plantations. But the evolution of the population of Central America is explained more in terms of internal demographic movements than in terms of immigration.

Within Central America, the growth of coffee and banana production provoked considerable internal migration. In Guatemala, for example, coffee production developed in previously sparsely populated regions – the Pacific coast and its immediate hinterland – which were then settled. In the same country, the coffee harvest each year caused a considerable seasonal migration of workers from the Indian communities of the western highlands to the coffee zone and back again. Since the wages paid by the banana plantations were higher than average in Central America, from the beginning these plantations attracted a steady movement of people from the central highlands to the Caribbean lowlands, and from El Salvador and Nicaragua to Honduras and Costa Rica.

Coffee expansion

In Central America natural conditions for the production of high-quality 'mild' coffees are outstanding, notably in the central volcanic highlands.

Table 1. *The population of Central America, c. 1870–c. 1930*

	Population (thousands of inhabitants)	Average annual rate of growth (%)	Density (per square mile)
Guatemala			
1880	1,225	—	29.2
1893	1,365	0.8	32.5
1921	2,005	1.4	47.7
El Salvador			
1878	554	—	68.4
1892	703	1.7	86.8
1899	758	1.1	93.6
1930	1,459	2.1	180.1
Honduras			
1881	307	—	7.1
1895	399	1.9	9.2
1910	553	2.2	12.8
1930	948	2.7	21.9
Nicaragua			
1875	373	—	6.8
1906	505	1.0	9.2
1920	638	1.7	11.6
1930	742	1.5	13.5
Costa Rica			
1864	120	—	6.1
1883	182	2.2	9.3
1892	243	3.3	12.4
1927	489	2.0	24.9
Central America[a]			
1870	2,370	—	14.1
1900	3,533	1.3	21.0
1915	4,915	2.2	29.2
1930	6,019	1.4	35.8

[a] Without Belize.

Sources: Guatemala: Censuses (for 1880, 1893, 1921). El Salvador: Rodolfo Barón Castro, *La población de El Salvador* (Madrid, 1942) (for 1878, 1892, 1899); *Anuario estadístico* (for 1930). Honduras: Héctor Pérez Brignoli, 'Economía y sociedad en Honduras durante el siglo XIX. Las estructuras demográficas', *Estudios Sociales Centroamericanos*, 2/6 (1973), 51–82 (for 1881, 1895, 1910); Nicolás Sánchez Albornoz, *La población de América Latina* (Madrid, 1973) (for 1930). Nicaragua: Alberto Lanuza Matamoros, 'Estructuras socioeconómicas, poder y Estado en Nicaragua (1821–1875)' (San José, 1976, unpublished dissertation) (for 1875); *Censo Nacional de Población* (Managua, 1950) (for 1906, 1920); Albornoz, *La población de América Latina* (for 1930). Costa Rica: Censuses (for 1864, 1883, 1892, 1927). Central America: Woodward, Chapter 1 of this volume (for 1870); Albornoz, *La población de América Latina* (for 1900); Ralph L. Woodward, Jr, *Central America. A Nation Divided* (New York, 1976) (for 1915, 1930).

Most of the countries of this region achieved full integration into the world market through the production and export of coffee. Here the expansion of the coffee economy will be studied in three countries only: Costa Rica, Guatemala and El Salvador. Honduran attempts at coffee production failed, and in Nicaragua, although coffee exports became important after 1870, they did not normally attain as high a percentage of the total value of exports as in the three selected countries, because the new crop competed in the Nicaraguan economy with cattle raising, the traditionally dominant economic activity.

It is perhaps advisable to point out at the outset the sharp contrast between the process of coffee expansion in Costa Rica on the one hand and Guatemala and El Salvador on the other. Because of the absence of strong colonial structures, Costa Rica moved straight into the coffee era a little more than a decade after Independence from Spain, without any significant internal upheavals, and much sooner than the rest of the isthmus. In both Guatemala and El Salvador, by the time of Independence strongly entrenched interest groups had developed. The Liberal reforms demanded by the spread of coffee cultivation were only put into effect following the decline of the world market for dyestuffs, hitherto Central America's main exports, during the 1860s and 1870s, and after a bitter struggle between rival groups. We shall also see that the social structure shaped in Costa Rica by the coffee economy was very peculiar, whereas the rest of the Central American coffee countries shared similar social features.

From the 1830s, coffee became Costa Rica's main cash crop. Its cultivation went through three main periods of growth in three areas of the country. Until the late 1840s it was confined to the central highlands around San José (*Meseta Central*); between 1850 and 1890, following the road to the port of Puntarenas (on the Pacific coast), it spread out towards the heavily forested western edges of the central highlands, in the province of Alajuela; and from 1890, and closely related to the railway developments of the time, it expanded into the Reventazón and Turrialba valleys, to the east of San José. Notwithstanding this expansion, the *Meseta Central* remained by far the most important coffee zone in Costa Rica: in 1890 13,800 (77 per cent) of the 17,940 hectares then planted with coffee bushes were in that region, and in 1935 59 per cent (27,600 of 46,920 hectares) were there.

In Guatemala, cochineal, a product of high value per unit of volume demanding relatively little capital and labour for its production, did not have a strong multiplier effect on the national economy. Guatemala lacked a road network, a modern system of rural credit, and a viable system of labour supply. The Indian communities were left almost free of heavy labour demands for several decades. But from the middle of the nineteenth century, as cochineal became an increasingly weak base for the national economy, the government began to encourage, timidly at first, the production of coffee and other cash crops (sugar, cotton), granting tax exemptions, attempting to spread the necessary technical knowledge and importing machinery. Nevertheless, the Conservatives, who depended on the support of the Indian communities, would not put into effect the necessary reforms without which coffee production could not reach its full potential. Coffee is a product which demands an efficient and cheap transport system (it has a relatively low value per unit of volume), the development of credit institutions (it is necessary to wait several years before any profits are earned by a new coffee-grower), and an abundant supply of land and labour. The Liberal revolution, which introduced the radical reforms needed by coffee interests, was launched in 1871, the same year in which coffee first became Guatemala's main export crop.

The process in El Salvador was quite similar. From around 1850 a sudden drop in indigo exports induced the government to encourage the production of coffee, cocoa, agave and other cash crops. The expansion of coffee cultivation between 1864 and 1880 made it a viable solution for the threatened national economy. Beginning in 1881 – when coffee first became El Salvador's leading crop – considerable reforms were undertaken, changing the country's economic structures in order to favour the interests of the coffee-growers.

In Costa Rica, three processes marked the formation of the territorial basis for coffee expansion: the appropriation of public lands; private land transactions; and the dissolution of communal forms of property. This last process was of little consequence, since the communal lands belonging to Indian communities and to Spanish towns – a form of property abolished from 1841 to 1851 – were not a very important feature of the Costa Rican countryside. At the time of independence Costa Rica had approximately only 60,000 inhabitants. So waste and public lands were plentiful even on the *Meseta Central*, where most of the small population lived. The expansion of coffee production tended to reinforce and extend the fragmented smallholding structure inherited from the colonial period, as the access to public lands remained easy until the 1890s. As for private land transactions, with the development of coffee exports from the 1830s, land prices began to rise rapidly, particularly for lands of the *Meseta Central* suited to coffee groves. From 1800 to 1850, the average price of land in the central valley increased by 1,773 per cent. The degree of land concentration in Costa Rica has been a matter of some dispute. Recent research, however, has shown beyond any doubt that it was not considerable before the 1930s. The causes of this local peculiarity of land tenure in the major coffee zone in Costa Rica – *sui generis* in overall Latin American terms – were mainly the chronic shortage of labour, the excessively high price of land, and the limited financial resources of the principal coffee-growers.

In Guatemala there were also three processes which together form the so-called Liberal agrarian reform, but they are quite different from those in Costa Rica. In the first place, the extensive landed property of the church was seized by the Liberal state in 1873, and later disposed of by sale or even by grants free of charge, sometimes with the specification that the lands so acquired should be planted with coffee or other cash crops. Then a law of 1877 abolished a form of land rent, the *censo enfitéutico*. Most of the lands involved were communal, and as many of the occupants did not have enough money to buy their plots within the decreed six months, the law thus assured their confiscation. These plots, amounting to 74,250 hectares, were seized by the state and sold in public auctions. The third reform was the Liberal decision to sell, on very easy conditions, public lands to the coffee-growers and the producers of other cash crops. Between 1871 and 1883, 397,755 hectares of wastelands were sold. The agrarian reform carried through by the Liberals is one of the factors which explains the development of coffee production in Amatitlán, Suchitepéquez, Sololá and Quezaltenango. As in Mexico, the first Liberal governments wished to foster small and medium-sized holdings and to avoid the formation of very large estates, but in this, even though their agrarian laws were promulgated again in 1888 and 1894, they failed.

In Guatemala most communal lands survived the Liberal reforms. This was not the case in El Salvador. From 1864, when the big expansion of coffee cultivation began, there is some evidence of the usurpation of communal lands. Nevertheless, in 1879 the *ejidos* and communal plots still represented 25 per cent of the total land surface of the small country. Moreover, they were located exactly in the central volcanic highlands where the soil was most favourable to coffee cultivation. President

Zaldívar (1876–85) decided in 1879 to grant full tenure to occupants who planted coffee, cocoa, agave or other cash crops. The communities, Indian or *ladinos* (*mestizos*), yielded to this pressure and tried to produce coffee, but they did not have the necessary techniques and had no capital or access to credit. In 1881, a law abolished the communal land system, and the following year this was extended to the *ejidos*. These lands had to be purchased by their occupants, within a term which was extended several times, but in the event most *comuneros* lost their holdings, which were acquired by the coffee-growers.

Labour was very scarce in Costa Rica throughout the nineteenth century and so wages tended to rise. The causes of this were varied. To begin with, even though demographic growth was not insignificant, the population was still quite small in 1900, and as we have seen there was no large-scale immigration. But undoubtedly the most important factor was the pattern of land tenure. The large number of small proprietors and the peasant smallholding structure, which were inherited from the colonial era and which expanded in the first decades after independence, have already been noted. The fact that he had a small plot of land did not deter the peasant from working as a rural labourer or as a carter as well, but it is nevertheless a fact that the widespread distribution of small landholdings limited the supply of labour. Moreover, from 1899, the lure of the higher wages paid by the United Fruit Company, established in the Atlantic lowlands, provoked internal migrations towards the banana plantations, thus draining labour from the coffee zone. These factors explain why, although personal dependence was not altogether absent, the Costa Rican rural worker was basically an employee, a wage labourer, and not a 'serf'.

In Guatemala, most of the inhabitants were Indians and lived in communities provided with lands. The coffee haciendas were located in sparsely populated zones near the Pacific coast. In 1877, the Liberal government issued the Reglamento de Jornaleros (day-labourers). It allowed the coffee-growers to recruit as labourers, for limited periods, a certain number of Indians from the highland communities, even against the *comuneros*' will. This system was retained throughout the period under consideration, even though some measures were adopted to improve the condition of the coerced rural labourers, for example the establishment of minimum wage levels guaranteed by law from the beginning of the twentieth century.

Though El Salvador had a big population for its small territory, before the Liberal reforms most people lived in communities. The coffee-growers were obliged to seek varied ways of obtaining labour, but the problem vanished after the 1880s as a consequence of the agrarian policy of President Zaldívar. Thousands of peasants were divested of their communal lands and could not obtain new plots. They had to establish themselves on the haciendas as resident workers (*colonos*), or else they lived as squatters for most of the year, working with their families as hired labourers during the coffee harvest. Social unrest was a common feature of the Salvadorean countryside after the reforms, particularly in the western region where the Indian population was greater; the repression of peasant movements was entrusted to the rural guard (*policía montada*) created in 1889.

The beginning of coffee expansion in Costa Rica was financed with small amounts of capital, accumulated during the colonial period and the first decade of independence from cacao and tobacco cultivation, the export of a dyewood (*palo brasil*), and the extraction of precious metals from the mines of Monte del Aguacate, which had been discovered in 1815 and exploited particularly after 1820. When regular exports of coffee to Britain started in 1843, commercial houses in London and Liverpool began to advance credits against future harvests, channelling them through the Costa Rican commercial houses which were established, mostly by the richest coffee-growers, from the 1840s onwards. These commercial houses in turn granted credits to the small producers, who were drawn into economic dependence on the large coffee-producers and on the merchants. This enabled the well-to-do coffee-growers to exercise a high degree of pressure and social control over the small farmers, in order to guarantee them the additional labour needed for the harvesting of their own coffee and even more for working at their large processing plants. In 1857, the government of President Juan Rafael Mora (1849–59) made a contract with the merchant Crisanto Medina to create the Banco Nacional Costarricense, which was to receive deposits, give credit, and issue notes. The bank was inaugurated on 1 January 1858. Its creation seemed to present a dangerous threat to the coffee-producers who practised usury and used it as a form of social control. They thus brought about a *coup d'état* which toppled Mora. The bank ceased operations not only because of this opposition but also due to losses caused by the collapse of a Liverpool firm to which it was connected. From the 1860s onwards, credit-giving establishments multiplied in number, many of them short-lived. The most important were the Banco Anglo-Costarricense, established in 1863, and the Banco de la Unión (1877) which later became the Banco de Costa Rica.

During the long period of Conservative rule in Guatemala before 1871, the structures of credit and finance were very primitive. The rural mortgage was practically unknown, because there was almost no legal security for the money lender. Interest rates could attain 50 per cent, even though the annual legal rate was a mere 6 per cent. The usurers were able to prevent the creation of several banks. With the Liberal revolution there were attempts to create a modern financial system. The church properties, seized in 1873, were used by the government to back the Banco Nacional, established in 1874 as a commercial bank receiving deposits, issuing notes and giving credit. But this bank could not resist the financial panic provoked in 1876 by the war against El Salvador, and disappeared the next year, thus opening the way to the creation of several private commercial banks, all of them authorized to issue notes by the Code of Commerce (1877). This also regulated the mortgage system and established an obligatory public register of landed property and of mortgages. The main banks were the Banco Internacional (1877), Banco Colombiano (1878), Banco de Occidente at Quezaltenango (1881), Banco Americano (1892), Banco Agrícola Hipotecario (1893) and Banco de Guatemala (1894). Nevertheless, credit was still difficult to obtain, and the coffee-growers depended on a personal and commercial credit with high interest rates (12 per cent annually). The banks and other money lenders obtained cheap credit in Europe and then granted loans at high interest rates in Guatemala. By these means, German coffee-producers who kept in contact with the banks of Bremen and Hamburg profited from the long coffee crisis at the end of the nineteenth century, seizing the estates of Guatemalan coffee-growers who owed them money and were unable to pay it back.

The first stages of coffee expansion in El Salvador were financed – at least in part – by mortgaging properties where indigo was produced. Many indigo-growers sold their lands and equipment in order to cultivate coffee. Landowners and city-dwellers (merchants, military, priests, civil servants, etc.) obtained enough credit to initiate the coffee economy. As in Costa Rica, British capital financed future harvests. The first banks appeared after 1880, all of them issuing notes: Banco Occidental, Banco Salvadoreño, Banco Agrícola Comercial. Their credit went to the big landowners, who in turn granted loans to smaller producers. Bank credits especially destined to finance the production of coffee only began around 1920.

Throughout the period under study, the cultivation of coffee remained extensive and quite primitive, except to some extent in El Salvador. On the best lands of the Costa Rican *Meseta Central*, the decline in the average yield per hectare, already evident in 1881, is confirmed by the quantitative data available for the twentieth century. From 1909 to 1956, average yield declined by 52.5 per cent.[1] Production increases were obtained by extending the cultivated area. Central American coffee groves were established as permanent plantation enterprises (unlike in Brazil, where coffee was a frontier or migratory crop), but the use of fertilizers was seriously limited. In the second half of the nineteenth century the custom was established of planting shade trees to protect the coffee bushes from winds and excessive rainfall, and to shield the soil against erosion. Guatemalan cultivation techniques were similar to those used in Costa Rica. But in El Salvador, the sheer scarcity of adequate soils, and sometimes the fact that the coffee groves covered steep hillsides, led to better agricultural techniques, to the extent that the yields in some of the largest coffee farms were the highest in the world.[2]

In contrast to cultivation, processing techniques became increasingly mechanized and technically specialized. Costa Rica led the development of these techniques and taught them to the rest of Central America – and to Columbia. *Beneficio húmedo* (wet processing) began to be used in Costa Rica as early as 1838. The coffee berries were piled in heaps to soften the pulp, and then placed in tanks through which a stream of water passed; there they were continually stirred to free them from the outer pulp. The coffee beans were then spread out upon a platform to dry in the sun, and then the inner husk was removed by water mills. The use of *beneficio* steam machinery imported from England and later from the United States began to spread during the 1850s. Obviously the increasing costliness and technical complexity of the new processing techniques led to the concentration of this stage of production in a few coffee mills. Around 1888 there were only about 256 *beneficios* in Costa Rica, whilst four years earlier there were 7,490 coffee farms.[3] Costa Rica passed on the

---

[1] See Carmen S. de Malavassi and Belén Andrés S., 'El café en la historia de Costa Rica' (unpublished dissertation, San José, 1958), 35–6.

[2] David Browning, *El Salvador. Landscape and society* (Oxford, 1971), 224.

[3] Joaquín Bernardo Calvo, *Apuntamientos geográficos, estadísticos e históricos* (San José, 1887), 47.

knowledge of the processing techniques to Guatemala and El Salvador. In those countries too the processing stage tended to be concentrated in a few large estates or coffee mills. In Guatemala, German coffee-growers used better techniques and so obtained a higher output: in 1913 they owned 10 per cent of the Guatemalan coffee farms, but produced 40 per cent of the processed beans.

In the three countries under study, the growth of coffee cultivation provided the leading impulse towards the modernization of the transport system and decisively influenced the form of the road and railway networks. In Costa Rica, a road capable of taking ox-drawn carts was needed to carry the coffee to the Pacific port of Puntarenas. It was built between 1844 and 1846, financed by a tax levied on coffee exports. The ships carrying the coffee to Europe and the Atlantic coast of the United States took the Cape Horn route, which lengthened the voyage and consequently raised freight charges. The building of the Panama Railway linking the Atlantic and Pacific oceans (1851–5) opened up another possibility, without really solving the problem. In the same period, the Costa Rican government of Juan Rafael Mora signed a contract with the Pacific Mail and Steamship Company, to ensure that their ships called at Puntarenas; this contract was extremely favourable to the Company. Nevertheless, it was still felt necessary to open a road – or a railway – to the Atlantic, and to build a new port on the Caribbean coast. Puerto Limón was established in 1870, but it was not until 1890 that the Atlantic Railway was completed, linking San José to this new outlet. Henceforth Costa Rica enjoyed lower freight charges (due also to the spread of steamships on the Atlantic routes), and direct access to its main markets. The Pacific Railway was also under construction at this time, but was not completed until 1910.

From 1873, the Liberal regime in Guatemala endeavoured to build better and more numerous roads, linking the capital city to Quezaltenango, Huehuetenango, the Pacific ports and later the Atlantic port of Santo Tomás. These projects were financed by the issuing of treasury bonds and the levy of a tax on rural property. Any adult male was forced to work three days each year on the construction and maintenance of roads, or else to pay a certain sum in order to obtain an exemption. The first railway contract which worked was established in 1877–80 with William Nanne: the railway, built with national capital, linked the port of San José with Escuintla (1880) and with the city of Guatemala (1884). A new contract was signed in 1881 for the construction of a railway to the port of Champerico from Retalhuleu to guarantee the transport of coffee produced there; it was completed in 1883. In 1884 a port (later called Puerto Barrios) was established on the Caribbean coast, and a railway leading there was begun with national capital. But its building was interrupted, to be completed only in 1908, after a contract (in 1900) with the Central American Improvement Company Inc. This contract – which marked the beginning of American control over Guatemalan railways – granted the Company the concession for 99 years of the exploitation of Puerto Barrios, lands at both sides of the rails and tax exemptions. In 1912, all the Guatemalan railway network fell under American control through the Guatemala Central Railway Company, which was absorbed by the International Railway of Central America. Between 1881 and 1884, the government of Justo Rufino Barrios signed contracts with ten foreign steamship companies. These contracts included, on behalf of the companies, annual government subsidies, land concessions and tax exemptions.

In El Salvador, the roads needed to ensure coffee transportation were built at the end of the nineteenth century, financed by national and municipal taxes on coffee production and trade. As in Costa Rica and Guatemala, the government attracted foreign steamship companies to Salvadoran ports (Acajutla, La Libertad) through very generous contracts. The railways were built in part with government and national capital (Sonsonate–Acajutla, La Unión–San Miguel). The Salvador Railway Company (which was British) was granted in 1885 a concession to construct a railway linking the main coffee zones to the port of Acajutla. Another railway built later on with American capital connected with the Guatemalan network thus permitting the export of Salvadoran coffee through Puerto Barrios. Deprived of an Atlantic coast, before the construction of the Panama canal El Salvador was more isolated than Costa Rica and Guatemala from the more important world markets for coffee.

The main buyers of Costa Rican coffee during the nineteenth century were Britain, France, Germany and the United States. The commercial and financial links with England only began to weaken after the first world war, as those with the United States became more important. To begin with, Guatemala sold its coffee mainly to Britain. The British remained Guatemala's most important suppliers, but first the United States, then Germany, then during the first world war the United States again, replaced Britain as the principal importers of Guatemalan coffee.

El Salvador, at the beginning of the twentieth century, sold coffee mainly to France, the United States, Germany, Italy and Britain, in that order.

Coffee became the most important export crop first in Costa Rica (during the 1830s and 1840s), then in Guatemala (where it displaced cochineal in 1870) and finally in El Salvador (where it displaced indigo in 1880). Its value as a percentage of total exports reached a maximum at the end of the nineteenth century in Guatemala (92 per cent in 1880) and Costa Rica (91 per cent in 1890). In El Salvador it did not dominate the export trade so thoroughly until the twentieth century, when the Salvadoran economy came to be the most dependent on coffee exports.

It is therefore easy to understand that the crises in the world coffee market – caused by overproduction or occurring as a result of general capitalist crisis – had very serious economic consequences for Central America. The most important of these crises occurred during the period 1897–1907 (as a result of a worldwide overproduction of coffee) and during the 1930s following the crash of 1929; coffee prices did not recover their 1929 level until 1946.

The main effects of the expansion of coffee during this period were similar in Costa Rica, Guatemala and El Salvador. Subsistence agriculture activities were steadily displaced by coffee in certain zones. The development of monoculture not only changed the countryside, it provoked severe crises in the national food supply. Sometimes the food shortage forced governments to pass laws prohibiting the export of grains and cattle and encouraging their importation, setting maximum prices for basic foodstuffs, and so on, but these measures never added up to an effective solution of the problem. In Costa Rica, as the best lands of the central valley were gradually taken over by coffee, the production of maize, beans, sugar-cane (for internal consumption) and cattle for meat and milk supply was relegated to waste lands around the coffee zone. As the sources show abundantly, subsistence crises became frequent and foodstuffs, which had been very cheap at the time of independence, became very costly. In Guatemala, a report from the department of agriculture (a section of the ministry of development) in 1902 declared that the supply of staple products for popular consumption had been adequate and their prices low before the expansion of coffee; but coffee had changed all that, and foodstuffs were now often imported and were expensive. Measures were then adopted to encourage the production of maize, potatoes, beans, rice and wheat, with scarcely any noticeable effect. In the central and most densely populated zone of El Salvador, although later than in Costa Rica and Guatemala, coffee cultivation also ousted maize and other basic foodstuffs, which had began to be produced on less fertile soils, and sometimes on land occupied by squatter peasants during the months separating one coffee harvest from the next.

There can be little doubt that the coffee-growing elite exercised a decisive influence over the social, political and economic life of these countries (particularly Costa Rica). The coffee export tax was the one great source, apart from foreign loans, of finance for important projects such as roads, railways and public buildings. Gradually in Costa Rica, and more precipitously in Guatemala and El Salvador, coffee expansion provoked a thorough reorganization of social and economic structures and was instrumental in the full integration of these countries into the world market, with all the accompanying advantages and disadvantages.

Enclave economies[4]

Banana plantations and gold and silver mines constituted enclave economies in Central America. The plantations, far more important historically than the mining ventures, were at the beginning a kind of projection or consequence of the railway contracts, but they came to be a central feature of the Central American economies on their own account.

Bananas became an object of international trade in 1870, when regular exports from Honduras to New Orleans were established by the New Orleans Bay Island Fruit Company. Rival companies soon appeared. The expansion of the American market then provided a strong incentive for the establishment of banana plantations in Central America from the 1890s.

The first stage in the development of the banana business was marked by strong competition both at the level of production and trade. Bananas were cultivated by independent labourers, with very small investment and good probabilities of profit. The American merchants who shipped the fruit to the United States, while bringing pressure on the Central American producers to keep prices low (as bananas are a very perishable product, the farmers were in a hurry to sell), had to face risks of heavy loss during the voyage and also fierce competition in New Orleans. As a

[4] For a definition of enclave economy, see Fernando H. Cardoso and Enzo Faletto, *Dependencia y desarrollo en América Latina* (Mexico, 1973), 48–53. This section follows closely Ciro Cardoso and Héctor Pérez Brignoli, *Centroamérica y la economía occidental (1520–1930)* (San José, 1977), chapter 9.

result specialization began in the export business. Transport in bigger ships provided with refrigeration and the building of adequate storage and loading facilities in some Central American ports demanded large outlays of capital. In addition, the spread of banana cultivation away from the coastline required an adequate transport system to the ports, provided by railway networks.

The consolidation of the big banana companies was a complicated process, involving land concessions by the Central American states, the construction of railways and ports, the introduction of foreign tech nology and capital, the acumen and skill of certain entrepreneurs, conflicts and mergers between the companies themselves, the confiscation of lands occupied by native independent farmers, and even border conflicts between neighbouring countries.

The United Fruit Company (UFCO), formed in 1899, began its operations in Guatemala by an agreement with the International Railways of Central America, which had received an important concession of waste lands. From 1906, through purchases and new concessions, the banana company expanded its holdings in the Motagua valley. In 1928, using a subsidiary company, the UFCO began to buy lands on the Pacific coast as well, developing its plantations in this region from 1936.

In Honduras, banana production until 1913 was in the hands of native farmers. Several companies, like the Vaccaro brothers, the Hubbard–Zemurray, the steamship line Oterí and the UFCO, shared the shipping and distribution. Around 1913, prices fell and a severe drought affected the plantations, causing a crisis during which some of the companies withdrew. This moment was seized by the powerful UFCO for a large-scale penetration in Honduras. In fact, since 1912 two of its subsidiary companies – the Tela Railroad Company and the Trujillo Railroad Company – had signed substantial railway contracts with the Honduran government, thus obtaining vast land concessions. During the 1920s Honduras produced the majority of UFCO's bananas. The company of the Vaccaro brothers operated in the region of La Ceiba and in the Aguán valley. It was reorganized in 1924 and 1926, becoming the Standard Fruit and Steamship Company. Samuel Zemurray also began his enterprises by buying and selling bananas, but in 1902 he obtained a concession of public lands at the Honduran side of the Motagua river. In 1911, after a crisis which almost ruined him, his enterprise became the Cuyamel Fruit Company. The government of Honduras granted this company new concessions near the Guatemalan frontier, but as the border between the two countries was not clearly delimited, a series of conflicts between Honduras and Guatemala began in 1913; these were in fact merely the effects of the rivalry between the Cuyamel and the UFCO. The conflicts ceased in 1929, when the two companies merged. From 1920, Cuyamel's main plantations were located in the Ulúa valley.

In Nicaragua, banana production was of less importance. The UFCO operated on the Atlantic coast from the 1890s, but exports were quite small. During the 1920s the Cuyamel Fruit Company became established there, and the plantations experienced a certain expansion. Nevertheless, most of these plantations were located on inadequate soils. In 1930, the UFCO sold its properties in Nicaragua, and after that occupied itself exclusively with commercial operations through a subsidiary enterprise, the Cukra Development Company.

In Costa Rica, the beginning of the banana trade was linked to the activities of Minor Keith and the complicated history of the Atlantic Railway. In 1899 the UFCO obtained the use of the concessions granted earlier to Keith. United Fruit managed to manipulate all of the banana business in the country, after ousting two rival enterprises, the American Banana Company and the Atlantic Fruit Steamship Company. In 1927, two new companies on the Pacific coast began to export bananas, but the UFCO soon purchased their plantations and expanded them during the 1930s. In 1930, throughout Central America, the UFCO had overtaken all its rivals: it owned 63 per cent of the 103 million bunches of bananas exported.

The Caribbean coastline of Central America, which saw the first development of banana production, was only sparsely populated. The building of the railways and then the banana plantations generated some migratory currents: from the central highlands to the coast; and from the West Indies and from China to Central America. Honduras also received immigrant workers from El Salvador. And the spread of the banana plantations led to the development of a significant rural proletariat. Although the wages paid by the fruit companies were generally higher than those offered elsewhere in Central America, the position of the plantation workers was prejudiced by several payment practices. For instance, in Honduras it was usual to pay workers in vouchers which were accepted only at the companies' stores, called *comisariatos*; or else to fix their wages in dollars and then to pay them in Honduran currency at an exchange rate below the legal rate. Furthermore, whereas Honduran workers were used to weekly payments, at certain times the companies paid only every 40 days.

The Costa Rican banana exports expanded rapidly after 1880, reaching a maximum of eleven million bunches in 1913, even though starting in 1904 the plantations were plagued by a disease called *mal de Panamá*. After the first world war, exports diminished slowly, to around seven million bunches during the 1920s. The UFCO began at this time to abandon its Atlantic plantations, and to establish itself on the Pacific coast. In the Caribbean zone, banana production was now pursued by Costa Rican farmers, who sold their fruit to the company. In 1927–8 they formed a Costa Rican banana co-operative.

In the 1890s, the Honduran banana exports amounted to around 1.5 million bunches per year. With the penetration of the fruit companies, exports rose sharply: 9.8 million bunches in 1920, 16.3 million in 1925, 29 million in 1929. During the 1920s, Honduras became the world's leading producer of bananas. The *mal de Panamá* appeared in 1926, mainly at the plantations of the Trujillo Railroad Company, provoking the complete abandonment of Puerto Castilla in 1935, which led in turn to the elimination of 125 kilometres of railway in this region.

Exports from Guatemala, which entered the banana market later, amounted to three million bunches in 1913, reaching six million per year during the 1920s and 1930s. In Nicaragua, from 1900 to 1920, banana exports reached a little over 1.5 million bunches per year. They increased to 3 million bunches between 1920 and 1930, but their decline was swift after 1935.

Since 1864, numerous mine concessions had been claimed and granted in Honduras. In the 1870s, mining production began to be encouraged by the government, and to recover from a long period of depression. During the Liberal presidency of Marco Aurelio Soto (1876–83), who in the past had proclaimed agriculture as the cornerstone of Honduran development, the mines were declared to be the mainstay of the national economy. His policy, favourable to mining and foreign interests, was followed by his successors, especially Luis Bográn (1883–91). The concessions to foreign companies were numerous, although only one of them dominated the mining business: the New York and Honduran Rosario Mining Company. This enterprise, between 1921 and 1937, obtained a net profit of 36 per cent and paid dividends which amounted to some $8 million. The main Honduran mineral production was silver, and the most important mining zones were located around the capital, Tegucigalpa. In 1887, minerals represented some 50 per cent of the value of Honduran exports, but with the rise of the banana trade their importance diminished steadily (to only 6 per cent in 1928).

In Nicaragua, gold mining, which guaranteed high profits to some foreign companies, was responsible in 1912 for 23 per cent of the total exports of the country. But as in Honduras, it tended to become less important, especially after 1923. The mines were to be found at Nueva Segovia (San Albino Gold Mining Ltd, Nicaragua Development Syndicate), Chontales, Matagalpa and the Atlantic region.

In Costa Rica, on the other hand, gold and silver mining, located in the north-western region of the country, became more significant after 1920, reaching a peak in 1928. But here, as in Guatemala and El Salvador, mining was not of great importance; it never provided as much as 3 per cent of the country's total exports.

The enclave economies of Central America had little dynamic effect on the national economies as a whole; the economic expansion they generated tended to limit itself to the zones of mines or plantations.

The original concessions granted to the foreign companies were extraordinarily favourable to them. In the case of the banana enterprises, these concessions consisted of lands, the use of other natural resources, tax exemptions, and free import of numerous products (which had a deleterious effect on the development of national industries, as imported goods entered the country free of tax and were sold to the plantation workers at the *comisariatos*). The railway contracts handed the control of all internal transport to the banana companies. The *comisariatos* ousted petty commerce from the plantation zones. The exemptions – above all those of customs duties – generated weak states, with poor financial resources. This was particularly the case in Honduras, where the banana plantations and exports were the core of the national economy. In 1917–18, the exemptions granted to the fruit companies surpassed the total revenue of the Honduran state.

The banana business being highly concentrated, the few possibilities of industrialization it opened up were made good use of by the companies themselves, as a complement to their agricultural activities, which were gradually diversified. Thus in Honduras, the Standard Fruit Company owned from the 1920s sugar mills, liquor manufactures, industrial plants producing vegetable oil, soap and fertilizers from the seeds of cotton, coconut and other products cultivated on its lands or purchased from local farmers.

The most harmful effects of the enclave economy were probably the consequence of frauds and the fact that the conditions under which the concessions were granted by the governments of the small and weak Central American countries remained unfulfilled: clandestine loadings, tax evasion, the building of clandestine railways (in Honduras), the fact that the companies at times failed to construct some of the railway tracts specified in the concessions (which were of national interest, but not of export interest), their practice of varying freight charges on their trains so that the companies were favoured against local producers, and so on.

A different aspect of this question is the foreign companies' absolute lack of respect for the sovereignty of the Central American countries, the sometimes open pressure on local governments, and the intervention in national affairs. United States military intervention on behalf of these enterprises occurred frequently, though generally short-lived: the landing of marines or the arrival of warships in Central American ports might occur any time that the North American properties and citizens felt or declared themselves threatened.

SOCIETY

Social structures

In examining the extent to which economic and political change in the period under discussion affected Central American social structures, it should be noted first that the composition of the upper, dominant groups in society was not significantly changed by the coffee expansion and Liberal reforms. Following the Liberal revolutions, many Conservatives did lose their personal wealth and position through confiscation, or were even forced into exile, while the Liberals used their newly acquired political power to obtain economic advantages (for example, through grants of public and former communal lands). Nevertheless, there is no doubt that the Liberal order allowed a more widely based foundation of power, by including in the new dominant groups many members of the old oligarchies. Even so, this did not avoid fierce struggles within the dominant class. The degree to which former oligarchies were absorbed varied from country to country. It was perhaps minimal in Guatemala and Nicaragua, while in Costa Rica a notable continuity since colonial times has been demonstrated.[5] Important changes were a diminution of the political power and influence of the Catholic church and the professionalization of the national armies; the latter provided one of the few possibilities for social mobility.

The marked presence of foreigners within the dominant social groups deserves some attention. In the coffee business, production was mostly under the control of Central American growers. But in the case of banana plantations, local producers were displaced by North Americans almost everywhere. Foreign economic influence was decisive in trade, transport and finance. Resident foreign merchants – mainly British, German, North American, French and Middle Eastern – became even more numerous during the twentieth century, joining the earlier immigrants who had come as coffee processors and traders. The integration of foreign residents into Central American society was generally incomplete, although in Costa Rica they were often naturalized.

For the general populace, predominantly rural, the great contradiction of Central American liberalism was between the proclamations of equality for all citizens and the actual social situation, which included forced labour (which in Guatemala was even legal). Costa Rica, with its firm structure of smallholdings, was a different sort of country altogether, but in the other Central American countries the surviving Indian communities (mostly in Guatemala) and the rural labourers – either permanently established on the farms (*colonos* or *peones*) or employed as day-labourers (*jornaleros*) – suffered the forced labour system. This reenacted and extended colonial procedures like the *mandamientos* (advance payments creating debts and often tying the peasant to the farm), and the laws against vagrancy. The peasants were cruelly repressed by the landowners and by government troops whenever they tried to organize or to act against their situation. The typical Central American farm had resident labourers who reproduced their labour force partly through a subsistence economy (plots alloted within the farm as part of or a complement to the wage), and day-labourers hired only during harvest time and practising for the remainder of the year a subsistence agriculture as squatters or leaseholders. This system allowed substantial savings in the farmer's expenditure,

[5] Samuel Stone, *La dinastía de los conquistadores* (San José, 1975).

and constituted a serious obstacle to the formation of a real capitalist labour market and of a proper rural proletariat.[6]

However, a more typical proletariat did originate from the foreign enclaves, whether mine or plantation. The spread of the banana plantations led to the settlement and economic exploitation of the Caribbean lowlands. The United Fruit Company began the struggle, necessary to make human settlement possible in that region, against yellow fever, malaria and other tropical diseases, and was followed in these efforts by the other fruit companies. As we have seen, migratory currents brought in labour, mainly from the West Indies and from the Central American highlands. The presence of West Indians, not entirely assimilated until the present day, and speaking their own dialects, created a new kind of social and ethnic problem. In Costa Rica, for example, the Chinese and West Indians were not really national citizens for several decades, and they were seriously limited in their freedom to go where they pleased. Before the construction of railways and docks began, and the beginning of the plantation system, what amounted to an ethnic (or 'racial') problem in Central America was the social discrimination suffered by the Indians, mostly in Guatemala – where they formed a clear majority of the population – and in western El Salvador. The rest of El Salvador and the whole of Honduras and Nicaragua were predominantly *mestizo*, and in Costa Rica most of the population (some 80 per cent in 1925) were of European stock.

The heyday of the export economy brought about some urbanization and modernization, which had effects on the social structure of Central American countries. At the end of the nineteenth century, the capital cities began to grow steadily. The varied services needed by the export activities and the strengthened bureaucracy generated by the consolidation of the national states attracted many rural dwellers to the cities. This led to the beginning of an urban middle class, mainly in the capital cities, which was important for the political evolution of the region. On the other hand, the first signs of an urban proletariat appeared also, following the creation of some small factories (textiles, foods and drinks) in San Salvador, Guatemala and San José. Nevertheless, it must be stressed that the artisans still predominated, with full industrialization only occurring in Central America in the 1950s. Urbanization also meant

6 See Edelberto Torres Rivas, *Interpretación del desarrollo social centroamericano* (San José, 1971), 75–82.

the carrying out of public works such as the paving and lighting of streets, the spread of modern transportation, the construction of large buildings and parks, the proliferation of daily newspapers, some advances in medicine and modest progress in education, even though the latter – except in Costa Rica – remained almost exclusively available to the upper and middle classes. During the first decades of the twentieth century, students arose as a new political force. Needless to say, social conditions being what they were, urbanization also brought about the spread of some very poor districts, including slums.

As we have already noted, Costa Rica had a peculiar economic structure, and the same can be said of its social organization, marked by wider popular participation in education and even in politics, and by a faster development than in the remainder of the isthmus of state assistance to the workers in matters of health, education and labour legislation.

Social struggles

At the beginning of the 1870s, the only social movements which can easily be identified are those which have been called by George Rudé the 'preindustrial crowd': for example, the peasant uprisings in western El Salvador during the 1880s, after the confiscation of communal lands by the Liberal government. The first labour organizations, which appeared at the end of the nineteenth century, were mutual aid societies, clearly following the pattern of the traditional artisan guilds. During the 1920s, in all five countries strong advances in the organization, actions and – though to a lesser extent – the political consciousness of the workers took place. This can be seen in the foundation of the first trade unions and of the Central American Labour Council (1926), which aimed to unify the labour movements throughout Central America and was responsible for the spread of socialist ideas until 1930. The first Communist parties were also founded between 1920 and 1931.

A number of catalysts can be perceived which explain, or help to explain, what happened next to popular movements and organizations. First of all, we have the beginnings of an urban lower and an urban middle class which provided leaders such as Agustín Farabundo Martí (who had rural roots but was educated at a secondary school in San Salvador, where he also began his university studies) or Miguel Mármol (a cobbler). Secondly, despite being actively repressed, the development of a large proletariat at the mines and plantations owned by foreign corporations created an environment favourable to the occurrence of 'modern' strikes, mainly after 1920. The political document which launched the Sandino insurrection was written in 1927 at the Nicaraguan mining centre of San Albino. Finally, there was the clear influence of factors such as the lessening of repression in some Central American countries during the 1920s, the Mexican Revolution, the Russian Revolution and the creation of the Third International.

Nevertheless, the development of trade unions and of popular ideology and struggles was in Central America much slower and less profound than in other Latin American countries such as Mexico, Argentina or Chile. Even the 'modern' strikes at the plantations and mines were, up to 1930, strictly economic and had no political overtones; and the movement led by Augusto Sandino was much more nationalist than socialist. The social effects of the economic depression following the crisis of 1929 permitted, during the 1930s, an accelerating of the pace of the labour movement and organization, gave a big push to the guerilla war in Nicaragua and provided the occasion for the great peasant uprising of 1932 in El Salvador.

Intellectual development

The small cities of these poor countries, where education was restricted to a tiny minority (with Costa Rica a partial exception), could not boast a cultural life comparable to that of their larger Latin American neighbours. However, in this period we have an obviously important exception: Rubén Darío (1867–1916), born in Nicaragua – although living mainly outside Central America – is considered by many to be the greatest of all Hispanic American poets. Under his influence, modernism flourished in Central America, with such names as Alfonso Cortés and José Coronel Urtecho (Nicaragua), José Valdés and Vicente Rosales (El Salvador), Enrique Gómez Carrillo and Máximo Soto Hall (Guatemala), Juan Ramón Molina and Froilán Turcios (Honduras), Rafael Cardona and Julián Marchena (Costa Rica). Apart from modernism, at least two other literary trends deserve mention: Costa Rican *costumbrismo*, which tried to convey the life of the countryside in poetry (Aquileo Echeverría, Joaquín García Monge) or in prose (Manuel González Zeledón); and, also in Costa Rica, the very interesting mystical poetry of Roberto Brenes Mesén.

While some Central American writings are known and read in other Hispanic American countries, it is difficult to find comparable instances in other fields. The Guatemalan composer Jesús Castillo, for example, or the Costa Rican sculptor and painter Max Jiménez are nowadays almost forgotten outside their own countries.

Liberal reforms and Liberal dictatorships

Central American Liberal reforms have distinct similarities when compared from an exclusively institutional point of view. Constitutions, codes, laws regarding the laicization of education and other aspects of social life have a definite resemblance in all five countries, as they were inspired by the same European and North American models. But striking differences are found when the actual meaning and consequences of these reforms are studied (although between the Guatemalan and Salvadoran cases there are close similarities). With regard to the social and political results of Liberal transformations, Costa Rica is the only country where a comparison of laws with reality shows any consistency on points referring to the liberty, equality and rights of the citizens.

The first country to experience a genuine Liberal reform was Guatemala. After a movement which failed (in 1869), a Liberal revolution toppled the Conservative regime of Vicente Cerna in 1871. This revolution was planned on Mexican territory, with the support of the Liberal government of Juárez. Its leaders were Miguel García Granados, president from 1871 to 1873, and Justo Rufino Barrios, president and virtual dictator from 1873 until his death in 1885. The main economic measures of the new Liberal regime have already been mentioned. In the political field, the Liberal constitution of 1879 established a form of government with a strong presidency, centralized and representative, and with a one-house legislative assembly. It also brought about the complete separation between state and church, thus crowning several anti-clerical and secularizing measures taken since 1871. The reality of Liberal political power in Guatemala, however, as in the remainder of the isthmus, was embodied in harsh dictatorships favouring the local oligarchy and export-led economic growth, exercising a repressive vigilance over the working classes and systematically thwarting the constitution. The most important dictator in this period, after Barrios, was Manuel Estrada Cabrera (1898–1920).

In El Salvador, the Liberal reforms were started – after an early failed attempt – by Liberal leaders very much influenced by Guatemala, Santiago González (1871–6) and Rafael Zaldívar (1876–85). Zaldívar was toppled by General Francisco Menéndez (1885–90), under whom the Liberal process was completed by the constitution of 1886. This was the most stable of all Central American Liberal regimes; there were no civil struggles from 1898 to 1931. From 1913 until 1927 the country was governed by the so-called dynasty of the Meléndez–Quiñónez, under three related presidents – Carlos Meléndez (1913–18), Jorge Meléndez (1919–23) and Alfonso Quiñónez Molina (1923–7). As in Guatemala, despite the constitution and other Liberal documents, oligarchic dictatorship is a more apt label for the Salvadoran Liberal regime than representative republic.

In Costa Rica, Liberal measures were undertaken early by mildly Conservative governments such as those of Braulio Carrillo (1835–42) and Juan Rafael Mora (1849–59). The constitution of 1844 was already clearly Liberal. So the *coup d'état* of 1870 led by Tomás Guardia, who became president (1870–82), and the Liberal constitution of 1871 were only a part of a very gradual process of transformation, which saw less dramatic upheavals than those occurring in Guatemala and El Salvador. However, the Liberal state in Costa Rica was, socially as well as politically, less of a grotesque farce than elsewhere in Central America. As early as 1889, the Liberals suffered electoral defeat and accepted it. It is true that in 1917 the constitutional process was interrupted by the dictatorship of Federico Tinoco Granados, but only briefly. The political participation of the popular masses (mainly peasants), and the attitude of most Liberal and Conservative governments, less repressive and more prone to social reforms, gave more stability to the Costa Rican regime. This explains its stronger position with regard to the owners of banana plantations, who in Costa Rica were taxed from 1909 onwards, before the other Central American countries were able to enforce taxation, and who were forced to fulfil their commitments concerning railway construction.

Honduras is a clear case of frustrated Liberal reform. In other words, although the reforms were carried out and the institutional frame of a Liberal state was built, the lack of a strong dominant class at the national level proved it to be, in the long run, a very empty process. During the nineteenth century Honduras had an economy and society consisting of numerous but unimportant local activities which were not really linked to each other within an integrated framework: silver mines (Tegucigalpa), timber (Atlantic coast), cattle raising (Olancho and the southern region), tobacco (Copán), and so on. Local geography made communications difficult, and its effect was reinforced by the destruction and massacre which occurred during the civil wars and 'pacifications' after independence. Between 1876 and the first years of the twentieth century, under the influence of Guatemalan Liberals and of such leaders as Marco Aurelio Soto and Ramón Rosa, a real attempt at Liberal reform was made, with the laicization of state and society, new legal codes, a new tax organization, a railway policy, strong support offered to mines and coffee plantations, and so on. But the lack of a dominant class capable of giving sense to the state and its overall reform policies, and of integrating the country and its local oligarchies, was responsible for the failure of this attempt and for a very unstable and weak government, which was an easy prey to the banana companies. As in the remainder of the isthmus, Honduras suffered dictatorships during this period: those of Marco Aurelio Soto (1876–83), Luis Bográn (1883–91) and Policarpo Bonilla (1893–9).

In Nicaragua a late but quite typical Liberal reform took place under José Santos Zelaya (1893–1909), with such measures as the Agrarian Law of 1902, which established a strong control over the labour force. But Zelaya's nationalism in economic matters (although quite moderate) led many foreign residents to seek the alliance of the Nicaraguan Conservatives, still a force to be reckoned with in spite of the Liberal reforms. The revolt of 1909, which overthrew the Liberal leader and restored Conservative rule, was supported by the United States. Three years later the United States intervened militarily and administered Nicaragua for the next twenty years (see below).

Liberal leaders in Central America shared a positivist ideology. Unlike the old Liberals of the period of independence, even if they did not formally renounce the democratic political ideal, they believed that the national economies of the isthmus had to progress, with the help of strong political and social control, before democracy became feasible. They felt also profound contempt for the Indian and peasant masses, whom they distrusted, and whom they submitted to a harsh repression. It should be clear, however, that the contradiction between strongly Liberal imported institutions and evident social oppression was to be expected. The kind of dependent economic growth experienced in Central American countries had no use for workers with full labour rights and citizenship. On the contrary, it needed firm political and social control and low wages. Costa Rica was an exception, but only a partial one.

The dream of union as a basis for foreign intervention

By the end of the nineteenth century, most Central American states were sufficiently consolidated to make the restoration of their union in a federation difficult. Moreover, such a project had never obtained the support of the dominant classes, and lacked any popular or economic base. It was a dream of middle-class intellectuals and occasionally a tool or a pretext in the hands of ambitious politicians, or even foreign countries such as Mexico and the United States.

Trying to build a new Central American union for his own profit, Justo Rufino Barrios, for example, provoked a war between Guatemala and El Salvador in 1876; he was defeated and killed in Salvadoran territory in 1885. The next unionist project was a consequence of the last British attempt at gunboat diplomacy in Central America in 1894–5. Following a diplomatic incident, British warships blockaded the Nicaraguan port of Corinto, but the intervention of the United States led to a settlement by which Britain recognized Nicaraguan sovereignty over the Mosquito Coast in return for the payment of an indemnity. After that, British withdrawal and American pre-eminence in the isthmus, as in the entire Caribbean, were accepted trends. Seizing the occasion of that last British threat, the Honduran president, Policarpo Bonilla, invited his Central American colleagues to Amapala, where a pact was signed by Honduras, Nicaragua and El Salvador, which were to unite in a Greater Republic of Central America (20 June 1895). The United States seemed at first to accept this measure, but in 1896 the US government did not recognize the ambassador sent to Washington by the new united Republic. In fact the whole project was very fragile, and it was not long before it collapsed, soon after a draft constitution had been written (1898).

At the beginning of the twentieth century, the United States and the Mexican regime of Porfirio Díaz decided to join efforts to intervene in Central American affairs. The United States had already supported the Corinto Convention of 1902, which was signed by all the Central

American republics except Guatemala and which agreed to submit any disputes arising between them to a regional tribunal of arbitrators. When in 1906 Guatemalan revolutionaries tried to overthrow the dictator Manuel Estrada Cabrera with the aid of the Salvadoran government, the result was a war which eventually involved Honduras as well. The United States and Mexico acted together and, with Costa Rica, organized a meeting aboard the North American ship *Marblehead*, where a pact was signed in July 1906, ending the current war and planning a further meeting at San José. But Nicaragua refused to recognize the interference of the United States in Central America, and sent no envoy to the meeting. In San José, the other four countries decided that the presidents of Mexico and the United States would arbitrate the possible aftermaths of the recent war, while a Central American tribunal would settle future problems within the region. The first tribunal, a few months later, failed to settle a complicated affair involving first Nicaragua and Honduras and then Guatemala and El Salvador. Porfirio Díaz and Theodore Roosevelt then convinced the Central American governments to send representatives to a conference in Washington.

The meeting at Washington (1907) decided to promote an important programme of co-operation between the countries of Central America, to establish a Central American Bureau which was to promote reunification, and a Central American Court of Justice to settle future disputes. Soon after this conference, in 1908, the tribunal acted successfully in a question involving Guatemala and El Salvador against Honduras. It functioned until 1917, when it was ended because of its inability to condemn the Bryan–Chamorro Treaty between the United States and Nicaragua. Further attempts at Central American union were made without success in 1921 and 1923.

The question of the inter-oceanic canal: illegitimate birth of Panama and intervention in Nicaragua

Plans for the eventual building of an inter-oceanic canal underwent substantial changes after the Clayton–Bulwer Treaty (1850). Colombia conceded rights in Panama to a French company, the Universal Inter-Oceanic Company, which began construction of the canal in 1882, under the direction of Ferdinand de Lesseps. But the company went bankrupt in 1889 without having completed its work. Its chief engineer, Bunau-Varilla, sold the French concession in Panama to the United States. The

North Americans, however, only became interested in the Panama route after an attempt to build their own canal in Nicaragua failed around 1895, because of extreme difficulties and costliness, and financial problems linked to the world economic depression of the time.

By the time the North Americans resumed their interest in an inter-oceanic canal, new developments had taken place. The second Hay–Pauncefote Treaty with Britain (1901) opened up the possibility of complete control by the United States of a fortified canal. This was of great importance from a strategic point of view, due to growing North American interests both in the Caribbean and in the Pacific ocean. But the Nicaraguan president, Zelaya, was adamant in his decision not to permit foreign control over any part of his country's territory. So negotiations began in 1902 with Colombia over the building by the United States of a canal in Panama, and including the question of North American sovereignty over the canal zone. But in 1903 the Colombian Congress refused to ratify the Hay–Herrán Treaty, because of a military intervention by the United States in Panama without the consent of either Colombia or the local authorities (September 1902). The North Americans then supported the secession of Panama from Colombia, promoting a Panamanian movement led by Dr Manuel Amador. The new country was recognized immediately by the United States, and a treaty was swiftly negotiated (1903) permitting the construction of the canal and establishing North American control, for a century, of a canal zone ten miles wide. The canal opened in 1914, and Panama became the most typical enclave economy of Latin America, utterly dependent on the new inter-oceanic route and the services it demanded. Moreover, it was politically a sort of protectorate of the United States, very much like Cuba.

In the meantime, the possibility of an alternative Nicaraguan inter-oceanic canal was being negotiated by Zelaya with European capitalists. This was contrary to the economic and strategic interests of the United States and, with other factors, led to the rupture of diplomatic relations between the two countries in 1908, and the overthrow of Zelaya in 1909. The United States then seized on the chaotic state of finance in Nicaragua as an opportunity to intervene, landing Marines (1912), confirming a puppet Conservative regime established in 1911, obtaining control over the Nicaraguan customs, railways and National Bank, and creating a National Guard under North American officers. The situation was best encapsulated in the Bryan–Chamorro Treaty (1916), which granted the

United States the perpetual and exclusive right to dig and operate in Nicaragua an inter-oceanic canal, and cemented the *de facto* North American protectorate over this country, even if the provisions which would establish a formal protectorate had to be eliminated from the treaty to secure its ratification by the United States Senate.

The Liberal resistance became a real revolution in 1925–26, with the support of Mexico, when the marines withdrew for the first time. But the Liberal army chief José María Moncada negotiated an agreement with the United States in 1927 in order to win the Nicaraguan presidential election the following year (which he did); his lieutenant, Augusto César Sandino, rejecting this agreement, then became the leader of a national guerilla struggle. He denounced the Bryan–Chamorro treaty and all kinds of United States intervention in Nicaraguan life, and destroyed North American property. For some six years he and his small group, enjoying considerable popular support, successfully challenged not only the National Guard, nurtured and trained by the United States, but US marines as well. Then, with the change in foreign policy brought about by Franklin D. Roosevelt, the marines left the country and Roberto Sacasa was elected. Sandino ceased to fight in January 1933 and approached President Sacasa, only to be treacherously murdered the next year by the National Guard, on the order of its leader Anastasio Somoza García, who already exerted a *de facto* control over the Nicaraguan government.

CONCLUSION

By 1930, the model of economic growth, social control and political organization established by the Central American Liberal oligarchies five or six decades earlier seemed to be exhausted and doomed to failure, assailed by the middle-class and popular movements of the 1920s and having to face the economic crisis of 1929. But as no alternative model to that built during the heyday of the export economy was in sight, the transition to new social, economic and political structures was a very long and difficult process.

The definitive integration of Central America into the world market, which brought about a long period of economic growth, also brought about a dilemma born of the new structures it helped to create, and which is not completely solved even today. The Liberal order, except in Costa Rica, excluded the vast majority of the population, not only from the profits derived from economic growth, but also from any political participation. The peasant masses never completely accepted the new pattern of domination, and the cultural, economic and social abyss between the dominant groups and those they dominated became more profound than ever. Under such conditions, it is difficult to build viable modern nations, or stable political and social structures.

Central America

Caribbean Sea

PACIFIC OCEAN

MEXICO

BELIZE
Belize City

GUATEMALA
Puerto Barrios
Puerto Cortés
San Pedro Sula
HONDURAS
Tegucigalpa
Chalatenango
Quezaltenango
Santa Ana
Guatemala
San Salvador
EL SALVADOR
San Miguel
Gulf of Fonseca

Puerto Cabezas

NICARAGUA
Jinotega
Matagalpa
León
Corinto
Managua
Granada

Bluefields

COSTA RICA
Puntarenas
San José
Cartago
Puerto Limón

PANAMA
Colón
Panama City

COLOMBIA

300 km
200 miles

3

CRISIS AND CONFLICT, 1930 TO THE PRESENT

The establishment of stable nation states and permanent economic links with the world market through agricultural – especially coffee – exports took place in Central America during the second half of the nineteenth century. This process occurred first and most successfully in Costa Rica; later, and after much bloodshed, in Guatemala and El Salvador; and belatedly and incompletely in Honduras and Nicaragua. The backwardness inherited from the Spanish colonial period, the cyclical crisis in the international coffee market and the political struggles of the oligarchy for control of the government all slowed down economic growth, social progress and the development of institutional stability. Nevertheless, by the beginning of the twentieth century important changes had taken place in social stratification with the appearance of a coffee bourgeoisie and a small urban middle class, and political life was stable, though not democratic.

In 1914 the total population of Cental America was a little under 4 million, of whom nearly 60 percent lived in Guatemala and El Salvador. The basis of society – the agrarian structure – had three characteristics: large coffee estates controlled by national farmers producing for export; banana plantations, foreign-owned, with a vertically integrated production and marketing structure tied directly to the North American market; and small landholdings belonging to peasants who cultivated basic grains and other products for their own consumption or to satisfy internal demand. (Coffee and bananas accounted for 80 per cent of Central American exports.) The labour market was composed of *mozos colonos,* farmhands tied to the coffee haciendas by lifelong indebtedness; agricultural workers on U.S.-owned banana plantations; and – the largest sector – peasant smallholders, sharecroppers and migrant day-labourers who worked for wages

This chapter was translated from the Spanish by Elizabeth Ladd.

during the harvest season. In Costa Rica, this last category did not exist on a significant scale, and in Honduras subsistence farmers were predominant, partly as a result of that country's mountainous terrain.

Before 1930, the advantages of the export agriculture model were never doubted. On the contrary, the high degree of economic specialization and the freedom to sell in the foreign market were seen as a great opportunity for material progress in certain regions and among a few small groups. It is certainly true that a number of important changes came about under the impetus of export production. More than 80 per cent of the railway lines that exist today in Central America had already been built by about 1910. On the Atlantic coast the ports of Puerto Cortés, Puerto Barrios and Limón (in Honduras, Guatemala and Costa Rica, respectively) were renovated to reduce the cost of direct transport to European and North American markets. A financial and banking system was gradually established; before the First World War there were twenty-three banks in the region, most of them based on national capital. Although the electricity system was limited and served only the capital cities of Guatemala, San Salvador and San José before 1917, the telegraph linked the major cities and the most important economic areas of the region.

Central America came under U.S. influence in the late nineteenth century and this intensified when Britain in 1901, under the Hay–Pauncefote Treaty, agreed to diminish its presence there. The United States began to construct an inter-oceanic canal in Panama, which had, with U.S. assistance, secured its independence from Colombia in 1903; the canal was opened in 1914. The United States intervened in Nicaragua in 1912 and remained there, with a brief interruption, until 1933. At the same time, Washington imposed its will on the other Central American republics through military and diplomatic means during various episodes of political instability. After the First World War the U.S. economic presence in Central America was extended beyond investments in agriculture, railways and ports. For example, electricity services in three of the five countries passed into North American hands. More than 75 per cent of foreign trade was to or from the United States (an increase from the pre-war period largely at the expense of Germany). Such developments contributed to a period of relative prosperity, particularly in the 1920s and especially for Guatemala, El Salvador and Costa Rica. The export model became even more firmly entrenched. In the years immediately before the world crisis of 1929–30, income from coffee and bananas accounted for nearly 90 per cent of export revenue in Costa Rica, Guatemala and El

Salvador, and 70 per cent in Honduras and Nicaragua (where the mining of gold and silver remained significant). The 1920s were also characterized by a political stability in which – at least in Costa Rica, under the Liberal 'Olympians' represented by Juan Ricardo Jiménez Oreamuno and Cleto González Víquez; in Guatemala, where José María Orellana and Lázaro Chacón, both Liberals, were successively elected; and in El Salvador under the leadership of the Liberal Meléndez–Quiñónez family – the functioning of the oligarchical structures of control and domination were compatible with a form, albeit limited, of electoral, representative democracy.

When the international economic crisis of 1929 reached Central America, it immediately changed the dynamics of foreign commerce through a drop in international demand for the region's traditional agricultural products as well as in the traditional sales of manufactured goods from more economically developed countries, especially the United States. The impact of the world depression varied from country to country. The highest levels in foreign trade were in fact achieved in Nicaragua in 1926, in Guatemala in 1927, and in Costa Rica and El Salvador in 1928, whereas Honduras did not see its foreign-exchange earnings decline until 1931. Similarly, the lowest point in the depression cycle was experienced in different ways.

It is possible, however, to generalize about the effects of the economic crisis on the region as a whole, although there were certain distinctive features in each country. The depression was not felt locally as a financial catastrophe paralysing economic life; it was experienced as a period of stagnation lasting more than a decade, scarcely interrupted by moments of transitory recovery. Because Central American society generally had agriculture as its economic base and the external market as its dynamic factor, and because more complete indicators do not exist, statistics for the production and export of coffee and bananas or, even better, data on foreign trade more generally are used to show the external origin of the crisis in the form of declining international demand, which recuperated only after 1945 and whose counterpart was a parallel decline in imports. These were the combined effects of the international crisis of the decade and the Second World War at the end of the depression.

As seen in Table 3.1, there was no spectacular crash in regional production or exports, but rather a zigzag pattern, which during the first years showed an average decline equivalent to 50 per cent of the value of exports in relation to the highest point of the preceding decade, and which imposed severe limitations on the capacity to import. The international

Table 3.1. *Central America: Value of Foreign Trade 1930–45 (in millions of current dollars)*

Year	Guatemala		El Salvador		Honduras		Nicaragua		Costa Rica		Central America	
	Export	Import	Export	Import	Export	Import	Export	Import	Export	Import	Export	Import
1930	51.6	33.0	22.0	20.0	54.9	26.0	13.4	16.0	27.5	11.0	169.4	106.0
1931	33.2	26.0	19.0	12.0	55.8	17.0	10.4	12.0	24.1	9.0	142.5	76.0
1932	23.3	15.0	9.0	9.0	55.6	12.0	7.0	7.0	14.4	5.0	109.3	48.0
1933	16.5	12.0	9.0	8.0	60.0	10.0	6.1	6.0	14.0	6.0	105.6	42.0
1934	19.2	12.0	9.0	5.0	52.6	12.0	4.6	5.0	8.2	9.0	93.6	46.0
1935	16.1	15.0	10.0	9.0	17.1	6.0	4.6	5.0	7.3	7.0	55.1	42.0
1936	22.0	18.0	10.0	8.0	11.2	5.0	3.5	6.0	7.8	8.0	54.5	45.0
1937	23.0	26.0	15.0	10.0	12.2	6.0	6.2	6.0	10.8	12.0	67.2	60.0
1938	23.5	26.0	10.0	9.0	15.9	10.0	4.3	6.0	9.3	13.0	63.0	64.0
1939	24.3	24.0	12.0	9.0	22.5	11.0	4.8	7.0	8.6	17.0	72.2	68.0
1940	15.6	20.0	10.0	8.0	22.3	11.0	3.7	8.0	7.0	17.0	58.6	64.0
1941	18.8	19.0	10.0	8.0	21.3	11.0	4.6	12.0	9.8	18.0	64.5	68.0
1942	26.7	14.0	17.0	9.0	20.3	12.0	5.6	8.0	10.2	12.0	79.8	55.0
1943	26.3	18.0	21.0	12.0	9.0	10.0	7.7	16.0	12.2	20.0	76.2	76.0
1944	31.1	21.0	22.0	12.0	19.8	14.0	7.8	12.0	10.4	22.0	91.1	81.0
1945	39.7	23.0	21.0	13.0	27.6	15.0	6.9	14.0	11.5	27.0	106.7	92.0

Source: CEPAL: *América Latina: Relación de Precios de Intercambio* (Santiago, 1976), pp. 35, 43, 45, 49, 53.

collapse of the gold standard in 1931 created problems with the exchange
rate; Guatemala and Honduras resisted devaluation, while Costa Rica and
El Salvador, after letting their currencies float, devalued between 1931
and 1933. (Nicaragua followed suit in 1937.) The countries most affected
by the crisis were Honduras and Nicaragua, and in both recovery was slow
and at levels lower than those of the rest of the region. In Nicaragua,
moreover, the balance of trade remained persistently unfavorable for fifteen years. Stagnation lifted slightly in 1936–9, and especially in 1937,
in Guatemala, El Salvador and Costa Rica, but the paralysis of international commerce precipitated by the war in Europe contributed to the
problems of the external sector at the start of the Second World War (see
Table 3.1). The levels of foreign trade, public spending and the gross
domestic product (GDP) in general recovered only after 1945, and in some
cases, such as Honduras, even later.

The existence of an internal market economy was important because
most agricultural production and that of the small artisan-manufacturing
sector was consumed domestically. It is difficult to make precise calculations of the value of production destined for the foreign market and that
which went into domestic consumption; the latter contained an important
element of self-consumption which was centred not only in peasant economies but also in the traditional estates whose owners lived on an extensive
system of sharecropping. Calculations made for the beginning of the
1940s suggest that on average less than half the value of agricultural
production was destined for export trade.[1]

The nature of the agricultural sector was determined by the functioning
and relations among its three sub-sectors. The banana industry was modern and controlled by North American capital, its operations internationally integrated. Thus, the banana industry was affected by the crisis not
only in the decline in the volume of trade and the fall in the price of
bananas but also by changes in investment strategies on the part of the
parent company. In the 1930s the United Fruit Company, unable to
combat the 'Panama disease' effectively, decided to transfer its plantations
to the Pacific region: Tiquisate in Guatemala, and Quepos in Costa Rica.

The second sub-sector was the coffee industry, which had a different
level of capitalization. Coffee enterprises were able to continue even with
decreased revenues because of the permanent character of coffee cultivation

[1] E. Torres-Rivas, 'Centroamérica: algunos rasgos de la sociedad posguerra', Working Paper of the
Kellogg Institute, no. 25 (Washington, D.C., 1984), table 1, p. 49.

and also because of previous experience with depressed cycles followed by periods of prosperity. The decline in income in the coffee sector affected the system of production only in a relative way, by inhibiting the expansion of cultivated areas and improvements in productivity. The decrease in international demand affected coffee earnings, which could be absorbed by the land-ownership structure without affecting basic production resources on the estates.

The third sub-sector was the peasant economy, whose production was distributed more in the form of family self-consumption than through sales of surpluses in local markets. In fact, only this sector of the economy improved its level of production. The crisis stimulated the conditions to strengthen a simple mercantile economy as an alternative to the relative weakness of the mercantile export sector. Increased production of basic grain crops, especially corn and beans, confirmed that the mercantile economy could reappear or invigorate itself wherever independent producers maintained their means of production, the availability of food stimulating domestic demand. Figures for this period indicate that there were times when grain and beans were quite abundant, being especially so, for instance, in 1937. Using logical deductions based on a knowledge of the structure of production, we can conclude that such yields came from small properties. Undoubtedly, it is this information that has enabled Bulmer-Thomas to analyse the diverse mechanisms which palliated the crisis, one of which was the substitution of agricultural imports during the second half of the 1930s.[2] Domestic agriculture grew in importance for some time, and more because of internal conditions that reduced the ability to import than because of governmental decisions.

The absorption capacities of the peasant economies were put to the test when they became a refuge for the rural unemployed masses. As happens in mono-export economies, where dynamic impulses originate in foreign demand, the loss of such impulses translates into a partial decadence in the monetary sector of the internal market, but without catastrophic consequences. Coffee production depended only partly on wage relations, as can be seen from the position of the *mozo colono* in Guatemala, El Salvador or Nicaragua, or the sharecropper in Costa Rica. In both situations coffee producers avoided the problems of paying wages, leaving the matter of maintaining and replacing the labour force as marginal to the cost of production.

[2] V. Bulmer-Thomas, *The Political Economy of Central America since 1920* (Cambridge, 1987), chap. 4.

During this period, too, coffee earnings, derived from and subject to international prices, were relatively independent of the internal cost of production, which only indicated a lower limit; cycles of growth or depression were not reflected in wage levels or other living conditions of the labour force. The standard of living of the peasant population was tied to the level at which production itself yielded enough to support a subsistence economy. Nevertheless, there was unemployment on the national urban level, less visible in the country, where 80 per cent of the population lived.

Government response to these problems in all five countries can be described as a policy of confronting the economic cycle in a traditional and orthodox manner. The traditional element was determined by the culture of the coffee producers, whose mentality, strongly influenced by economic liberalism, led them to insist upon the inefficacious nature of state action. The orthodoxy of policy lay in its application of the principle that state spending stimulates demand only to the extent that it exceeds tax revenues; therefore, fiscal deficit had to be avoided at all costs. Central American governments carried out immediate budget cuts as a consequence of the appreciable fall in fiscal revenues which came largely from taxes on imports and exports. The most surprising development in this regard occurred in the mid-1930s, when the reductions in public spending reached the level where they began to produce small surpluses, which, for example, in Guatemala and El Salvador, accumulated as unspent savings.

Of the five governments, that in Guatemala was the most orthodox, and after 1932 managed to balance the budget, henceforth generating a growing surplus which accumulated unproductively until the end of the war. The government not only reduced public employment, it also cut salaries and instituted a policy of road construction – based on free labour – all of which did nothing to stimulate domestic demand. The other governments were in a different position, and hampered by the same shrinkage of public spending to prevent annual deficit balances, they resorted to internal debt. The budgets of Honduras and Nicaragua were managed at the lowest level of purely administrative expenses, a level so low that the next step would have been total paralysis. The year 1937 saw only a fleeting improvement in foreign trade, but this was important in that it signalled a turning-point after which state spending began a slow growth.

The orthodox attitude in public policy, influenced by the defense of the landowners' interests, ensured that state spending during this epoch of crisis not only failed to address the effects of the depression cycle but also indirectly contributed to them. The growth of debt incurred to cover budget balances always proved unproductive while the governments' contribution to the GDP was always small and, during these years, declining. Programmes of public works, purchase of crops or credit expansion were practically unthinkable. In general, there existed no fiscal policy capable of 'curing' a depression that had foreign origins or of limiting the dislocation caused by a boom in exports when this originated entirely in price movements rather than in the growth of the productivity of labour.

In sum, except for variations of minor significance, the Central American states responded to the economic crisis with a set of orthodox liberal economic policy measures. Their policies (or absence of them) weakened domestic consumption, drastically cutting public spending, reducing salaries or limiting the mobilization of financial resources.

At the same time, as we shall see, a profound fear of social unrest found expression in a defence of the traditional political order by heightening authoritarian mechanisms already deeply rooted in the culture of the region.

The impact of the Second World War on the Central American economies was considerable because Europe was an important market for the region's exports. In the short term the most important consequence was the loss of first the German and then the British markets for coffee and the reorientation of Central American trade towards the United States, consolidating a tendency that had been growing since the First World War. This shift was particularly important because the region's trade balance with the United States was in deficit whereas it had been in surplus with Britain and Germany. Central America was converted not only into a good neighbour but also into a good partner. Among the most important measures was the Inter-American Coffee Agreement (November 1940) that established quotas for the first time for the expanding U.S. market. Banana exports, on the other hand, declined. The reduction or loss of South East Asian markets produced a degree of agricultural diversification through the emergence of 'war crops', such as rubber, basic oils and vegetable fibres, the strategic production of which the U.S. government encharged to the United and Standard Fruit companies in Guatemala, Honduras and Costa Rica. However, the importance of these crops proved to be temporary, and after the war only abacá and African palm continued to be subordinate products of the banana enclaves.

None of the Central American countries was at this time in a position to encourage industrial growth through import substitution. Although the war greatly impeded imports, there was little effort to establish the domestic supply of manufactured goods. By 1944–5 the countries of Central America, especially Guatemala and El Salvador, had perforce accumulated sizeable reserves of foreign exchange and gold which were not employed in productive activity but were largely used to pay the external debt, especially the oldest loans, those advanced by the British. At the same time, the inflow of external earnings contributed to inflation, which was particularly acute in Honduras and Nicaragua.[3] The fiscal problems that had prevailed since 1930 continued, to varying degrees, until 1942, but it was only in Costa Rica under the Calderón Guardia regime that they caused serious problems.

The most important political phenomenon at the beginning of the 1930s was the recrudescence of the peasant war in the north of Nicaragua. As is well known, Nicaragua had been invaded on 3 October 1912 by the United States, when a squadron of warships entered the Pacific port of Corinto and 1,500 marines landed in an effort to end the struggle between Conservatives and Liberals. The North Americans eventually left (August 1925), but Nicaraguan fratricide caused them to return, in larger numbers, in 1926. When this renewed intervention led to what they considered to be a shameful accord between the foreign military forces and the traditional Nicaraguan politicians, Augusto César Sandino and a group of dissident Liberal officers rose up in rebellion in July 1927, opening an intermittent but prolonged civil war.

At the beginning of 1930 the marine units stationed in Nicaragua were concentrated in the cities and left the principal operations of the war in the hands of the National Guard (Guardia Nacional), which they had recently created. The course of the war was irregular, but the offensives carried out by Sandino and his men gained strength during the winter of 1931–2, possibly as a result of the economic crisis and its effects among the impoverished peasantry of Las Segovias, one of Nicaragua's most important coffee-producing areas. U.S. President Herbert Hoover announced his intention to withdraw the last of the marines after the Nicaraguan presidential elections in November 1932. Washington wanted the Nicaraguan government to reach an agreement directly with the Sandinistas or con-

[3] V. Bulmer-Thomas, *Political Economy of Central America*, p. 100.

tinue the war without United States military aid. As a result, on 2 January 1933, the day after Dr. Juan Bautista Sacasa took office as president and put Anastasio Somoza in command of the National Guard, the last foreign troops sailed from Corinto. At the beginning of February 1933, Sandino reached a peace agreement with the new liberal government, but a year later, on 21 February 1934, he was assassinated by the National Guard. In the meantime the guerrilla war that developed in Nicaragua had considerable repercussions throughout Latin America but especially in Central America where it inflamed the social discontent arising from unemployment, low wages and shortages caused by the economic crisis.

These factors, without doubt, lay behind the bloody peasant rebellion in the Izalco region in El Salvador in January 1932. However, the uprising and slaughter that followed it should be seen in the context of the election in January 1931 of a popular leader, Arturo Araujo, who in the name of 'laborism' won more than 50 per cent of the vote and defeated the candidate of the powerful coffee oligarchy, Alberto Gómez Zárate. This election, hailed as the only free poll ever held in the country, constituted a popular victory that was rapidly countered by the military coup of December 1931 led by General Maximiliano Hernández Martínez. The rupture of constitutional order created profound internal and international discontent, and, in accordance with the provisions of the Peace and Friendship Treaty signed between the five Central American governments and the United States in 1923, Washington refused to recognize the new regime. However, General Martínez was easily able to hold on to office once the 1932 revolt had been suppressed, eventually obliging the United States to recognize his government in an act that effectively terminated both the 1923 original peace treaty and Washington's policy of boycotting non-elected regimes.

The leadership and programme of the popular rebellion of January 1932 have never been sufficiently clarified, but it was certainly a peasant uprising and in some areas, such as Nahizalco and Juayúa, it was vigorously supported by indigenous communities. For three days well-armed government troops fought the insurrectionary groups armed with machetes and clubs who were overrunning the western part of El Salvador in a random fashion, peace being restored at the price of twenty-five or thirty thousand deaths. The severity of this repression created a climate of terror which extended beyond the frontiers of this small country and lasted for many years.

What happened in El Salvador was not a well-planned revolutionary action but rather a disorganized display of deep popular discontent that was far from an isolated event in the region. The artisanal base of Central American manufacturing and the existence of a vast peasant class effectively confined organized protest to that sector of the agricultural proletariat linked to the banana plantations. The social discontent of a population which lacked traditions of organization and struggle was general but unstructured. In Costa Rica, though, it took on a relatively more systematic and active character when, in August 1934, popular malaise finally led to the banana-workers' strike in the Limón region. This strike lasted for more than forty-five days, enjoyed a broad class-based solidarity and finally turned out to be a decisive event in the social history of Costa Rica since it marked the birth of an independent union movement in that country.

There were also social unrest and protest in the plantation areas of northern Honduras. In February 1932, a broad-based but short-lived strike movement broke out in the Tela Railroad Company as a consequence of the dismissal of eight hundred workers and a general salary cut. The government of Vicente Mejía Colindres initially backed the Honduran workers' demands, fearing that the company's actions – which exacerbated the effects of the economic crisis – would lead to the generalized spread of collective unrest. On the other hand, discontent among the banana-workers in the Izabal zone in Guatemala failed to generate a strike movement or other forms of collective protest. All that remains in the historical record of the social struggles in this country is the pre-emptive repression ordered by President Ubico, alarmed by the news from neighbouring countries. The incipient union movement started by socialist-inspired artisans was destroyed when the government ordered the execution of fourteen militant student and labour organizers and imprisoned more than twenty persons, who remained in jail without judicial process until 1944.

It is necessary to stress that during this period institutional stability was achieved by means of diverse processes which had nothing to do with democratic mechanisms and which were, in fact, as much the results of the depression and its social consequences as of the authoritarian tradition and political *caudillismo*. The most wide-spread opinion among analysts of this era is that the system of oligarchical domination in general was directly threatened by popular discontent, the almost universal reaction being to install military governments which had a great capacity for repression and were legitimated precisely by their ability to keep things under control in the face of the risk of rampant social disorder. With the passage of time the most negative aspects of a political system that seemed to be always on the defensive were reinforced. Central among these was the inability of the regime to tolerate any opposition.

The electoral system which seemed to have been consolidated in the previous decade was *formally* upheld in all the countries except El Salvador, where the coup by General Hernández Martínez was validated in 1932 by the National Assembly, which installed him as president. Even he, however, continued to govern through successive re-elections until his fall in 1944. In Guatemala the Liberal general Jorge Ubico was elected, though without opposition, in February 1931. His position as *caudillo* was soon confirmed when he annulled municipal autonomy, seriously interfered with the independence of the judiciary and generally concentrated power in his own hands. Ubico was reelected in 1937 and again in 1943, after successive modifications of the Constitution. In Honduras General Tiburcio Carías Andino was elected in February 1933, after two previous efforts; like Ubico, he managed to endow the executive power with total authority, centralizing in his hands the control of the country's political life, except for activity in the areas reserved to the jurisdiction of foreign plantation-owners. A constitutional assembly in 1936 promulgated a document modifying the length of the presidential term and authorizing it to continue for six additional years after its legal expiration in 1939; further extensions authorized by the parliament enabled Carías to rule until 1948. In Nicaragua, the government of the Liberal Juan Bautista Sacasa, elected under U.S. supervision in 1932, was overthrown by a coup d'état led by the impatient General Somoza, also a Liberal and Sacasa's nephew. After a brief period of transition, Somoza was elected in November 1936 and became President of Nicaragua on 1 January 1937. Thus began the long period of the dictatorship of this family, which did not end until 1979.

Costa Rica merits separate mention because its democracy, which took the form of liberal *caudillos* elected on the basis of their prestige, acting through small parties of notables (land-owners, lawyers, etc.) and characterized by their capacity to tolerate the existence of oppostition, largely survived the test of the social effects of the depression. In fact, the last liberal *caudillo,* Ricardo Jiménez, was not elected but appointed in May 1932 by Congress, which first proposed him as candidate and then proclaimed him president. The attempt at a coup in Bella Vista, albeit a failure, revealed the limitations already evident in the old oligarchical model. Yet, in February 1936, León Cortés was elected without a major crisis, and in 1940, Dr. Rafael Angel Calderón Guardia likewise assumed the presidency. Calderón's government is notable not so much for his election landslide (84 per cent of the vote), as for the character of his presidential leadership. There are disputes over whether his exceptional social policy was a product of his social christian background in Europe or of his firm alliance with the Catholic Church – at that moment led by Archbishop Sanabria – or his association with the Communist Party. Whatever the case, during his government the Costa Rican Social Security Fund was set up in 1941; and in 1943 a comprehensive labour law was passed and important modifications made to the Constitution, establishing a set of civil rights distinctly advanced for the time. The social reforms of the Calderón Guardia administration were consolidated under that of his successor, Teodoro Picado (1944–8). However, Calderón Guardia's attempt to regain office in 1948 by means of electoral fraud and in the context of violence unusual in the political life of the country, led, as we shall see, to the civil war of 1948.

The military dictatorships set up in the 1930s in four of the region's countries experienced a twofold pressure towards the end of the Second World War which provoked what has been called the 'crisis of the oligarchy'. On the one hand, the international climate provoked by the defeat of European fascism encouraged people to value local democratic experiences; on the other, internal social forces which had been contained for so many years of stagnation and dictatorship now sought to establish a democratic process through elections, party competition and popular organization. The anti-oligarchical programme was not radical in its ideology – it merely sought to re-establish the rule of law – but the struggles against the dictatorships towards the end of the war initially took the form of urban insurrection.

In April 1944, a general strike obliged General Hernández Martínez of El Salvador to resign. This was a multi-class movement, led by professionals of the middle class and young military officers. The campaign failed to become a national movement or introduce profound changes because its leaders were discovered and shot. As a result, the crisis was resolved internally in the armed forces; the decrepit dictator was replaced by his chief of police and later by another hastily elected general, Salvador Castañeda Castro (1945–8). A movement of similar stamp, also led by young military officers, academics, professionals and middle-class businessmen, managed to oust the dictatorship of Jorge Ubico in Guatemala between June and October 1944. This anti-oligarchical movement was more radical and more successful because the generals of the old army of the dictatorship were expelled from the country, the Liberal Party disappeared and the field was open for free popular organization. With the election of Dr Juan José Arevalo in December 1945 a process of reform with broad popular participation was initiated.

The democratic struggles against the oligarchy and military authoritarianism were not triumphant in Honduras and Nicaragua because the social forces mobilized were weak, although the programme was similar to those of the other countries. In Honduras, the 'anti-oligarchic' campaign led by the Liberals assumed a limited dimension and was essentially a battle against the dictator Carías, who had the support of the foreign plantation interests and thus a sufficient base for governmental stability. Nevertheless, social discontent limited General Carías' ambitions; he had no choice but to agree to hold presidential elections in 1948 and to allow the Liberals to participate, although the victor was his Minister of War, Juan Manuel Gálvez. In Nicaragua the truly democratic interests of social renovation, for which a generation of intellectuals and workers had been fighting, were obscured by traditional Liberal–Conservative rivalry. The Conservative Party, through its youth groups, participated actively in the struggle against Somoza's dictatorship, but neither of the parties managed to give its platform a popular anti-oligarchical content. All the same, Anastasio Somoza was obliged to desist from having himself openly re-elected in 1947. Under both national and international pressure, the dictator had Dr Leonardo Arguello elected 19 February 1947, only to remove him on 24 May. Benjamin Lacayo Sacasa was hastily installed, and after twenty-two days of provisional government, elections were held in which another compliant Liberal, Victor Román y Reyes, emerged the victor. Both were relatives of Somoza, who never left his post as chief of the National Guard and became president again in January 1950.

In Costa Rica the liberal democratic experience had deep historical roots, yet the political forms which characterized it seemed to come to an end in the 1940s. It was the end not only of the liberal *caudillos* but also of a style of government. The pre-electoral period of 1947–8 was characterized by a growing intransigence on the part of the government, which disturbed the conciliatory tradition of the country. Never before had there existed the distrust and political violence now manifested by both the government and the opposition. Under considerable political pressure because of Calderón Guardia's plans for re-election, the government ceded control of the National Electoral Tribunal to one of the opposing factions. Elections were held on 8 February 1948, but the results were not known until the 28 February, when the defeat of Calderón's National Republican Party and the victory of Otilio Ulate was announced. On 1 March the National Congress, whose majority favoured Calderón, annulled the presidential elections. Insurrection would not wait, and the "revolution of '48" broke out on 10 March.

The military events of the two-month civil war in Costa Rica are of minor importance compared to the social and political phenomena which accompanied its unfolding and its resolution. In effect, the social policy of Calderón in the early 1940s had constituted a preliminary rupture of the traditional oligarchical order. The so-called social guarantees he introduced had two decisive but contradictory respects: on the one hand, the beginning of the incorporation of the popular masses into political life through a party of the left (the Communists); and on the other hand, Calderón's connection with the clergy, an outcome of his social christian inclinations learned in Europe that broke with a long anti-clerical tradition of liberal inspiration. The anti-Calderón alliance was itself cleft by even deeper contradictions. On one side was the powerful landed-commercial oligarchy based on coffee, which mounted the most militant opposition in defence of their economic and social interests. On the other were the urban middle class intellectuals and politicians, who had entered the political scene more recently motivated by an interest in modernization and change. They were led by José Figueres, Rodrigo Facio and members of various groups who eventually formed the National Liberation Party in 1951. The crisis was above all a crisis within the ranks of the bourgeoisie, yet precipitated by the new role of labour, which at that time reached a level of organization and influence it would never achieve again.

José Figueres, who led the triumphant coalition of the urban middle class and a fraction of the oligarchy, proclaimed himself chief of the Founding Junta of the Second Republic and governed the country for eighteen months (April 1948 to November 1949). The set of measures taken at this time paradoxically continued the reformist impetus initiated by Calderón and the Communists. For example, Figueres lifted the tax on wheat to lower the price of bread, faciliated wage increases for agricultural workers and established the Consejo Nacional de Producción and the Instituto Costarricense de Electricidad, which nationalized production and reduced the cost of electricity. On 21 June 1948, he imposed a 10 per cent

tax on capital and nationalized the private banks; to the present day these
are considered the most audacious steps ever taken under reformist inspiration. A new constitution, drawn up by a constitutional assembly with a
conservative majority in 1949, did away with the army and established in
its place a rural National Guard and urban police forces. Figueres' transitional government was then replaced by that of Otilio Ulate (November
1949 to November 1953), a conservative leader but one of those who
participated in the victory over Calderón Guardia. The Partido Liberación
Nacional (PLN) was established 12 October 1951 as the result of the
fusion of diverse social forces under a social democratic inspiration, an
ideology already contained in one of its founding currents. In the elections
of 1953, Figueres, as candidate of the PLN was finally constitutionally
elected President of Costa Rica (1953–8), and during his term he pursued
a reformist policy with even greater vigour, which contributed to the
social and economic modernization of the country, the perfecting of
strictly electoral processes, and the definition of a new role for the state.

The political changes begun in 1948 favoured not only a broadening of
political democracy but also a stage of economic growth based on the
diversification and modernization of agriculture and the establishment of
light industry based in the urban centres. The nationalization of the banks
weakened the links between commercial-finance capital and the coffee
exporters, but socio-economic policy did not have a well-defined anti-
oligarchic purpose; it promoted a vast programme of modernization of the
coffee plantation which benefited all the planters at the same time as it
created a co-operative system for marketing coffee in order to limit the
commercial monopoly. In essence, this established a new role for the state
in active economic intervention in order both to modernize the productive
bases of the bourgeoisie and to limit its monopolistic features.

The social policies vigorously pursued by the PLN allowed it to create a
new base of support in the country's peasantry. It should, at the same
time, be noted that after 1948 the urban labour movement, under the
influence of the communist Partido Vanguardia Popular (PVP), was badly
defeated and disorganized. In Central American terms the social-
democratic ideology and policies of the PLN constituted advanced forms
of bourgeois thought, which bore a certain resemblance to the radical
reformism of the governments of Guatemala at the time.

Guatemala's experience is distinct in that the new period of democratic
life lasted less than a decade. The overthrow of the dictatorship of General
Ubico in June 1944 and of his immediate successor General Ponce on 20

October 1944 as the result of a broad-based national movement, was immediately consolidated by the election of a constitutional assembly promulgating a modern constitution with socialist leanings to replace the old liberal-oriented constitution in effect since 1877. A civilian–military junta called elections which Dr Juan José Arévalo won by a landslide. Arévalo's government (1945–51), encouraged the modernization of a socially and culturally backward country, established programs for the promotion and diversification of agriculture, and introduced social security and a labour law; but above all, Arévalo created the conditions for the organization of diverse social interest groups and extended mandatory free public education. He was succeeded by Jacobo Arbenz (1951–4), also elected by a large majority, whose government continued Arévalo's programme but in a more nationalist and radical style.

Between 1951 and 1954 an attempt was made to renovate the old system of land-ownership by imposing an agrarian reform that constituted the most profound challenge to the traditional social order in the entire region. The reform attempted to punish unproductive large land-owners, prohibit any form of personal servitude and utilize the land as a means of production and labor. The implicit purpose was to dismantle the old rural class structure and create an internal market capable of supporting industrial growth under the control of national and state capital. In this sense, Arbenz's programme not only was anti-oligarchic but also contained an obvious anti-imperialist purpose. Probably the most significant feature of the period, begun by Arévalo and intensified by Arbenz, was the importance acquired by union and peasant mobilization and organization.

The expropriation of more than 100,000 hectares of land accompanied by an intense peasant mobilization in Guatemala in the early 1950s was the culminating moment of the anti-oligarchical offensive which swept over Central America during the post-war years. Here mention should be made of two different factors which contributed to the defeat of Arbenz's nationalist programme. One was that the United Fruit Company was the largest land-owner in the country; under the law more than 15,000 hectares of company land were to be expropriated. The other was the Cold War and the confrontation with the Soviet Union which had exacerbated the anti-communist tendencies in U.S. foreign policy and the anti-communism of conservative groups which constituted the internal opposition to the revolutionary reformism of Arbenz and the parties of the Democratic Front.

A conspiracy within the senior ranks of the army nurtured by U.S.

ambassador John Peurifoy was the culmination of a long anti-communist campaign that had an important religious content. This campaign weakened the Democratic Front's political support for President Arbenz, who had to resign on the night of 27 June 1954, after receiving an ultimatum from his Minister of Defence and chief of the armed forces. The form of Arbenz's resignation at the peak of popular mobilization and organization provoked enormous internal confusion and ensured that within a short time the parties and popular organizations would be declared illegal and subjected to brutal repression. The offensive was especially violent against the peasantry, who had benefited from the redistribution of land. Within a week the changes in the armed forces left power in the hands of the leaders of the conspiracy. On 5 August 1954, Colonel Carlos Castillo Armas was named head of state, opening a new stage in the political life of Guatemala.

There was no stable consolidation of power after these events. Castillo was assassinated by one of his own partisans on 26 June 1956, and this unleashed a new crisis in the army. Successive coups d'état and a fraudulent election in 1957 led finally to the election in 1958 of General Miguel Ydígoras Fuentes, who presided over a conservative transition towards political democracy. Freedom of organization, speech and the press were reinstated as Ydígoras tried to impose contradictory measures of national reconciliation that alienated the sympathies of the coalition which had brought him to power. He was removed by a military coup in March 1963.

In Honduras during this period, the election of Juan Manuel Gálvez (1949–54) amounted to an attempt to prolong the Carías regime, although there were a number of important new developments. The first was the great banana strike in May 1954, which started as a simple protest over the dismissal of twenty-five workers at the Tela Railroad belonging to the United Fruit Company and developed into a campaign for higher wages and better working conditions. The favourable attitude towards change and the search for democratic experimentation, both of which took different expression throughout the region, explain why the conflict spread rapidly to the plantations of the Standard Fruit Company, the El Mochito mine, and the entire foreign-owned agro-industrial zone in the region of San Pedro Sula. The conflict, which attracted the active support of more than 40,000 workers, ended in July after sixty-nine days of strike. It was important not only for its victorious conclusion but also because it had decisive effects on the whole of political society, the most important of these being the creation of real possibilities for working-class and peasant organization. This was the starting-point for labour and social security legislation as well as the creation of the Ministry of Labour and the new awareness that the national problem was closely linked to the social problem. The incorporation of labour and, later, the peasantry, as relatively autonomous political forces was a decisive feat in the framework of a backward agrarian society. It must be added, however, that the strike had a negative impact on the labour market, reducing employment on the banana plantations from 35,000 workers in 1953 to 16,000 in 1959, and its effects on production were compounded by a hurricane in December 1954. These events do not fully explain the slowness of overall growth, but they were undoubtedly important given the weight of the fruit plantations in Honduran economic life.

A second central phenomenon of this period was the entry of the armed forces into the political arena. In the elections of 1954 the traditional Liberal and National parties were unable to resolve their differences because neither could claim an absolute majority. Although the Liberals won 48 per cent of the total, a second vote was corrupted by fraud, provoking the intervention of the army, for the first time, as an institution in 1956. It is of some significance that the victor of the new national elections held under military supervision in September 1957 was Dr. Ramón Villeda Morales (1957–63), returning the Liberals to power after twenty-five years of conservative government.

By contrast, political life of El Salvador remained marked by a permanent military presence, both because the army had been a decisive factor in the struggle for power since 1932 and because senior government officials had always come from the military establishment. In the period under analysis, the oligarchical crisis and its counterpart, institutional and democratic modernization, were expressed in the so-called Revolution of '48, a movement of young officers who carried out a coup d'état on 14 December 1948.

Thereafter a variety of measures were taken to improve the economy and state institutions. All of these may be described as conducive to a relative modernization of Salvadorean society, albeit without recourse to the risks of democracy and without touching the economic bases of the coffee oligarchy. In spite of these limitations, the acts of both the revolutionary junta and the regime of Major Oscar Osorio (1950–56) were marked by a willingness for change. A new constitution, promulgated in 1950, gave legal support to the whole of the transformation process. The general climate of this epoch explains why, as in the other countries, the social rights of workers were recognized in the Constitution, in specific legislation, and in the appearance of a more functional concept of the role of the state in the economy and of the changes which the economy should undergo.

Perhaps the most important feature of these years was the effort to promote industrial growth by various means. In this area the construction of the Río Lempa hydroelectric plant, which is the largest in Central America, and the port of Acajutla, which is modern and was built to fortify foreign trade, are significant. Both autonomous state enterprises were built with the participation of the private sector. In fact, the reformist thought of these young Turks continued beyond Osorio's regime, prolonging itself into the first years of the government of Colonel José María Lemus (1957–60). The political life of the country, however, continued to be marked by government repression and a distinctly authoritarian democracy.

During this period Nicaragua also passed through a stage of important economic growth based on cotton exports, which lent a certain legitimacy to the continuation of the regime of Anastasio Somoza. In the middle of his campaign for re-election, however, he was assassinated on 21 September 1956, in the city of Léon. The Somoza family's control over the state mediated through the National Guard (which was in the hands of Anastasio Somoza, Jr.) and the Congress (presided over by Luis Somoza) ensured that the mechanisms of succession were resolved within the family, supported by the Liberal Party against the fierce opposition of groups of independent Liberals and the Conservative Party. The death of Somoza provoked violent repression against the opposition even though the assassination was the personal act of a young poet, Rigoberto López Pérez. Luis Somoza was promoted to president and his election was ratified by Congress in February 1957. He ran a shadow government which profited from the cotton boom and the first investments stimulated by the Central American Common Market. Luis Somoza died a few days before the poll of February 1963, in which the dictatorship of the family was interrupted to allow the election of a friend of the family, René Schick, who helped pacify the growing opposition to the Somozas and create a space for the future ascent to power of Anastasio Somoza, Jr., in 1967.

The end of the Second World War marked the slow and contradictory beginning of a new stage in the economic life of the countries of Central America. The international context was generally favourable because of the recovery of the European economy and the re-establishment of trade and investment links with the United States. In fact, despite minor recessions in 1949 and 1954, Central America benefited from the effects of the longest phase of prosperity ever seen in the world economy. At the same time, post-war economic growth was accompanied by a quantitative and qualitative transformation of Central American society. Most significantly, population growth rates for the entire period 1945–80 exceeded 3.2 per cent. In 1945 the region had a little more than 7 million inhabitants while in 1980 its population was 20 million. Several other socio-demographic changes were also decisive. In particular, the level of urbanization increased from 14 to 43 per cent between 1945 and 1980, expanding in particular the population of the capital cities, which came to account for more than 25 per cent of the total population.

One other phenomenon of the post-war period deserves mention: the role the state began to play in the promotion of development by means of the modernization of its institutions, such as central banks, and the creation of others, such as development banks and public electricity companies.

The importance of the economic changes during the post-war period must be seen in the context of the revival of international trade once the restrictions imposed by the exigencies of the war were lifted. Central America's traditional production, which had continued to respond to internal demand but had been depressed by the decline of the international market, was soon stimulated again from outside.

During the first few years the economic cycle was based exclusively on the rise in international prices and the reopening of traditional external markets. No important productive investment can be attributed to Central American exporters, who reacted slowly through the route of increases in the extent of land under cultivation, adding to the acreage in production. This operation was carried out through the utilization of land that was in the hands of the peasant sector and by substituting export crops for those destined for the internal market. The cultivation of new land and the risks of capital investment in improved techniques appeared only at the end of the period under consideration.

Despite this, the improvement in the value of foreign trade in Central America was the first factor that favourably affected the economies of the region. The increase in the value of the terms of trade (see Table 3.2) until 1954 demonstrates how, for a while, the capacity for exchange in the region improved, and how it had an immediate effect on the more than

Table 3.2. *Central America: Value of foreign trade (in millions of dollars),*
terms of trade and purchasing power of exports (1970 = 100), 1946–58

Year	Exports	Imports	Terms of Trade	Purchasing power of exports
1946	128.4	127.0	93.5	21.2
1947	192.4	197.0	87.7	24.4
1948	238.9	221.0	95.9	29.5
1949	242.1	215.6	108.4	31.8
1950	299.6	233.3	135.0	40.2
1951	343.4	279.7	149.9	43.0
1952	367.9	322.1	144.4	44.5
1953	390.1	338.0	152.7	48.4
1954	410.8	380.8	176.6	48.5
1955	420.0	414.5	159.3	50.7
1956	438.8	469.2	162.1	51.5
1957	469.5	524.9	151.9	54.4
1958	453.6	509.9	132.6	52.8

Source: James W. Wilkie and P. Reich (eds.), *Statistical Abstract of Latin America* (Los
Angeles, 1979), vol.20, table 2730, p. 412.

proportional increase of imports which had been held back for a long time,
especially during the war years. The most critical case was that of Honduras, whose economic life continued to revolve around banana production.
During the Second World War, due to the so-called Panama disease
(sigatoka), which affected a large proportion of the plantations, production was almost paralysed and the plantations had to be moved from the
Trujillo zone to new lands between San Pedro Sula and La Ceiba. The
investments of foreign companies seem to be recorded as capital entries
which were not reflected in the growth of either production or exportation. According to Bulmer-Thomas' calculations, the GNP of Honduras,
which was $257 per capita in 1929 (1970 prices), fell to $191 in 1939 and
only recovered to $225 in 1949, a notable contrast to the figures of
neighbouring countries.[4]

The three coffee-growing countries reacted at different times. El Salvador, the largest producer in the region, was the first to take advantage of
the new post-war opportunities and by 1949 was already producing
73,000 metric tons of coffee, a quantity not surpassed until 1957, with
83,200 tons. Guatemala started to increase its production from 1951,

[4] Ibid.

when it was 63,000 tons, and maintained a steady growth during the entire period. Costa Rica did not increase levels of production until 1954, and then only very slowly. All the countries benefited from the rise in prices that occurred in the international market, which rose by 600 per cent between 1940 and the peak period reached in 1954–7. At the end of the Second World War (average of 1940–4), the quoted price of a pound of coffee in New York was about 11.7 cents; in 1949 it had risen to 28.7 cents, and between 1955 and 1957 it was worth 57.4 cents.[5]

This period is important not only because the production of a traditional product like coffee increased but also because it witnessed the beginning of a decisive diversification of agricultural commodities such as lumber, cocoa, hemp and, above all, sugar and cotton. The sowing of cotton reached extraordinary levels in El Salvador and Nicaragua and later in Guatemala, and it merits specific discussion both because of its economic consequences and because of its effects on society and politics. The cultivation of cotton changed the rural landscape in important areas of the humid Pacific coast of Central America. The rapidity with which areas were taken over for this product occurred because the lands used were old tenancies which had been devoted to extensive cattle-grazing, estates devoted to 'lease agriculture', land owned by peasants and, of course, unproductive terrain. 'Cotton fever', which began in 1945 in Nicaragua and El Salvador and in 1950 in Guatemala, not only disrupted vast areas traditionally occupied by a peasantry dedicated to subsistence farming combined with the cultivation of basic crops for the market, it also modified the state of unproductive and sharecropping estates, thus shattering the social equilibrium of thousands of peasants. The ecological balance was also altered to an extent that is still not appreciated; old forested areas and pastures were destroyed in the zones of Escuintla and Retalhuleu in Guatemala, La Paz and Usulután in El Salvador, and Chinandega and León in Nicaragua.

The modernization of Central American agriculture began with cotton, which immediately became a conspicuous example of modern agricultural enterprise. The structure of such enterprises has common characteristics in all three countries. The typical cotton entrepreneur was formerly a civil or military functionary, political leader or businessman, and only occasionally a former farmer. This was linked to the role played by the state, which so promoted and protected the planting of cotton that it has been dubbed

[5] James Wilkie (ed.), *Statistical Abstract of Latin America*, (Los Angeles, 1980), table 2526, p.340.

'political cultivation'. The industry arose, in effect, through the creation of large state facilities for bank credit plus 'know-how' acquired abroad and, most essentially, by planting on rented lands. This last factor constitutes a novelty inasmuch as the capitalist renting of land converted the cotton planter into an entrepreneur linked to the land in the most modern manner, by means of rent, which formed part of the investment capital.

The production and export of cotton grew at a regional average of 10 per cent during the first years; by the end of the 1950s it accounted for 6.6 per cent of the total of world exports and the third largest production in Latin America. Production reached 843 kilos per hectare in El Salvador, 700 in Guatemala, and 580 in Nicaragua. Egypt, another producer of unirrigated cotton, was producing 520 kilos per hectare during this period.[6] El Salvador initiated a so-called cotton boom which is worthy of note because before 1945 national production was extremely low and available land was relatively scarce. The 13,000 hectares planted in 1945 increased to 40,000 in 1956; in one decade the land area, yield and the value of production increased to occupy the country's entire Pacific coastal region. The growth of productivity was rapid and after 1954 El Salvador had, according to official sources, the highest yields in the world, next to Nicaragua.

It was in Nicaragua that the cultivation of cotton presented the best opportunity for constructing an agricultural economy for export that was modern and had far-reaching social and political implications. In effect, by 1950 Nicaragua was already the primary cotton producer in Central America, with more than 18,000 metric tons, and in 1954 it was exporting more than 47,000 tons. In that decade cotton exports occupied first place, accounting for 35 per cent of total exports. The production and export of this crop consolidated an already important entrepreneurial group, which oversaw the most dynamic period of expansion Nicaragua had ever experienced. Contrary to what has been mistakenly observed about the cotton adventure, capital participation was provided not only by the 'Somoza group' but also by the country's Liberal and Conservative business groups.

In the three producing countries the cultivation of cotton was important not only for high rates of growth in production, which increased from 11 thousand metric tons in 1947 to 110 thousand tons in 1958 (excluding

---

[6] CEPAL, *Análisis y proyecciones del desarrollo económico. El Desarrollo Económico de El Salvador* (Mexico, 1959), p. 21.

cottonseed and its derivatives), but also for the installation of agro-industrial cotton gins and as a source of social transformation on the part of business on the one hand, and the mass of agricultural labor on the other.

It was also during the post-war period that the production of cane sugar and livestock for export was started on a large scale. Both areas constituted significant sources of modernization in agriculture and economic diversification, contributing to the end of the mono-export tradition which had prevailed in most of the societies of the region. The stimulus for the conversion to sugar began before the Cuban quota was re-allocated among the small economies of Central America and the Caribbean. From 1947 the proportion of land planted, production and productivity began to grow slowly, increasing from 96,000 tons in 1949 to 236,000 in 1958. In the following decade volume increased even more and sugar became the third most important regional export. As with cotton, it was Nicaragua which most rapidly developed the modern sugar plantation with an agro-industrial infrastructure and skilled personnel, although Guatemala always had the largest volumes of production and exportation. All five countries became self-sufficient and, after 1953–4, began exporting to the United States. Nonetheless, the regional sugar industry never attained profitable production costs. With the fall of prices on the world market during the 1970s the industry found itself in a state of crisis without foreseeable recovery. Beef production was more successful, with exports beginning after 1955 and growing with North American demand from 3.2 million kilos at the end of the 1950s to 8.6 million in 1972.

The impulse to export agriculture directly provided by the United States aggravated rural domestic imbalances, on the one hand by sacrificing the best land to cattle-grazing and cotton, and on the other, by displacing the cultivation of basic grain crops to poor land and reducing the acreage allotted to the cultivation of products for the domestic market. In other words, the type of agrarian structure which carries with it unequal forms of tenancy was reinforced during this phase; the number of peasants engaged in the process of proletarianization increased, as did the standard of living and opportunities for work. It should not be forgotten that the historical formation of commercial agriculture for export produced a distribution of functions whereby the peasant sector of the economy became the producer of goods destined to feed the national population. The sharecropping economy continued to function in a very backward technological state, without capital resources and with difficult access to the marketplace.

In this regard, one should note the newest tendency towards shortages of foodstuffs like corn, rice, beans and so on. The period under consideration (1945–60) tested the capacity of Central American countries to maintain their self-sufficiency in food production. In fact, despite variations from one country to another, internal market production was already stagnating or in frank recession by 1948. The growth of population and the diminution of the supply of basic foods for popular consumption produced a regression in the nutritional levels of some sectors of the population, and this situation tended to worsen. The production of corn in 1949 was 950,000 tons, of rice 63,000 tons and beans 106,000 tons; in 1958, the total regional production of corn barely reached 1,023,000 tons, with rice at 77,000 tons and beans at 103,000 tons, which meant that the amount available on a per capita basis first stagnated and then decreased in each product category, most notably corn. The average rate of cumulative growth between 1949 and 1959 was 2.58 per cent, but exportable products increased at 7.14 per cent compared with 1.6 per cent for internal consumption.[7]

This picture presents us with paradoxical conclusion: that Central American agriculture had grown at a faster rhythm than that of nearly all other Latin American countries, yet it had not translated into an increase in employment opportunities for the rural population or an improvement in the levels of food consumption for the low-income population in general. At the same time, the growth and transformation of the export sector was based on an agriculture that increased in value not only through rises in prices but also because after the early post-war years, and especially during the 1950s, there were increases in productivity and modernization in some of its sectors.

After 1945 the rate of capital formation was very low, giving the definite impression that these were economies without capital accumulation in the sense that the augmentation of productive capacity did not play any relevant part. After 1950 there was growth in capital investment, closely associated with improvements in the capacity to import, which maintained an ascendant rhythm in spite of the accelerated growth of imports. The process of the slow destruction of urban and semi-rural

The statistical information in this section was obtained from CEPAL, *Primero y segundo compendio estadístico centroamericano* (New York, 1957, 1962).

artisanry and its replacement by small- and medium-sized industrial enterprises has not been sufficiently studied. No doubt this phenomenon is connected with the improvement in internal demand resulting from a new political and cultural climate bolstered by a rise in the incomes of the better situated social groups in the structure, the growth of population, and urbanization. Another factor was an improvement in the facilities for obtaining the supply of capital goods, primary materials, fuel and the like, which accompanied the rapid rise in imports throughout the period.

The censuses taken around 1950 record the presence of numerous manufacturing establishments with fewer than five employees, artisanal in character and generally known as 'workshops', which supplied nearly the entire demand for food, beverages, shoes, textiles, wood products, leather goods and so on. In the midst of this sea of tiny enterprises there existed two or three large factories, with ample capital, high concentration of labour and a monopolistic nature. Examples of these are the beer factories which had existed in Guatemala and El Salvador since 1890, a textile factory in Costa Rica, the cement factories in Nicaragua and Guatemala. In addition, there were agricultural concerns which were categorized as industries, the coffee-processing plants, the cotton gins, the sawmills, the rice-threshing plants and so on.

Obviously, the domestic supply of products for immediate consumption was highly restricted, a fact amply demonstrated by the composition of imports after 1945. It is only from the late 1950s that capital goods grow in importance, and during the first decade of the period under consideration, that is to say before the end of the 1950s, one finds no official policy of import substitution. The propensity for external consumption, which grew with both the relative increase in income and the capacity to import, was disadvantageous to the existence of Central American manufacturing and initiated the decline of artisanry, that would become more evident during the era of the Latin American Common Market.

The value of industrial production in the region as a whole amounted to about 12 per cent of the gross domestic product (GDP), with greater development in Nicaragua and Guatemala and less in Honduras and El Salvador. In 1946 the value of the production of food, textiles and beverages was $29 million in Guatemala, $31.7 in Nicaragua, $21.2 in Costa Rica, $7.6 in El Salvador and $6.3 in Honduras. Eleven years later, in 1957, the value of production of the same products for immediate consumption had climbed to $50 million in Guatemala, $73.1 in Nicaragua,

$50.6 in Costa Rica, $35.4 in El Salvador and $17.2 in Honduras.[8] We might add that this represents a modest growth, less in some cases than that in population and insufficient to satisfy the expansion of domestic demand, which relied increasingly on imports. Foreign commerce in Central America expanded, with the import ratio rising from 16.3 per cent in 1950 to 21.1 per cent in 1960.

As we have seen the end of the Second World War marked the beginning of a new stage in the economic history of Central America; the average annual rate of growth of GDP for the region as a whole was more than 5.3 per cent for nearly twenty-five years. However, for the ten years between the late 1950s and the late 1960s – the period known as the 'golden decade' of the Central American economy – economic performance was even better. The factors which invigorated the regional economy in the 1960s were of a diverse nature, and produced important differences among countries and in the nature of the cycle. The establishment of the Central American Common Market (CACM) in 1960 was the principal factor, although this itself was the effect of two other concurrent developments: the relative homogeneity of the regimes, and the growth of the international economy and the recovery of foreign demand. The historical factor – a common colonial experience and union in the immediate aftermath of independence as well as more than a dozen attempts at a Central American union since then – is also important.

Economic integration did not result from the exhaustion of the external sector. Indeed, it was precisely the dynamism of this sector which favoured the process that, announced on 16 June 1951, preceded similar initiatives elsewhere in Latin America. Between 1951 and the signing of the Multilateral Treaty for Free Trade and Economic Integration on 10 June 1958, economic relations were conducted on the basis of short-term bilateral treaties limited to specific goods. The idea of a larger market itself had the programmatic and technical support of the United Nations Economic Commission for Latin America (ECLA/CEPAL), whose pioneering work emphasized the importance of regional planning and the role of the state. At this time both local commercial interests and the politically dominant groups in the various Central American republics favoured the objective of economic cooperation although they had little experience of it and were

---

[8] The value of production in El Salvador and Costa Rica is calculated in 1950 dollars; that of Honduras, 1948 dollars, and Nicaragua, in 1958 dollars. CEPAL, *Primero y segundo compendio estadístico*.

Table 3.3. *Intra-Central American exports: value (in millions of dollars) and percentage of total exports, 1950–87*

Year	Value	% of total exports	Year	Value	% of total exports
1950	8.5	2.9	1970	286.3	26.1
1951	10.7	3.2	1971	272.7	24.6
1952	10.4	2.9	1972	304.7	22.9
1953	11.0	2.9	1973	383.3	23.0
1954	13.4	3.3	1974	532.5	25.2
1955	13.6	3.1	1975	536.4	23.3
1956	14.9	3.5	1976	649.2	21.6
1957	17.6	3.8	1977	785.4	19.1
1958	20.9	4.7	1978	862.7	22.4
1959	28.7	6.7	1979	891.7	19.9
1960	30.3	6.9	1980	1,129.2	25.4
1961	36.2	8.0	1981	936.8	25.5
1962	44.7	8.7	1982	765.5	22.4
1963	68.7	11.7	1983	766.6	21.6
1964	105.3	15.6	1984	719.2	18.9
1965	132.1	17.4	1985	488.4	13.9
1966	170.3	20.4	1986	447.9	11.1
1967	205.6	24.0	1987	525.9	13.8
1968	246.9	26.1			
1969	250.1	25.7			

Source: SIECA, *Series Estadísticas Seleccionadas de Centroamérica* (Guatemala).

unsure as to how to proceed towards it. There is little doubt that the new groups that had come to control state power in the post-war era were far more open to such an enterprise than the landed oligarchy, which, looking primarily to the overseas market did not fully understand its possibilities. Thus political and ideological as well as economic factors converged to favour the signing of the 1958 treaty, which led to the General Treaty of Central American Economic Integration signed on 13 December 1960. The 1960 treaty established a free trade area for a period of five years, laid the basis for a customs union and introduced a series of fiscal, credit and service incentives that promoted the growth in intra-regional trade shown in Table 3.3.

If the original ideas proposed by CEPAL are compared with the final draft of the 1960 treaty, it is evident that several key features had been abandoned, particularly the notion of gradualism and reciprocity as a means by which to establish local industries within the five signatory countries according to a plan for the region as a whole. This shift reflected the interests and influence of the United States as much as those of Central American entrepreneurs. Both were willing to liberate commerce from all restrictions and to reduce the role of the state to that of a mere administrator of free trade.[9] The project of regional co-operation, which fell short of total economic integration, sought to counter the historical deterioration of the agrarian export model by providing employment to a growing supply of labour, raising national per capita income and the standard of living of the urban population, and reducing the external vulnerability that had been determined from the beginning by the nature of the dependent relationship with the world market. In the decade of the 1960s average annual growth of industrial production was in fact 8.5 per cent, almost double the growth rate of the GNP.[10]

It has been rightly said that the project of integration was, above all, a project for entrepreneurs. They were the ones who took direct advantage of it and the ones who in the course of daily events moulded it to suit their needs. Among these investors one must decidedly include North American capital. When we speak of entrepreneurs, we refer as much to businessmen as to a nascent industrial elite, little differentiated in social terms from the agrarian oligarchy. The programme of the 'common market' created an important industrial base without necessitating reforms in the countryside; in both conception and application it included a tacit agreement not to interfere with the great rural interests. According to some, the mechanism of building an economic space out of five small markets postponed the political task of reforming the old rural structure.

In sum, the common market project initially advanced rapidly because the governments agreed without major problems on the establishment of a common external tariff, abatements in taxes on local products, and the promulgation of laws to foment industry. These last created competitive little fiscal 'paradises' for foreign investment. As has been seen, the result

---

[9] In February 1959, Douglas Dillon, U.S. Assistant Secretary of State, 'put an end to the initial U.S. objections, identified Washington's requirements for regional trade in Latin America – the freest possible movement of goods, capital and labour – and moved rapidly to have these applied'. A. Guerra Borges, *Desarrollo e Integración en Centroamérica: del pasado a las perspectivas* (Mexico, 1988), p. 20. On the emergence and development of the Central American Common Market, see in particular SIECA, *El desarrollo integrado de Centroamérica en la presente década*, 13 vols. (Buenos Aires, 1973).

[10] CEPAL, 'Industrialización en Centroamérica 1960–1980', in *Estudios e informes de la CEPAL*, no. 30 (Santiágo, 1983).

was an active zone of free trade, the emergence of industries which substituted imports on the most basic level of products for immediate consumption, and a hitherto unknown flourishing of transportation, insurance and other services linked to the growth of new industrial parks.

The programme of economic integration has been the object of eulogies and critiques that sharply contradict one another concerning its significance as a mechanism of growth and development. Today judgments can be made with the benefit of hindsight. During the 1960s the economic policies which sought to foment industry through this programme were successful within apparently inevitable structural limitations. At its peak, more than 85 per cent of the total value of intra-zonal exchange consisted of industrial goods, defined to include commodities for immediate consumption (beverages, food, shoes, shopwork and some textiles). The substitution of imports was, literally speaking, a substitution at the level of assembly, which meant that the co-efficient of imports rose parallel with the growth of industry, at an average rate of 25 per cent in the last five years of the decade. The use of imported capital goods, obsolete in their countries of origin, was novel and saved labour so the manufacturing sector did not utilize an excessive supply of labour. Finally, under the influence of North American policy, a competitive industry was essentially established in the hands of foreign capital, resulting in denationalization and new dimensions of financial dependence.

In the sixties the participation of the agricultural sector in regional production continued to decline, thus ratifying a historical tendency which started after the war. Accordingly, in the middle of the 1970s its share approached a little more than 30 per cent, but it absorbed 60 per cent of the economically active population and contributed about 80 per cent of extra-regional exports (foreign currency). Central American development manifested a cruel paradox; economic growth had always depended on the production and export of agricultural products, but social development in the countryside was sharply limited and contradictory. Agriculture had grown more rapidly than the Latin American average yet this did not improve opportunities for work or the standard of living of rural inhabitants, who are the majority of the population.

No dualist explication is pertinent in examining the modernization of the internal market economy in the hands of small, increasingly impoverished owners. The increases in exportable goods occurred above all in cotton and meat, especially in El Salvador, Guatemala and Nicaragua, and

Table 3.4. *Central America: Increase in volume of agricultural production, 1950–4 and 1975–6 (in percentages)*

	Total production	Food	Export products
Latin America	106	124	117
Costa Rica	143	130	142
El Salvador	136	116	188
Guatemala	250	254	309
Honduras	85	68	102
Nicaragua	199	148	337

Source: CEPAL, Cuadro 19, 'El Crecimiento Económico de Centroamérica en la Postguerra', in 'Raíces y Perspectivas de la Crisis Económica', *ICADIS,* no. 4:93.

sugar in Guatemala and Costa Rica. But the fact that a high percentage of the agricultural population continued to receive low incomes meant that the general process of dynamism created employment or generated income for other sectors.

The Central American experience in industry as well as in agriculture (and in general economic growth) provides a good example of how a rise in wealth in societies with great social inequalities creates greater disparities. The 'trickle-down' theory has been a myth for many long years. It is nothing but a wish or an academic hypocrisy. What actually happens is a permanent 'competitive exclusion' in which the losers are always the peasants. Agricultural dynamism undoubtedly changed the rural landscape; it modernized important agrarian sectors, creating an entrepreneurship distinct from the traditional image of absentee land-ownership. On the other hand, the advance of agrarian capitalism caused the disappearance of the *mozo colono* (the peasant whose attachment to the land is permanent) and substituted temporary agricultural labourers whose position as such is not influenced by whether or not they own a small piece of land. This semi-proletarianization meant, above all, a relative but increasing impoverishment. The phenomenon was particularly acute in Guatemala and El Salvador. In Nicaragua, the displacement of the production of basic grain from the Pacific coast to the interior and its replacement by cotton created a labour market formed by transient wage-workers to the degree that the 'salarization' of the rural labour force was complete by the sixties.

On the political plane the decade of the sixties witnessed repeated defeats of reformist movements of different signatures, expressions of a democratizing will which encouraged popular participation in parties, unions and elections. The failure of gradualist programmes illustrates the crisis of the oligarchical–liberal order, later to become completely bankrupt.

During the last years of the 1950s Latin America as a whole had experienced sluggish growth. The need to open up new channels of development through cooperation was signalled by the establishment of the Inter-American Development Bank in 1961. Concern over this issue was expressed at Punta del Este, Uruguay, in March 1961 immediately following the Kennedy administration's declaration of an Alliance for Progress to stimulate U.S.–Latin American co-operation through economic growth and political democratization in the wake of the challenge presented by the Cuban Revolution. Although the Alliance for Progress resulted in increased loans for Central America and provided greater legitimacy to the idea of agrarian reform and structural change, it also led to a rise in military aid, particularly for Guatemala and Nicaragua, and introduced the doctrine of national security, the concept of the 'internal enemy'. The result of this combination assigned to put brakes on the revolution in Central America was the fortification of counter-insurgent political–military structures and the complete absence of substantive reform.

The most concrete outcome of this set of external and internal conditions in the political arena was the emergence of profoundly repressive governments. These were, however, the result of a certain type of electoral opinion; they respected the alternation of executive power, but only within the narrow circle of military choices. The cycle of these 'facade democracies' began in El Salvador with the creation by the army of the Partido de Conciliación Nacional (PCN), created in the image of the Mexican Partido Revolucionario Institucional (PRI). Although the Mexican party had to some extent resolved the problem of legitimacy by holding periodic elections, and the problem of succession by naming, through secret mechanisms, the candidate who would win, the historical context was very different in Central America. The PCN was created in 1961 following the military coup that put an end to the reformist tendencies of a civil–military junta (1960) and the cautious modernization projects attempted by Colonels Osorio and Lemus (1956–60). This coup marked the installation of a new period of political monopoly by the army, which, in totally controlled elections, secured the election of Julio Rivera (1962–7), Fidel Sánchez (1967–72) and Carlos Humberto Romero

(1977–9). In Guatemala, a similar experience was established with the same sequence of a coup d'état (Colonel Peralta Azurdia, 1963), a constitutional assembly, a new constitution and presidential elections. First to be elected under this system was Julio César Méndez (1966–70) himself a civilian but leader of an essentially military government, which was subsequently controlled directly by officers: Colonel Carlos Arana (1970–4) and Generals Kjell Laugerud (1974–8) and Jorge Lucas García (1978–82). For more than sixteen years El Salvador and Guatemala lived under a military control characterized by the observance of legal formalities. The regimes tolerated limited opposition but only within the parameters of strict rules of the game; Congress was under the control of political forces closely tied to the army, and periodic elections were held in which the parties could elect representatives but not presidents, whose selection was always in the hands of the high military command. This experience was accompanied by a permanent demobilization of popular organization and a general depoliticization of political life parallelled by brutal repression against reformist and radical political forces. As a result of this the union movement, the university (professors and students), sectors of the Church and even the reformist parties themselves, which were temporarily allied with the army, and above all the peasants, were beaten down in a permanent and bloody manner.

The base of these regimes was a solid alliance with the business sector, the economic interests of which were assiduously promoted by official policy. To this was added the multiple support of the United States, which cannot be described solely as military and economic assistance since it also included important cultural and ideological elements within the framework of an explicit objective: security against counter-insurgency.

One result of this was the rejuvenation of the military institution, modernized and trained in special operations, covert activities, intelligence operations on a national scale, and so on, as if waging a war against an internal enemy, although this did not yet exist. Another consequence was the corporate consolidation of the business groups, which perfected their associations so meticulously that they became not only a powerful united pressure group but also a political force with a much higher level of aggressiveness with regard to their economic interests.

The years of this period were also characterized by intense social struggle and efforts to introduce reforms. Between 1964 and 1968 the first guerrilla war was started in Guatemala by a group of ex-rangers from the army after the failed military insurrection of 13 November 1960. Later they were joined by radical groups of students and urban workers and the communist Guatemalan Labour Party itself. The creation of the Thirteenth of November Movement and the Rebel Armed Forces (Fuerzas Armadas Rebeldes, or FAR) did not constitute a military challenge in the strict sense, but it undoubtedly expressed the profound popular discontent produced by the anti-peasant policies of the governments which followed the fall of Arbenz and the deception practiced on the reformist groups by the military coup of March 1963, which, as we have seen interrupted an electoral process and frustrated a democratizing project of institutional normalization.

The entry of the middle sectors into regional political life is an important phenomenon which is associated with the crisis of oligarchic domination in the sense that the latter exercised power on the basis of exclusion. The middle-class groups were not alone; in Central America they invariably favoured popular and union organization, party competition and universal suffrage. Also associated with the parties and organizations of the middle sector were a major intellectual and cultural renewal and the formation of a relatively modern 'public opinion'.

The history of Central America begins to change under these social and political influences, even when fraud — more in the counting of votes than in the elections themselves — preventive coups d'état and repressive violence underscored time and again the weaknesses of the democratic foundations. The electoral history of the region does not exhibit a continuous or ascendant progress, or irreversible phenomena of democratic affirmation.

In Honduras, Ramón Villeda Morales governed with a modernizing hand, re-established a bipartisan system and initiated changes which were always incomplete and backward despite the support of the Alliance for Progress. On 3 October 1963, weeks before the scheduled elections, a group of officers headed by Colonel Osvaldo López Arellano broke the law under unjustifiable pretexts and expelled the civilian president. This coup d'état inaugurated the epoch of full military intervention in politics, bringing Honduras into line with the rest of its neighbours. López Arellano had himself elected president by a constitutional assembly and was promoted to the rank of general. But he found he was facing the most important peasant mobilization in the history of Central America with the mass occupation of large tracts of land which were not only uncultivated but also held under very questionable terms of tenancy. The occupation of state and common lands often revealed them to be illegally possessed by large landlords. The dynamic of the agrarian 'invasions' was paralleled by the organization of several peasant federations whose importance in political life began to be decisive. To alleviate the pressures and the growth of conflicts in the countryside, López Arellano's government promulgated in 1967 a programme of land distribution which affected hundreds of Salvadoran families who lacked title to properties they had occupied in Southern Honduras for a long time.

No one has ever been able to identify the precise and immediate causes of the aptly called 'useless war' between Honduras and El Salvador which broke out in July 1969.[11] Abuses against Salvadorean peasants by the Honduran authorities doubtless occurred, more than 100,000 persons being expelled during a three-month period. Honduras itself suffered from a permanent and substantial commercial deficit with El Salvador as a result of the common market. A football game erupted into a riot, whose seriousness resides neither in itself nor even in the number of supposed deaths that occurred. The Salvadorean Army, which was the better equipped, invaded Honduras but only stayed seventy-two hours because of mediation by the Organization of American States (OAS) and U.S. pressure. The rupture of all relations between the two countries weakened the project of economic integration and established a focus of discord that remained unresolved, owing as much to the frontier's lack of definition as to the continual aggravation of nationalist sentiment. The event seriously affected the structure of Salvadoran exports, 20 per cent of which were directed at the Honduran market, and created a serious demographic-economic problem in the poorest rural region of El Salvador, which was already over-populated.

The event pointed up serious social deficiencies in Honduras, especially injustices in the countryside and the futility of internal conflict. López Arellano first tried for re-election on the pretext that the dangers of a new war required his presence, but he finally accepted a project of national unity proposed by the army, COHEP (Consejo Hondureño de la Empresa Privada) and the union movement. A bipartisan solution was attempted in the Colombian style by electing a president but splitting government posts in a fifty-fifty ratio between the Liberal and National parties. Thus, in June 1971 the aged lawyer Ramón Ernesto Cruz of the National Party was elected. The formula for national reconciliation did not, however, work, more because of the political backwardness of the traditional

---

[11] See Thomas P. Anderson, *The War of the Dispossessed: Honduras and El Salvador 1969* (Lincoln, Neb., 1981); and D. Slutzsky et al., *La Guerra Inutil* (San José, 1971).

caudillos than the senile ineptitude of the President. On 4 December 1972, López Arellano again shattered the feeble legal order that had been achieved, breaking the army's word in open contempt of the bipartisan project for stability.

Nicaragua was no stranger to the reformist projects of the decade, both the kind that adopted a more or less ritual aspect, such as those inspired by the Kennedy Administration and those originating from a real desire for change. The death of President Schick in 1966 created the possibility that the temporary interruption in the Somoza family's control of the government would develop into a longer period of democratic competition. However, the historical opportunity was lost with the electoral imposition of Anastasio Somoza Debayle, who also retained his post as head of the National Guard. At the beginning of 1967, before his election, the most important popular mobilization ever seen in the country was staged to repudiate the electoral fraud in advance. It was especially true of Nicaragua at this time that the geopolitical priorities of the United States favoured neither a civil government nor a democratic perspective.

Nicaragua's history was marked by frequent pacts between the two 'historical' parties, Somoza's Liberals and the Conservatives. In 1972 one of these pacts took place, when Dr Fernando Aguero, the leader of the Conservatives, agreed to act as a member of a triumvirate established to preside over the country until new elections in 1974. The earthquake of December 1972 interrupted this arrangement and must be mentioned because its strictly telluric effects were as disastrous as the ones it had on the political situation in Nicaragua. In the first place, it revealed the internal weakness of the National Guard, which was incapable of maintaining order when what was required was not merely physical repression; it made a shambles of the formality of the bipartisan 'triumvirate', because Somoza immediately had himself elected co-ordinator of the National Emergency Committee, which monopolized international aid and converted itself into an arbitrary executive power; it revealed in a dramatic manner the misery of the popular masses and mobilized them, especially in the city of Managua, where manifestations of external solidarity never reached. These conditions did not prevent Somoza from having himself elected president of the country again in 1974.

The history of this period in Costa Rica follows a more civilized path. The 'war' of 1948 and the succeeding events were the Costa Rican way of settling accounts with the old coffee oligarchy, with its political culture and with the need for institutional and economic modernization. This design was carried out in the context of the new conditions that emerged in the 1950s with the rise of the PLN and the renewed strength of an important generation of politicians and intellectuals, many of whom were militants of this social-democratic current. The force of political tradition permitted the perfection of electoral mechanisms and extended to the construction of a state capable of stimulating growth and development. The governments of Figueres (1953–8), Mario Echandi (1958–62), Francisco Orlich (1962–6), José Joaquín Trejos (1966–70), José Figueres again (1970–4) and Daniel Oduber (1974–8), evince a pendulum swing in the exercise of the electoral process, which included two victories – in 1958 and 1966 – for the opposition.

The renewal of Costa Rican society included the reconstruction of a state which defined its relation to the economy and the society by promoting a social economy where the influence of the market was less disorderly; it strengthened small-and medium-sized businesses, especially in agriculture; it democratized credit, not only with the nationalization of the banks but also with the creation of local juntas to administrate them. There was a broadening of the varieties of coffee and an increase in state control of basic services like electricity, transportation, insurance, telephone service, ports and other services, all through a regime of autonomous and semi-autonomous institutions. The education sector was expanded. Entry into the Common Market, which had been delayed by a persistent isolationist viewpoint on the part of economic groups, permitted a gradual development of light industry that become important by the 1970s. Since Costa Rica is a poor country one can draw the elementary conclusion that it prospered because it had been well administered.

In the middle of the seventies the political crisis completed a long cycle of gestation when it took the form of an armed and massive challenge to the institutional order in Nicaragua, Guatemala and El Salvador. The roots of the crisis were long and diverse and varied from one country to another. What they had in common was a dominant agrarian class which allowed the exercise of power to reside with the army and in the permanent violence of the state rather than in the search for consensus and respect for legality. The emotional and political difficulties of negotiation were compensated for by relative success in the capacity for repression; the struggle for the economic surplus was almost always resolved in the political field rather than in the marketplace despite the liberal roots of the economic culture of the landed class.

If it is true that the crisis was the last expression of a will for social change, the forms it assumed in each country can be described as the collapse of the weak channels of legal participation. In societies that are blocked politically, subordination, whether lived or imagined, is superior as a mobilizing force to economic exploitation as such. Class contradiction is inferior to the rotation between what may generically be termed dominant and subordinate groups. This explains the multi-class character of the social forces expressed through the guerrilla organizations. Nothing could have been farther from the *focos* of the 1960s than these genuinely poly-class coalitions, carriers of a will for radical change more through the experience of mobilization used than through the ends vaguely inscribed in their programmes. The social heterogeneity stimulated a multiple convergence of ideology, which explains this original combination of the theology of liberation, radical Jacobinism and various breeds of Marxism.

The features just described reflect the social and ideological nature of the Frente Sandinista de Liberación Nacional in Nicaragua (FSLN); the Frente Farabundo Martí para la Liberación Nacional (FMLN) in El Salvador (composed of four political–military organizations); and the Union Revolucionaria Nacional Guatemalteca (URNG) (comprising three different-sized organizations).[12] The activity of these guerrilla organizations began with varying degrees of success. The Guatemalan groups had the precedent of 1964–8, but they only appeared between 1975 and 1978 as a strongly established force in the central and northeast highlands. In El Salvador the organizations formed successively between 1971 and 1976, when they began to perform propaganda actions armed with great audacity. In Nicaragua, the FSLN was formed early (1961) but, battered by repression and lost in secrecy, it only became a real presence in December 1974.

The political crisis was neither characterized uniquely by manifestations of armed violence nor confined strictly to guerrilla actions. Before and after peak insurgent activities there were mass mobilizations of unprecedented magnitude, such as the march of the miners in Ixtahuacán (November 1977); the general strike of public employees in 1978; and the agricultural-workers' strike on the south coast (February 1980) in Guatemala. The occupation of the Labour Ministry, the seizure of churches and the general strike of 1977–8 in El Salvador, and the great urban uprisings together with the general strikes that followed the assassination of Pedro

---

[12] These designations correspond to the ones adopted by the unitary organizations after 1979, and not 1977–8.

Joaquin Chamorro in Nicaragua between 1978 and April 1979 reflect the same process. For the most part these mass phenomena were linked to military resistance, although in Guatemala and El Salvador the height of mass mobilization did not coincide with the timing of guerrilla offensives, which would have doubtless provoked a crisis of major, perhaps definitive dimensions. The political crisis reached its breaking point in July 1979 in Nicaragua, almost coinciding with the beginning of the most severe economic crisis since 1930, which punished the Central American societies with the worst breakdown in their republican history.

At the end of the 1970s, it was evident that Central American society and economy were different from what they had been immediately after the Second World War. Between 1950 and 1980 GDP rose from $1,950 million to $7,520 million (1970 prices) and the population from 8 million to 21 million inhabitants. Social stratification diversified in several senses, some calling it more segmented and others more pluralistic. The urban population jumped from 15 to 45 per cent of the total during this period and became 'rejuvenated' in the sense that the age group between fifteen and twenty-four years increased proportionally, especially in the cities. Manufacturing activity also grew from 14.6 to 24.1 per cent of GDP, and in general the productive apparatus was modernized. National integration was achieved through networks of roads, electricity and telephone services, and in 1980 the region had a physical level of communications greatly superior to conditions even ten years earlier as a result of large investments in the infrastructure. Intra-regional commerce reached $1.1 billion in 1980.

Similar advances were not registered in the provision of services in education, labour, health and housing; even those important changes which did take place had specific social limitations due to the excessive sway of the laws of the marketplace, against which the laws of the state were especially weak in Guatemala, El Salvador and Honduras. The dynamic of modernization was limited and exclusive, and social and cultural lag was sometimes concealed by statistical rhetoric or by the urban image of a small group of modern constructions. The traditional structure was not altered but had a modern structure superimposed on it, producing contradictory effects and delays in social change in general.

In the seventies economic problems had begun to escalate as a result of the rise in the price of oil in 1973, the beginning of disorder in the international financial market in 1974, swings in the prices of Central

American export products and several droughts and three natural catastrophes of major proportions in Honduras, Nicaragua and Guatemala. The real growth rate was still an average 5.6 per cent a year, but external vulnerability kept rising (from 16.2 to 27.3 per cent of the co-efficient of imports). From 1981 negative rates of growth were generalized throughout the region.

Import substitution industrialization had experienced a growing dependence upon imported primary materials, intermediate components and capital goods. When the economic crisis took the form of reduced loans, diminished investment and falling prices for agro-exports, the industrial sector was directly affected, prompting a crisis in intra-regional trade (see Table 3.3). Nonetheless, the project of economic integration had been positive in that it stimulated industrial production, modified economic structures, encouraged employment, altered patterns of production and consumption and, above all, introduced new economic, political and cultural linkages between Central Americans. Some of these were later evident in the declarations of the regional presidents at the end of the 1980s (Esquipulas II, August 1987, and Costa del Sol, February 1989) which produced important initiatives towards the solution of political conflict.

Even before the full scope of the post-1979 economic crisis was evident, the situation was exceptionally poor for the majority of the population of Central America. Toward the end of the seventies, 20 per cent of the highest income groups earned more than 50 per cent of the wealth, with substantial variation among countries (see Table 3.5). The social breach widened and the number of Central Americans living in situations of extreme poverty was growing.[13]

After thirty years of steady, though sometimes erratic, growth in per capita income there was a collapse of socially incalculable magnitude. At the end of 1985, per capita income in Costa Rica and Guatemala was the same as it had been in 1972; in Honduras, it had dropped to 1970 levels; and in El Salvador and Guatemala, to 1960 and 1965 levels respectively. External factors unleashed the crisis but their effects were multiplied by the backwardness of the existing social structures and, above all, by the factors that produced profound political instability.

The 1970s produced new economic problems, most particularly the first major oil price rises in 1973 but also the erratic price of coffee and other regional exports. As a result, great importance was given to the use

---

[13] M. E. Gallardo and R. López, *Centroamérica: la crisis en cifras* (San José, 1986), table 1.8, p.158.

Table 3.5. *Central America: distribution of income and levels of income in 1980 (in 1970 dollars)*

Strata	Costa Rica		El Salvador		Guatemala		Honduras		Nicaragua	
	Percent	Mean Income	Percent	Mean Income	Percent	Mean Income	Percent	Mean Income	Percent	Mean Income
Poorest 20%	4.0	176.7	2.0	46.5	5.3	111.0	4.3	80.7	3.0	61.9
30% below the median	17.0	500.8	10.0	155.1	14.5	202.7	12.7	140.0	13.0	178.2
30% above the median	30.0	883.0	22.0	341.2	26.1	364.3	23.7	254.6	26.0	350.2
Richest 20%	49.0	1,165.2	66.0	1,535.5	54.1	1,133.6	59.3	796.3	58.0	1,199.8

Source: CEPAL, based on official figures of the countries.

of foreign capital, largely in the form of loans, to avoid fiscal deficits and enable governments not only to compensate for the lack of local investment but also to respond to periodic droughts and a series of natural catastrophes (the Nicaraguan earthquake of 1972; Hurricane Fifí, which hit northern Honduras in 1974; and the Guatemalan earthquake of 1976). By the time of the second major 'oil shock' in 1979 Central America was already registering the impact of the international recession through the fall in its growth rate, which had historically stood at around 5 per cent per annum. Oil purchases, which had accounted for 2.7 per cent of imports in 1970, rose to 21.1 per cent in 1982, accelerating inflation and producing a veritable disaster in the current trade account. Capacity to meet payments on a debt which rose from $895 million in 1970 to $8,456 million in 1980 and $18,481 million in 1987 was radically diminished as exports encountered major problems, interest rates rose and the trade balance worsened. The prospects for development were gravely impeded on every front.[14]

The regional economic recession of the 1980s was most acute in Nicaragua and least pronounced in Costa Rica, which was the only country to register any growth (in 1985–6). Structural adjustment and stabilization measures designed and effectively imposed by the IMF were begun in Guatemala in 1981 and soon applied to all the countries with varying degrees of failure. The objectives of reducing inflation, controlling the fiscal deficit and improving the balance of payments were not even met at the cost of stagnation, this being assured by a fall in imports of more than 50 per cent and sharp cut-backs in government expenditure. U.S. preoccupation with this serious situation led to the establishment of the bipartisan Kissinger Commission and, in 1984, to President Reagan's 'Caribbean Basin Initiative'. However, the tariff concessions under the CBI had little impact on the overall economic crisis in the region.

The fall of the Somoza family dictatorship in July 1979 was a moment of historical proportion in the Central American crisis for a variety of reasons. In the first place, it was not only the end of a long familial, military and hereditary dictatorship but also produced the collapse of a form of bourgeois power and a weak state constructed on very personalized social and economic bases, which made use of non-national, traditional and

---

[14] Inter-American Development Bank, *Progreso económico y social en América Latina* (Washington, 1980–7).

violent political resources. Second, it was the political and military victory
of a broad multi-class coalition of national character with a programme for
the cultural, moral and political regeneration of a backward society.
Third, it was the downfall of a conspicuous expression of U.S. foreign
policy expressed through aid and military protection; the power resources
of Somoza's dictatorship were basically North American. Finally, it constituted a revolutionary form of resolving the crisis which affected El Salvador and Guatemala, where massive insurrectionary movements were also
preparing the way for a take-over of power.

At the beginning of 1980 the combined guerrilla groups in Guatemala
amounted to more than 8,000 fighters, with non-fighting civilian support
including about 250,000 persons in the over-populated indigenous zones
of the central and northeast highlands. The mobilization of the indigenous
peoples was the most outstanding feature of the crisis because it raised the
question of ethnic-national revindication and, in effect, constituted the
largest indigenous revolt since the era of the conquest. In El Salvador the
first guerrilla organization grouped in the FMLN included more than
4,000 armed men, a level of organization and discipline superior to that of
their counterparts in Guatemala, and a qualitatively different implanta-
tion in the population, not least because they were fighting against an
incompetent and corrupt army. If they had not immediately received U.S.
assistance in massive proportions, the armed forces in El Salvador would
have been incapable of resisting the popular insurrection.

The results of the civil wars have been different. In both cases the
internal war was the historical result of the 'oligarchical way of conducting
politics' and of the deep class divisions within society. The counter-
insurgency operations were directed with a 'crusading spirit' against the
infidels. The offensive of the Guatemalan army (1981–2) did not annihi-
late the guerrillas, but it forced them to retreat to their former areas while
physically destroying 440 indigenous villages, killing 75,000 peasants
and producing a population displacement that affected between 100,000
and 500,000 people. Operation 'Victoria 82' was an act of genocide that
destroyed the material and social bases of the indigenous culture. In El
Salvador, the FMLN launched its final offensive in January 1981, which
failed but did not prevent its consolidation in important zones of the
country.

In the midst of these contradictory military outcomes there was an
inevitable crisis of the 'facade democracies' based on periodic elections and
the consolidation of a counter-insurgent state structure. The crisis oc-

curred first in El Salvador and then in Guatemala. In both cases it began within the army and demonstrated the difficulties of maintaining an alliance in which the military was the axis of power. The coups, against General Romero in El Salvador (October 1979) and General Lucas García in Guatemala (March 1982), opened up a period of successive illegal changes which moved in the direction of transferring power to the political parties. In this 'twist of the fist' they were forced by the pressure of North American policy to 'civilize' the power structure, to present a democratic image based on the reinforcement of a political centre that the counter-insurgency itself had debilitated or destroyed.

Between the first civil–military junta in El Salvador and the last (October 1979 to December 1980), the Christian Democrats had gained strength while in 1982 the banker Alvaro Magaña was installed as provisional president. This was the period in which the North American presence consolidated itself firmly as the most important factor in political power. The U.S. Senate urged the 'legalization' of power and elections were called for a constitutional assembly (March 1982); to everyone's surprise the poll was won by a coalition of parties to the extreme right headed by Roberto D'Aubuissón, although the Christian Democrats emerged from the election as the single most important party in the country. Successive coups d'état in Guatemala (March 1982 and August 1983) also led, under the somber leadership of General Mejía Victores, to constitutional elections (June 1984). The results were similar; a strong representation of rightist parties, yet the Christian Democrats possessing the largest relative majority. There was an orderly retreat of the army to the barracks that looked like nothing less than a military defeat. In May 1984 and December 1986 the Christian Democrat leaders José Napoléon Duarte (El Salvador) and Vinicio Cerezo (Guatemala) were elected president in polls without fraud and with practically no abstentions. For the first time in fifty-five years in El Salvador and twenty years in Guatemala, civilian opposition candidates were victorious.

The democratizing wave in the midst of crisis, war and open U.S. intervention also came to Honduras. The erosion of the military governments who controlled the country from 1971 (López Arellano, 1971–5; Juan Alberto Melgar Castro, 1975–8; Policarpo Paz García, 1978–80) was substantial. The political weariness of the Honduran colonels did not originate in the duties of war. López Arellano and two ministers were denounced on charges of flagrant bribery, after his own government had imposed, for the first time in history, taxes on the production and export of bananas. His successors practised a policy of cautious reform, but they, too, found themselves involved in scandals concerning contraband trafficking in drugs and emeralds as Honduras was converted into an appendix of the international Colombian corruption. Yet as the Sandinista revolution imposed, against its own intent, the militarization of Honduras and the liberalization of the government, there took place a now inevitable Central American ritual of holding constitutional elections to draw up a new Magna Carta and thus hand over the reins of power with a clear legal conscience.

The elections of April 1980 opened the way for the return of civilian government, the return of the Liberals and the reinforcement of U.S. influence. The Carter administration greatly assisted the victory of Roberto Suazo Córdova, and U.S. presence gained a new regional dimension directly articulated against the Sandinista government of Nicaragua.

The strategy of national security reinforced by the obsessive vision of the recently elected President Reagan transformed Honduras not only into a 'sanctuary' for mercenary Nicaraguan bands organized by the U.S. administration, but also into an offensive establishment which included several military bases and a site for the aggressive staging of an endless series of joint manoeuvres that began in 1982. Honduran society has been disturbed in many ways by becoming the seat of various non-Honduran armies and having been converted into the aggressive military axis of U.S. foreign policy. The survival of civilian power under these conditions is only one of the basic formalities which are convenient to maintain and has little to do with the internal crisis of the Honduran army, especially in the Consejo Superior de las Fuerzas Armadas (CONSUFFAA), which forced Generals Gustavo Alvarez Martínez and Walter López out of power and the country.

During the government of Suazo there was a serious confrontation between the executive branch, Congress and the judiciary, which was resolved through a mediation by the army, the unions and the U.S. embassy. Another conflict, internal to the traditional parties and resolved by the intervention of these same entities, produced a virtual end to Honduran bipartisanship. In the presidential elections of 24 November 1985 there were three candidates from the Liberal Party and two from the National, the candidate who had the most votes (Rafael Leonardo Callejas) losing, and Azcona de Hoyo, who had 200,000 votes less, winning because his count was inflated by the votes of all the other Liberal candidates. At any other point in the history of the country, a crisis like this would have rapidly provoked the intervention of the armed forces.

In Costa Rica institutional stability has remained undisturbed, in spite of the fact that the conservative government of Rodrigo Carazo (1978–82) tried to follow a liberal economic policy. Contrary to what was expected, Carazo refused to negotiate with the IMF and permitted the use of the territory by the opposition to Somoza in Nicaragua,. The elections which followed allowed the return of the PLN under Luis Alberto Monge (1982–6), but the economic crisis was already starting to bite and North American policy tried to convert Costa Rica into a key part of its anti-Sandinista offensive. Monge's government acted in a contradictory manner as a result of economic helplessness, U.S. pressure and the general move to the right in Central American politics. In January 1984, Monge proclaimed the permanent, unarmed and active neutrality of Costa Rica, but in August he got rid of important officials who belonged to the progressive wing of his party in order to facilitate the activities of the anti-Sandinistas in the country.

In 1986, in spite of the difficulties experienced in social and economic policy, the PLN won the elections again under the leadership of Oscar Arias in the party's first experience of running against a conservative opposition organized into a party with a clear ideological identity. As this movement consolidated itself, the country would enter into a U.S.-style political model, one of bipartisan structure in which there is little programmatic difference between the parties. The forces of the left in Costa Rica entered a crisis and lost their already slim electoral support.

The most important aspects of Arias' government were his effort to bring the country to a position of effective neutrality and his initiative to achieve peace after calling a meeting of presidents in February 1987 to which President Daniel Ortega of Nicaragua was not invited. Successive efforts culminated in the Esquipulas II meeting held in Guatemala in August 1987, where the five Central American presidents signed a document calling for regional pacification. This proposal received the support of the countries of the Contadora group active since 1983 in favor of peace (Mexico, Panama, Colombia and Venezuela), those belonging to the Support Group (Brazil, Argentina, Peru and Uruguay), the European Parliament, and four of the five permanent members of the United Nations Security Council. Yet it was stubbornly opposed by the Reagan administration, which continued to support and promised increased aid to the mercenary groups known as 'contras'. On this count, the conduct of the United States seemed to be the greatest obstacle to the eventual pacification of Central America.

The situation in Nicaragua in this period was characterized by a set of novel features, some positive, some negative, presented as a total reorganization of society with intensive support among the mobilized masses, directed by the FSLN yet in the framework of respect for private property, aside from that of the Somoza family. The FSLN proclaimed as basic principles a mixed economy, political pluralism and nonalignment; on the basis of these they created a state economic sector and an alliance (the Frente Patriótico Revolucionario, or FPR) which included various parties situated to the right and the left of the FSLN.

Notwithstanding these intentions the dynamic of change in Nicaragua has been limited, on the one hand by the economic and political backwardness of the country and, on the other, by the fierce opposition of the Reagan administration. With the indefinite suspension of bilateral assistance by the United States (February 1981) and the blocking of loans by international organizations (starting in November 1981) the country's economy was slowly paralysed by the difficulty in replacing parts as well as intermediate goods, capital and raw materials. This position illustrates the economic backwardness of a society tied by a thousand strings to the U.S. economy. The collaboration of the private sector was made difficult by these deficiencies provoked from the outside, because the market lost its total decision-making sovereignty in exchange for a growing intervention by the state, because of a new attitude on the part of workers, and even because a bourgeoisie without an army, as one civilian leader noted, is not a bourgeoisie. The fundamental behaviour of the economic system passed from a type consistent with the principle of accumulation to a system for the satisfaction of basic needs of the population and one in which businessmen speculate, decapitalizing their companies and taking resources out of the country.

On the political front, the FSLN constituted itself as a party and the mass organizations formed a broad base of social support through the Comités de Defensa Sandinista. A field of opposing forces formed immediately on which the Consejo Superior de Empresa Privada (COSEP) and the upper levels of the church hierarchy played complementary leading roles. In December 1981, the U.S. National Security Council took the initiative in organizing the so-called contras and initiating a chain of covert actions (including the mining of Nicaraguan ports).

The victories in the political and social arenas were not matched by the development of the economy, which dramatically signalled the limits of the new arrangement. Between the efforts at national reconstruction and the defence of territory a few important events occurred: the conflictive development of the ethnic question (with the Miskitos of the Atlantic coast), in which mistakes made at the beginning later gave way to an original and daring solution: reclaimed autonomy. Political pluralism was put to the test in a backward political culture; the first elections, held in November 1984, were won by the FSLN with 67 per cent, a constitutional assembly was elected and Daniel Ortega voted in as president. Even before the elections it was evident that the opposition lacked a meaningful alternative policy with respect to the revolutionary project. The Reagan administration granted substantial aid – of public and of private origin – to a counter-revolutionary military force which was better organized and financed but which had no ability to govern. The effect of the 'low-intensity war' was nevertheless successful. The Sandinistas secured effective military victories against the contras, especially in 1983–7, but the exhaustion of the economy imposed by the mobilization of resources, the gradual destruction of co-operatives, bridges, schools, numerous civilian deaths, and so on, created an extremely difficult situation for the Sandinista government.

This set of political and economic phenomena constituted a renewed example of the enormous difficulties a small country has to face in order to win national independence and overcome under-development. The war imposed on Nicaragua only made this task more difficult, bringing with it social sacrifice for the population. Agrarian reform and other measures in the countryside contributed to the alteration of social structure and the partial alleviation of production difficulties, but the economic crisis affecting the rest of the countries of Central America afflicted Nicaraguan society in greater measure, and obliged its leaders to seek peace as a condition for any kind of internal arrangement.

By now the Central American crisis possessed an important international dimension involving new actors as U.S. hegemony in the region began to manifest some signs of decline. Significantly, the only diplomatic initiative to endure was the Contadora Accord signed in January 1983 by Mexico, Venezuela, Colombia and Panama in an effort to secure a framework for negotiating the end to the various and distinct conflicts. Although the peace of the region as a whole was never placed in significant danger, the conflicts in Nicaragua and El Salvador did pose a major threat to stability and democracy. In August 1987 the Central American presidents signed the Procedures for the Establishment of a Firm and Lasting Peace in Central America, generally known as the Esquipulas II agreement. This accord led to a series of meetings to consider and resolve the socio-political crises of the region and improve inter-governmental relations. Thus, conversations between the Nicaraguan government and the Contra rebels were held at Sapoá in February 1988, and a year later the FMLN guerrillas made wide-ranging proposals for the cessation of the civil war in El Salvador. Neither initiative seemed remotely likely at the time Contadora was set up. The inauguration of a new president in Washington in January 1989 increased hopes of a more modulated U.S. policy towards the region. Nevertheless, the solution to the crisis depended above all on the political initiatives of the Central Americans themselves.

4

GUATEMALA SINCE 1930

Although the 108,900 square kilometres of its landmass made it smaller than both Nicaragua (148,000) and Honduras (112,000), Guatemala had in 1930 the largest population in Central America (1.7 million). The capital – Guatemala City – had, however, a population of only 130,000 and the country's second city, Quezaltenango (20,000), was no more than a modest provincial town. With a minuscule manufacturing base and an export sector almost completely dominated by coffee (which generated 77 per cent of export revenue) and bananas (13 per cent), Guatemala conformed to the stereotype of a backward plantation economy in which large commercial farms coexisted with a patchwork of small peasant plots dedicated to subsistence agriculture and the provisioning of a limited local market in foodstuffs. On the eve of the depression, GDP stood at $450 million, making Guatemala's economy considerably greater in size than those of the other states of the isthmus. (The second largest was that of El Salvador, with a GDP of $227 million; the weakest, that of Nicaragua with a GDP of only $129 million.) Moreover, Guatemala still retained much of the regional political influence it had enjoyed under Spanish colonial rule, when it was the seat of civil and ecclesiastical administration as well as the centre of commerce for the entire area. Hence, although it was a decidedly small and impoverished state compared to most in Latin America, and was dwarfed by Mexico to the north, Guatemala remained the strongest power in Central America, which constituted a distinct political arena just as much in 1930 as it does today.

The assumption of the presidency by General Jorge Ubico in February 1931 following an election in which he won over 300,000 votes against no competition began a thirteen-year regime of personalist dictatorship that both mirrored those of his regional peers – Maximiliano Hernández Martínez in El Salvador, Tiburcio Carías Andino in Honduras and Anastasio

Somoza in Nicaragua – and continued Guatemala's long-standing tradition of prolonged autocratic government. This had begun early in the republican era under Rafael Carrera (president from 1838 to 1865). Carrera, a man of humble origins, had vigorously upheld a backward-looking conservative order in the face of precipitate liberal efforts to abolish the colonial restraints on the free market. The political and economic chaos that attended independence and the Central American Confederation established in its wake had produced a strong backlash not only among Guatemala City's powerful merchant class, under threat of losing the effective regional monopoly upheld by the Spanish crown, but also among the bulk of the peasantry, which rapidly found the paternalist controls of the colonial regime preferable to the atheism and high taxes associated with liberal 'modernization'. Carrera could, therefore, give his rule what might now be called a populist character, his platform of clericalism, defence of the Indian community, and conformity with the social norms of the imperial order receiving wide-spread support from the mass of the population. Correspondingly, following the collapse of the Confederation, which was irredeemably tarnished as a liberal artefact, the dictator sought to revive Guatemala's control over the weaker states of the isthmus. This had now necessarily to be imposed by occasional intervention rather than through any formal channels, but Carrera was remarkably successful and the country's political influence extended to the Colombian border throughout the middle decades of the nineteenth century.

In the 1870s the advent of coffee and a second generation of liberalism that promoted it through policies of free trade and opening up the market in land – primarily that of the Church and the Indian communities – witnessed no reduction in Guatemala's ambitions as a regional power. The great liberal *caudillos* Justo Rufino Barrios (1873–85) and Manuel Estrada Cabrera (1898–1920) not only preserved an absolutist regime at home but also meddled incessantly in the affairs of their neighbours, although the scope for this was greatly diminished by the consolidation of the United States as a regional power at the turn of the century. Following the overthrow of Estrada Cabrera, who had long been supported by Washington in return for his generous concessions to the United Fruit Company (UFCO) that began to cultivate bananas early in the twentieth century, there was a brief and disorganized attempt to revive the union of Central America, but this came to nought in an era when U.S. marines were being regularly dispatched to impose order in neighbouring states such as Honduras and Nicaragua. If Guatemala remained Central America's strongest power, its political elite could no longer reproduce the regional authority and privileges held under the colony or, indeed, during most of the nineteenth century. The outlook bred of this past was increasingly turned inward, manifesting itself above all in the social arrogance of a provincial seigneurial class.

The rise of U.S. hegemony was not the only factor in Guatemala's introversion. While the oligarchy could afford to harbour ambitions to the south, it viewed its large northern neighbour Mexico with considerable apprehension. Immediately after independence the Mexican General Augustín de Iturbide had made an abortive attempt to take control of the isthmus, and although Mexican liberalism had been welcomed by many of the elite in the 1870s, ideological affinity never erased a residual suspicion about expansionism and, as evidenced by the secession of Chiapas in the 1820s, even annexation. Such a jealously guarded political identity on the part of the white and *ladino* upper classes was greatly fortified by the Mexican Revolution, which traumatized the Guatemalan landlords and sharply curbed any efforts to reduce the authority of the military or relax a particularly rigid social system determined as much by racism as by the demands of the plantation economy. Thus, although the 1920s witnessed a degree of intra-oligarchic dispute and a number of challenges to the contracts conceded to the United Fruit Company, the short-lived regimes of Generals José María Orellana (1921 5) and Lázaro Chacón (1926–30) did not indulge opposition to nearly the same degree as elsewhere in Central America. Ubico's rise to power was as firmly based on his support for United Fruit, the only fruit company operating in Guatemala as well as the single most important representative of U.S. interests and largest employer of waged labour, as it was on his suppression of popular discontent in the wake of the crash of 1929 when he was Minister of War.[1] The economic crisis, it should be noted, had provoked an outbreak of popular mobilization in Central America, and particularly in that region of El Salvador bordering on Guatemala, summoning up fears of a Mexican-style revolt. Hence, although social order was disrupted to a quite modest degree in Guatemala, Ubico experienced little difficulty in gaining oligarchic support for his policy of harsh repression that limited upper-class political life as well as subordinating the lower orders.

[1] Details of contracts signed by UFCO and the Guatemalan government are given in Alfonso Bauer Paiz, *Cómo opera el capital Yanqui en Centroamérica: el caso de Guatemala* (Mexico, 1956). This highly polemical text reflects the depth of feeling generated by the company's activities in the late 1940s and early 1950s.

The absence of a system of open and competitive politics within the Guatemalan landlord class, such as the system tenuously established elsewhere in the first decades of the twentieth century, may largely be attributed to the country's large Indian population – some 70 per cent of the total population in 1930 – and the tendency of debt peonage – the principal mechanism for providing coffee plantations with seasonal labourers from the highlands – to strengthen the coercive characteristics of the central state. Although the tasks of engaging more than 100,000 workers for the harvest and then guaranteeing their arrival at the *finca* were technically undertaken by independent *habilitadores* (money-lenders) who dispensed cash advances for local fiestas and when the surplus of corn was low, in both law and practice the state was committed to supporting this system, upon which depended both the country's staple export and general social control in the countryside.[2] The fact that the great bulk of migrant workers came from the eight densely populated 'Indian' departments of the western highlands placed particular importance upon the control of the *jefes políticos* (regional executive officers) of these zones, but even in those areas, such as Alta Verapaz, where plantations had been established in the midst of dense peasant settlement and drew much of their labour force from the locality the *finqueros* depended upon a much higher degree of state support than was the case in El Salvador or Costa Rica. Moreover, at the time Ubico took power German planters concentrated in Alta Verapaz produced more than half the national coffee crop and yet had not converted this economic power into political authority to the extent achieved by their peers in the other two countries. Ubico, who had served as *jefe político* in Alta Verapaz and often enjoyed less than harmonious relations with the local land-owners, was by no means a puppet of the coffee bourgeoisie, although he sought throughout his regime to provide it with optimum conditions during a period of recession. At the same time, he continued Estrada Cabrera's policy of full cooperation with the United Fruit Company in making generous concessions of land and tax exemptions about which both coffee planters, prejudiced by the company's effective monopoly over rail transport and manipulation

---

[2] For a contemporary account of relations in the countryside, see Chester Lloyd Jones, *Guatemala Past and Present* (Minneapolis, 1940). Over the last two decades theoretical and historical work on rural labour relations has advanced significantly. The best historical overview is given in David McCreery, 'Coffee and Class: the Structure of Development in Liberal Guatemala', *Hispanic American Historical Review* 56, no. 3 (1976), and 'Debt Servitude in Rural Guatemala, 1876–1936', *Hispanic American Historical Review* 63, no. 4 (1983).

of freight charges, and the small but burgeoning urban middle class expressed some discontent.

Although Ubico maintained the formalities of a liberal democratic system and even resorted to a further election as well as to a referendum in order to confirm constitutional changes that enabled his continuation in office, he permitted no opposition candidates, scarcely ever convened his cabinets, and employed a formidable secret police force to invigilate not only the population at large but also the army, upon which his power ultimately depended. The jailing of radical activists and the execution of their leaders in 1932 was facilitated by a 'red scare' easily conjured up in the wake of the abortive peasant rebellion across the border in western El Salvador. No less decisive, however, was the regime's repression of more traditional opposition in 1934, when the device of a discovered 'assassination plot' was employed to eradicate the last vestiges of dissident organization with the loss of several hundred lives. On this basis Ubico was able to outlaw all civic organization independent of the government – including the Chamber of Commerce – command large numbers of votes, direct a hand-picked and compliant Congress, and personally undertake the daily supervision of the state, a task greatly assisted by his enthusiasm for the radio and the motorcycle, which made him a much more ubiquitous autocrat than suggested by subsequent literary depictions of the culture of the dictator during this epoch.[3] In other respects Ubico's ability to give full rein to personal eccentricity – such as a proclivity for providing the populace with advice over the airwaves and in the desultory press on issues from cooking to musical taste and mechanics – corresponded more directly to the bitter whimsicality of unencumbered power projected by novels of the genre established by the Guatemalan Miguel Asturias, whose *Señor Presidente* (1946) was in fact modelled on Estrada Cabrera. These activities were also authentic political devices, serving to maximize the potential of personal authority. Over time, of course, both human frailty and the inexorable political logic that places the requirements of collectivities over those of individuals undermine such systems, but for a dozen years Ubico was able to supervise Central America's largest nation-state without significant challenge while lacking either the decisive military victory obtained by General Martínez in El Salvador or the fulsome backing given by the United States to Somoza in Nicaragua. Insofar as it did not derive from such a profound rupture with existing patterns of

---

[3] See Kenneth J. Grieb, *Guatemalan Caudillo: The Regime of Jorge Ubico* (Athens, Ohio, 1979).

government, Ubico's regime was perhaps less remarkable than those of his regional counterparts.

In responding to the economic crisis the Ubico government was far from inactive, seeking to protect the agricultural system and the socio-ethnic structures upon which it rested by a degree of innovation as well as conservation. Between 1927 and 1932 the value of coffee exports fell from $34 million to $9.3 million, and the value of banana exports dropped barely less precipitously. Annual average growth of GDP collapsed from 5.4 per cent in 1920–4 to minus 0.6 per cent in 1930–4 as a result of the decline in world prices, producing great difficulties for coffee farmers, for whom the payment of cash advances to seasonal labourers constituted a major item of expenditure. As plantation wages were cut and prices of basic grains tumbled, peasant farmers became less responsive to the mechanisms of debt-based seasonal labour at a time when economic logic required greater export volume and thus an expanded harvest work force. Predictably, Ubico defaulted on the external debt, left the gold standard but retained the quetzal's parity with the dollar, which was to last until 1984, and reduced state expenditure by 30 per cent in order to avert a progressive fiscal crisis. His response to growing difficulties in agriculture was to transform the principal mechanism for labour supply by abolishing debt peonage – an act undertaken with full exploitation of its 'progressive' and 'democratic' implications – and replacing it in 1934 with what was a far more extensive and directly coercive system based upon the obligation for all those who farmed less than approximately 3 hectares to work between 100 and 150 days a year on the *fincas*. The number of peasants classified by the new decree as 'vagrants' was sufficiently large not only to make good the loss of indebted labourers but also to provide a ready supply of workers for the *corvée*, with which the state undertook an ambitious road-construction programme. At the same time, Ubico bolstered legal protection for landlords, by granting immunity for all crimes committed in defence of property, and he replaced the traditional system of indigenous mayors, who had hitherto co-existed with *ladino* local authorities and received state recognition, with that of centrally appointed intendents. This latter initiative undoubtedly reduced indigenous autonomy and further prejudiced the position of communal culture, which had been under pressure since the liberal revolution of 1871 and the emergence of the coffee estate. On the other hand, it was not an unambiguous assault upon Indian society because the new authorities sometimes proved more resistant to landlords' demands than had Indian leaders, the requirements of the *finca* being balanced by an evident need to protect the subsistence economy upon which it depended for labour and food crops at the same time as the two competed for land and control over resources.

Ubico directed these policies with enough paternalist patronage of the indigenous population to persuade some students of his regime that he enjoyed appreciable popularity among the peasant masses. This is to be doubted. It is nevertheless true that, despite a slow but steady expansion of the frontier of the agro-export plantation, subsistence agriculture remained relatively buoyant after the initial impact of the depression through to the 1950s when the growth first of cotton and then cattle ranching renewed pressure on peasant plots without providing compensatory opportunities for waged labour. In this respect the stagnation of the economy caused by the depression offered a degree of protection for Indian society and the peasant economy (and as under the Carrera dictatorship in the middle of the nineteenth century this coincided with conservative rule). At the same time, the denial of autonomous organization and the enhanced demands on labour through the vagrancy law amounted to more than negotiated and incremental exactions within a traditional division of social and racial power. When Ubico fell in 1944 these were among the first measures to be reversed in the name of democracy, and even after the counter-revolution of 1954 they could not be restored.

As elsewhere in Central America, the Second World War weakened the dictatorship. In economic terms Guatemala was somewhat protected in that Ubico had for some time been reducing commercial ties with Germany because the Nazi regime insisted upon paying for coffee in Askimarks (which could only be exchanged at face value for German goods), while trade with Britain was very modest indeed. The 1940 Inter-American Coffee Agreement provided a guaranteed U.S. market at modest but acceptable prices for the country's primary staple, and the decline in banana exports was to some degree off-set by cultivation of the strategically important crop *abaca* (hemp). At the same time the Guatemalan State received considerable revenue from the management of the extensive coffee estates and other property (nationalized in 1944) of the German nationals Ubico had deported at the start of the war. However, the rapid fall in imports caused by the conflict soon reversed the gradual decline in consumer prices witnessed in the late 1930s. And the middle class, which was particularly prejudiced by war-time inflation, was exposed for the first time in a dozen years to democratic ideals inextricably associated with the Allied campaign. The dictator's sycophantic press could not fully suppress this important external influence, and yet the *caudillo* was unable and unwilling to accept the political consequences of the 'geographical fatalism' that had underpinned his declaration of war on the Axis powers whose ideologies and regimes he so admired. In June 1944, when confronted with street protests by the students of San Carlos University demanding the free election of faculty deans and the rector, Ubico belligerently declared, 'While I am President I will not grant liberty of the press nor of association because the people of Guatemala are not prepared for democracy and need a firm hand'.[4] By this time, however, his regime was gravely threatened not only by the students but also by the bulk of the middle class of the capital and, most critically, by junior army officers dissatisfied with incompetence and corruption in the upper echelons of the military as well as with a broader sense of social stagnation. The students' demonstrations at the beginning of June were met with predictable police repression but over the following weeks they returned to the streets, encouraged by the success of their Salvadorean counterparts in removing General Martínez, clear signs that the Ubico regime no longer had U.S. support, and popular backing for increased demands that extended first to complete university autonomy and then to liberty of the press and association. On 24 June the UN Charter was read to the crowd at a public meeting and a petition was presented to the president signed by 311 distinguished public figures; together these proved sufficient to persuade the ailing autocrat that it was time to stand down.

Ubico's departure from power was precipitate but not the result of a decisive revolutionary moment; he was able to pick out a member of his lacklustre entourage, General Federico Ponce, to replace him and ensured ratification of the succession by Congress. The peasantry did not intervene significantly in these manoeuvres; a few compliant or confused groups manipulated by the authorities endorsed Ponce's accession to power. The working class was still very small, lacked trade unions and desisted from independent action. Even the middle class, which had headed the campaign against Ubico, displayed every sign of being somewhat taken aback by its rapid success, for which there was no obvious next step or political leadership. Prolonged authoritarian government had left a political vacuum. However, the resolutely personalist nature of the dictatorship also deprived the new regime of great authority, political skill or a clear mandate beyond sustaining an '*ubiquismo* without Ubico'. Despite the temporary advantages

[4] Quoted in Carlos Samayoa Chinchilla, *El Dictador y Yo* (Guatemala, 1950), p. 176.

gained by conceding the principal demands of the students and sheer relief
at the dictator's removal, there was only limited potential for such a policy
succeeding for more than a few months; its demise was hastened by Ponce's
ineptitude in calling elections in October and then declaring himself the
winner with more votes than had been cast. This was, under the circumstances, no more plausible than Ubico's refusal in June to make any concessions to the students. It prompted the junior officers to rebel against a
regime that lacked any popular following and was further weakened by the
disorganized ambitions of the military old guard.

The password of the military rising of 20 October was *'constitucion y
democracia'*, and its leaders – Majors Francisco Arana and Jacobo Arbenz –
took the bold step of distributing weapons to civilians supporters, thereby
averting the possibility of a popular anti-militarist movement feared by
the officer corps. Such an initiative converted a regular military coup,
eventually won by dint of a fortuitous artillery hit on the capital's arsenal,
into a much broader movement, although at no stage over the following
ten years did the military lose its leading role in the management of the
state. The rising of October was to all intents and purposes a continuation
of the demonstrations of June; it obeyed the logic of the moment in
yielding a junta – Arana, Arbenz and a lawyer, Guillermo Toriello – that
proclaimed itself strictly provisional and called for free and fair elections
for the presidency and a constituent assembly.

The revolt of October 1944 opened a singular decade in Guatemalan
political history, the character of which is perhaps better captured in the
phrase 'ten years of spring' than in the term 'revolution' that is more often
applied to the governments of Juan José Arévalo (1945–50) and Jacobo
Arbenz (1951–4). Notwithstanding differences in style and a critical
deterioration of relations with Washington following the onset of the Cold
War from 1948, those two administrations combined cautious economic
reform with an unprecedented extension of civic and political freedoms,
and in this respect they may legitimately be distinguished from all subsequent governments, which resorted to authoritarianism and resisted all
but the most minimal adjustments to the economy. As a result, the
'revolution', which is remembered by a small but significant portion of the
population, has often been viewed in Manichaean terms, by the left as a
solitary experience of freedom and progressive redistribution, and by the
right as a sobering example of ingenuous reform acting as hand-maiden to
communism.

Returning from a decade of exile in the provinces of Argentina, the mild-mannered schoolteacher Arévalo rapidly won broad support for his candidacy because he appeared to personify all the civic virtues associated with democratic government, and his lack of party affiliation was viewed as a distinct advantage for the formation of a broad progressive coalition. Arévalo's victory, by 255,000 out of a total of 295,000 votes, in the elections of December 1944 was the product of individual popularity and the 'bandwagon' effect of his artfully managed campaign rather than any clear ideological preference on the part of the electorate. Although both he and Arbenz sought to build a government on the Mexican model, the reform period was characterized by the relative diffusion and weakness of the political organizations that supported it. Drawn principally from the middle class and promulgating programmes that differed in tactics rather than strategy within a common acceptance of the broad reformist and nationalist motifs of the day, forces such as the Frente Popular Libertador (FPL), Renovación Nacional (RN) and the Partido de Acción Revolucionaria (PAR) were marked by personalism and a failure to establish an organized mass membership, thereby accentuating the role of the presidents who were obliged to negotiate their disputes and orchestrate their deputies. Although there existed throughout this period a more radical current seeking to remedy the absence of a national Communist Party, a great many of the young parliamentarians elected to the new constituent assembly supported Arévalo's idealist 'spiritual socialism' that combined recognizable motifs of secular mysticism with the less familiar cadences of a developmentalist vision:

We are socialists because we live in the Twentieth Century. But we are not materialist socialists. We do not believe that man is primarily stomach. We believe that man is above all else the will for dignity. . . . Our socialism does not aim at an ingenious distribution of material goods or the stupid equalization of men who are economically different. Our socialism aims at liberating man psychologically and spiritually. . . . The materialist concept has become a tool in the hands of totalitarian forces. Communism, fascism and Nazism have also been socialist. But theirs is a socialism which gives food with the left hand while the right mutilates the moral and civic virtues of man.[5]

Such statements heralded a primarily political rather than economic programme for change, but recognition of a spectrum of civil liberties in a country with such entrenched divisions determined by race as well as class prompted significant shifts in the balance of social and productive power.

[5] Juan José Arévalo, *Escritos políticos* (Guatemala, 1945), p. 199.

The charter of 1945 abolished the vagrancy law of 1934 and thereby terminated an epoch in which rural labour had been organized by predominantly extra-market forces. At the same time, suffrage was extended to many of those who had been obliged to work under such systems, but the democratic impulses of the assembly fell short of giving the vote to illiterate women, an appreciable sector of the population. In keeping with the juridical mode of the time, property was declared to be inviolable but also subjected to a 'social function' that provided for state intervention, the prospect of which was viewed with some alarm by landlords already disturbed by Ubico's appropriation of German-owned estates. Building on the Constitution, the new government provided for the holding of municipal elections in 1946 – a measure of considerable importance for a rural population deprived of autonomous organization for over a decade and generally more concerned with local government than that at a national level. The following year Arévalo consolidated the constitutional freedom of association by introducing a comprehensive labour code – the first in Guatemala's history – which guaranteed trade unions and collective bargaining, and established legal norms for working conditions. The prevailing political atmosphere precluded an outright opposition to this singular measure, and it is significant that resistance to it on the part of the United Fruit Company was sustained in the name of democracy because the code permitted the organization of rural workers only on estates of at least five hundred employees when at least fifty wished to form a union, of whose members 60 per cent had to be literate. In imposing such sharp restrictions the government had sought to inhibit wide-spread unionization in the countryside – in 1948 only eleven rural unions were registered – but such an evidently conservative policy was not unjustifiably construed by United Fruit as prejudicial to the interests of large commercial concerns. Under pressure from the company and the State Department, Arévalo amended the statute in 1948, thereby laying the basis for far more extensive rural organization over the following years, although outside the banana enclave this rarely assumed the form of a coherent and politically unified mass movement.

No less apprehensive about the possibilities of the urban labour force trespassing the bounds of legal ordinance, Arévalo was quick to close down the Escuela Claridad, a workers' night-school run by Marxists who were unable to establish an independent Communist Party because the Constitution prohibited parties with international links. In both this measure – repeated in 1950 – and his assiduous insistence that the restrictions as well as the liberties stipulated by the labour code and the constitution be respected, the cautious President was fully supported by Colonel Arana, who, as commander of the army, sought to restrict advances made by the popular movement and often had to be held back from acts of direct repression as workers began to make use of the unfamiliar tactic of the strike. Nonetheless, under Arévalo this was far from a frequent occurrence, and the general rise in wages in both town and countryside derived principally from government initiatives and a generally buoyant economy now liberated from the constraints of the war and benefiting from the postwar rise in the coffee price.[6]

Such conditions amounted to a great deal less than a boom in production, but they did assist the cessation of coerced labour and provide the new regime with some leeway for its reforms under what remained remarkably tight fiscal constraints. Thus, while Arévalo established a state credit institute – one of the very few measures taken in the name of development that antagonized neither local entrepreneurs nor the U.S. government – his personal enthusiasm was much more consistently directed towards precisely those 'spiritual' advances made possible by changes in the superstructure rather than the substance of Guatemalan society. As leader of a 'teachers' revolution', the President found a ready constituency for promoting education, nearly doubling the number of schools and teachers from the level obtaining in 1940. The number of books published and level of cultural activity in the towns underwent a marked increase, while brave attempts were made to establish rural literacy campaigns. By 1954 the standard of education in Guatemala still remained the lowest in the region, those who had been taught to read and write being numbered in the tens rather than hundreds of thousands. Yet even such limited advances had a discernable effect within the country, not least in augmenting the quantity of state employees, whose work increasingly included economic management as the apparatus of intervention – incarnated in the establishment of a central bank – was slowly expanded.

Arévalo's attachment to the cause of Central American union was not uncharacteristic of Guatemalan civilian politics, within which this ideal was more prominent than elsewhere in the isthmus, yet it proved no more successful in practice than had previous endeavours. Support for the 'Caribbean Legion', a loose grouping that held no brief for political union but

[6] A sense of both the objectives and the limits of Arévalo's programmes may be gleaned from Leo A. Suslow, *Aspects of Social Reform in Guatemala 1944–1949* (New York, 1950).

congregated non-Communist opponents of dictatorial regimes from the Dominican Republic to Nicaragua, was altogether more adventurous in its open patronage of insurrectionary activity. The Guatemalan president's assistance of the force of José Figueres in the Costa Rican civil war of 1948 contributed to the downfall of less a reactionary autocracy than a Communist-backed populist regime, but it had the effect of temporarily stemming the growing sentiment in Washington that his government was excessively indulgent towards domestic radicals who were exploiting democratic liberties in their campaign against US interests. However, Arévalo's involvement in the Legion's affairs greatly antagonized Colonel Arana, whose ambitions to succeed him as president had been rebuffed by the major parties. Arana had accumulated considerable power by virtue of almost constant activity in suppressing ill-organized revolts against a government with which he felt decreasing sympathy as the impetus of social change began to parallel that of political adjustment. In July 1949, Arana, by this stage widely suspected of preparing his own coup, was assassinated while returning from an inspection of a cache of arms confiscated from Arévalo's colleagues in the Caribbean Legion. Culpability for this act that removed the principal conservative challenger to the reformist regime was generally ascribed to Arana's colleague Arbenz, who despite being Minister of Defense was notably sympathetic to the left and the prospect of introducing more substantial economic reforms. Although responsibility was never proved, a significant portion of the military reacted to Arena's death by staging a major revolt that was defeated only with considerable loss of life and the calling of a general strike by the Confederación de Trabajadores de Guatemala (CTG) under a predominantly Marxist leadership.

The collapse of this rebellion shifted the locus of political activity to the left precisely at a time when the Cold War was setting in and the initial anti-dictatorial impetus evident elsewhere in the region had been brought to a halt. Until 1950, U.S. investment in Guatemala had been increasing, and although the State Department harboured reservations as to Arévalo's ability to control the radical forces within the parties that supported him, Washington's pressure was exercised with a modicum of restraint. With the effective disintegration of the domestic forces of conservatism, the growing strength of the left within the unions, and control of the military in the hands of an officer pledged above all to nationalism but also amenable to its radical interpretation, the U.S. government shifted its policy from lack of sympathy – evident in the arms boycott of 1948 – to increasing aggression, which was by 1953 to take the form of concerted destabilization.[7] This progression was certainly influenced by the replacement of the Truman administration by that of Eisenhower, which saw the promotion to Secretary of State and Director of the CIA of the brothers John Foster and Allen Dulles, who had worked for and held shares in the United Fruit Company, the largest U.S. company in Guatemala. Nevertheless, the State Department was scarcely less preoccupied under Dean Acheson than under Foster Dulles for although the transfer of office from Arévalo to Arbenz in March 1951 introduced policies that thirty years later would seem unremarkable in their objectives of limiting foreign control of infrastructure and effecting a modest redistribution of land, these were undeniably accompanied by greater popular activity and a discernable fortification of the left as the political forces of the middle class that had underwritten the revolution of October 1944 began to lose momentum and break up.

The first signal of a more consolidated approach towards the inequities of land tenure was given by Arévalo's 'Law of Forced Rental' of December 1949. This statute provided for provisional usufruct of some uncultivated lands, but in practice it affected the less densely settled *ladino* zones of the south-east rather than the Indian departments of the *altiplano*. It was under Arbenz, a less 'political' but more administratively resolute leader than Arévalo, that both the policies of the Guatemalan government and the political objectives of some of its supporters became a matter of considerable concern for the United States and the local landlord class. Since its foundation in 1944 the CTG had been led if not comprehensively controlled by the left, personified by Víctor Manuel Gutiérrez, the confederation's secretary-general. This leadership had provoked a split in the union movement, with the more cautious sectors of the urban labour force led by the railway workers clinging to their mutualist past and resisting an overtly political role. However, in October 1951 the undoctrinaire and skilful Gutiérrez achieved a rapprochement, and the establishment of the Confederación General de Trabajadores de Guatemala (CGTG) effectively represented a unification of what was still a very small labour movement — there were fewer than 100,000 members in 1954 — under radical leadership. In 1950 the disparate rural unions were unified in the Confederación Nacional Campesina de Guatemala (CNCG), and on the eve of the counter-

[7] Although written from a deeply anti-communist stance, Ronald M. Schneider, *Communism in Guatemala* (New York, 1958), contains a wealth of detail on the left between 1944 and 1954.

revolution claimed to have 345 affiliates with 256,000 members. Although such figures may have been inflated, they were not grossly exaggerated, and despite the very diffuse and informal character of the rural *sindicatos*, they combined with the communal-based *uniones* to confront the landlords with an unprecedented organization of a peasantry that had hitherto been contained with only very irregular interruptions by a deft mixture of patronage and coercion. The leaders of the CNCG were largely from the middle class, profoundly suspicious of the Marxists heading the urban movement, and in no sense could be described as the 'Bolshevik menace' so often perceived by the large land-owners. However, shortly after the establishment of the CGTG, Gutiérrez was able to reach a tactical accord with the rural leadership largely as a result of the small Communist vanguard having settled its often heated internal disputes and accepted the need for an agrarian reform of a non-collectivist character. Gutiérrez had been at loggerheads over this and other critical issues with José Manuel Fortuny, the leading ideologue of Guatemalan communism and architect of the tactic of 'entryism' inside the Partido de Acción Revolucionaria from 1947. As a result, the small caucus of Marxists had been debilitated for a number of years, and its divisions were not fully healed until the constitutional difficulties of public registration were finally resolved in the formation of the Partido Guatemalteco de Trabajo (PGT) in December 1952. Recognition of this party by the Arbenz government was seen in the United States as tantamount to an official imprimatur of communism, but the organization's militants never exceeded two thousand in number; of these, none served in the cabinet, fewer than half a dozen held senior posts in the civil service and a similar number won seats in Congress. The influence of the PGT derived largely from its members in the leadership of the trade unions, but even there programmatic positions were frequently sacrificed for tactical ends and were in any case rarely out of keeping with a much broader accord between supporters of the government that the primary tasks of the 'second phase' of the revolution lay in an agrarian reform and the curbing of United Fruit's control over the economy, principally through its monopoly of rail transport to the Caribbean port of Puerto Barrios. Although the PGT was anathema to Washington by virtue of its very existence, a more profound threat was seen to lie in the fact that it formed part of a broad consensus that was prejudicial to U.S. corporate interests in the country and thus constituted a challenge to the security of the hemisphere. Insofar as the retiring, upright Arbenz also formed part of this consensus he was doomed to be depicted as a Communist 'stooge'.

It was less from the tenets of communism than from the recommendations of the World Bank's 1950 mission to Guatemala that the Arbenz government drew many of its economic initiatives, including the building of a public road to Puerto Barrios to compete with UFCO's railway and the construction of a state-owned electricity plant that also stood to prejudice U.S. corporate interests. The World Bank's report had mentioned but not made detailed proposals for an agrarian reform, which was recognized to be a major and politically sensitive undertaking. The statistical evidence of an exceptionally regressive pattern of land tenure presented in the 1950 census indicates why the government felt obliged to confront this issue and why a constituency for change existed well beyond the ranks of the radical left: some 2 per cent of the population controlled 74 per cent of all arable land, whereas 76 per cent of all agricultural units had access to only 9 per cent; 84 per cent of all farms possessed an average of less than 17 acres and 21 per cent less than 2 acres when 9 acres was considered the minimum size for the sustenance of an average family. The government's response to this extreme imbalance resulting from the consolidation of the coffee estates and banana plantations was to adopt a distinctly moderate proposal for redistribution with the explicit objective of developing capitalist agriculture through building up the 'small farmer' sector while protecting most commercial enterprises. Arbenz himself was scrupulously clear on this point: 'It is not our purpose to break up all the rural property of the country that could be judged large or fallow and distribute the land to those who work it. This will be done to latifundia, but we will not do it to agricultural economic entities of the capitalist type'. Accordingly, Decree 900 of 27 June 1952 left untouched farms of under 90 acres and provided extensive exemptions to units over this size on which significant cultivation was undertaken. Moreover, nearly a third of the land distributed was already owned by the state, so that although a total of 918,000 acres were expropriated and distributed to 88,000 families in two years, less than 4 per cent of all privately owned land beyond that controlled by UFCO was affected by the measure. In the highland departments only 15 per cent of 19,000 farms were touched by the law, and there is little evidence of any reduction of harvest labour supply as a result of it.

Although it drew its inspiration far more from the models of Italy and Mexico than from those of the Soviet bloc, aimed at increasing production rather than curbing the power of the landlords, and left almost the entire productive base of the large commercial farmers untouched, the reform was resolutely boycotted by the oligarchy. The first concerted effort since the Liberal revolutions of the 1870s to adjust the terms of landed society in Central America was viewed as a major assault upon the political culture erected upon the traditional hacienda, already under threat from independent peasant organization. Yet, if the opposition of local land-owners proved to be largely ineffectual and failed to coalesce into a significant political campaign despite the support of the Church, that of UFCO – the enterprise most severely affected by dint of the extent of its uncultivated lands – ultimately proved to be decisive. Over 15 per cent of the 650,000 acres owned by UFCO were marked for expropriation with compensation to be paid in line with the company's 1950 tax declaration. According to the government the corporation was owed $627,527 at $2.99 per hectare, whereas UCFO rapidly gained Washington's support for its counter-claim for $15.8 million, at $75 per hectare. Arbenz's refusal to pay such a sum served to accelerate the U.S. government's campaign against his regime, which could now be attacked for a tangible infraction rather than on the basis of questionable ideological comportment. Such a policy was greatly assisted by UFCO's ability to harness much of the U.S. press to its cause, but this itself was not without official assistance and was underpinned by the shrill political atmosphere of the McCarthy years, during which the logic of anti-communism was all-encompassing.

By the end of 1953 the efforts of the State Department to organize a diplomatic offensive against the Arbenz government had effectively been overtaken by plans for direct destabilization and a CIA-supported intervention, although these were throughout provided with diplomatic backing through less than subtle tactics in the Organization of American States and the United Nations. Furthermore, at no stage did 'Operation Success' deviate from its objective of presenting Guatemalans as the principal protagonists and Central Americans as the sponsors of the overthrow of a government that, albeit elected, internationally recognized and manifestly in control of national territory and institutions, was now unreservedly denounced as a pawn of Moscow and a threat to the security of the Western Hemisphere. The fact that this government had no allies in Central America and could not even rely upon a sympathetic neutrality from states such as Mexico, Argentina and Bolivia, which still followed a foreign policy discernably autonomous from that of Washington, gravely debilitated its diplomatic defence under conditions in which direct physical resistance was broadly accepted to be beyond serious consideration. In this respect Washington's decision to remove Arbenz may be contrasted with the not dissimilar campaign against the Sandinista government in Nicaragua thirty years later.[8]

Notwithstanding this unprecedented situation on the international plane, the final intervention come close to failure. The 'invasion' of Guatemala from Honduras in June 1954 by a group of insurgents led by Colonel Carlos Castillo Armas and supported by air-raids on the capital undertaken by CIA pilots was only assured success once the army, which had hitherto maintained a neutral stance despite reservations as to Arbenz's policies, halted its initial resistance, obliged the President to stand down, and entered into negotiations with U.S. envoy John Peurifoy over the terms of succession. The signal failure to distribute arms to the population, absence of viable preparations for resistance on the part of the unions, and extensive disillusionment within the middle class ensured that once the high command had taken this step further opposition to the intervention was destined to fail. Moreover, so great was Washington's political investment in the operation that it was not prepared to parley for long over its outcome. Castillo Armas, the firm U.S. candidate for the presidency, was installed in office within a matter of weeks and began to oversee a comprehensive dismantling of the reforms of the previous decade.

During the year following the counter-revolution of 1954 there was plenty of evidence, particularly in the countryside, of a 'settling of accounts', but there was more encarceration, exile, politically motivated unemployment and removal of civil liberties from the supporters of the 'revolution' than actual bloodletting. The level of violence cannot plausibly be compared with that prevalent both in Guatemala and elsewhere in Latin America in the 1970s. Nonetheless, the intervention of 1954 opened a new political era in which almost every effort at reform was stalled by a ruling class determined to protect its economic and social interests at any cost. Both the decade-long experience of mounting radicalism and final reliance upon U.S. intervention in order to eradicate it marked the political instincts of the landlords and an emergent urban bourgeoisie; the culture of anti-communism was seeded before the example of Cuba affected the rest of the region. Not only did the civilian elite set its face determinedly against concessions to the lower orders of society but the army, first traumatized

---

[8] The intervention of 1954 and its background are surveyed in detail in Stephen Schlesinger and Stephen Kinzer, *Bitter Fruit: The Untold Story of the American Coup in Guatemala* (New York, 1982), and Richard Immerman, *The CIA in Guatemala: The Foreign Policy of Intervention* (Austin, Tex. 1982).

and then thoroughly purged, undertook a marked and apparently irreversible shift away from its anomalous acquiescence in social change and became increasingly dedicated to the tasks of coercive control. Within fifteen years it had not only regained many of the attributes of the pre-1944 epoch but was also demonstrating itself to be one of the more efficient and most ruthlessly repressive bodies in the subcontinent. At the same time, both the urban working class and the peasantry were subjected to a decisive political and organizational defeat from which there was evidently no easy or rapid means of recovery. The regional and international balance of power in 1954 was such that these developments appeared neither greatly surprising nor, indeed, as decisive as later transpired to be the case. Two Guatemalan generations were to grow up in a political atmosphere that certainly registered distinct, sometimes important, shifts in character but always remained determined by the trauma of the 'liberation'/'counter-revolution', which was consolidated in an extended and predominantly authoritarian regime.

Castillo Armas abolished both the CGTG and the CNCG, cancelled most of the provisions of the 1947 labour code, and withdrew legal recognition from 553 trade unions while devolving nearly all the expropriated private lands to their original owners and handing over control of the state electricity plant to the very U.S. company against which it was originally designed to compete. Generously funded by Washington, which between October 1954 and the end of 1957 disbursed aid of $100 million when grants to the rest of Latin America amounted to less than $60 million a year, the new president argued that an election would be excessively costly. However, because he was the leader of a movement championed as democratic he permitted the holding of a referendum over acceptance of his appointment, gaining the support of 95 per cent of the vote. The extreme vagueness of his 'New Life' programme for social harmony served to veil increasing division within his supporters, unified by opposition to Arbenz rather than agreement over a positive post-revolutionary platform. Yet not even the quasi-fascist convictions of his principal adviser Mario Sandoval Alarcón, leader of the extremist Movimiento de Liberación Nacional (MLN) for the following two decades, could persuade Castillo Armas to run the risk of reverting to coerced labour or formally cancelling the extension of suffrage. Such measures were justifiably viewed as unnecessary for the eradication of the reformist legacy once the agrarian reform and labour organizations had been suppressed. However, the absence of a coherent project on the part of the regime beyond these objectives provoked increased discontent within the *'liberacionista'* camp, and in October 1957, Castillo Armas was killed in an internal feud. Such a precipitate termination of what the United States had presented as a model government was further complicated by the resort of the defunct president's party to fraud in order to thwart the electoral challenge of General Manuel Ydígoras Fuentes, a traditional conservative whose Redención party artfully projected the need for social and political rapprochement, questioned the extent of U.S. influence, and combined appeal to the middle class with the prospect of a return of the old guard of the Ubico era. The electoral fraud of 1957 was to presage resort to this tactic over the ensuing years, but this time it was employed without the backing of the military, which still retained misgivings as to *liberacionista* ambitions and intervened, with U.S. support, to guarantee a new and relatively honest poll the following year, from which Ydígoras emerged as the clear victor.

The Ydígoras administration (1958–63) halted the ascendency of the arriviste hardliners of the MLN, but it did so in the form of a disorganized, backward-looking enterprise increasingly accused of corruption and soon revealed to be both unwilling and incapable of restoring a genuine openness to political life. Ydígoras, once Ubico's Minister of Public Works, undoubtedly possessed more of the flair of a *caudillo* than had Castillo Armas and initially reaped the benefits of his predecessor's repression of the left and the unions, but neither the auctioning of the *fincas nacionales* nor the stentorian revival of claims on Belize (British Honduras) were sufficient to consolidate a new political order at a time when coffee prices were falling and the Cuban revolution was providing an example of radical change comparable to that snuffed out in Guatemala just five years previously. Lacking any consistent ideological appeal and heavily dependent upon distribution of the spoils of office to sustain its supporters, the regime was confronted by a diverse but growing opposition within its second year in power. In November 1960 a military revolt by junior officers dismayed at the degree of official venality and still influenced by the Arbenz period was subdued without great difficulty, but two of the ringleaders – Captain Marco Antonio Yon Sosa and Lieutenant Luis Turcios Lima – failed to surrender and were by 1962 embarked upon a guerrilla campaign in which their military skills were adjusted to the strategy of Castro's insurgents. The establishment of the Fuerzas Armadas Rebeldes (FAR) in three fronts in the eastern departments of Zacapa and Izabal opened a guerrilla war that subsequently underwent important shifts in intensity, strategy and popular support but persisted for over two decades as a central factor in Guatemalan political life. Under Ydígoras this development was still of minor political and strategic importance, but it served to harden the attitude of the military hierarchy as the regime attempted its own electoral fraud – winning all but two seats in the congressional poll of 1961 – and then lost the support of many of these deputies, which obliged the President to rely upon a military cabinet in order to cow the parliamentary opposition and provide protection against the rising number of coup threats.

It is likely that this hybrid administration would have collapsed well before the end of its official term were it not for the growth resulting from the establishment in 1960 of the Central American Common Market (CACM), within which Guatemala was the most powerful economy, and the support given to incumbent elected governments by Kennedy's Alliance for Progress. However, as the elections of 1963 drew near, Ydígoras increased political tension by tabling an income-tax bill and thereby alienating a bourgeoisie notable for its ability to resist even the most minimal fiscal demands. (Guatemala was the last Latin American country to introduce such a tax and would for the next twenty years maintain the lowest level of taxation in the Western Hemisphere notwithstanding repeated attempts by civilian and military regimes to increase both direct and indirect levies in order to expand the capacity of the state.) Moreover, the President appeared, after an initial period of judicial skirmishing, to acquiesce in the candidacy of the still exiled Juan José Arévalo in the approaching poll. Since neither the governing party nor the MLN seemed set to win a majority and several new centrist organizations quickly rallied to Arévalo's cause, this move was perceived by the military high command as little less than tantamount to the restitution of the reform era, a prospect made all the more threatening by the expansion of FAR operations in the countryside. The absence of discernable opposition by Washington to the resulting overthrow of Ydígoras by his Minister of Defence, Colonel Enrique Peralta Azurdia, suggested that even under Kennedy the U.S. government was of the same opinion.

The Peralta Azurdia regime (1963–6) was in many respects a logical consequence of Ydígoras's resort to a military cabinet. It represented an effort by a now well-funded and progressively more confident institution to establish a stable system of political control in the wake of the excessive partisanship and incompetence of Castillo Armas and Ydígoras. Although the view of Peralta and his colleagues was that only the military possessed the capacity to mediate competing interests within the dominant bloc as well as guarantee discipline within the working class and peasantry, they did not seek an exclusively military regime. Instead, the Guatemalan officers took their model in part from the Mexican Partido Revolucionario Institucional (PRI) and in part from from the successful enterprise of their Salvadorean counterparts, whose Partido de Conciliación Nacional (PCN) had to all intents and purposes monopolized office since 1950 through a system wherein limited opposition and congressional representation by non-radical forces was tolerated but tightly controlled elections continued to return the official party to power. The success of the PCN derived in no small degree from the Salvadorean military's ability in the late 1940s to forestall an authentic reform movement of the Guatemalan type by incorporating some of its motifs into their own discourse. The potential for such a strategy was, therefore, much more limited in Guatemala itself, but in founding the Partido Institucional Democrático (PID), Peralta obtained the acquiescence not only of Sandoval's ultramontane MLN but also of the centrist Partido Revolucionario (PR), established in 1958 under Mario Méndez Montenegro, a former leader of the FPL and supporter of Arévalo. The comparably moderate forces of Democracia Cristiana Guatemalteca (DCG) and Francisco Villagrán Kramer's Unidad Revolucionaria Democrática (URD) remained outside this uneasy concordat, lacking the influence to pose a major challenge to it. As a result, they fell foul of the principal device designed to protect the new system enshrined in the Constitution of 1965 – the stipulation that no party could contest elections without previously submitting a list of at least 50,000 members that satisfied the government-controlled electoral commission. Although the traditional means of manipulating the contents of ballot boxes was never jettisoned, this precautionary measure gave the PID and the high command a legal procedure with which to organize an acceptable field of contestants. Hence, in the poll of 1966 only the PR was permitted to present a notionally reformist programme against the trenchantly anti-communist campaigns of the PID and the MLN, the party's inclusion owing less to a genuine breadth in the system – the PGT and almost all independent trade unions remained outlawed – than to the expectation that it would continue its informal alliance with the PID. However, the mysterious death prior to the poll of Mario Méndez Montenegro, whose policy of extreme caution had provoked a number of internal rifts, elevated his brother Julio César to the leadership of the PR and enabled the diffuse forces of the centre-left to close ranks behind a more resolute commitment to reform. Indeed, such was the conviction of Méndez Montenegro's campaign that even the leadership of the FAR endorsed his candidacy in the hope of a democratic opening, even though shortly beforehand the army had captured and executed a score of trade unionists and militants of the PGT – including Víctor Manuel Gutiérrez – with which the guerrilla was allied. Taken unawares by this rapid consensus behind the opposition candidate, the PID felt obliged to recognize Méndez Montenegro's victory, which they could not plausibly deny without jeopardizing the entire project of controlled constitutionalism at its first trial. However, the PR failed to secure an overall majority and the prospective president thus required the endorsement of the outgoing legislature dominated by the right. After a week of private bargaining and a public exchange of threats not witnessed in more than a decade, Méndez Montenegro finally obtained the acceptance of his victory by the MLN and the military. Yet the price he agreed for this – complete non-intervention in the affairs and operations of the army – soon proved to be so high that it effectively reduced his programme to little more than a collection of pious intentions, and his administration to a weakling apparatus incapable of restraining a military counter-insurgency campaign of considerable ferocity.

At the time of the PR's assumption of office in 1966 the guerrilla campaign in eastern Guatemala had been under way for four years and was at its peak.[9] Although the rebel forces were small – at no stage more than three hundred militants – and failed to generate a broad base of peasant support as prescribed by the *foco* theory held by their leaders, they provided an unprecedented challenge to the military and threatened to provoke the rural revolt constantly feared by the landlord class. Yet the guerrillas were not concentrated in the area of greatest Indian population and were badly divided over political strategy, with Yon Sosa, whose operations centred on Izabal, inclining to the advice of Trotskyists in establishing the breakaway MR–13 in March 1965 while Turcios maintained the original FAR on a more orthodox course in alliance with the PGT. Although the FAR had endorsed Méndez Montenegro's candidacy, it rejected his offer of an amnesty once it became clear that the new government could not restrain the operations directed against the guerrillas by Colonel Carlos Arana Osorio from his headquarters in Zacapa. Combining a scorched-earth policy of generalized repression with a U.S.-

[9] For a valuable survey of the guerrilla movement in the 1960s, see Richard Gott, *Rural Guerrillas in Latin America* (London 1971).

sponsored 'civic action' programme whereby certain communities were politically and economically favoured by the army, Arana's campaign resulted in the death of some ten thousand people in the space of five years while close co-operation with MLN militants and the establishment of a system of 'military commissioners' in the villages laid the basis for the death squads of the 1970s and the civil patrols of the 1980s. The similarities of this operation to many of the methods employed in Vietnam owed much to the fact that for a while U.S. strategists considered Guatemala to be a case of comparable severity. However, by 1968 both wings of the guerrilla had been driven into retreat, their reduced forces seeking both protection and a new strategic arena in the capital in direct contravention of the ruralism of the *foco* theory, which had already lost its chief protagonist, Che Guevara, in an even more abortive effort to employ an urban vanguard to awaken the peasantry to revolutionary consciousness in the Bolivian countryside. Turcios had already died – in a car crash – in 1966; Yon Sosa was shot by Mexican troops in the border area in 1970; and the new strategy of executions and kidnappings was soon shown to provoke much greater repression than political support from the populace. For both the guerrillas themselves and their natural constituency the cost of this failure was very high indeed. Yet its lessons were not ignored. The next generation of insurgents, most particularly the Ejército Guerrillero de los Pobres (EGP), was established around a core of survivors from the FAR and on the conviction that immersion in the Indian society of the western highlands in a prolonged campaign of political education and collaboration before initiating combat represented the only viable strategy for a popular revolution in Guatemala.

For some years matters of this nature were to remain part of a suppressed and esoteric culture, but the counter-insurgency campaign of the late 1960s polarized political activity to such a degree that the negotiation of some space for even modest reform was viewed as a doomed venture by all except the most ardent advocates of constitutionalism. Even before Méndez Montenegro's term expired it was evident that the military would no longer brook anything bar the most formal and limited pursuit of democratic politics. Arana's zeal in repression and excessively aggressive political views eventually won a spell of diplomatic exile in Nicaragua – where he was assiduously patronized by Somoza – but the army continued to tighten its control, having a free hand in the declaration of states of siege at the same time as its programme of pacification fortified the confidence of the right wing and nullified the President's efforts to adjust the social and economic legacy of 1954. Government proposals for sales and property taxes were sabotaged with ease, further complicating recovery from the down-turn in the economy and stagnation of the CACM, while the emergence of death squads such as Ojo por Ojo and Mano Blanca hastened the retreat of the centre and left into the semi-clandestine shadows. By the 1970 elections the PR was comprehensively discredited and the right in such ascendency that Arana could return from Managua to campaign on an explicitly repressive platform: 'If it is necessary to turn the country into a cemetery in order to pacify it, I will not hesitate to do so'.[10]

There was no place in such an atmosphere for the degree of indecision and flexibility that had attended the 1966 poll. Threats from the new vigilante groups replaced rejection of membership lists as the most efficacious means of cowing the already disorganized opposition. Arana's victory with the support of some 5 per cent of the population, in an election in which fewer than 50 per cent of registered voters cast a ballot, marked the first of a string of polls in which population disenchantment paralleled the successes of the official, military-sponsored candidate. The diminishing efficacy of such a system was to become apparent within a decade, but in 1970 lack of popularity was manifestly of minor importance to the colonels compared to the aim of eradicating not only the radical left, which was already in disarray, but also any opposition to a regime that was no longer simply defending the social order established in 1954 but upholding the interests of a new generation of commercial farmers and entrepreneurs who had emerged through the CACM and the expansion of the economy beyond the staple exports of coffee and bananas. In pursuit of this objective Arana imposed a state of siege for the first year of his regime, during which more than seven hundred politically motivated killings took place, exiles both official and voluntary abounded, the university was intervened and the military occupied the centre stage of politics. Although the MLN and the paramilitary gangs that it readily admitted to fostering played an important part in the early phase of this activity, many in the army resented the party's autonomous capacity for violence and were scornful of Sandoval's brash political credo, which was so decidedly inquisitorial that it could not serve as a viable vehicle for government. Accordingly, the MLN was progressively reduced to the status of a minor partner as the officer corps used the PID to consolidate an institutional regime. By

---

[10] *New York Times*, 8 May 1971, cited in Jim Handy, *Gift of the Devil. A History of Guatemala* (Toronto, 1984).

the time of the 1974 elections the success of Arana's offensive was sufficiently evident that Sandoval could be offered the vice-presidency to General Kjell Laugerud, the former chief of staff (of Norwegian extraction). The main opposition was provided by the DCG, whose leaders tried to circumvent official impediments to their campaign by fielding a conservative officer, General Efraín Rios Montt, as their candidate. The PR was now a spent force, and the only other reformist organization of any influence, Manuel Colóm Argüeta's Frente Unido Revolucionario (FUR), was excluded by the authorities' refusal to accept the validity of its list of ninety thousand supporters. As in 1966, the logic of the opposition was to fall behind the most viable challenger, and Rios Montt polled particularly well, but despite discernable differences within the dominant bloc and the fact that their principal opponent was renowned for his role in the counterinsurgency operations of the 1960s, the system functioned without major flaw. The DCG claimed that 180,000 votes were altered to provide Laugerud with victory, and the party was sufficiently confident of its support that for a while a major crisis seemed to be pending. But Rios Montt bowed to the pressures of his fraternity and accepted a diplomatic post in Spain in exchange for recognizing Laugerud's triumph.

The events that attended Laugerud's elevation to the presidency may have persuaded the new incumbent of the desirability of a more modulated regime. In any event, the need for the degree of inflexibility shown by Arana was no longer apparent. Moreover, Laugerud was soon at odds with his predecessor, whose personalism threatened to undermine institutional unity at a time when military participation in the economy was on the rise and responsive to a technocratic direction of the type offered by the new president. As a result, Laugerud permitted a very limited relaxation of the political climate, allowing some unions to make a public appearance and accepting a number of DCG policies as valid proposals for economic growth and social amelioration. For two years it seemed as if the military might accept some measured qualification to the policies of extreme economic conservatism and political dictatorship, and the Christian Democrats responded by moving closer to the government while rank-and-file organizations began a tentative process of reorganization. However, in February 1976, Guatemala was struck by a major earthquake in which thousands of people were killed and extensive damage caused. Although administrative chaos was less than that in Nicaragua four years earlier, control of the National Reconstruction Committee was the object of fierce and sometimes violent competition within the ruling class, and the after-

Table 4.1. *Guatemala: rural sector, c.1950–c.1975*

	Year	Area (× 1,000 hectares)	Production (× 1,000 metric tons)
Coffee	1950	162	57.6
	1977	270	147.0
Bananas	1950	17	185
	1974	59	450
Cotton	1948–52 average	5	2
	1970	120	146
Sugar	1961–5 av.	32	1,960
	1977	85	6,800
Cattle	1947–52 av.		977 (per 1,000 head)
	1974		1,916 (per 1,000 head)
Maize	1948–52 av.	538	437
	1978	522	760
Beans	1948–52 av.	63	30
	1978	135	80

Source: Edelberto Torres Rivas, 'The Beginning of Industrialization in Central America', Working Paper no. 141, Woodrow Wilson Center (Washington D.C., 1984).

math of the disaster saw an upsurge in political conflict as the military and its right-wing allies sought to contain the effects of independent political and organizational activity in the relief campaign. Renewed recourse to the death squads closed off any potential latitude in the political system and compounded the effects of the deteriorating economy in encouraging the development of a radical opposition that had been dormant since 1968.[11]

In terms of global production the Guatemalan economy advanced considerably between 1950 and 1980. Although the population grew at about 3.2 per cent per annum (from 3.0 million to 7.3 million), so also did GDP (from $767.1 million to $3,067 million) and even GDP per capita (from $293 to $575). In the rural sector this expansion was primarily due to growth in agro-export activity, which in terms of both area cultivated and production, advanced more rapidly than did domestic food crop agriculture. As Table 4.1 demonstrates, the expansion of large-scale commercial agriculture took the form of greater cultivated area as well as improve-

[11] See Roger Plant, *Guatemala: Unnatural Disaster* (London, 1978).

ments in yield, and it was frequently the domestic food crop sector, both subsistence and locally marketed, that bore the brunt of this expansion because the agricultural frontier as a whole moved imperceptibly over these thirty years. Thus, although the size and infrastructure of the economy progressed steadily, distribution of what was still an exceedingly modest national income did so at a notably slower rate with the result that, according to estimates for 1970, the poorest 50 per cent of the population earned only 13 per cent of income (at an average of 73 Central American pesos per head), while the top 5 per cent accounted for 35 per cent (2,023 pesos per capita). In the countryside this disparity was even greater, mirroring the pattern of land tenure too closely for land poverty to be disregarded as a central factor despite complex and plausible technical arguments as to the efficiency of commercial farming. According to the 1979 agricultural census, units of less than 7 hectares accounted for 87 per cent of all farms and yet possessed a mere 16 per cent of cultivated land. At the other end of the spectrum the 482 estates of more than 900 hectares constituted less than 1 per cent of farms whilst possessing 22 per cent of the cultivated land. Perhaps most significantly, 167,000 plots (31 per cent of all farms) were less than 0.7 hectare in size.

The growth in the population and greatly reduced opportunities for temporary labour in the new agro-export sector – neither cotton nor sugar require a harvest work force for as long as coffee does, and cattle-raising produces a minimal labour demand – meant that despite increases in production, overall land–labour ratios fell, income distribution remained markedly regressive, and the degree of landlessness also rose. By the mid-1970s the historic poverty of the rural population of the country had palpably not been alleviated, and for many thousands of peasants it was increasingly being determined by pressure at both poles of the traditional exchange between harvest labour in the lowland plantations and cultivation of a subsistence plot subjected to an unprecedented degree to incursions by cattle ranchers and other commercial farmers, who were expanding their holdings under the law or outside of it. By the mid-1970s per capita grain consumption was, with the exception of rice, one-fifth lower than that in the previous decade, and although the average calorie-intake remained constant over the decade – in the rest of Central America it rose by 4 per cent – that of proteins fell.

The prospects of a rural population in such a position finding some escape in the new urban industrial sector were exceptionally limited, since this, too, had registered a notably uneven form of development. Although between 1950 and 1978 the share of GDP attributable to manufacturing rose from 11.1 per cent to 15.1 per cent and the total value added from $98.0 million to $531.7 million, with nearly half of all foreign investment in 1970 being directed to this sector, the structure of industry remained largely traditional and highly dependent upon foreign inputs and investment. Between 1960 and 1978 perishable goods fell from 86 per cent to only 70 per cent of all production, while capital goods rose from 4.7 to less than 9 per cent. In 1975 only the food, tobacco, textile and wood industries drew more than half their primary materials from the national economy. The nature of production was little transformed from that prevailing at the establishment of the CACM, with an industrial labour force of 219,000 representing only 11.5 per cent of the economically active population (compared with 128,500 and 10 per cent in 1962) and still predominantly concentrated in workshop production (68.4 per cent of workers employed in enterprises with five or fewer workers, against 75.6 per cent in 1962). Expansion of the urban and industrial economy encouraged the growth of the capital as the sole urban centre of metropolitan proportions – in 1980 Guatemala City had a population of 1.2 million, Quezaltenango, the second town, 92,000 – but it had not produced any major social transformation by the time the world recession of the 1980s hit commodity prices, stalled and then reversed growth rates, and provoked an increase in indebtedness highly unfamiliar in an economy traditionally directed along extremely conservative lines. Popular discontent resulting from the inequities of growth was already evident before the onset of economic decline at the end of the 1970s, but it was significantly deepened by the recession, which hit the urban economy especially hard and, as elsewhere in Latin America, compelled a large sector of the labour force to depend upon precarious strategies for survival in the informal economy. Although an economy as backward as Guatemala's had long nurtured such a sector of petty vending and independent marketing of small-scale services, this now expanded considerably, further prejudicing the condition of the majority of a population: 44 per cent were illiterate; 43 per cent were younger than age fifteen and yet only 18 per cent of school-age children were enrolled in education; the average life-expectancy was fifty-six years; the level of infant mortality was officially estimated at 79 per 1,000 live births but generally agreed to be very much higher, particularly in the countryside. Since the government's budget allocated more to military expenditure (22.4 per cent in 1985) than to health (7.5 per cent) and education (13.3 per cent) combined, it is not surprising that indices such as these were broadly perceived to derive not just from the backwardness of the economy and its powerless position in the contracting world market but also from the social policy of a state opposed to redistribution and instinctively inclined to the maintenance of the status quo through force of arms.

The years 1977 to 1983 were marked by open social and political conflict in which both government and military were increasingly hard-pressed to maintain control in large areas of the countryside, and sometimes in the capital itself; the bulk of the 100,000 people estimated to have been killed for political reasons since 1954 lost their lives during this period. In the towns, most particularly in Guatemala City, much of the violence was attributable to the actions of anonymous death squads operating against individual or small groups of activists of opposition parties and unions, but it was primarily the indigenous peoples of the western highlands who suffered its effects. This campaign – for which there are few parallels in the history of twentieth-century Latin America – incorporated the traditional derision shown by the *ladino* towards the *indio,* whose distinct dress, languages and autochthonous customs were, and remain, widely construed as primitive and an impediment to both material progress and the consolidation of a republican and Hispanic culture. Although the period since 1944 had witnessed appreciable *ladinización,* more than 40 per cent of the country's population had one of the five main Indian languages – with more than twenty distinct dialects – as their mother tongue and remained more attached to the society of the sixteen principal ethnic groups than to that of a Guatemalan nation.[12] The preponderance of Indian peasants in the harvest labour force and their overwhelming majority of the population of the eight departments of the *altiplano* region had since the last quarter of the nineteenth century required the managers of the state to negotiate as well as to impose a form of apartheid with limited advantages for the *indio* insofar as it tolerated a degree of cultural autonomy, albeit under persistent pressure. Nonetheless, from the 1950s onwards the expan-

---

[12] Debate over the social character and political dynamics of ethnicity in Guatemala is highly charged and sometimes obscure in its terms of reference. Severo Martinez Peláez, *La patria del criollo* (Guatemala, 1973), remains the most controversial text. For alternative views, see Carlos Guzmán and Jean-Loup Herbert, *Guatemala: una interpretación histórico-social* (Mexico, 1970), and Carol Smith, 'Indian Class and Class Consciousness in Pre-revolutionary Guatemala', Working Paper no. 162, Latin American Program, Woodrow Wilson Center (Washington, D.C., 1984). A quite extraordinary account of such consciousness is Elizabeth Burgos Debray (ed.), *I . . . Rigoberta Menchú* (London, 1983).

sion of commercial agriculture had posed an increasingly serious threat, not solely to communal lands dedicated to the cultivation of local food crops but also to a distinct socio-cultural way of life indivisible from the *milpa* (plot). In the 1970s the pattern of economic growth markedly accelerated this pressure, challenging the indigenous universe and provoking a response both peasant and Indian in its nature. This movement, often unseen at the level of formal and 'national' politics, may in some senses be compared with that of the early independence period in that it sought to defend both a specific economic circuit and a culture; however, it was at the same time a modern phenomenon that incorporated syndicalist organizational forms and adopted unfamiliar political discourses, such as that of radical Christianity as well as the notion of liberation for oppressed peoples.

The most palpable single threat to the indigenous population was the establishment of the Northern Transverse Strip (Franja Transversal del Norte, FTN) by the Laugerud regime in 1976. This project amounted to the declaration of a 'development zone' close to the areas of most dense Indian settlement on the Mexican border and in the department of Izabal on the Caribbean coast. Designed primarily to meet the needs of agribusiness and the petroleum and nickel industries, in which great expectations were invested, the FTN provided extremely generous incentives for capital in a concerted attempt to open a new frontier where the interests of the established peasant economy were accorded minimal protection. The success of the project in attracting both local and foreign enterprises, led to inflated land prices and threw existing patterns of ownership, both legal ones and those based on precedence, into confusion, thus compounding the trauma caused by the earthquake. The FTN represented a signal effort to impose a modern, capitalist economy in the heartland of subsistence agriculture. Yet it was less a break with than an acceleration of the existing tendencies within the rural economy.

After the earthquake the initial advances made by the opposition were modest in character, but the establishment in 1976 of the Comité Nacional de Unidad Sindical (CNUS) and the growth of the Confederación Nacional de Trabajadores (CNT) — which together increased the number of unionized workers from 1.6 per cent to 10 per cent of the labour force between 1975 and 1978 — were developments of some consequence. Moreover, the revival of confidence and militancy frequently took place outside the confines of organized — still less, officially recognized — structures; the protest march of the miners of Ixtahuacán to the capital in November

1977 combined with that of sugar-workers to prompt impressive displays of spontaneous popular sympathy. These examples also provided encouragement for a nine-day strike by 85,000 public-sector workers, many of them middle class, in February 1978 – the single largest instance of industrial action since 1954. In each case the unions were strengthened, although they still remained highly vulnerable to shifts in the popular mood and dependent upon the resolution of rank-and-file militants, the most prominent example of which was the prolonged endeavour of the workers in Guatemala City's Coca-Cola plant to obtain official recognition. This campaign over five years cost the lives of a dozen activists and attracted international attention precisely at the time when the Carter administration was insisting upon greater respect for human rights from its allies. The shift in U.S. policy affected the Guatemalan military in much the same manner as it did their counterparts in the rest of Central America, as well as in Chile and Argentina. But whereas the regimes in El Salvador and Nicaragua were obliged to adjust their repressive tendencies somewhat, the Guatemalans refused to do so and were subjected to an arms embargo. Developing a more autonomous foreign policy and turning to the Southern Cone and Israel for logistical support, the army was able to retain its control without major difficulty in the election of 1978. General Romeo Lucas García was elected in a poll in which 69 per cent of registered voters abstained and 20 per cent of the ballots were spoiled. Colóm Argüeta's FUR and its Social Democratic allies led by Alberto Fuentes Mohr were prohibited from standing, and the DCG won acceptance only by omitting from its platform many of the proposals for which Rios Montt had campaigned in 1974. Lucas had passed over the discredited MLN and picked the respected Villagrán Kramer as his vice-presidential candidate, thereby bestowing upon the official ticket a degree of credibility. But such a move neither persuaded the U.S. government to alter its hardening position nor, indeed, resulted in anything more than the isolation and abuse of Villagrán, who was eventually forced to abdicate his solitary campaign for social consensus and seek exile in Washington.

The absence of any change in policy was sharply reconfirmed in May 1978 when some hundred Kekchi peasant farmers from the town of Panzós, Alta Verapaz, were shot down by the army when meeting in the town square to discuss the defence of their lands threatened by cattle ranchers granted, or claiming, concessions under the FTN. The Panzós massacre is widely and justifiably perceived as opening a new phase of rural confrontation out of which emerged the Comité de Unidad

Campesina (CUC) and a disposition on the part of many inhabitants of the countryside to support the armed organizations of the left. However, it was in Guatemala City that public order first broke down on a major scale when, following a large demonstration earlier in the year against both the Panzós massacre and the assassination of CNUS leader Mario López Larrave, extensive rioting took place in October 1978 against a rise in bus fares. The regime, surprised by the depth of public feeling on this issue, gravely misjudged its impact on an already poor transport system heavily used by workers living on the outskirts of the city. Much less accustomed to controlling angry street crowds than to eliminating individual oppositionists, the security forces were able to reinstate order but with enough difficulty to suggest that the customarily subdued city might once again be the site of unpredictable outbursts of discontent.

Both the public sector strike of February and the riots of October were marked by a lack of control and decision on the part of unions, themselves unaccustomed to managing movements on such a scale. Nevertheless, the events of 1978 encouraged organizational consolidation and underscored the opposition's need for agreement on a broad platform. Early in 1979 steps were taken towards this with the formation of a loose alliance of centrist parties and the major unions in the Frente Democrático Contra la Represión (FDCR) which, despite restricting its demands to those for respect of basic civil liberties, posed enough of a threat to provoke the execution by unidentified gunmen of the Social Democrats' leader Fuentes Mohr as well as, less than eight weeks later, the FUR's Colóm Argüeta, both of whom the military hierarchy viewed as potential victors of the 1982 elections. These were but two further instances of state-sponsored assassination for which Guatemala had long possessed a formidable reputation, but they also marked a readiness to kill both distinguished popular figures and proponents of modest reform as well as the traditional targets on the left. According to the young leader of the DCG, Vinicio Cerezo, 120 of his party's members were killed in the space of ten months in 1980–1 when the Christian Democrats were in sharp competition with the radical currents for popular support. In a political culture such as Guatemala's, the macabre task of disaggregating the death toll by party affiliation is often needed to help identify shifts in government policy.

Although this increase in repression further alienated the Lucas García government from Washington, it was not without a certain logic. In July 1979, Somoza was overthrown in Nicaragua, and in October reformist elements in the Salvadorean army staged a coup to end the PCN regime, some of their number deliberately seeking a rapprochement with a progressively more militant popular movement; the prospect of a break-down of the established order throughout Central America was viewed with great gravity. That the Guatemalan military hierarchy was not absolutely rigid in its response to this threat, which was little less real than it was perceived, may be seen in its decisions in the spring of 1980 to concede most of the demands made in an unprecedented strike by cotton- and sugar-harvest workers supported by the urban unions as well as CUC. The scale of the strike, and its well-organized threat to the most modern sectors of agribusiness, obliged the regime to impose a wage agreement on the farmers, yet, in contrast to the government's climb-down over bus fares, this was later allowed to lapse by default and did not signal any relaxation of the counter-insurgency campaign in the highlands. Such a tactic proved highly efficacious; but what it gained in terms of stealth and the avoidance of further prejudice to the regime's unenviable international reputation was lost in January 1980 in the much publicized police attack on the Spanish embassy, which had been peacefully occupied by a score of Indians seeking the services of Madrid's sympathetic envoy to intercede with the military controlling their villages. The killing of all the demonstrators – including that of the solitary protestor evacuated alive only to be taken from his hospital bed and shot – and the narrow escape of the ambassador himself revived concern abroad about methods to which international opinion had become wearily familiar. Hence, despite the regime's sanguine expectation that the Reagan administration would reopen full and friendly relations, it subsequently proved difficult for the new administration to overcome profound congressional disdain for the Guatemalan military, making full support for the campaign against the left dependent upon a much more substantial political reorganization than the colonels and, indeed, Reagan himself had anticipated.

Such a strategy, clearly signalled by the end of 1981, was delayed by a number of years partly as a result of the military's ability to resist pressure from Washington and partly because the challenge posed by the guerrilla was manifestly serious. Drawing on a ground-swell of sympathy engendered both by economic pressure and by the army's operations, organizations established in the early 1970s – such as the EGP and the Organización del Pueblo en Armas (ORPA) – had succeeded in extending their activity throughout much of the *altiplano*. By 1980 the EGP controlled large tracts of Quiché and Huehuetenango while ORPA's fighters were moving with ease in the departments of San Marcos, Sololá and

Chimaltenango. Concurrently, the very much smaller reincarnation of the FAR had established a presence in the outlying and under-populated Petén region, posing little threat to either the state or economic infrastructure, yet tying down valuable military units. The strategy of armed struggle also gained adherents among a fraction of the much weakened PGT, although this group failed to build an urban campaign of great significance. Such a pattern of support reflected the relatively subordinate influence of the orthodox left in a movement that owed much to shifts in the doctrinal and pastoral attitudes of the rural priesthood, many of whose members had for more than a decade been developing the traditionalist structures of Acción Católica into a much broader and politically independent system of organization of the laity. Although the Guatemalan Church hierarchy was notably more reactionary than those (until 1979) in El Salvador and Nicaragua, where similar developments were taking place, it proved difficult to impede the encouragement of co-operatives, the spread of catechism and novel interpretations of the Gospel in a country noted for popular piety but where Catholicism had for many years been subjected to competition from evangelical Protestantism and where the number of locally born priests was very low. However, the traditional attachment of the military to the mores and hierarchy of the established Church did not stop it attacking what were perceived, often justifiably, as subversive clerics and their proselytising acolytes in the catechist movement. The persecution of the clerics reached such a point that in 1980 the Bishop of Quiché ordered the evacuation of all religious from his diocese in order to assure their safety and to protest the anti-clerical campaign. As both radicalized priests, and many of those who had followed them out of a position of traditional respect into one of political commitment, became treated as enemies of the state, collaboration with guerrillas, who frequently came from local communities and espoused recognizable aspirations, became correspondingly more compelling an option. In those areas where the military had effectively declared what since Vietnam have been termed 'free-fire zones', such collaboration was little less than a strategy for survival. By 1981 this pattern was sufficiently generalized to cast considerable doubt upon the army's control of the western highlands, where the rebels were staging operations on a scale that belied accusations that they were isolated Communist agitators divorced from the local population. The Guatemalan armed forces appeared to be in a situation no better than that encountered by Somoza's National Guard early in 1979, or that of the Salvadorean military at the same time.

The severity of the army's position provoked unease inside both the military and the dominant bloc as a whole. In 1981 garrison officers publicly voiced their misgivings over the lack of a coherent strategy and the poor conditions in which they were obliged to stage a highly exigent campaign while senior commanders appeared to be reaping considerable personal rewards from their management of the state and, in particular, the FTN. Army discontent was somewhat reduced by the appointment of the president's brother, General Benedicto Lucas García, a French-trained officer of some ability, to direct operations. However, the regime's failure to register the extent of disenchantment led it to stage the 1982 elections in customary style, presenting the Minister of Defence, General Aníbal Guevara, as official successor to Lucas García without paying heed to the claims of the junior officers who sought greater institutional participation in political decision-making. This, in turn, provided encouragement for the outcast MLN, which had taken to crying fraud at what seemed to some a rather late stage in its life, while the guerrillas demanded a boycott of the poll and theatened to disrupt it in much of the countryside. In the event, the tactical difficulties of attacking places where numbers of civilians were gathered meant that this disruption did not extend much beyond the traditional degree of popular abstentionism, but Guevara's predictable victory prompted demonstrations of protest by the upper-class followers of the MLN and other small rightist parties which, most unusually, were subjected to less than gentle treatment at the hands of the police. This anomalous situation of a military regime lacking support from the right wing and a significant portion of the officer corps by virtue of professional inefficiency, political dishonesty and economic corruption did not last for long. Within days of the poll a bloodless coup by middle-level officers ousted Lucas García and Guevara. They were replaced with a junta of whom the most celebrated member and eventual leader was General Rios Montt, brought out of retirement to provide the movement with a figurehead who was staunchly anti-communist yet not part of the ruling cabal.

The political character of the junta was initially confused. However, in the subsequent in-fighting the MLN and its allies were excluded from influence, and Rios Montt, who had become a 'born-again Christian' prone to launching into millenarian disquisitions, dedicated himself to a maverick style of government which gave central attention to the counter-insurgency campaign yet also harrassed the upper class with new tax proposals and the prospect of a Bonapartist regime restoring a greater degree of autonomy to the state at their expense. The populist potential in such a project was never realized, partly because Rios Montt was disinclined to abjure his professional proclivities or his vocation as a martinet but largely because he was obliged to dedicate himself principally to defeating the guerrilla. Although a comprehensive eradication of the armed groups in the highlands – now unified on paper but scarcely in practice as the Unión Revolucionaria Nacional Guatemalteca (URNG) – was not achieved, the adoption of an extensive scorched-earth campaign reminiscent of tactics employed in Algeria and Malaysia as much as in Vietnam did succeed in delivering a major blow to the rebels from which it would require several years to recover. This campaign, known as 'fusiles y frijoles' for its policy of relocating friendly communities with a modicum of economic assistance while freely treating those seeking protection from the rebels as if they were enemy combatants, revealed the guerrillas' inability to provide such protection or maintain control over large areas for any length of time. By mid-1983 it was clear that the destruction of many villages, construction of fortified hamlets and enforced conscription of tens of thousands of able-bodied men into poorly or unarmed 'civil patrols' had achieved much success in exploiting the guerrillas' loss of popular confidence, if not sympathy, and reducing their rebellion. Subsequently this system of rural control was further expanded and presented by the army as a complete strategy for rural development, although one of its principal effects was to prevent many communities from having access to their traditional lands and practising the customs attached to them.[13] By 1985 the rebel forces were beginning to regroup and resume operations at a more modest level, but the abrupt set-back they had suffered stood in stark contrast to the ability of their Nicaraguan and Salvadorean comrades to sustain, respectively, a successful insurrection and a prolonged resistance against the state's forces. This further reduced the prospects of a regional radical upsurge that a few years before had seemed imminent but was now sorely threatened by Washington's obvious preparedness to intervene militarily in Central America.

The requirements of containing the domestic insurgency prompted not only Rios Montt's regime but also those that followed it to pursue a foreign policy little more amenable to the amicable Reagan than it had been to Carter. Already accustomed to a degree of distance from Washington, the military studiously desisted from enthusiastic support for U.S.

---

[13] Christine Krueger, 'Security and Development Conditions in the Guatemalan Highlands', Washington Office on Latin America (Washington, D.C., 1985).

plans to revive the regional military alliance Consejo de Defensa Centroamericana (CONDECA) and give the battle against communism a truly regional character. No less reactionary than their peers, the Guatemalan officers were not prepared to sacrifice their own precarious advantages for what they often considered to be questionable logistical and political enterprises, and although manifesting unrefined contempt for the Sandinistas, they were also prepared to adopt a pragmatic approach towards the new Nicaraguan government once it became clear that neither it nor Cuba was providing the URNG with significant material support. However, both the political traditions of the ruling class and the experience of the military tended towards close collaboration with the United States, and there was little dissent from the view that the regime could not permit differences in appreciation of the region's strategic position to prejudice both ideological affinity and the resolution of mounting economic difficulties. Within a year of Rios Montt's taking power, it was clear that he was incapable of negotiating such a delicate balance, especially since his unpredictable conduct had diminished support not only among the bourgeoisie but also within the high command. His eventual removal, in August 1983 at the hands of General Humberto Mejía Victores, was widely anticipated and corresponded to a resurgence of confidence within a ruling bloc temporarily thrown into confusion by the events surrounding the 1982 election. Mejía's return to the established mode of military government in greater collaboration with the business sector and a desistence from flamboyant pronouncements was, however, carefully shorn of the excessive partisanship witnessed under Lucas García, and provided a secure guarantee that compliance with Washington's desire for the restitution of civilian rule would be undertaken in a disciplined fashion, retaining full operational independence for the military and excluding the forces of the left from the *apertura* (opening). Although somewhat perplexed by the profusion of party-politicking that ensued, and more deeply concerned at another sudden outburst of street protests in the capital caused by the deteriorating economic situation (most sharply illustrated by the collapse of the sixty-year parity of the Quetzal with the dollar), the high command gravely stuck to its pledge, overseeing elections to a constituent assembly in 1984 and a further poll for the presidency and a new congress in 1986. This second, and more important, contest was handsomely won in the second round by Vinicio Cerezo and the DCG, which finally reached office after thirty years. Having taken advantage of the many candidacies on the extreme right in the first round, in the second round the DCG represented the obvious choice for those discontented with the existing order. In keeping both with its political traditions and with a resolutely pragmatic assessment of the prevailing balance of forces, the party held back from any move towards judicial investigation of the violation of human rights by the military – although it did take some limited action against sections of the police – and sought to exploit support from more prescient commanders aware of the international conditions in order to obtain a working neutrality from the majority of the officer corps inclined to a glowering scepticism. At the same time, Cerezo studiously avoided raising the issue of an agrarian reform because this more than any other single issue threatened to destroy the tenuous concordat that had permitted him to take office.[14] Benefiting from a clear margin of electoral support from a populace that had apparently voted for a policy of social rapprochement and an end to the violence, backed by a conservative administration in Washington anxious to maintain civilian governments in the region, and exhibiting exceptional caution, the new government offered the prospect of ending a long history of reactionary control. Nonetheless, such a scenario was not so different from the attending Méndez Montenegro's victory in 1966, and many commentators expressed reservations as to its chances of success. The failure either to curb the army's operations or to present a substantive programme of economic improvement for the peasantry and the urban poor suggested that a resurgence of popular organization and radical demands – already witnessed in the protests in Guatemala City in the autumn of 1985 and evident in the countryside within weeks of Cerezo's assumption of office – could not be discounted. If the pattern of politics since 1954 had indeed been subjected to major adjustment, it remained open to doubt whether the underlying tensions in Guatemalan society could be contained for any length of time simply by the adoption of formal democratic procedure.

[14] The background to the 1985 elections and first phase of the Cerezo presidency is succinctly but critically analyzed in James Painter, *Guatemala: False Hope, False Freedom* (London, 1987).

5

EL SALVADOR SINCE 1930

During the first three decades of the twentieth century the economy of El Salvador became the most dynamic in Central America. Unlike the rest of the region, El Salvador had no banana enclave, but the success of its coffee economy was such that the country gained a reputation as 'the Ruhr of Central America'. The efficiency of the coffee sector owed a great deal to the capacity of a new generation of landlords to exploit the comprehensive alienation of communal lands in El Salvador's central zone in the years which had followed the Liberal revolution of 1871. The altitude and fertility of these lands was particularly well suited to the crop, and because El Salvador is by far the smallest Central American state (21,040 square kilometers) while possessing a large population – even in 1930 it was approaching 1.5 million – the density of settlement was extremely high and the opportunities for peasant migration correspondingly low. As a result, large numbers of rural inhabitants were not so much physically displaced as deprived of their status as small freeholders or members of the municipal commune and converted into waged harvest labourers or *colonos* paying labour rent for subsistence plots on the edges of the new coffee *fincas*. Thus the Salvadorean agro-export sector was unique in the isthmus in that it was blessed with a high availability of local labour. Moreover, the remarkably rapid and all-encompassing alienation of common land – the Church, that other traditional target of nineteenth-century liberalism, possessed very little rural property – encouraged an early concentration of commercial estates and propelled the formation of one of the most compact and confident landed oligarchies in the world.[1] The landed oligarchy of El Salvador is often referred to as 'the fourteen families', although in

---

[1] For discussion of this process, see David Browning, *El Salvador: Landscape and Society* (Oxford, 1971), and Rafael Menjivar, *Acumulación originaria y desarrollo del capitalismo en El Salvador* (San José, 1980).

1930 there existed sixty-five large commercial enterprises and some three hundred fifty estates of more than 100 hectares, which is large by Salvadorean standards. Four decades later, well into an era in which agrarian reform had elsewhere ceased to be 'subversive' and was included in the mildest of political programmes, the distribution of land was still the most inequitable in Latin America while the economic power of the oligarchy remained concentrated to an impressive degree: twenty-five firms accounted for 84 per cent of all coffee exports and forty-nine families possessed farms of more than 1,000 hectares.[2]

The conversion of El Salvador into an oligarchic state and an agro-export economy based on private property was by no means a smooth process. It depended as much upon the exercise of class and ethnic violence as it did upon the entrepreneurial zeal and political confidence so celebrated in the opening years of the new century. Indeed, it was in El Salvador that Liberalism had first been challenged by Indian resistance in the aftermath of Central American independence; in 1833 the popular uprising led by Anastasio Aquino had required the deployment of troops from outside the province and wide-spread repression before social order was restored and the *ladino* state secured. In the 1870s and 1880s the expropriation of common land provoked a series of local revolts, residual violence being higher than that attending similar measures in the rest of the region. This conflict prompted the formation of a powerful army that simultaneously provided some protection against Guatemala, with which relations were always strained, and supported the regional designs of Liberalism, for which El Salvador had long been a spiritual home. Internal and external dependence upon armed force sustained for a while a political culture based upon the coup d'état, yet if the Salvadorean landlords lagged behind those of Costa Rica in subduing upstart army officers and introducing government by civilian grandees, they were not far behind. Within a decade of its establishment by coercive means, the Liberal state was provided with a comprehensive legal apparatus; and by the turn of the century, political life had been freed from both military intervention and the

---

[2] The character and development of the oligarchy have yet to be analysed exhaustively. However, much useful information and suggestive discussion may be found in Robert Aubey, 'Entrepreneurial Formation in El Salvador', *Explorations in Entrepreneurial History*, second ser., vol. 6 (1968–9); Everett Wilson, 'The Crisis of National Integration in El Salvador, 1919–1935', unpublished Ph.D. dissertation, Stanford University, 1970; Eduardo Colindres, 'La tenencia de la tierra en El Salvador', *Estudios Centroamericanos* 31 (1976); Manuel Sevilla, 'El Salvador: la concentración económica y los grupos del poder', Cuaderno de Trabajo no. 3, Centro de Investigación y Acción Social (Mexico, 1984).

instability this cultivated. The economic resource and political confidence of landed capital was fully manifested in the monopoly over office held by the Melendez and Quiñonez families, who passed the presidency calmly between each other through formal elections and in a manner comparable to that of the Costa Rican 'Olympians'.

So assured was this regime that even after the Mexican Revolution, towards which it displayed a notably unflustered attitude, the oligarchy was prepared to sanction a degree of popular organization, in the towns, at least, albeit of a severely supervised nature. In the 1920s artisanal guilds were permitted to operate, legislation was introduced to regulate the conditions of urban workers, and reformist opponents of the Liberal order were allowed to compete for office. When the boom years of the 1920s were brought to an abrupt end, however, the Salvadorean oligarchic regime was revealed not as a stable and organic means of social control capable of mutating into 'tradition' but as an extraordinarily fragile construction which had been built upon the exceptional performance of the agricultural economy, the termination of which it was unable to survive.

The distinctiveness of the Salvadorean agricultural system, in contrast to that of Costa Rica, for example, lay in the absence of a buoyant class of medium-sized farmers and the abundance of land-poor harvest workers. The dominance of the *finqueros* was based less on their indirect control of an internal market in coffee than on the direct control they exercised over land and production. This system may also be contrasted with that in Guatemala insofar as labour control in El Salvador depended much less upon moving large numbers of temporary Indian labourers to the plantations from separate zones of peasant settlement and subsistence agriculture, than upon supervision of workers living on or near to *fincas* where they were employed, either for the harvest or throughout the year. On the one hand, the weakness of what might be termed a 'middle peasantry' made landlord domination less the product of a negotiated hegemony than that of direct and emphatic control. On the other hand, both the relatively low importance attached to the 'Indian question' – by 1930 indigenous culture in El Salvador was limited to the regions around Izalco and Santiago Nonualco – and the marginal need for extensive coercive mechanisms to ensure a supply of labour reduced the tendency of the state towards centralism and authoritarianism. After the subjugation of the conflict that attended the first phase of appropriation, the role of the army in maintaining order was increasingly replaced by paramilitary forces – particularly the National Guard (Guardia Nacional) established in 1912 – which were often based near major farms and were more directly answerable to individual land-owners than was the regular military.

This rural regime was marked by neither flexibility nor a philanthropy beyond that normally associated with an omnipotent but prescient *patrón;* wages and conditions on Salvadorean estates were among the poorest in the region and contributed towards the relative efficiency of the export economy. However, the maintenance of a coherent system of political control at the level of the state depended not only upon stable terms of competition within a very small capitalist class but also upon the restriction of social contradictions to the locus of the *finca*. By 1930 it was evident that this second condition no longer obtained as a peasantry in particularly onerous circumstances, even by Central American standards, began to manifest a wide-spread discontent. The Liberal order, already losing momentum, entered a period of crisis, and late in 1931 the landlord class withdrew from government, accepting the claims of the military to direct control of the polity. At the same time, the structure of the coffee economy ensured that the oligarchy continued to exercise the social power of a formidable ruling class, including that of veto over the economic policy of regimes which remained in the hands of the army, with one short break, from 1932 to 1982. Nowhere else in the isthmus was such a division of power so clear and systematized, or so much in contrast with the pattern of politics up to the 1930s. One of its characteristics – evident from the late 1970s as much as in the early 1930s – was a marked incidence of conflict within the dominant bloc in times of social crisis when the concession of political power by the landed bourgeoisie to the military could no longer be guaranteed to support their economic interests.

The origins of this singular division of power may be located in the turbulent weeks between November 1931 and February 1932, when the failure of a reformist Liberal administration to contain popular discontent caused by the collapse of the economy in the world depression led to a military coup and then, at the end of January 1932, to insurrections in both San Salvador and the western regions of the country. The suppression of these rebellions was of such ferocity that what became known as La Matanza could be described as the single most decisive event in the history of Central America until the overthrow of Somoza in Nicaragua in July 1979. It traumatized both the peasantry and the oligarchy, laying the basis for a fifty-year regime that, notwithstanding prolonged periods of general tranquillity, drew its underlying strength from the memory, both real and cultivated, of the violence of 1932 and the fear that it might recur. When this fear was realized in the civil war of the 1980s, some of the vestiges of 1932 were still plainly visible in the low level of armed conflict in those areas where the revolt had taken place, as well as in the extreme reluctance of the landlords to accept a civilian regime pledged to reform and strongly sponsored by Washington in preference to proponents of open militarism and unabashed conservatism.

In 1930 the Salvadorean economy was more narrowly based on coffee than any other in the region. During the 1920s high prices had prompted both an extension of the agricultural frontier close to its limits – 90 per cent of land under coffee in 1960 was under coffee in 1930 – and concentration on a single crop that was considered risky by more than cultivators of sugar, *henequen* and cotton. The fall in the price of coffee – from 25 cents a pound in 1925 to 9 cents in 1935 – as a result of the world depression had, therefore, a catastrophic effect and generated wider and more directly politicized social conflict than that witnessed elsewhere in Central America. Income from exports in 1932 was less than half of that in 1926, the average annual growth rate for 1930–4 was -0.7 per cent, and by 1939, after several years of gradual recovery, GDP per capita was still below that of 1929. Although there is evidence that the *cafetaleros* (commercial coffee farmers) held back from collecting the harvest of 1930, the most logical response to the crisis was to maximize the volume of exports, cutting wages to the increased harvest labour force required by expanded production. Thus, despite lay-offs of permanent workers, some extension of plantation lands, the calling-in of debts and tightening of terms of tenantry, the principal economic cause of popular unrest in the countryside appears to have been the sharp reduction in pay, which was cut from 75 to 15 centavos per day in two years. This measure provoked a series of rural strikes in 1931, markedly increasing political tension and providing growing support for the Federación Regional de Trabajadores de El Salvador (FRTS), which had been established in 1924 but which from 1930 was sharpening its activity under the direction of the newly formed Partido Comunista de El Salvador (PCS) led by the veteran agitator Agustín Farabundo Martí. The party itself, however, was very much less popular than the Partido Laborista (PL) recently founded by Arturo Araujo, a maverick member of the ruling class whose adoption of a vague but robust reformism had enabled him to win the presidency in 1931 despite profound oligarchic misgivings as to the outcome of an open poll. The greater advance of trade-union organization in El Salvador than elsewhere in the region during the 1920s had already obliged the Liberal governments to engage in some pre-emptive populist activity, but Araujo took this tendency to its limit in economic circumstances which precluded the possibility of both meeting popular expectations and safeguarding the interests of the landlords. Hence, although the President retained a strong personal following, his government soon lost its sense of direction and authority in the face of strikes and demonstrations, while the military began to manifest unfamiliar signs of disquiet and the oligarchy chafed under its failure to secure a devaluation of the currency. When, in December 1931, the army finally rebelled, principally because it had not been paid for months, few were surprised. Only Araujo loyalists were completely dismayed because even the PCS, which had strenuously opposed the government, did not believe that the coup presaged any major change in the political system as a whole. This view soon proved to be gravely mistaken when the new head of state, Araujo's Minister of War, General Maximiliano Hernández Martínez, withdrew his promise to hold elections in January 1932 after the voting lists had been drawn up and campaigning was well advanced. One persuasive interpretation of Martínez's timing in this manoeuvre was that it enabled the army to identify supporters of the PL and PCS, drawing them into the open before embarking upon their repression. In all events, the cancellation of the poll gave the proponents of insurrection within the PCS support for a hastily planned and several times postponed urban revolt. It also drove the leadership of the peasantry around Ahuachapán and Izalco towards a rebellion that had some links with the PCS but was at root an independent movement in pursuit of both immediate economic amelioration and a more deeply seated defence of the region's embattled communal culture.[3]

The urban uprising of 22 January 1932 was suppressed within a matter of hours because news of its preparation had already reached the high command; isolated mutinies by radical conscripts had already been contained and several important Communists, including Farabundo Martí, detained some days previously. The subsequent campaign of persecution in San Salvador was extended to supporters of Araujo and members of artisanal guilds who often had nothing to do with the rebellion. The adoption of a policy of summary execution of known opposition elements

---

[3] The events of 1931–2 are discussed in some detail in Thomas P. Anderson, *Matanza: El Salvador's Communist Revolt of 1932* (Lincoln, Neb., 1971); Rafael Guidos Vejar, *Ascenso del militarismo en El Salvador* (San José, 1982); Roque Dalton, *Miguel Marmol* (New York, 1987).

and extensive incarceration of suspects effectively decapitated the radical movement – Farabundo Martí was shot after a brief court martial – and was emphatic enough to eradicate all vestige of independent popular organization for a dozen years and to hamper its progress for a further two decades thereafter. In the west of the country – there was no fighting in the east – the jacquerie led by Indian *caciques* managed a somewhat less fleeting existence in that it exercised control over a number of small settlements for up to forty-eight hours. It was, nonetheless, directed without strategic ambition and in the traditional mode of peasant revolts, devoid of the 'Bolshevik' characteristics often ascribed to it, manifesting a notable reluctance to damage religious property, and generally preoccupied with imposing justice on individual representatives of the state and the landlord class in a brief flurry of disorganized and almost carnival repudiation of the regime of the *cafetaleros*. The level of violence inflicted by rebel forces almost entirely bereft of firearms was, however, quite low; fewer than fifty people died at their hands.

Apprehension over the consequences of both the economic collapse and the cancellation of elections had prompted the U.S. and British governments to dispatch warships to Salvadorean waters. Some Canadian marines were briefly disembarked. But this outside force was rapidly ordered to retire following Martínez's insistence that the army and civilian vigilantes had the revolt under control within two days. In the light of subsequent developments, this proved to be something of an understatement because the retreat of the rebels began on the first full day after their insurrection and was rapidly converted into a rout as the troops and 'fraternities' of irregulars organized by landowners exacted an awesome revenge for the challenge to a social order based not only on the coffee *finca* but also on a belligerently *ladino* republic. Given the summary and extensive nature of this repression, it is not surprising that assessment of its human cost has become the subject of rather macabre debate; but if the figure of 40,000 deaths presented by the opposition movement of the 1980s is often deemed too high, it is evident that the razing of villages and liquidation of many of their inhabitants throughout February 1932 produced a toll that may reliably be said to be in the tens of thousands. The impact of such attrition was no less cultural than political; it threw the peasant *cofradías* (socio-religious brotherhoods) into confusion and effectively suppressed the wearing of Indian clothes, which was now considered by the rural population to be a provocative act of cultural resistance – and rightly so since although the revolt was denounced as communist by the regime, for many local *ladinos* it was a revolt of primitive *naturales* against whom a genocidal solution was not beyond the realm of reason.

Although much of the violence of the spring of 1932 was undertaken by civilian vigilantes – the forebears of the death squads of the 1970s – its political outcome was the confirmation of the army's claim to office; and because the army remained a backward, garrison-based force lacking an institutional system for political decision-making, power stayed firmly in the hands of its commander, Martínez, who consolidated a regime of pronounced personalism. The decisiveness of the general's direction of operations enabled him to impose a number of limited constraints upon the oligarchy. He readily accepted its demands for a devaluation and weathered the difficulties of suspending the external debt within weeks of coming to power, but he later cut interest rates, established a central bank and withdrew rights of issue from private institutions, imposed exchange controls and provided for state participation in a credit bank. None of these measures severely prejudiced entrepreneurial interests, but some restricted short-term profitability and laid the basis for a modest state intervention in the economy, albeit usually in close collaboration with the powerful corporate associations of the bourgeoisie such as the Asociación del Café, which was transformed in 1942 into the Compañía Salvadoreña del Café and subsequently remained little less than a parallel economic cabinet through its control of the coffee market. By the end of the 1940s this process of modest qualification to a completely free-market model had proved to be sufficiently advantageous to the landlords and their commercial partners that they tolerated Martínez's introduction of some protectionist measures on behalf of an artisanate bereft of corporate representation and still in need of tariffs to assist recovery from the effects of the depression. There was nothing particularly adventurous in such initiatives – the exceptional economic conditions of the 1930s drew similar measures from equally conservative regimes in the region – and they never reached the point at which the land-owners' control of economic policy, through the relevant cabinet portfolios, or its capacity for non-compliance, through its representative bodies, came under serious challenge. (Indeed, this did not occur until the tabling of a bill for agrarian reform in 1976.) There was no further agitation over the exchange rate, which was maintained at its 1935 level of 2.5 colones to the dollar for more than fifty years.

Martínez ruled El Salvador for more than twelve years (1932–44) in a style broadly comparable to that of his peers in the neighbouring states, through a cycle of unopposed re-elections and with the retention of no more than a veneer of democratic procedures. It should, however, be noted that over time this became a formality of some consequence insofar as the Salvadorean military, unlike their counterparts in many South American countries, never fully jettisoned the protocols of the Liberal constitutional system. Under Martínez the survival of this political form was both ensured and yet evacuated of substance by a narrow concentration of personal power combined with a no less marked eccentricity of character that was later lampooned for its ostentatious mysticism – the President was an ardent advocate of theosophy and did not lack confidence in his ability to tap supernatural powers – but which also served to create an aura of unpredictability and distinctiveness around the person of a *caudillo* who could by no means be considered a mere cipher of the oligarchy. The predictability of his electoral successes sometimes provoked ill-fated stabs at revolt by disgruntled senior officers, but even before Washington reversed its refusal to recognize de facto regimes in 1936, Martínez's position was extremely secure. Thereafter it appeared little less than unassailable until the final stages of the Second World War. By this time the enforced expansion of trade with the United States had compensated for the very low level of direct U.S. investment and bestowed upon Washington an unprecedented degree of influence in El Salvador, albeit more circumscribed than in any other Central American state except Costa Rica. This influence was employed to reinstate a modicum of popular participation in the political process without at the same time undermining the landlords or threatening the army. Such an objective in the mid-1940s (as in the 1950s), pursued by Roosevelt by means short of direct intervention, was exceptionally difficult – arguably impossible – to achieve, but it nonetheless greatly debilitated a dictatorship which had declared war on the Axis on the basis of geographical necessity rather than ideological repudiation and increasingly at odds with the democratic sentiments of the 'Four Freedoms' propounded by the Allies.

By the time Martínez's authority appeared to be slipping in 1943 – a year in which, on the one hand, a tax on coffee exports agitated the *finqueros,* and, on the other, the railway-workers managed to revive their union – his dalliance with the fascist powers in the late 1930s had become but a minor feature of growing discontent with a long-standing and narrow autocracy, most forcefully expressed in the middle class, which had been hit particularly hard by the sharp rise in consumer prices induced by the war. By Central American standards the urban middle sector in San

Salvador was large and, despite a dozen years of obligatory absence from public life, not lacking in political traditions. Moreover, agitation over the corruption and bureaucratic inefficiency stemming from the favouritism inherent in Martínez's personalist regime found a strong echo in the ranks of the army, where many officers felt threatened by the President's growing patronage of the paramilitary forces, which were commanded by regular officers but not answerable to the Minister of War. When, early in 1944, the inflexible *caudillo* instructed a compliant Congress to amend the constitution to allow him yet a further term in office, he succeeded in maximizing antipathy towards his government. In April a section of the officer corps staged a revolt that was subdued only with difficulty by the National Guard and the execution by firing squad of the ringleaders, none of whom could be described as radical. Such a move, unprecedented in the history of the modern Salvadorean army, increased hostility between the various security forces, and outraged not only the victims' colleagues but also the urban populace at large. The students and doctors of the capital declared a civic strike, which did not last long but engendered enough support to persuade the President that he could no longer rely upon the army, Washington or popular acquiescence. However, both the cautious approach of the U.S. Embassy, which refused to support either side, and the desire of a majority of officers for a conservative and institutional succession restricted the immediate outcome of the anti-dictatorial movement to Martínez's replacement by a trusted colleague, General Andrés Ignacio Menéndez.

The strike of April 1944 was staged in support of the military dissidents and against Martínez rather than the ruling class as a whole; there was no significant movement in the countryside, and the working class played only a subordinate role. Although this was the first of a series of popular anti-dictatorial mobilizations in Central America during 1944 and opened a short but active period of political competition, there was no instant upsurge in radical activity once Martínez had gone and Menéndez had announced new elections for the autumn. The initially cautious mood appeared to confirm expectations of a restitution of the system that had obtained up to 1931. However, the accumulating impetus of the candidacy of Dr Arturo Romero, who gained the endorsement of the Communist-backed and rapidly expanding Unión Nacional de Trabajadores (UNT) despite his espousal of a programme less radical than that of Arturo Araujo's Partido Laborista, raised fears inside both the military and the oligarchy of uncontainable mobilization following an almost victory for Romero at the polls. Such apprehension was deepened by the removal of General Ubico in Guatemala in June and the popularly backed military coup of October. Thus, when a large crowd gathered in the central plaza of San Salvador on 21 October 1944 precisely to celebrate the Guatemalan revolution, Menéndez finally bowed to the pressure from his colleagues and permitted a pre-emptive coup by Colonel Osmín Aguirre, one of the leaders of the repression in 1932. The resulting massacre in the city centre within six months of Martínez's departure not only marked a return to the methods of the ex-president but also underscored the extreme vulnerability of any effort to sustain a civilian political system without the unambiguous imprimatur of the army. Attempts to stage a second general strike and then to invade the country from Guatemala were suppressed without quarter even, as in the case of the ill-organized student invasion, when the opposition was middle class and far from extremist. Aguirre's coup imposed unity on the military apparatus and ensured that no civilian candidate stood in the elections of January 1945, the 'overwhelming majority' of votes being cast in a manner quite distinct from that envisaged by the United Nations, for an old ally of Martínez, General Salvador Castañeda Castro, heading the aptly named Partido Agrario (PA).

Castañeda presided over a four-year holding operation during which time the Cold War set in and the international conditions for a return to democracy deteriorated under the weight of a pervasive anti-communism. The same period also witnessed a steady economic recovery as coffee prices were freed from war-time agreements, opening possibilities of agricultural diversification and encouraging ideas of some industrial development. This encouraged a degree of differentiation within a capitalist class which, although exceptionally tight, was not fully integrated and had always incubated some tension between landlords and merchants. Competition rarely went much beyond sectoral tussles over positions in the markets, but within such a compact community it had enough resonance to disturb unity over the prospect of a simple retreat to the restrictions of the Martínez years. This was politically reassuring yet also out of keeping with the new phase of economic growth. Moreover, many junior officers who had supported the coup of April 1944 considered that of October, with its personalism and rejection of an institutional system of apportioning office and regulating policy, to have defrauded them. Hence, when Castañeda endeavoured in 1948 to prolong his lacklustre regime, he was overthrown in what became known as 'the majors' coup', which marked both a consolidation of the military around the objectives of the 1944 revolt and a clear shift towards modernizing the style of control. A regime of complete political prohibition and economic conservatism moved towards one that promoted an increased level of state intervention in the economy, tolerated a number of closely watched-over urban unions and civic associations, accepted some political competition within the middle class as well as the oligarchy, and gave a degree of support to those elements of capital seeking to invest in new sectors of agriculture, particularly cotton, and the manufacturing industry. The principal figure in this movement was Colonel Oscar Osorio, who manoeuvred diligently and forcefully to establish the Partido Revolucionario de Unificación Democrática (PRUD) in 1949 as the military-sponsored official party of government that would in 1961 mutate with little change beyond that of title into the Partido de Conciliación Nacional (PCN), which ruled until 1979.

The junta that held power until 1950 was young, middle-class and technocratic, initially attracting wide-spread sympathy for the military in what was seen as a reprise of April 1944. But the *apertura* that many expected was never granted. Anti-communism remained resolutely at the centre of a system that replaced Martínez's narrow autocracy with a more dynamic style of domination predicated upon the belief – as expressed by Colonel José María Lemus – that 'the only truly efficient way to achieve [social and economic] equilibrium and avoid the evils of dangerous doctrines is to promote broad transformative doctrines within the framework of co-operation between government, the capitalists and the workers'.[4] *Transformismo* was a much-used term in Central America at this time, yet although the Constitution of 1950 included stipulations in favor of agrarian reform and the 'social function' of all property, the Salvadorean officers desisted from implementing the former in the countryside and implemented the latter only with great caution in the towns. The new regime could be described as anti-oligarchic only insofar as it confirmed Martínez's exclusion of civilians from political power and adjusted the terms of that exclusion to incorporate some statist and developmentalist currents. This fully assuaged Washington, while absolute prohibition of popular organization in the countryside and tight control of the urban unions through both co-optation and direct coercion ensured that for the mass of citizens, the system was only marginally different from its predecessors.

The governments of Oscar Osorio (1950–6) and José María Lemus

---

[4] Quoted in Robert E. Elam, 'Appeal to Arms: The Army and Politics in El Salvador, 1931–1964', unpublished Ph.D. dissertation, University of New Mexico, Albuquerque, 1968, p. 146.

(1956 – 60) consolidated military power in a period of generally buoyant coffee prices, agricultural diversification and some modest growth in manufacturing. The election of 1956 was, as usual, contested by parties of the civilian right, but the PRUD received 93 per cent of the votes once a reshuffle in military appointments had ensured full institutional support for the official candidate. Such a reassuring result enabled Lemus to start his period in office with great confidence and to relax some of the controls imposed by Osorio. However, towards the end of the decade coffee prices began to fall and the example of the Cuban Revolution excited the enthusiasm of the students, who subjected the government to increasingly vociferous opposition through their union, and the newly established reformist party named after the movement of 1944, the Partido Revolucionario de Abril y Mayo (PRAM). At first Lemus attempted to field this challenge with some flexibility since the alliance built around the PRAM won the mayoralty of the capital and five other towns in the spring of 1960 elections. Nevertheless, government refusal to permit any opposition victories in the congressional polls only encouraged their campaign to the point at which, in August 1960, Lemus declared martial law and sent the army into the university. These measures, and the vigorous clamp-down that ensued, signalled a refusal to accept a genuinely independent and active opposition. Although Communist influence and the economic slump certainly caused consternation within the officer corps, there was a lack of unanimity over the wisdom of restricting political participation so tightly. Hence, when a section of the army overthrew the now highly unpopular President in October 1960 and established a junta with civilian technocrats and sympathizers of democratic reform, there was apprehension but no immediate resistance from more conservative elements. Yet, once it became clear that the junta would permit the left to stand in new elections, this caution was rapidly reversed and the counter-coup led by Colonel Julio Rivera in January 1961 received majority military support for its restitution of institutional government. Just as in 1944, when open elections and civilian government emerged as a tangible possibility, political concessions by the military were soon curtailed. However, Lemus' precipitate prohibition of all authentic opposition not from the right was henceforth adjusted by the newly formed PCN to permit some congressional and municipal representation as a form of safety-valve and to refurbish the image of the regime within the Alliance for Progress. The Partido Demócrata Cristiano (PDC), established in 1960, was permitted to win fourteen congressional seats against the PCN's thirty-two in 1964, and in

1966 one of the party's young leaders, José Napoleón Duarte, was allowed to take the mayoralty of San Salvador which he soon converted into a platform for the PDC's policy of social rapprochement and measured reform.[5] On the other hand, the Partido de Acción Renovadora (PAR), which had had a tenuous existence since the late 1940s to be revived under a new leadership in the early 1960s, was banned in 1967, having won 29 per cent of the vote on the basis of a much more extensive programme of reforms. Its effective successor, the Movimiento Nacional Revolucionario (MNR), led by Guillermo Manuel Ungo, was allowed to contest the poll of 1968 on a Social Democratic platform that included the call for an agrarian reform – not a leading item on the PDC agenda – but it lacked great popular appeal and failed to win any seats in 1970, which may well have guaranteed its continued existence.

The presence of an opposition was integral to the PCN regime, which continued to exploit its control over elections to maintain a 'continuist' system of government under the presidencies of Colonels Julio Rivera (1961–7), Fidel Sánchez Hernández (1967–72), Arturo Molina (1972–7) and General Carlos Humberto Romero (1977–9). Although the more devout and philanthropic aspects of Catholic social policy promulgated by the PDC, or demands for redistribution emanating from the Social Democrats, were at times unsettling and threatened to attract considerable support, their mere existence served to sustain the appearance of democracy and kept the system from being a full-fledged dictatorship, even though it was guaranteed by the regular army at elections and more generally upheld by the paramilitary forces. From the end of the 1960s these were assisted by a powerful, semi-official organization known as ORDEN, which functioned principally as a vigilante force in the countryside. In contrast to previous bodies of this type, ORDEN was designed to have a mass membership, and many who joined it were less attracted by its reactionary ideology than by the possibility of minor official favours or often simply the need to protect themselves against persecution, usually at the hands of the National Guard, which firmly suppressed dissident activity and ensured the prohibition of independent rural unions.

In the 1960s, rural unions often originated from the co-operatives and communal associations sponsored by the Church, posing little ostensible threat to the established order until rising violence and support for the

<hr />

[5] The origins and development of the PDC are analysed in one of the very few published studies of a Central American political party: Stephan Webre, *José Napoleón Duarte and the Christian Democratic Party in Salvadoran Politics, 1960–1978* (Baton Rouge, 1979).

'preferential option for the poor' in the pastoral work and theological convictions of many rural priests engendered potent currents that acquired organizational autonomy in the 1970s.[6] Radical Catholicism was perhaps stronger in El Salvador than elsewhere in Central America, and it matched the influence of the secular left in politicizing rural labour and the students, if not the urban working class. By the mid-1970s this was plainly depleting the rank-and-file support built up by the PDC, but it did not deprive the party of large numbers of tactical votes in elections where the left either could not or would not stand. The strength of the movement was nowhere more clearly signalled than in the positions adopted at the end of the decade by Archbishop Oscar Arnulfo Romero, a cleric of hitherto conservative persuasion who, on the basis of his forceful condemnation of violence, was considered by the military and the right to be a major hindrance and, with somewhat less justification, an active supporter of the left. The shock caused by Romero's volte-face paralleled that generated by the scale of rural organization, which, because it remained largely outside the pattern of formal national politics, diffuse, and almost by definition absorbed with local tactics, was not for a long time perceived by the military as posing a markedly greater threat than the tame co-optational entities out of which it grew. As a consequence, efforts to establish an agrarian reform against landlord opposition were pursued with minimal energy and the demands of the centrist opposition for a strategic resolution to the rural question generally dismissed as demagogy. When, however, it was recognized that an authentic challenge existed in the countryside, the political instincts of the armed forces were permitted to run free in a repressive campaign that frequently compounded rather than cowed opposition.

In the towns, particularly San Salvador, the marked growth of manufacturing and regional trade in the 1960s prompted by the Central American Common Market (CACM) provided some space for trade-union expansion. Moreover, although the number of organized workers remained very low and many of these were enrolled in federations controlled by government supporters, independent action such as the general strike of 1967 reflected an erratic trend towards militancy and away from the mutualist traditions of the artisanate.[7] That this was still vulnerable to co-optation as well as coercion may be seen in the wide support for the government's invasion of

---

[6] Carlos Cabarrús, *Génesis de una revolución* (Mexico, 1983); Jenny Pearce, *Promised Land: Peasant Rebellion in Chalatenango, El Salvador* (London, 1985).

[7] See Rafael Menjivar, *Formación y lucha del proletariado* (San José, 1982).

Honduras in the 'Soccer War' of 1969, when nationalist fervour captured the PDC, which enjoyed appreciable support among workers, and elicited minimal opposition from the Communist Party (PCS), which was the major leftist force inside the unions.

This conflict had little to do with clashes during various football matches in the first round of the World Cup, and was aggravated less by border disputes than by El Salvador's considerable commercial superiority over Honduras and the large number of Salvadorean migrant workers in that country. The imbalance in trade resulted from Salvadorean exploitation of its already existing advantages under the more favourable commercial climate given by the CACM, but emigration from densely populated and intensively farmed El Salvador had provided its oligarchy with a valuable safety-valve for many years. More than half a million people had left the country since 1930, the majority to Honduras. This population provided a ready target for the embattled Honduran regime of Colonel Osvaldo López Arellano, which sought both to resist Salvadorean economic hegemony and to reduce popular opposition by appropriating the lands of Salvadorean settlers for redistribution. At least 100,000 migrants were driven back to their homeland, and this produced long-term problems that far outweighed the short-term political gain of a momentary boost to Salvadorean nationalism. Many of these refugees had trade-union experience from working the Honduran banana plantations, and most necessarily sought to re-establish their lives in the capital since the prospects for rural labour were now far worse than when they had left the country. The size of the influx was in itself a problem, but many of the refugees were less inclined to be grateful for their deliverance than discontented by the absence of opportunities that attended it, which was also a factor of some consequence. The capacity of the urban economy to absorb more labour was already exhausted, and the war effectively ended the CACM. More immediately the regime's resettlement programme provided little or no relief.

Thus, not only was a strategic outflow of poor Salvadorean workers brought to an abrupt halt by the war with Honduras, but a large number of displaced and dispossessed people were added to the expanding population of the shanty-towns around the capital, accelerating an already visible process of 'marginalization'. Between 1950 and 1980 the country's urban population grew from 18 per cent to 44 per cent of the total – an average increase by regional standards – and that of the city of San Salvador from 116,000 to 700,000 – this, too, by no means exceptional in Central

America. However, by the mid-1970s the department of San Salvador, containing more than a fifth of the national population, had a population density of 843 per square kilometre against a national average of 170, itself five times the Central American average. Thus, although the social conflict of the 1970s and 1980s could not be explained plausibly just by population density, which had been high for centuries, it was the case that this phenomenon was reaching chronic proportions and creating in the political centre of the country conditions of settlement that both exacerbated the economic difficulties of the mass of the people and promoted extra-occupational patterns of unrest and organization. As with the rapid expansion of the student population – by 1974 more than 30,000 were enrolled in the Faculty of Humanities alone – a major new political constituency came into being and unsettled the familiar socio-political balance between town and country.

The war with Honduras generated a crisis within the PCS, which was seen by many radicalized youth as incapable of providing a decisive challenge to the regime. Continued devotion to the 'peaceful road to socialism' through elections and cautious work in the unions were in keeping with Moscow's advice – increasingly harmonious with that issuing from Havana – and the organizational instincts of a party that had been all but destroyed by the adoption of an insurrectionary strategy within two years of its birth. Critical of this approach and of the 'idealist' belief that democracy could be obtained with the support of a 'national bourgeoisie' of anti-oligarchic entrepreneurs, the secretary-general, Salvador Cayetano Carpio, together with several important union and student leaders, left the party to establish a 'politico-military organization', the Fuerzas Populares de Liberación – Farabundo Martí (FPL), in 1971. This guerrilla organization did not begin operations immediately, because it rejected the *foco* theory derived from the Cuban example as well as notions of rapid insurrection in favour of a strategy of 'prolonged people's war' on the Vietnamese model. In the 1972 a more middle-class and adventurous group of disenchanted PDC supporters broke from legal politics to set up the Ejército Revolucionario del Pueblo (ERP) on the basis of a more militarist *foquismo*. Internal disputes over the validity of this model of an elite vanguard bringing the masses to revolutionary consciousness through example more than organizational collaboration reached a bloody apogee in the execution by the ERP leadership of the distinguished writer Roque Dalton in 1975. Supporters of Dalton's criticisms of the ERP subsequently formed the third major guerrilla force, the Fuerzas Armadas de Resistencia Nacional

(FARN) on more cautious political and military lines. The relatively late emergence of these groups in El Salvador compared with the rest of Central America may be attributed in large part to the fact that although there appeared to be some prospects for democratic progress in the 1960s, these were progressively reduced over the following decade as the PCN prevented the reformist opposition from obtaining office despite, or more probably because of, their growing popular support.

Since the principal mechanism for this containment continued to be government manipulation of the polls – particularly flagrant in those for the presidency in 1972 and 1977 – the pattern of polarization tended to follow the electoral calendar, popular discontent at scarcely credible opposition defeats provoking significant break-downs in public order as well as accumulating a more general disenchantment with the political system as a whole. Although the parties of reform might be criticized for a misguided belief in their ability to take office or cajole the regime into introducing progressive change, they acted with appreciable skill in seeking to exploit the opportunities available to them. By forming the Unión Nacional Opositora (UNO), the PDC, MNR and the Unión Democrática Nacionalista (UDN) – effectively a front for the outlawed PCS – not only suppressed what were little more than tactical and confessional differences between themselves but also presented the government with an impressive challenge behind the candidacy of the able Duarte, supported by the less colourful but more intellectual Ungo. Indeed, so high were expectations of a UNO victory in 1972 that when Colonel Molina was finally declared the winner by less than 10,000 votes after a suspiciously abrupt suspension of public information on the count, a section of the officer corps was prompted to stage a coup. Although the rebels refused to distribute arms to civilians, they were defeated only after troops from neighbouring states organized in the Central American Defence Council (Consejo de Defensa Centroamericana, CONDECA) were flown in to assist the disorganized loyalist forces and the ever-faithful paramilitary police. Duarte had hesitated to support the rising and held back UNO followers from staging their own street protests, but he was deemed too threatening an opponent to be afforded further guarantees and was arrested, severely beaten and exiled to Venezuela. The treatment administered to one of the most talented leaders of Latin American Christian Democracy enhanced his profile abroad and greatly increased his popularity at home.

The Molina regime, though shaken by the events of 1972, did not thereafter impose markedly tighter control than had its predecessor. It even reduced pressure on the formal opposition in an effort to maintain its participation in the system. This temporary relaxation was most evident in the regime's preparedness to acquiesce in opposition control of some congressional committees. Although this was won more by tactical skill than official concession, such acquiescence enabled the presentation in 1976 of a bill for limited agrarian reform which the government did not immediately block. However, the oligarchy staged a resolute resistance through its principal pressure groups – the Asociación Nacional de Empresas Privadas (ANEP) and the Frente de Agricultores de la Región Oriental (FARO) – thwarting the proposed legislation and signalling to the high command that the limits of concession had been exceeded. This stance was brutally supplemented by the growing activity of right-wing vigilante groups (death squads) such as FALANGE and the Unión Guerrera Blanca (UGB), which undertook selective assassinations and established a pattern of repression that was henceforth to be a sadly persistent feature of Salvadorean life.

Both the ground yielded to the opposition and the Molina regime's own disposition to countenance some form of reform in the rural sector drove the military farther to the right. The PCN candidate for the 1977 poll, General Romero, was an extreme conservative. In an effort to protect its candidate against a reprise of the events of 1972, UNO put forward a retired officer, Colonel Ernesto Claramount, who represented a minority liberal current within the military. This forced the hierarchy to carry out a frantic reorganization of army commands in order to assure support for an official candidate more resolute in his convictions than skilled in defending them. However, the scale and clumsiness of the machinations employed to return Romero both before and during the poll provoked the occupation of the capital's centre by his opponent's followers, wide-spread street violence and a short-lived general strike. Although the guerrillas were responsible for some of this activity, much of it stemmed from popular organizations and trade unions whose members had voted for UNO but were inclining to direct action in pursuit of both economic and political objectives. The post-electoral repression of 1977 assisted the growth of this tendency because President Romero, unlike his predecessor, maintained and increased coercive control, courting a rupture with the Carter administration as official government forces, ORDEN and the death squads embarked upon a violent campaign against both the orthodox left and the Catholic radicals which had already begun to construct broad-based popular organizations, fronts or 'blocs' around the much smaller guerrilla groups: the Bloque Popular Revolucionario (BPR) (1975) for the FPL; the Ligas Populares – 28 de Febrero (LP–28) (1977) for the ERP; and the Frente de Acción Popular Unificada (FAPU) (1974) for the FARN.[8] These bodies were still in fierce dispute over political and military strategy and unable to stage more than small-scale operations, usually against individuals connected with the oligarchy or military. But in the wake of UNO's manifest failure to secure reform through constitutionalism, the extension of the left's influence and growing acceptance of armed struggle were not without a certain logic. This, combined with continued sectarian divisions, gave rise to a string of organizations which were to compete for popular support until, with the country standing on the verge of civil war early in 1980, they were forced into unification.

It is certainly true that the final collapse of the PCN regime as a result of the coup of 15 October 1979 was influenced by developments at a regional level, particularly the Nicaraguan revolution of July but also the poor and deteriorating relations between the Romero regime and Washington as a result of Romero's suspension of constitutional guarantees and reluctance to halt escalating violence by the military and its informal allies, who were not afraid to promise the liquidation of the country's entire Jesuit order unless its members left. However, the momentum of domestic conflict had reached such a point by mid-1979 that a major political crisis appeared inevitable in any event. The acquiescence of the United States in a change of regime merely facilitated a relatively bloodless and essentially pre-emptive coup initiated by reformist junior officers but soon captured by less ambitious conservative rivals to Romero anxious to meet the accumulating radical challenge with both a more resourceful strategy and badly needed U.S. economic and logistical support. Romero had been obliged to lift his state of siege earlier in the year, yet this proved insufficient to stem the tide of strikes, demonstrations and guerrilla operations; both the suspension of the Constitution and its restitution in unaltered circumstances confirmed the exhaustion of the PCN strategy of combining repression with formal liberties. Neither was adequate by itself, and when organized separately they simply cancelled each other out. An essentially tactical arrangement had decomposed into confusion whereby the populace was aggrieved at the absence of proclaimed freedoms and insufficiently cowed by the violence. The younger officers behind the

---

[8] Latin America Bureau, *El Salvador Under General Romero* (London, 1979).

October coup generally associated with Colonel Majano sought to provide space for negotiation (although, unlike their forebears in 1944 and 1961, they held back from promising immediate elections). In this they enjoyed the tacit support of Washington, still shocked by the overthrow of Somoza and concerned to avert open military rule. Nonetheless, the reformists remained a minority inside the army and enjoyed even less support in the powerful paramilitary forces; and since the radical left refused to halt popular mobilization or abdicate armed activity – only a truce was agreed – on the basis of changes in the military hierarchy, conservative officers were able to harness the logic of maintaining public order to their rapidly organized campaign to sabotage economic concessions. For both internal and external reasons it proved impossible to resolve these tensions inside the dominant bloc with any speed. As a result, although the reformists progressively lost authority, political conflict within the military and ruling class endured long after El Salvador had entered a low-level but prolonged and very brutal civil war in which the military and oligarchy were ranged against a popular bloc composed of the majority of the erstwhile legal opposition and the organizations of the radical left.

In economic terms the outbreak of major social conflict in El Salvador in 1979 was perhaps more predictable than even the Nicaraguan revolution; the steady increase in production and agro-exports during the post-war period had been matched by a no less impressive tendency to reduce access to land for subsistence, prompting increased unemployment and underemployment and a regressive distribution of income in the countryside more pronounced than in the rest of Central America and certainly beyond hope of significant alleviation from growth in the urban economy. Between 1950 and 1980, GDP grew from $379.6 million to $1,526 million at an annual average rate of 5.2 per cent while the population expanded at 3.3 per cent. The increase in GDP per capita from $185 to $289 over this period appeared to indicate an improvement in the wealth of the population at large consonant with a threefold increase in the number of vehicles, fourfold rise in paved roads and in the number of telephones, and other infrastructural advances of a similar order. Yet if the global stock of wealth had increased faster than that of people and the forces of production had advanced considerably, the impression of a comprehensive modernization was belied by the indices for income distribution and land tenure. In 1977 the wealthiest 6 per cent of the population earned as much as the poorest 63 per cent. In 1975, 41 per cent of rural families were completely landless, 34 per cent farmed less than 1 hectare (insufficient for subsistence) and 15 per cent possessed less than 2 hectares.[9] Moreover, although since before the turn of the century, the Salvadorean peasantry had been much more restricted in its access to plots of land than had small farmers in neighbouring states, land poverty had accelerated appreciably since the late 1950s as commercial estates dedicated to both coffee and new crops such as cotton and sugar as well as cattle-ranching occupied greater space within a virtually static agricultural frontier. The rise in production that supported the post-war growth in GDP may be explained in part by better yields – that for coffee rose from 655 kilos per hectare in 1950 to 1,224 in 1977 – which also had the effect of at least maintaining demand for harvest labour. However, while the expansion of land under coffee was relatively modest – from 112,000 in 1950 to 147,000 hectares in 1977 – that under cotton more than trebled (to more than 60,000 hectares) while sugar increased by comparable degree (to 38,000 hectares) and the area in pasture for cattle – the sector that demanded least labour and most land per unit – rose by 50 per cent. In many cases this expansion was achieved at the direct cost of peasant holdings on the periphery of established coffee country and outside the traditional zones of large estates. Although cotton was an established crop and could be extended on the basis of existing patterns of tenure, the rise in cattle-raising trespassed deep into the less fertile and marginal lands that had hitherto provided a modicum of space for subsistence. This expansion did not produce an absolute stasis in the domestic food crop acreage – which may be broadly but not exclusively associated with peasant agriculture – but it did impede growth in land cultivated for the domestic market. Between 1948 and 1978 land given over to maize expanded by 30 per cent; to beans, by 23 per cent; and to rice, by just 12 per cent. Modest improvements in yield assisted increases in production of 75 per cent, 43 per cent and 67 per cent respectively over a period when El Salvador's population nearly trebled in size.[10] Thus, while harvest labour demand was maintained and agro-exports grew in both volume and value, the subsistence economy declined relative to both the commercial estates and the population. The import of increasing quantities of basic grains was necessary to maintain levels of consumption.

[9] Ministerio de Planificaíon, 'Distribución del ingreso y gasto por deciles de hogares', (San Salvador, 1981); Censo Agropecuario, 1975, cited in J. Mark Ruhl, 'Agrarian Structure and Political Stability in Honduras', *Journal of Inter-American Studies* 26, no. 1 (1984): 47.
[10] Edelberto Torres Rivas, 'The Beginnings of Industrialization in Central America', Working Paper no. 141, Latin American Program, Woodrow Wilson Center (Washington, D.C., 1984), p. 17.

Lacking virgin lands in which to settle or even a culture of socio-economic 'refuge' comparable to that sustained by the Indian farmers of Guatemala, the expanding Salvadorean peasantry was caught in a pincer movement between loss of opportunities for direct cultivation and those for temporary waged labour. This by no means compelled a break-down in rural order, still less open revolt, but it did aggravate discontent with the landlord regime while dislocating large numbers of rural labourers from the economic and social controls of the *finca*, opening the traditionally cautious political consciousness of the peasantry to the unsettling influence of local priests, schoolteachers and lay activists opposed to the established order. The sharp contrasts in the human condition in El Salvador, where the wealth of the landlord class was as impressive and as ostentatiously paraded as anywhere else in Latin America, were naturally prone to excite sentiments of Jacobin egalitarianism as much as resignation to an historic and unremovable order.

As we have seen, a significant proportion of the rural population moved either permanently or temporarily to the towns as the manufacturing sector began to grow. Between 1950 and 1977 industry expanded by an average of 6.3 per cent a year. The share of GDP attributable to manufacturing production rose from 12.9 per cent to 18.7 per cent, which was high by regional standards. Much of this growth took place under the CACM in the 1960s when the share of foreign, principally U.S., investment in manufacturing rose from 0.7 per cent in 1959 to 38.1 per cent in 1969.[11] Such progress was not of the type envisaged by many planners in the period after the Second World War insofar as there was very little heavy industry – capital goods accounted for 8.6 per cent of production in 1978 – and the bulk of output (64.7 per cent) was of perishable commodities frequently related to agricultural production. Nevertheless, the amount of locally produced inputs was lower than this structure might suggest, the textile industry importing 45 per cent of its raw materials and the paper industry nearly 90 per cent. This, combined with the 'assembly and finishing' character of many of the new enterprises, limited the trickle-down effects of sectoral growth to the rest of the economy. Furthermore, since much of the new industrial plant was foreign-owned and capital-intensive, the overall rise in the labour force (from 87,300 in 1962 to 118,000 in 1975) was much more modest than that in production

---

[11] Gert Rosenthal, 'El papel de la inversión extranjera directa en el proceso de integración', in *Centroamérica hoy* (Mexico, 1976), p. 125.

and masked a fall in the size of the working class relative to the economically active population as a whole (from 10.2 per cent to 9.3 per cent) as well as the fact that nearly half of this manufacturing labour force was still employed in artisanal workshops of five employees or less.[12] Thus, not only did industrial growth fail to supply alternative employment for most of those leaving the countryside, it also resulted in the properly 'proletarian' character of the urban labour force being diminished from the early 1960s onwards – a matter of no little importance for sociological theories of revolution. The influence of assembly-line and factory syndicalism cannot by any means be excluded from the urban unrest of the late 1970s, but these were often subordinate in terms of both numbers and political impetus to the role of radicalized white-collar and skilled workers (particularly the teachers and power workers), the impoverished 'self-employed' in the informal sector, and locally based community organizations that usually dominated the plebeian fronts to the fore in popular mobilization until open activity was halted by repression following the general strike of August 1980. Nonetheless, it is of some consequence that once a modicum of public organization and activity again became possible after the elections of 1984, the trade unions, particular those in the white-collar and public sectors, revived remarkably quickly, suggesting that urban discontent could not be reduced simply to a revolt of a marginalized lumpenproletariat.

It is evident that neither economic stagnation nor mere poverty caused the social conflict of the late 1970s, the former because it simply did not occur until the civil war had begun – and the international economy entered recession – and the latter because poverty in itself was no novelty in Salvadorean society nor as great as in Honduras, which remained relatively free of violence, although undoubtedly people were getting poorer faster than ever before. What lay behind the collapse of a social order established a century before was a process of concerted growth dominated by the export sector that dislocated tens of thousands of rural labourers from the security of both their lands and harvest wages but failed to replace this disaggregation of the peasantry with a process of socially stable and economically compensatory urbanization. This imbalance not only accelerated impoverishment but also created a significant population devoid of 'pure' class character, often geographically as well as socially mobile, outside established circuits of control, and subjected to decreas-

---

[12] Ramón Mayorga, *El crecimiento desigual en Centroamérica* (Mexico, 1983), pp. 60–6.

ingly efficacious strategies for survival. This population cannot be accounted as exclusively urban or rural since the symbiosis between town
and countryside is too strong in El Salvador, as later became evident in the
relatively fluid exchange between the two spheres in terms of military
operations. In this respect, at least, the crisis was as 'modern' as it was
traditional, combining features of the late twentieth century (the guerrillas' use of video for propaganda and education) with those familiar for
centuries (the struggle over land; cultural antipathies; inter-communal
violence).

Between October 1979 and January 1980 there was considerable confusion
in Salvadorean politics as a junta combining both reformist and conservative officers, representatives of the legal opposition (including the PCS),
the oligarchy, and some sectors of the radical bloc endeavoured to agree
upon policy while the military continued to attack popular demonstrations. By the end of 1979 those reforms the progressive elements had
managed to introduce were plainly being stalled by the right, and the
refusal of the military to accept government control over its operations
resulted in the resignation of all the reformists except members of the
PDC. In January 1980 the plebeian fronts held a large demonstration in
the capital to mark the anniversary of the 1932 rising and the formation of
the Coordinadora Revolucionaria de Masas (CRM), which unified the
popular organizations and was joined two months later by most of the
reformist parties and many unions to form the Frente Democrático
Revolucionario (FDR). Henceforth the FDR acted as the principal political body of the opposition. This consolidation of the popular bloc was
hastened by the assassination of Archbishop Romero in March, a crime
widely attributed to the paramilitary forces nurtured on the periphery of
the army and publicly lauded by extremist politicians of the right, such as
Roberto D'Aubuissón, who considered as subversives even those depleted
and cowed representatives of reform still in government. Romero's death
indicated how far such forces were prepared to go in their campaign
against reform, and it split the PDC, a minority leaving both government
and party on the grounds that it was no longer politically possible or
morally acceptable to collaborate with the right in order to fortify the
centre against the left. The majority of the party, however, continued to
support their leader José Napoleón Duarte, who was receiving support
from Washington for his vehement campaign against his old UNO allies
for being the dupes of Communism. The opposition retorted with equal

predictability that he had made common cause with those who not only oppressed the people but had also tortured and exiled him when he championed democratic rights.

Although Duarte was henceforth vilified by the left and centre as a puppet, he maintained a position independent of the extreme right and most of the military in that he insisted upon an agrarian reform as a necessary means by which to reduce polarization in the countryside. Since the Carter administration supported this strategy and the high command was now prepared to accept it as the price for much-needed U.S. logistical backing, a still disorganized oligarchy failed to impede its formal introduction in May 1980. The reform subsequently underwent a very chequered history in that redistribution of large coffee estates either fell outside its compass or was postponed *sine die,* and the conversion of a number of less efficient and 'over-sized' haciendas into co-operatives often amounted to little more than an alteration of deeds, since sabotage and violence impeded a genuine adoption of control by the labourers. There was some progress in granting title to small plots, but this proceeded far more slowly than planned and certainly did not produce the stratum of small capitalist farmers envisaged by the U.S. planners in charge of the programme. Harried particularly by the forces of the right but also sometimes by those of the left, the recipients of long-awaited lands were largely incapable of realizing a significant change in their circumstances while the great majority of the rural population remained excluded from the reform. Yet even those limited steps that were taken proved anathema to the landlords, who began to exercise their de facto powers of veto with the help of officers who accepted the reform as a requirement of U.S. support but whose political instincts were to hinder any change in the traditional order. The exceptions to this rule were notable for their small number, but as the war became more extended some of the more able commanders not known for their progressive views began to accept the programme on purely logistical grounds.

Even before this attitude began to take root, the oligarchy was being obliged by the thrust of the junta's policies to move beyond spoiling operations and stage a political challenge for formal office. This was compelled both by the fall of the PCN and Washington's strategy of making military support conditional upon at least the promulgation of some social reforms, a quid pro quo greatly facilitated by the PDC's presence in the junta but justifiably viewed by the extreme right as susceptible to adjustment should it gain power and the left-wing challenge continue to perturb the U.S. administration. The establishment of the Alianza Republicana Nacional (ARENA) under the leadership of the reactionary populist Roberto D'Aubuissón may, therefore, be seen as the first genuinely independent intervention of the landlord class in open political competition since 1932, a development that was somewhat obscured by the adoption of modern methods of campaigning in the style of U.S. parties to complement the power of patronage and retribution over voters employed by, or vulnerable to, the party's leading supporters. ARENA's unqualified repudiation of economic reform and advocacy of a purely military solution to the conflict was nothing if not simple and coherent – the electoral appeal of which was often underrated by its opponents – and it effectively obliged Washington to desist from any major challenge to the landed bourgeoisie. Yet if D'Aubuissón's well-publicized connections with the death squads and chilling proclamations engendered diplomatic embarrassment, his opposition to the government lent some credibility to the notion that formal political competition existed in El Salvador, thereby facilitating the presentation of both the government and its legal opponents as constituting a democratic system worthy of protection against Communist subversion.

The programme drawn up by the Coordinadora Revolucionaria de Masas (CRM) in January 1980 and adopted by the Frente Democrático Revolucionario (FDR) a few weeks later was not a charter for Communism, but it did include a comprehensive agrarian reform and the nationalization of strategic economic infrastructure as well as the banks and foreign trade. (These last two measures were, in fact, implemented in part by the junta on rational capitalist grounds, and although they were resisted by the oligarchy, were allowed to stand when the right was in control of the constituent assembly and presidency in 1982–4.) Although the FDR contained a number of powerful and openly Marxist bodies seeking some form of socialism through revolutionary change, none of its members was in a position to impose a programme of socialist transformation or indeed considered it viable in even the medium term, and the alliance had been made possible only through agreement on a 'popular democratic' platform that postulated a social policy comparable to that held by UNO in the early 1970s. Yet under the conditions of extreme violence obtaining from early 1980 the political methods of the FDR predictably took on a more radical tone, and opposition strategy increasingly came under the influ-

ence of the guerrilla groups. This shift began following the failure of the
general strikes of June and August 1980 when the reformists were obliged
to accept that there was no alternative to armed struggle.

The establishment of a combined military command in the Frente
Farabundo Martí para la Liberación Nacional (FMLN) in the autumn of
1980 marked the end of a period of ambiguity in opposition tactics and
the beginning of a civil war in which some 70,000 people lost their lives
over the following six years. The precipitate attempt by the FMLN to
stage a 'final offensive' in January 1981 not only provoked greater U.S.
intervention but also obliged the guerrilla to alter its tactics from a
predominantly urban and insurrectionary approach to a more rural and
low-level campaign punctuated with occasional large-scale attacks, particularly in the north and east of the country. The rebels were strongest in
Chalatenango (where the FPL was dominant), Morazán (ERP-dominated)
and around the Guazapa volcano to the north of San Salvador (where all the
groups possessed forces), although a total force of perhaps 7,000 combatants had the capacity to harass an army over 30,000-strong beyond these
zones and particularly in the rich farming country around San Miguel and
San Vicente. Under the Reagan administration military assistance to El
Salvador was substantially increased but also limited in its efficacy by the
army's lack of experience in combat, the low quality of the officer corps,
and the proclivity of the paramilitary forces for killing unarmed peasants.
Such resort to the traditional methods of control greatly prejudiced the
international image of the regime and prompted the French and Mexican
governments to recognize the FMLN-FDR as a representative political
organization. Yet even though the Salvadorean military acquired a formidable reputation for both inefficiency and brutality, the waging of a war of
attrition did eventually reduce the inhabitants of combat zones to strategies for survival beyond that of supporting the guerrilla. Thus, by the end
of 1982 it was evident that although it had established a remarkable
capacity for resistance, the rebel army lacked the ability to defeat the
military in the foreseeable future.

In the spring of 1982 elections were held for a constituent assembly
which produced a working majority for a revived PCN and ARENA over
the PDC, which had dominated the junta under Duarte's provisional
presidency. Unable to halt the poll, the guerrilla was now faced with a
regime that was certainly more conservative than its predecessor but could
also claim to have a popular mandate. Even though such claims were
rebutted with evidence of electoral irregularities that appeared convincing

to many beyond the rebel ranks, and despite the fact that the change in administration barely affected military operations, the poll did mark a shift in political conditions insofar as it opened up a second sphere of contest. This was boycotted by the FDR on the plausible grounds that since so many of its leaders and supporters had been killed there was no possibility of its being permitted to participate without precipitating a massacre. The notion that a political competition between parties of the right under the conditions of a civil war constituted a genuine democratic process was subjected to much scepticism both within the country and abroad, especially given El Salvador's questionable electoral traditions. On the other hand, it was apparent that however insufficient a reflection of public opinion, the restitution of the formalities of democratic government was a major development. This opened tensions inside the opposition on both tactical and ideological grounds, differences inside the left only finally being resolved following the death of two veterans of the FPL – Cayetano Carpio and Mélida Anaya Montes. As a result of these disputes, early in 1984 the FDR issued a new programme that was appreciably less radical than that of 1980; it suppressed concrete economic and social objectives and concentrated upon the mechanisms for a ceasefire and the establishment of a provisional government combining representatives of both the existing regime and the FDR. The opposition continued to denounce the formal political system as a charade, but the Reagan administration's decision to stage a concerted campaign against the left in Central America and the retreat of the embattled Sandinista government in Nicaragua from its early logistical support for the rebels indicated that expectations of a victory achieved in the short term and by military means were misconceived. The shift towards negotiation was further encouraged when, in May 1984, Duarte narrowly beat D'Aubuissón (by 54 per cent to 46 per cent of the vote) in an election that, although neither free of suspect practices nor reflective of the sympathies of a considerable section of the population, did nevertheless indicate a widespread desire for peace. By campaigning in the name of rapprochement, Duarte was able to match the well-funded and agile anti-communist crusade staged by D'Aubuissón, and although Washington made no secret of its preference for the PDC, the extent of the slaughter, economic crisis and forced migration undoubtedly convinced many to vote for what seemed the quickest and least terrifying path to terminating hostilities. However, if the exhaustion of the populace stemmed the progress of the radical right, expectations that the war would now be halted dissipated rapidly as Duarte, threatened by the powerful and suspicious high command and lacking U.S. support for negotiations, rejected proposals for a ceasefire and a new government, made by the rebels at the town of La Palma in November 1984. For the next two years peace talks foundered upon the president's insistence that the opposition lay down its arms without condition and the rebels' refusal to accept these terms as anything distinct from surrender. As the economy continued its steep decline, Duarte lost both popularity and authority, and the military failed to extend its containment of the FMLN to a decisive victory. The prospects of a government victory appeared as distant as those of a resolution that favoured the rebels who, confronted with absolute opposition from Washington, were unable to escape the logic of a *guerra popular prolongada* that offered their supporters no relief from violence and economic hardship.

Under such conditions, which produced a death toll of some 70,000 between 1980 and 1988, both sides had reason to consider the merits of the regional peace plan proposed by President Oscar Arias of Costa Rica in February 1987 and ratified, in amended form, by the regional heads of state in August of that year as the Esquipulas II agreement. Although both the armed forces and the FMLN remained profoundly reluctant to countenance concessions on the part of their political allies, President Duarte was unable to escape the logic of his earlier initiative to negotiate, while the left, now under pressure from Managua and Havana to display strategic flexibility, perceived the need to broaden its campaign on both domestic and diplomatic fronts.

The obstacles confronting a negotiated settlement were more substantial than in Nicaragua – where the Contra rebels had failed in their military campaign and remained almost entirely beholden to Washington – or, indeed, in Guatemala – where the Union Revolucionaria Nacional Guatemalteca (URNG) was too weak to expect reasonable terms from a civilian administration which was patently cowed by the military. Yet the political leadership of the Salvadorean opposition had never fully rejected the electoralist road or entirely dedicated itself to the capture of state power through insurrection. Equally, the civil war had greatly prejudiced the economic interests which challenged Duarte from the right and which now perceived some advantage in launching a nationalist campaign against the government's dependence on the United States, not least perhaps because this opened up the possibility of conducting an independent overture to the guerrillas. Although both the level of violence and the degree of ideological polarization underwent no diminution, it became apparent that U.S. involvement in Salvadorean affairs had produced some unforeseen consequences.

The strength of ARENA's conservative challenge to the PDC was not immediately obvious because the Christian Democrats secured control of Congress in 1985 and their opponents remained tarnished abroad by D'Aubuissón's association with the death squads. However, the Duarte administration was hamstrung by more than its extreme dependence upon U.S. aid, which by 1988 amounted to half the national budget. Although the army was bolstered by U.S. assistance, it was the government that suffered from its failure to translate this into victory over the guerrilla. At the same time, North American largesse provided ample opportunity for official corruption, which particularly damaged a confessional party that made much of its high moral purpose. Moreover, from the time that Duarte had obtained the provisional presidency his party had excused its failures in terms of the extreme right's control of the judiciary and, after 1982, the legislature; after 1985 such an explanation appeared threadbare indeed to those who had voted for the PDC, which failed to develop an organized popular movement based on its voters and then began to suffer from divisions within its elite. ARENA, by contrast, was able to stage a significant recovery as the government failed to realize the promises made between 1981 and 1984. As a result, the extreme right scored a sweeping victory in the legislative elections of 1988. Recognizing that this paved the way to ousting the PDC from the presidency in the poll of March 1989, the ARENA leadership turned its attention to improving its international image and making some gesture towards a negotiated settlement of the conflict so as to placate regional concerns as well as the preoccupations of many voters. These moves ran directly counter to the party's frequent calls for a 'final' military solution to the civil war, suggesting it had registered the importance of U.S. influence but was unwilling to alter its fundamental outlook. This, certainly, was the interpretation of many when D'Aubuissón was replaced as party leader by Alfredo Cristiani, a mild-mannered coffee grower who, educated in the United States, soon proved to be an extremely adroit advocate of the 'modern' ARENA in Washington.

Faced with a number of important developments both within the country and in Central America as a whole in 1987–8, the left responded with some unexpected initiatives of its own. In the autumn of 1988 the FDR leaders Guillermo Manuel Ungo and Rubén Zamora returned openly to San Salvador, secured personal guarantees and announced that they would participate in the March 1989 election in the name of Convergencia Democrática (CD), which, they claimed, would win a free and fair poll. The military leadership of the FMLN effectively dissociated itself from this move but desisted from directly attacking it. Then, as the election campaign got under way, the FMLN itself took the lead by proposing a postponement of the poll for six months as the principal basis upon which a cease-fire might be established, the left reincorporated into legal political life, the military dramatically reduced in size, U.S. military aid cut, and a true electoral test held. For a while the new Bush administration seemed prepared to consider discussion of this offer, and ARENA displayed even more willingness than the PDC to negotiate with its enemies. However, the FMLN's terms proved to be too steep and the initiative rapidly foundered. The guerrillas returned to their campaign to sabotage the poll but failed to impede Cristiani from easily beating the PDC candidate, Fidel Chávez Mena, while the CD predictably returned a very low vote.

In one sense these developments deepened the complexities of Salvadorean political life and appeared to open up possibilities not seen since the onset of the civil war in 1980–1. Yet even at the height of the manoeuvres it was difficult to envisage a stable resolution of the conflict in local terms. Indeed, ARENA's victory appeared to herald a return to the oligarchic mandate, uniting a fiercely reactionary dominant bloc under a reluctant but decisive North American imprimatur. A decade of bloody strife had failed to reduce political activity, but the practice of politics had equally proved incapable to putting an end to war.

6

HONDURAS SINCE 1930

In the first century after independence from Spain Honduras fought a mainly unsuccessful battle to overcome the constraints on national integration imposed by its geography.[1] The country's high mountains and narrow, steep-sided valleys had crippled internal communications, inhibited agricultural development and produced a marked localism in national politics. In the late 1920s, the land frontiers with Guatemala, El Salvador and Nicaragua were all still in dispute, leading to occasional military conflict, while the lack of national integration encouraged neighbouring governments to intervene in Honduran affairs. Even the off-shore territories were subject to the same centrifugal tendencies; the Bay Islands, recovered from Great Britain in 1860, remained largely autonomous, sovereignty over the Swan Islands was disputed with the United States, and possession of several islands in the Gulf of Fonseca was contested with El Salvador and Nicaragua. The country's difficulties were compounded by the size of its population. The 1930 census estimated the number of inhabitants at 854,184, giving a population density of less than 20 per square mile. The overwhelming majority were scattered throughout the rural areas, leaving the capital Tegucigalpa with a mere 40,000 souls. Large areas of eastern Honduras were virtually uninhabited.

Geography had given a different twist in Honduras to the liberal reforms which swept Central America from the 1870s. While Liberal *caudillos* implemented and participated personally in programmes to foster coffee and other agro-exports in the neighbouring republics, in Honduras Presidents Marco Aurelio Soto (1876–83) and Luis Bográn (1883–90)

---

[1] Richard Harding Davies tells the story of a Honduran congressman who demonstrated the nature of his country's geography by crumpling up a page of letter-paper, dropping it on his desk and declaring 'That is an outline map of Honduras'. See Richard Harding Davies, *Three Gringoes in Venezuela and Central America* (New York, 1896), p. 73.

emphasized mining, both becoming shareholders themselves in newly formed companies. Mining, on which the colonial economy had been based, offered the chance of eliminating the commercial disadvantage implied by poor internal communications since the high value-to-weight ratio of the leading minerals (silver and gold) reduced the relative importance of internal transport costs (almost prohibitive in the case of coffee). Furthermore, it was hoped that a mining boom might provide both the incentive and the fiscal resources with which to carry out long-overdue improvements in the communications system.

Some Honduran nationals participated in the recovery of mining after the liberal reforms, but the most successful ventures – stimulated by generous legislation – were foreign-owned, the New York and Honduras Rosario Mining Company acquiring a dominant position by the end of the century. The active promotion of foreign *direct* investment was no accident, because Honduras had been effectively excluded from the international bond market since the early 1870s as a consequence of a financial scandal, which became a cause célèbre and deeply scarred a whole generation of the political elite. The Honduran government had in the late 1860s raised three loans with a face value of nearly £6 million to construct an inter-oceanic railway link in a brave, if naive, attempt to improve communications and foster national integration. The scheme collapsed in 1872 with only fifty miles of track complete when it became clear that the Honduran government had been swindled; by the mid-1920s capitalization of unpaid interest had left Honduras with an external public debt of nearly £30 million – one of the highest in the world on a per capita basis.

The collapse of the railway venture led subsequent Honduran governments to hold exaggerated expectations of the impact of mining on national integration. The industry certainly expanded, but generous concessions limited the fiscal impact and the government's road-building programme remained pitifully undeveloped. Only one bank (Banco de Honduras) emerged in response to the mining boom, and the main beneficiary outside the mining sector was the small commercial enclave dominated by Arab, French and German merchants. Poor communications continued to inhibit the growth of a marketed surplus from agriculture and Tegucigalpa was the only capital city in Central America not served by a railway.

With this dismal background in view, it is not difficult to understand the enthusiasm with which successive governments greeted the overtures of foreign-owned banana companies at the turn of the century. The banana industry had been developing slowly since the 1860s with foreign ships calling at the Bay Islands and the Atlantic coast ports to purchase bananas from local producers. Growth was impeded, however, by transportation problems and the new breed of foreign entrepreneurs offered to develop railroads, improve port facilities and diversify exports in exchange for land and tax concessions. Since the land at the time appeared to have no other use, and since the fiscal privileges demanded were similar to those awarded to foreign-owned mining companies, the entrepreneurs were warmly received.

The first to enter Honduras in 1898 were the Vaccaro brothers, whose firm later became the Standard Fruit and Steamship Company. Four years later, in 1902, a similar concession was awarded to William Streich, but lack of funds forced him to sell his business to Sam Zemurray a few years later. Zemurray formed the Cuyamel Fruit Company in 1911, and the following year the United Fruit Company (UFCO) entered Honduras with the granting of concessions to two subsidiaries – the Tela and Truxillo Railroad Companies. These three companies (the Cuyamel, Standard Fruit and UFCO) soon came to dominate both the production and export of bananas and were responsible for the extraordinary boom which took Honduras to the position of the world's leading banana exporter by 1928. By that time more than a thousand miles of railways had been laid and even the sixty miles (ten had been added since the 1880s) belonging to the National Railway were managed by Zemurray's Cuyamel Fruit Company.

The price paid for this rapid expansion was high. Competition among the banana companies for government favours at first exacerbated the personalism and localism of Honduran politics. There were few, if any, elections in the first two decades of the century in which the competing candidates were not backed by rival companies. In the absence of alternative sources of funds, the companies became lenders of last resort and the successful candidate was expected to ignore irregularities in the implementation of existing contracts or award even more generous concessions. Tax privileges soon reached a point where the amount exempted far exceeded total government revenue from all sources, while duty-free imports sold through company stores undermined the fledgling manufacturing sector. Indeed, the few examples of industrial development by the end of the 1920s mainly represented diversification by the fruit companies themselves.

The spectacular growth of the banana industry did not solve the problem of poor communications inherited from the nineteenth century. By the end of the 1920s, an unpaved road linked Tegucigalpa with the Pacific port of San Lorenzo, but the centre of economic gravity was now firmly on the northern (Atlantic) coast, which was still not connected to the capital by road or rail. The banana zones on that coast were the purest form of enclaves with ports, railroads, telegraphs, and so on under foreign control and labour frequently imported (from the West Indies and El Salvador); a bank (Banco de Atlántida) founded by Vaccaro Bros. provided primitive financial services and the U.S. dollar (backed by gold) circulated freely, while the rest of Honduras remained on the silver standard in a rare example of bimetallism. One of the few links with the rest of the economy was provided by the fruit companies' lawyers, all Hondurans, who frequently doubled as politicians in remote Tegucigalpa.

The U.S. government had cast a jaundiced eye over Honduran internal affairs on several occasions since the turn of the century. Intervention by both Nicaragua and Guatemala had been one factor behind the decision to hold the conference of all Central American states in Washington in 1907 that produced the ill-fated Central American Court of Justice and a Treaty of Peace and Amity. Washington was also concerned by the geometric growth of the external public debt owed to European holders of the railway bonds, and in 1910 dollar diplomacy was invoked by Secretary of State Philander Knox to shift the debt from European to U.S. hands. The U.S. administration was thwarted, however, by Zemurray; he financed a revolution to topple the Honduran president, who favoured U.S. fiscal intervention.

Not for the first time, therefore, the State Department found itself at loggerheads in Honduras with one of the fruit companies, but a more active intervention was delayed until 1924. The presidential elections of 1923 had produced a three-way split with no candidate securing an outright majority. Congress refused to endorse any of the candidates, the outgoing President López Gutiérrez declared himself dictator and civil war ensued. This civil war, like its predecessors, might have been left to run its course if the U.S. administration had not recently persuaded all Central American countries to sign a new Treaty of Peace and Amity. U.S. prestige was, therefore, on the line, with the result that the marines entered Tegucigalpa in March 1924 and Sumner Welles was despatched to call a conference of the conflicting parties. The outcome was the Pact of Amapala, signed in May, which provided for the election to the presidency of Miguel Paz Barahona, one of the few participants in the 1923 election who had not participated in the civil war.

The marines departed almost as swiftly as they had arrived and Honduras entered on a period of stability such as it had not enjoyed since independence. This, however, was due not so much to U.S. intervention as to the growing maturity of the Honduran political system. The Liberal Party had gradually risen above the extreme factionalism of the nineteenth century into a political machine with national pretensions. The Liberals' opponents had finally coalesced into a genuine political party with the launch of the National Party in 1923. The two parties were distinguished less by the nineteenth-century ideological disputes between liberals and conservatives than by the conditions under which armed revolt was regarded as legitimate, the National Party demonstrating the greatest reluctance to use force as a means of settling political disputes.

Ironically, it was the National Party's presidential candidate – Tiburcio Carías Andino – who resorted to arms after the 1923 elections, but he did so only after López Gutiérrez had declared himself dictator. Both Carías and the National Party later demonstrated realism in accepting the stipulation of the Pact of Amapala that Paz Barahona (Carías' vice-presidential running mate) should be elected president. A more severe test for the National Party came when the Liberal candidate, Dr Vicente Mejía Colindres, defeated Carías in the 1928 presidential elections and became the first incumbent in Honduran history to win the presidency in peaceful elections against an official candidate. This rare experience was repeated in 1932, when Carías defeated the Liberal candidate in the October presidential elections. In the elections of both 1928 and 1932 the two parties presented a single candidate, giving the winner not only a plurality but also an outright majority. This made congressional intervention unnecessary and avoided the complications which had so frequently led to civil war in the past.

The period of relative stability that began in 1924 made possible the resolution of several problems from the past. In 1926, Congress ratified an agreement settling the outstanding external debt arrears; all unpaid interest was cancelled and the balance of the principal (£5,398,370) was to be paid off over thirty years with payment guaranteed by the consular revenues administered through the National City Bank of New York. These terms were not onerous, and Honduras was one of the very few Latin American countries not to default on its external debt in the 1930s.

Furthermore, the agreement permitted the Honduran government to return to the international capital market, and in February 1928 a loan was arranged with a U.S. bank to consolidate the public debts owed mainly to the fruit companies.

The renewed access to external finance might have increased the government's room for manoeuvre with the fruit companies, but the sale in December 1929 of Zemurray's Cuyamel Fruit Company to UFCO left the Mejía Colindres administration facing just two giant multinational firms: UFCO and Standard Fruit. The balance of power was revealed clearly during this administration when Congress first uncovered numerous irregularities in company behaviour that were ignored by the President and then failed to reverse Mejía's approval of contracts giving the fruit companies the right to utilize certain national waters without compensation. The sale of the Cuyamel Fruit Company did, however, have one desirable side effect: it ended the dispute between Zemurray and UFCO over concessions in the north-west of the country which had brought Honduras and Guatemala close to war in 1928. A treaty was signed between the two countries in 1930, and the boundary was settled by arbitration in 1933.

The banana boom had pushed specialization to the point where bananas accounted for nearly 90 per cent of Honduran exports at the end of the 1920s. Furthermore, the production of bananas formed such a large part of agricultural output that banana exports constituted around one-third of the gross domestic product (GDP). This dependence on one crop left the economy desperately vulnerable not only to fluctuations in the world market for bananas, but also to decisions by the two fruit companies on their global allocation of resources. The impact on Honduras of the world depression was therefore very severe, although it was delayed until 1931–2 by the decision of the fruit companies to concentrate production initially on their low-cost Honduran divisions.

The fall in the world price of bananas – nothing like as steep as for coffee – at first made no impact on Honduras. Since the 'price' was a book-keeping entry between different subsidiaries of the same vertically integrated firms, the returned value from banana exports was unaffected. By 1932, however, the companies were trying to transfer some of the burden to their Honduran divisions through a reduction in nominal wages and in the prices paid to independent producers. In the face of a series of strikes by the unorganized labourers (trade unions remained illegal in Honduras until the mid-1950s), the companies made some concessions on non-wage issues but were able to force through the salary reductions.

The artificial nature of the export price made the value of exports a meaningless statistic, but the value of imports started to fall after the fiscal year 1929/30 for a variety of reasons.[2] First, the fruit companies imported less as investment plans were shelved; second, the rest of the economy was not immune to the impact of world depression and, third, the dollar price of imports was itself falling. As a result of all these factors, customs duties fell and the government faced a major fiscal crisis in the run-up to the 1932 elections. Two foreign loans were arranged through UFCO with the Canal Bank and Trust Co. of New Orleans, but not for the first time in Honduran history public-sector salaries were 'postponed' and the floating debt (a euphemism for unpaid salaries) jumped from zero in 1929 to 8.1 million lempiras in 1933.[3]

THE CARIATO (1933 – 48)

When he finally assumed the presidency on 1 February 1933, Tiburcio Carías faced a very difficult situation. A rebellion launched by several of his Liberal opponents the previous November had still not been completely crushed, and the expenses of civil war had added to the fiscal crisis inherited from the Mejía Colindres administration. The decline in banana exports, which in turn reduced imports, government revenue and the general level of economic activity, was expected to continue and the fruit companies (especially UFCO) were pressing for favours from the government to off-set the impact of the world depression on the sharp decline in their global profits.

In the previous decade, Carías had done his best to establish an element of representative democracy in Honduras and end the cycles of civil war. The Liberal rebellion launched in November 1932 showed that the old habits had not yet died out, although neither Mejía Colindres nor the Liberal presidential candidate – Angel Zúñiga Huete – were directly implicated in the revolt. Faced with this challenge, Carías reverted to type and exploited the state of siege imposed as a consequence of the civil war to move against his political opponents. Zúñiga Huete went into exile in Mexico (not to return until 1948), gangs of convicts (with iron balls

---

[2] The fiscal year ended 31 July. This was changed to a calendar-year basis at the end of the 1930s.
[3] The lempira had been made the Honduran unit of account in 1926 by act of Congress, although the act did not go into force until 1931. The lempira was fixed at the rate of two per U.S. dollar, while the previous unit of account (the peso) had fluctuated around the same value since 1918. The lempira was fixed at two per dollar until 1990, giving Honduras one of the longest periods of exchange-rate stability in Latin America in the twentieth century.

chained to their legs) were employed on public works in the capital city, the authority of Congress to criticize the executive was progressively reduced, and local autonomy for mayors and municipalities was replaced by a much greater degree of central government control.

New presidential elections were due in October 1936, but shortly before that date Congress converted itself into a constituent assembly, extended the presidential term from four to six years and confirmed Carías in office until the end of 1942. This exercise in *continuismo* similar to that witnessed in El Salvador and Guatemala was taken a stage further in 1939 when Congress extended Carías' term in office to the end of 1948. The Cariato, as President Carías' sixteen years in office are known, finally broke the Honduran tradition of weak governments, civil wars and rapid presidential succession, although this was achieved at the expense of the nascent democracy which had begun to develop between 1924 and 1932.

Earlier Honduran presidents had attempted *continuismo,* but none had enjoyed Carías' success. This was due to various factors, perhaps the most important being the weak leadership provided by the Liberals, who remained loyal to the exiled Zúñiga Huete, incapable of exploiting the opportunities created by the arbitrary nature of Carías' rule and by the hardships of the depression years. A faction of the National Party led by Venancio Callejas split from Carías in 1936 over the new constitutional proposals, but a Callejas–Zúñiga pact signed in 1938 never commanded much respect. Even the unprecedented public demonstrations against the dictatorship in 1944, inspired by similar events in neighbouring republics, failed to galvanize the Liberal Party into decisive action. Zúñiga Huete failed to win the support of President Arévalo, Guatemala's champion of the anti-dictatorial Caribbean Legion, and the most vociferous campaign against Carías came from the more radical Partido Democrático Revolucionario Hondureño (PDRH), formed in 1947 to fight the dictatorship. The Liberals presented the same slate in the 1948 presidential elections as they had done in 1932, withdrawing only days before the vote through a combination of repression and fear of defeat.

While the Liberals were clearly expected to be the first line of defence against Carías' *continuismo,* the second could safely be assumed to be the armed forces. Occasional revolts occurred, the most serious in 1943, but Carías showed all his political skills in his relationship with the military and began the process of professionalizing the army which was completed by his Minister of War and presidential successor Dr. Juan Manuel Gálvez. As early as 1933 Carías established a training school for corporals and sergeants, and introduced obligatory military service in 1935; military officers began to receive U.S. training in 1942, following the entry of both the United States and Honduras into the Second World War. Carías purchased three war planes in 1934, having learned the importance of air power in the 1932–3 civil war where the services of the newly formed Transportes Aereos de Centroamérica (TACA) were used to support the government; additional military hardware was provided during the war by the Roosevelt administration. Carías also received support from neighbouring *caudillos;* General Maximiliano Hernández Martínez, the Salvadorean dictator, helped Carías during the civil war in the hope of breaking his own regime's diplomatic isolation, while General Jorge Ubico in Guatemala arranged for the murder of both a Liberal revolutionary (General Justo Umaña) and a leading Honduran Communist (Juan Pablo Wainwright).

The Cariato gave Honduras its longest period ever of political stability, but it was order without progress. Not only were the first tentative steps towards democracy sacrificed, but it also proved impossible to reverse the country's economic decline. At the end of the Mejía Colindres administration, the gross domestic product (GDP) per head was second only to that of Costa Rica in Central America; in 1934 the figure was exceeded by Guatemala and in 1937 by El Salvador, and in 1942 Honduras became the poorest republic in the region (and in all mainland Latin America) when it was overtaken by Nicaragua.[4] The healthy trade surplus which Honduras had enjoyed every year since 1925–6, and which enabled the government to maintain the lempira's parity with the U.S. dollar, finally disappeared in 1936–7, the shortage of domestic currency forcing the authorities to start importing U.S. notes and coins after 1942 to maintain monetary circulation.[5]

The root cause of these economic difficulties was the decline of the banana industry from the spectacular peaks it had reached at the start of the 1930s. At first the reduction was due to adjustment by the fruit companies to world recession – aggravated by serious flooding in 1934 – but by 1936 sigatoka disease had entered Honduras from the Caribbean

[4] See V. Bulmer-Thomas, *The Political Economy of Central America Since 1920* (Cambridge, 1987), table A.3.

[5] The Honduran trade balance is very sensitive to the price used to value banana exports. Since 1947, it has been customary to value exports at market prices which – if applied to the pre-war years – yields a large trade surplus in every year. Before 1947, however, Honduran authorities worked with a price which corresponded roughly to the local currency costs of the fruit companies; on this basis, a trade deficit was first recorded in the fiscal year 1936–7.

and wreaked havoc with banana plantations. No sooner had the companies developed a spray to counteract the spread of the disease than Honduras was plunged into the Second World War. The fruit companies' shipping fleets were requisitioned by the U.S. Navy with the result that Honduran banana exports in 1942–3 stood at 10 per cent of the 1929–30 peak. Exports, imports and general economic activity fell in line with the trend for bananas. By 1943 (its lowest point) GDP per head was 36 per cent below its peak in 1930.

The collapse of banana exports occurred despite the generous policy adopted towards the fruit companies by the government. President Carías, his Minister of War (Juan Manuel Gálvez) and the president of Congress after 1939 (Plutarco Muñoz P.) were all allied to UFCO (Gálvez and Muñoz as company lawyers), but Standard Fruit was equally successful in wriggling out of contractual obligations. Both companies collaborated closely in the 1930s, Standard Fruit accepting with equanimity its role as junior partner, and land titles were swapped in an effort to rationalize company holdings. In 1941 UFCO founded the prestigious School of Pan-American Agriculture and in the following year the company obtained a concession allowing the Truxillo Railroad Company to ship railway lines and other equipment to neighbouring countries in flagrant breach of the original contract.

The decline of the banana industry did lead to some agricultural diversification through a re-allocation of resources; the output of cereals, vegetables and other fruits all increased in the 1930s, but this could not compensate for the collapse of banana production, and the fruit companies retained firm control over both land and means of communication in the northern departments. The backwardness of the economy in general, and agriculture in particular, was captured vividly by a U.S. mission, led by E. M. Bernstein, which reported on monetary and credit conditions in 1943 at the invitation of the Carías government. The report, written in appropriately soothing terms, took the authorities to task for the weakness of banking institutions, the lack of attention to agriculture, the high cost of loans and the virtual anarchy surrounding the process of monetary emission in the absence of a central bank.[6]

The Cariato may have neglected economic development, but Carías could not ignore the fiscal crisis he had inherited from his predecessor.

---

[6] See E. M. Bernstein et al., *Informe de la Misión Técnica y Financiera sobre condiciones monetarias y de crédito en Honduras* (Tegucigalpa, 1943).

With payment on the domestic debt suspended since 1932 and public employees' salaries often unpaid, Carías was forced to use draconian measures. A loan was negotiated through UFCO with the Canal Bank of New Orleans, public-sector pay was reduced by 20 per cent (with a further 5 per cent deducted as payment to the Partido Nacional) and exchange control was introduced in 1934. This last measure was intended to generate exchange profits for the treasury rather than eliminate a shortage of foreign exchange (which was still plentiful), but it also served to restrict access to imports. The same purpose was served by tariffs introduced in 1934, although the following year a bilateral trade agreement with the United States forced on Honduras by Cordell Hull undermined the impact of the new trade restrictions; the tariff was revised again in 1938, following the Salvadorean example, with three scales designed to discriminate against countries enjoying a surplus on trade with Honduras. By 1937 Carías felt confident enough to force through a drastic reduction in the domestic debt, creditors receiving a mere 7 per cent in cash on the face value of their bonds. Coupled with the revenue-raising measures just described, this change produced an approximate fiscal balance from 1937 onwards while the tariff increases provided a stimulus for import substituting industrialization, a small number of modern factories opening their doors during the Cariato. War-time inflation – a product of import scarcity and monetary expansion – also stimulated fiscal receipts and permitted the government not only to carry on reducing the external debt (under the 1926 agreement), but also to lower the internal debt.

Despite Carías' neglect of economic development, some progress was made. The communications problem began to be solved during the Cariato. TACA was rewarded with a generous concession for its part in the civil war and within a few years internal air services were the most sophisticated in Central America. Then the outbreak of hostilities in Europe increased U.S. interest in highway construction in Central America; Honduras qualified for a two-thirds grant from the Roosevelt administration for its share of the Pan-American Highway and U.S. engineers completed the road link around Lake Yojoa, which finally connected Tegucigalpa with the national railway and the northern coast.

Honduras also played a part in hemispheric efforts to replace U.S. strategic imports cut off by hostilities in Asia. UFCO converted some of its banana plantations to the production of rubber, *abacá* and African palms, these programmes coming on stream by 1945. The country also collaborated in a U.S.-sponsored scheme to export fruits and vegetables to the Panama Canal Zone. Shortages of imports led to the expansion of forestry, the development of cotton production and the re-establishment of sugar-refining (sugar-milling had closed during the depression), all these products being exported on a modest scale after 1945.

The Second World War also brought an unexpected bonus for Honduran coffee producers in that the 1941 Pan-American Coffee Agreement gave the country a generous quota which had doubled by the end of the war. The improvement in communications, the post-war recovery in world prices and the greater availability of seasonal labour at harvest time as a result of demographic pressures all contributed to the emergence of Honduras as an important coffee-exporter, and by the end of the Cariato coffee production was twice its level at the beginning. With the return to normal commercial conditions after 1945, banana exports also recovered and stood at nearly half their peak level by the end of the Cariato. As a result, the Honduran economy enjoyed a modest boom in the last five years of the dictatorship, although GDP per head in 1948 was still below the pre-war peak.

Tiburcio Carías has frequently been grouped with the other long-serving dictators of Central America in the 1930s and 1940s, but there were differences between *caudillo* rule in Honduras and elsewhere.

The Cariato was not as tyrannical as *caudillo* rule in the neighbouring republics. Some leading Liberals continued to hold important positions, the Liberal press was generally allowed to function and the exile of the party leader, Zúñiga Huete, was self-imposed. Some of Carías' departmental governors, notably Carlos Sanabria in Colón, were petty tyrants, but Carías himself never shared his fellow *caudillos'* enthusiasm for European fascism, and Honduras' declaration of war on the Axis powers in December 1941 was not as cynical as some. Equally, Carías did not seek to dominate political life after his withdrawal from the presidency in 1948. Although he ruthlessly crushed the wave of protests against his rule in 1944, he had resolved as early as 1945 not to stand for re-election, and U.S. pressure was only of marginal importance in this decision. His handpicked successor, Juan Manuel Gálvez, stood uncontested in the presidential elections of October 1948 but subsequently demonstrated a certain degree of autonomy from the ex-dictator. Carías, furthermore, accepted his defeat in the 1954 presidential elections, when the Partido Nacional was split, without recourse to civil war. These differences should not, however, be exaggerated. Carías could be exceedingly ruthless when he felt it necessary, and the labour movement was given short shrift in a long dictatorship made worse by economic decline. The best that could be said for the Cariato was that it gave Honduras its longest period without civil war since independence.

Caudillo rule left unresolved a number of key issues. The relationship with the fruit companies, particularly UFCO, remained very unsatisfactory; the multinationals contributed virtually nothing to fiscal revenue as a result of the numerous concessions, yet they succeeded in evading most of their contractual responsibilities pleading in mitigation the state of the world economy. The weak fiscal position and the subordinate role of the government undermined the scope for economic diversification and left the economy dependent on an industry which appeared to be in structural decline. For most of the Cariato the fruit companies remained the lender of last resort, and foreign loans often depended on UFCO's support.

The 'commanding heights' of the Honduran economy (bananas, mining, external trade, railways, air transport and modern manufacturing) were still in the hands of foreigners at the end of the Cariato, the urban commercial sector was under the control of 'los Turcos'[7] and the one bright spot (coffee) had been developed by small- and medium-sized growers without political influence. The local political elite, including Carías, limited their economic activities to cattle-ranching, real estate or internal trade-activities which were safe from foreign competition. Yet the absence of a land-owning oligarchy, in contrast to El Salvador and Guatemala, was not without its advantages; the vast majority of rural Hondurans (with the exception of the relatively well-paid banana proletariat) still had access to land, and *ejidal* (communal) land ownership was widespread. The Cariato did not provide an alternative to the enclave development symbolized by the fruit companies, but at least it had not closed down all the options.

CAPITALIST MODERNIZATION AND SOCIAL REFORM (1949–63)

Juan Manuel Gálvez, president from 1949 to 1954, seemed an improbable candidate for the task of modernizing Honduras. As a former attorney for UFCO and Minister of War under Carías, he was expected to maintain the political stability achieved under the Cariato and change little else. Gálvez, however, laid the foundations for capitalist modernization and

---

[7] 'Los Turcos' was the name given to Arab immigrants from the Levant, many of whom arrived on Turkish passports after the First World War.

social reform and his work was continued by the three succeeding governments. By 1963, when the military seized power, Honduras had enjoyed fifteen years of almost unbroken social and economic progress under both Partido Nacional and Liberal Party rule. These changes – modest even by Latin American standards – were almost revolutionary in the Honduran context and prevented the state from becoming too closely identified with any single interest group. Although far from democratic and still dominated by *personalismo*, the political system moved away from the repressive model of neighbouring republics and came closer to the Costa Rican example, where well-organized pressure groups competed for official favours.

Gálvez began a six-year period of rule by introducing an income-tax law – the first in Honduran history – which obliged the fruit companies to pay 15 per cent of their profits to the government. Although UFCO only agreed to this long-overdue reform in exchange for fiscal concessions on its non-banana operations (e.g., *abacá* production), the change was dramatic; in its first full year (fiscal 1950–1), the new tax provided nearly 20 per cent of government revenue with most of the receipts coming from the fruit companies. The tax was raised again in 1955 to 30 per cent (following the Costa Rican example) and the fruit companies ceased to be the lender of last resort. While the relationship between the companies and the state was still very unequal, the income tax was the single most effective way of increasing the returned value from banana exports.

Gálvez also turned his attention to the weaknesses in the banking and financial system identified so clearly in the 1943 Bernstein mission. With support from the International Monetary Fund (IMF), a central bank was established in 1950 with a monopoly over the note-issue and exchange transactions and the resources necessary to guarantee the circulation of the lempira. For the first time, the Honduran currency was available in sufficient quantities to meet the demands of trade, while international reserves were more than sufficient to guarantee the rate of exchange with the U.S. dollar. A state development bank (Banco Nacional de Fomento – BNF) was also founded in 1950 to support the economic (particularly agricultural) diversification neglected hitherto by the private banks.[8] The BNF was given the resources to provide storage and marketing facilities, mate-

---

[8] A private bank (Banco Capitalizadora) was founded in 1948 with Salvadorean capital; this ended the duopoly exercised over Honduran banking for nearly forty years by the Banco Atlántida and Banco de Honduras, but did not at first contribute much to economic diversification.

rial inputs and technical advice, so that lending did not need to be restricted only to large-scale farmers.

Armed with higher fiscal revenues and aided by grants from U.S. agencies, the Gálvez administration turned to the neglected area of public works. The entire first chapter of a glossy book issued to commemorate Gálvez' years in the presidency was devoted to municipal drains – a sharp reversal of Honduran governments' usual priorities.[9] The most important progress came in the field of highway construction with feeder roads reaching into the agricultural frontier in the south, west and east of the country and major improvements in the railway–road link connecting the Atlantic with the Pacific coast via Tegucigalpa. Important advances were also made in electricity production and telecommunications, providing Honduras with the minimum social infrastructure necessary for capitalist modernization.

Capitalist development in Honduras had traditionally depended primarily on foreign initiative, but under the Gálvez administration a small national bourgeoisie began to emerge linked to agricultural diversification and urban growth. The banking reforms and improved communications helped production of coffee, basic grains, timber and meat. The increase in cotton production on the south coast (stimulated by the construction of the Pan-American Highway) was at first promoted largely by Salvadorean entrepreneurs, with the raw material being sent to El Salvador for ginning, but after the BNF set up a ginning plant Honduran participation increased. Agricultural diversification reduced the relative importance of bananas, whose contribution to exports finally dropped below 50 per cent in 1954. Industrial development was also stimulated, albeit from a very low base, by the Gálvez reforms and by the rapid growth of the urban population, which, particularly in San Pedro Sula and Tegucigalpa, far outstripped the population growth for the whole country. In 1950 nearly 20 per cent of the 1.37 million Hondurans could be classified as urban.

The reform movement under Gálvez was primarily of a developmentalist character and stopped far short of genuine political pluralism. The climate of repression under Carías was relaxed, political prisoners were released and the Liberal Party was free to operate normally, but the Gálvez administration harassed the small Marxist movement, banned the PDRH in 1952 and sided unequivocally with U.S. efforts to overthrow the Arbenz regime in Guatemala. Legislation favouring workers was passed in

[9] See *La Obra del Doctor Juan Manuel Gálvez en su Administración, 1949–1954* (Tegucigalpa, n.d.).

1952, but trade unions and strikes were still illegal, and Honduras remained outside the International Labour Organization (ILO), having abandoned its membership in 1938 under Carías.

The news, therefore, that a strike had been launched in April 1954 by workers belonging to one of the UFCO subsidiaries was greeted with unconcealed hostility by the Gálvez administration. This strike over pay and conditions occurred at a particularly tense moment in Central American history with the counter-revolutionary army of Carlos Castillo Armas assembled in Honduras and poised to invade Guatemala. Furthermore, an illegal Communist Party was formed in April by a faction of the banned PDRH and Communists were inevitably blamed for causing the strike. Gálvez arrested and imprisoned the leaders of the strike committee, and under intense pressure from the government the workers elected new, more moderate, leaders. But the strike spread to other activities on the northern coast and even found an echo in Tegucigalpa. The new anti-communist leadership gained the support of the American Federation of Labor (AFL) and the Gálvez administration began to press UFCO to reach a settlement. This was finally agreed on 9 July, a few days after the fall of Arbenz and the victory of the U.S.-supported counter-revolutionary forces in Guatemala.

In narrow economic terms, the strike was a pyrrhic victory for the workers. The modest wage increases (10–15 per cent) were swamped by wide-spread dismissals as both UFCO and Standard Fruit halved their work force over the next five years in response to production difficulties and the emergence of Ecuador as a major banana exporter. Yet the strike won legal recognition for the workers' right to organize and reversed UFCO's opposition to the existence of trade unions, which had been used by successive Honduran governments to resist progressive labour legislation. Within a short period, Honduras had rejoined the ILO and recognized 1 May as International Labour Day, while unions – under the watchful eye of the AFL – developed quickly along the northern coast and soon spread to the inland urban centres.

The 1954 strike also coincided with preparations for the October presidential elections. The Liberal Party had been revitalised under the leadership of the educationalist Dr Ramón Villeda Morales, but the Partido Nacional had been split by the decision of Tiburcio Carías to seek the presidency again. A breakaway faction – Movimiento Nacional Reformista (MNR) – led by Abraham Williams, vice-president under Carías, led to a three-way contest in which the Liberals won a handsome plurality but not a majority. In the time-honoured tradition, the losers refused to take their seats in Congress, a quorum could not be formed and Julio Lozano Díaz, who had succeeded to the presidency upon the retirement (on grounds of ill health) of Gálvez on 16 November, declared himself acting chief executive.

Lozano's intervention was at first welcomed by the three political parties. It avoided bloodshed and could be used to prepare the ground for fresh elections. Furthermore, Lozano maintained the reform programme of the previous few years, providing continuity with the Gálvez administration. The vote was extended to women and a Fundamental Charter of Labour Guarantees was introduced in 1955, covering virtually all aspects of labour relations from minimum wages to collective bargaining. In the same year, a national economic council later to become the Consejo Superior de Planificación Económica (CONSUPLANE) was founded to provide the rudiments of economic planning long before the Alliance for Progress would make this a condition for aid disbursal. Lozano, however, soon made it clear that he had no intention of handing over power in free elections, organized his own party (Partido Unión Nacional, or PUN), exiled Villeda Morales, and called elections for a constituent assembly in October 1956, which the PUN claimed to win with nearly 90 per cent of the 'vote'.

The other three political parties joined forces to protest against the Lozano dictatorship, but they were powerless to prevent it. The armed forces, on the other hand, had both the means and the motive to intervene. The professionalization of the military begun under Carías had accelerated during the Gálvez administration; funds for training and equipment had been poured in by U.S. administrations, concerned at the security implications of the Guatemalan Revolution. Honduras signed a military assistance pact with the United States in 1954, establishing the close relationship between the armed forces of the two countries, which has survived to this day. The unconstitutional character of the Lozano regime was an affront to the constitutionally minded officers of the Honduran armed forces, and within two weeks of the constituent assembly elections Lozano had been ousted by a military triumvirate including a son of former president Gálvez.

The military intervention was quite unlike the *cuartelazo* politics of the civil war eras. The military intervened as an institution and in defense of the constitution, promising fresh elections within a year. Moreover, it earned universal respect by keeping this promise. Nonetheless, military intervention came at a price; the armed forces demanded from the winners of the elections a high degree of autonomy for the military and the right to intervene in future in the event of a constitutional crisis. This privileged military position, established in the Constitution of 1957, accounts for many of the peculiarities of the Honduran political system in the last three decades.

The constituent assembly elections held in September 1957 produced an overwhelming victory for the Liberals. Villeda Morales, who had been posted to Washington by the military triumvirate and had calmed U.S. fears about his alleged Communist sympathies, assumed the presidency at the end of the year in indirect elections – three years after narrowly missing victory in direct elections. The new president went out of his way to accommodate the military, most of whose officers owed their positions to the Partido Nacional under Carías and Gálvez. Indeed, the suspicions held by some sections of the armed forces about Villeda Morales were the main reason for the President's agreeing to share power with the military under the Constitution of 1957 with disputes to be settled by Congress.

Villeda Morales' six-year presidential term (1957–63) saw a major extension of the reform programme undertaken by his predecessors. His more enthusiastic supporters claimed that Villeda Morales had introduced social democracy to Honduras and laid the foundations for genuine political democracy. Villedismo, however never fully surpassed the *personalismo* which had plagued Honduran politics since independence, and the President was more concerned with the threat to hemispheric security from Castro's Cuba than with that to political freedom from reactionary despotism in the neighbouring republics. The Liberal Party remained a loose amalgam of competing factions whose character was determined primarily by the man in charge. Thus, Villedismo could not survive Villeda Morales, and the party had to wait nearly twenty years before a new Liberal president emerged with the authority to stamp his own personality on the party machine.

The social reforms begun after the 1954 banana strike were extended in a variety of ways by the Villeda administration. The Labour Code of 1957 incorporated and extended the Labour Charter of 1955 and, after two failed attempts, a Law of Social Insurance was enacted in 1962. Coverage was at first limited to workers in the central district, but the principle of social security had been established and the proportion of the labour force receiving benefits rose steadily in the next two decades. Almost all labour disputes were settled through the conciliation procedures laid down in the

Labour Code. Industrial development was promoted through a Ley de Fomento Industrial, passed in 1958, giving fiscal advantages to new firms. Honduras also signed the 1958 Tripartite Treaty with Guatemala and El Salvador which provided for tariff reductions on intra-regional trade and preceded the formation of the Central American Common Market (CACM) in 1960.

Manufacturing growth was rapid under Villeda Morales and maintained the rhythm of the previous decade. Between 1948 (the last year of the Cariato) and 1963 (the last year of Villeda Morales' presidency), the share of manufacturing in GDP doubled to more than 14 per cent with foreign participation by no means dominant. Yet the years of Villeda's presidency were difficult ones for the Honduran economy; technical problems plagued cotton production in the late 1950s and the fall in coffee prices after the Korean War discouraged new coffee plantings. Some success was achieved in expanding meat exports to the United States, and sugar exports were boosted by the allocation to Honduras after 1960 of part of Cuba's U.S. sugar quota, but the continuing difficulties of the banana industry hung like a millstone round the economy's neck and kept the growth of real GDP well below that recorded in neighbouring republics. Honduras remained the poorest country in Central America and mainland Latin America.

Both the fruit companies experimented with new disease-resistant varieties of bananas after 1960 and the industry's fortunes began to recover. The massive dismissals after the 1954 strike were not reversed, however, and unemployment among banana-workers became a very serious problem. The government experimented with peasant colonization schemes on disused land handed back by the fruit companies, but social unrest in the banana zones continued and access to land for many families outside the zones was curtailed by the growth of agricultural export diversification (particularly cattle-raising and meat exports). With the help of dismissed banana-workers and the active participation of Communists, a militant peasant union – Federación Nacional de Campesinos Hondureños (FENACH) – was formed to press for radical changes in the land-tenure system. In 1962 the government responded with an agrarian reform law administered by the Instituto Nacional Agrario (INA), while the AFL and the anti-communist regional labour federation (Organización Regional Interamericana de Trabajadores, or ORIT) hurried to counter the influence of FENACH by helping to establish a rival peasant union, Asociación Nacional de Campesinos (ANACH). The agrarian reform law was not well received by the fruit companies, which were able to force through a number of amendments more favourable to their interests, but the measure remained on the statute book, providing a safety valve which could be opened or closed over the following years according to social conditions. Agrarian reform has never been radical in Honduras, but it was always more than a token concession to the Alliance for Progress and ultimately affected a significant minority of the peasantry.

Villeda Morales feared the consequences of the Cuban Revolution, but the real threat to his regime came from the traditional right. A series of minor revolts culminated in an uprising by the National Police in July 1959, which was suppressed with some difficulty. In retaliation, the President created a separate Civil Guard subject to presidential control (unlike the National Police, which had been subject to the control of the armed forces). Clashes between the 2,500-strong Civil Guard and the armed forces became frequent and contributed to a sharp deterioration in the relationship between the military and the Liberal government. A further rift was provoked when the party adopted as its presidential candidate for the 1963 elections Modesto Rodas Alvarado, a protégé of Zúñiga Huete in the 1940s and a man of known anti-militarist sympathies. The prospect of six years of Rodismo was too much for many officers, and the military, led by air force colonel Osvaldo López Arellano, overthrew Villeda Morales shortly after the President had agreed to disarm the Civil Guard and only ten days before the scheduled elections.

MILITARY RULE (1963–82)

The military regime, headed by López Arellano, was not recognized by President John F. Kennedy (to whom Villeda Morales had appealed personally at the moment of the coup), but the anti-communist stance of the new government produced a change of heart on the part of the Lyndon Johnson administration following Kennedy's assassination. This second military intervention completed the transformation of the armed forces as an institution and confirmed the army's role as a key actor in Honduran political life.

The real reason for the coup was the military's fear of an election victory by Rodas, who had committed the Liberal Party to revise the Constitution of 1957 and re-establish civilian control over the armed forces. Both Rodas and Villeda Morales went into exile, the former maintaining the loyalty of the Liberal Party through his well-organized Rodista faction, while the latter's Civil Guard was abolished and replaced by a police organization (Cuerpo Especial de Seguridad) subject to military control. The anti-communism of the military government was not all rhetoric designed to win U.S. support. Communists had helped to set up FENACH and had penetrated the union of Standard Fruit workers (SUTRASFCO). The new government promptly outlawed FENACH and purged SUTRASFCO, imposing restrictions on the rest of the labour movement. At a regional level, López Arellano joined forces with the neighbouring military governments to form CONDECA, a mutual defense pact with strong anti-communist overtones, supported by the U.S. administration, and in 1965 Honduras sent troops in support of the U.S. invasion of the Dominican Republic.

These initiatives, coupled with the underfunding of INA and the low priority given to land reform, confirmed the conservative nature of the new regime and won for it the enthusiastic support of the traditional land-owners. Such an alliance might have been sufficient to maintain an iron grip on affairs in neighbouring Guatemala or El Salvador, but in the Honduran context it represented a relatively weak coalition. Indeed, it was not until 1966, with the formation of the Federación Nacional de Agricultores (FENAGH), that the land-owners established institutional representation for their class interests. López Arellano, however, was able to consolidate his hold on power through a tactical alliance with the Partido Nacional, now unified under Ricardo Zúñiga A., who saw an opportunity to settle scores with the rival Liberal Party. The tactical and opportunist nature of the alliance was underlined by the fact that López Arellano had formed part of the junta which had paved the way for the Liberal government of 1957, in which he had occupied the post of Minister of Defence.[10] The new alliance with the Partido Nacional, however, was superficially effective and served to 'legitimise' López's rule, although the constituent assembly elections of 1965 were marred by fraud and strong-arm tactics orchestrated by the Mancha Brava – a shadowy para-military group linked to the Partido Nacional and the armed forces. The Partido Nacional majority in the new Assembly introduced a new constitution confirming the autonomy of the armed forces and promptly elected López Arellano (now promoted to brigadier general) as president for six years.

López's initial identification with the traditional land-owners and most conservative elements in Honduran society earned him the opposition not

[10] He was not originally a member of the junta, but joined it in 1957.

only of the organized labour movement but also of the new industrial groups. Within a few years, these two groups had made common cause and forged a powerful alliance with which the opportunist López was prepared to negotiate. This transformed the nature of political loyalties in Honduras: military rule in the 1970s acquired a reformist, almost populist, character which stood in marked contrast to the conservatism of the 1960s. Even in the 1960s, however, military government avoided the reactionary despotism so apparent in neighbouring countries; the reforms of previous governments in fiscal, labour and social policy were allowed to stand and in some cases were even extended.[11]

The purge of Communists from the organized labour movement strengthened the 'free and democratic' unions linked to ORIT and supported by the United States. Within a year of the 1963 coup, a national Confederación de Trabajadores de Honduras (CTH) had been formed, bringing together the banana-workers of the north coast, the unions of the central district and the peasantry organized in ANACH. The purged SUTRASFCO also joined the CTH, which was affiliated to ORIT and the International Federation of Free Trade Unions. The new confederation faced some competition from Social Christian peasant unions, organized on the south coast with the support of the Catholic Church, but this was not sufficient to challenge its hegemonic position at the national level.

The coup of October 1963 coincided with a resurgence of export agriculture in Honduras. Banana production soared as a result of the introduction of new varieties, while cotton, coffee, beef and sugar all benefited from improved world prices and greater credit availability. Demand for new land to support this expansion rose, driving up rents and leading to disputes over access to *ejidal* and national lands. The peasant organizations called on the government to revitalise the land-reform programme – virtually stalled since the coup – and began to undertake land invasions in support of their claims.

The main focus of peasant agitation was the agrarian reform agency INA, which in five years (1962–6) had distributed land to a mere 281 families. In a gesture designed to reduce the unpopularity of his regime, López appointed in 1967 as head of INA Rigoberto Sandoval Corea, who was also placed in charge of national planning. This proved a shrewd move because Sandoval managed to promote land reform without provoking

---

[11] The López government introduced, for example, a 3 per cent retail sales tax in December 1963 – the first government to do so in Central America.

excessive opposition from FENAGH or the fruit companies through the creation of co-operatives that often produced export crops.[12] Thus, the reformed sector did not undermine the export-led model favoured by the government and most of the land was obtained through 'recovery' of *ejidal* or national properties rather than through expropriation of private estates.

While the revival of INA and the land-reform programme reduced tensions in the rural areas, urban opposition to the regime was growing. The entry of Honduras into the Central American Common Market had undermined the government's income from import duties, the main source of revenue, and had obliged the López regime to introduce new taxes. These fell particularly heavily on urban areas, provoking a storm of protests in 1968, when the government introduced a new range of taxes on consumer goods and raised tariffs (in line with other Central American countries) on extra-regional imports. A general strike was called only to be met with a state of siege that soon forced it to be called off, but the strike cemented the informal relationship between the CTH and the industrialists of the Consejo Hondureño de la Empresa Privada (COHEP) who were also opposed to many features of the government's economic policies. This improbable alliance between workers and urban capitalists, both losers under the economic policies favoured by López in the 1960s, drove a wedge between the property-owning classes in Honduras and prevented the consolidation of a united anti-labour policy among the political elite.

The industrialists, with their main stronghold in San Pedro Sula, took exception to the way in which the CACM appeared to discriminate against Honduras. Although exports from Honduras to the rest of Central America had expanded since the CACM's formation, they had risen much less rapidly than exports by other CACM members to Honduras. As a result, the Honduran trade balance with the rest of Central America had turned negative at the start of the decade and increased in size in every year thereafter. Furthermore, many Honduran exports to CACM were agricultural goods sold at prices not unlike those ruling in world markets, whereas imports from CACM consisted of industrial goods whose price reflected the high common external tariff imposed by all CACM members. Honduras, the industrialists argued, had paid a high price for CACM membership and the rules of the game needed to be changed to serve the interests of the weaker members.

[12] These co-operatives, organized in 1970 by the Federación de Cooperativas de la Reforma Agraria de Honduras (FECORAH), often received financial support from state banking institutions and in some cases sold their output to the fruit companies for marketing.

With its close ties to traditional agricultural interests, the López regime at first paid little attention to the complaints of the industrialists, which surfaced as early as 1965. The trade deficit with CACM had to be paid in dollars, but the boom in agro-exports in the first half of the 1960s provided ample foreign exchange. This position soon changed, however, as cotton exports fell in response to falling prices after 1965 and banana exports hit their peak in 1967. Foreign exchange was now more scarce and the government joined the chorus demanding special treatment for Honduras within CACM.

The other CACM members were not insensitive to these Honduran requests, and by March 1969 agreement had been reached on a system of fiscal incentives for the region, which would have allowed Honduras to offer special privileges designed to attract foreign and local investment into its manufacturing sector. However, this concession soon became irrelevant since Honduras withdrew from the common market in December 1970, following the war with El Salvador, and proceeded to negotiate non-reciprocal bilateral trade treaties with Costa Rica, Guatemala and Nicaragua. [13]

The war with El Salvador in July 1969 was caused by a variety of factors, of which dissatisfaction with the functioning of CACM was only one. Salvadoreans had been migrating to Honduras in search of land and jobs for many decades, but two-thirds of the estimated 300,000 migrants who had entered Honduras since the 1890s had arrived since 1950. The overwhelming reason for Salvadorean out-migration was a desire for land, but land pressure had accelerated rapidly in Honduras, leading to an increase in the number of *microfincas* (farms smaller than one hectare) and landless workers. Tension over access to land was exacerbated by the unresolved dispute between Honduras and El Salvador over the border, which was still undefined for much of its length, but the flames were well and truly fanned when INA announced in March 1969 that the beneficiaries from the land-reform programme would be restricted to those of Honduran birth and that Salvadoreans without legal title would be expelled. The extremes of nationalist passion surrounding the World Cup qualifying matches between the two countries provided the final straw, and the Salvadorean army responded to the expulsion of their countrymen by invading Honduras on 14 July.

---

[13] The treaties allowed Honduras duty-free access to other countries, while permitting Honduras to charge tariffs on imports from these countries. Trade with El Salvador, however, remained blocked throughout the 1970s.

The war brought little glory to either side, and the Honduran army was rescued from an embarrassing humiliation only by the early intervention of the Organization of American States. A cease-fire was agreed, but diplomatic relations were broken and the border remained closed to normal commerce, jeopardizing Salvadorean exports to Nicaragua and Costa Rica. Although López Arellano's air force performed with some distinction, scoring a direct hit on Salvadorean oil-refining facilities in Acajutla, the President's authority was badly dented by the war, which provided the catalyst for the realignment of political forces in Honduras that had been simmering for some time.

The war had created a strong feeling of national unity in Honduras with all the political, business and labour organizations (except the Communist Party) responding to the call for patriotism. Within a few months of the war, COHEP had called a meeting of the 'Fuerzas Vivas', bringing business and labour leaders together with leading public officials. The meeting led to informal contacts with the President, who still clung to hopes for his own re-election. The discussions continued throughout 1970 and by the end of the year agreement had been reached on a political pact under which the traditional parties would unite behind a single non-political candidate in the 1971 elections leading to a government of national unity.

The agreement satisfied López, who was to be left in charge of the armed forces, but it failed to meet the demands of the traditional parties. It was therefore modified to allow for competition between the parties for the presidency, with the winner committed to appointing public officials on the basis of merit rather than party affiliation. Even this proved too much for the Liberal and National parties, however, and the day before the March 1971 elections, the pact was once again revised to allow for an equal sharing of the top government posts between the two major parties. Nevertheless, the Political Plan for National Unity (or *pacto*, as it was widely called) still committed the new administration to implement the reform programme thrashed out in the Fuerzas Vivas meetings.

The winner of the elections was the National Party candidate, Ramón Ernesto Cruz, who secured 49.3 per cent of the popular vote. A lawyer by training, the elderly Dr Cruz was neither politically nor temperamentally suited to leading a government of national unity committed to implementing a wide range of reforms. Sandoval Corea was replaced as head of INA by a conservative, peasant unrest was met with severe repression, and the Partido Nacional, with Ricardo Zúñiga occupying the key post of Minister of Government and Justice, concentrated its efforts on securing partisan control of the state bureaucracy. It became clear very quickly that the new administration was incapable of rising above the limitations of traditional party rivalries. Respect for civilian rule was badly dented, the workers' movement threatened a major demonstration in support of the original aims of the *pacto* and on 4 December 1972 the military intervened, with López Arellano once again becoming chief of state.

The collapse of the national unity government weakened the prestige of both traditional parties and left the military free to develop an informal alliance with COHEP and the labour movement, both of whose interests were promoted during the first (populist) phase of military rule. Decree No. 8, introduced before the end of 1972, provided for the transfer or forced rent of idle land; the landowners' organization (FENAGH) protested strongly and was able to force through some modifications to the law, but the pace of land reform accelerated with 11,739 families benefiting in the first two years (1973–4). The introduction of a new Agrarian Reform Law on 1 January 1975 took the process a stage further with upper limits set on the size of private landholdings and more explicit criteria established for determining idle or underutilized land. All the same, delays in implementing the law gave some large landowners a chance to subdivide their holdings, improve efficiency and escape the application of the law to themselves.

The second López administration, clearly influenced by the reformist military experiment in Peru, also addressed the question of national economic development in the post-CACM environment. A fifteen-year development plan published in January 1974 provided for state participation in the primary sector and co-operation with COHEP on new industrial ventures. A wide variety of parastatal organizations were set up, which were largely autonomous and free to raise funds on the international capital market. With competition from the rest of Central America much reduced and now aided by state support, the manufacturing sector grew rapidly and increased its share of GDP during the 1970s, while the exploitation of the country's enormous forest resources was pushed ahead under the watchful eye of the state Corporación Hondureña de Desarrollo Forestal (COHDEFOR).

The populism of General López concealed a weakness in his position inherited from the poor performance of the armed forces in the war with El Salvador. The junior officers, who supported the reform programme, agitated for a new command structure, designed to share power with the chief of state. The Consejo Superior de las Fuerzas Armadas (CONSUFFAA) was reorganized in March 1975 and took advantage of General López's temporary absence from the country to appoint Colonel Juan Alberto Melgar Castro as head of the military. General López remained chief of state, but he was forced to resign this post as well the following month when the *Wall Street Journal* reported that he had received a bribe from UFCO (now United Brands) to ensure that the government would lower the new export tax on bananas imposed by the Unión de Países Exportadores de Banano (UPEB), to which Honduras belonged.

CONSUFFAA, its authority now firmly established, appointed Melgar Castro as chief of state – replacing him as head of the armed forces with Colonel Policarpo Paz García. The collective nature of military rule was now clear, the chief of state being reduced to the first among equals. This shift was important because Melgar Castro – allied to the Partido Nacional – had conservative instincts, although the impetus in favour of the reform programme from other directions was still strong. Thus, Melgar Castro reappointed Sandoval Corea as head of INA and the land-reform programme continued until Sandoval's resignation in 1977, after which it slowed considerably.

The scandal over the bribe from United Brands offered the Honduran government an excellent opportunity to establish the relationship with the fruit companies on a more equal basis. Nationalist feelings were running high and the government took control of the north coast docks, set up its own marketing agency for bananas, Corporación Hondureña de Bananos (COHBANA), acquired railway lines from the companies, expropriated fruit company lands under the agrarian reform law and made the multinationals subject to the new export tax. The fruit companies, particularly United Brands, were in no position to argue, not least because three decades of export diversification had reduced their importance, the banana share of exports falling to 25 per cent by the end of the 1970s. However, the companies were by no means crushed and managed to fight off the challenge from COHBANA, while negotiating reductions in the export tax when international banana prices weakened.

Under Melgar Castro the military began to address the vexed question of a return to civilian rule. A Presidential Advisory Council set up early in 1976 was given responsibility for preparing an electoral law leading to constituent assembly elections. The prospect of handing over power to the discredited civilians divided the military, which was also split over the slower pace of agrarian and other reforms. Allegations that high officials were involved in drug-smuggling and other misdemeanours provided the justification for another change of government; CONSUFFAA intervened in mid-1978 to replace Melgar Castro by a triumvirate headed by Paz García.

The new government showed little sympathy for the progress recorded in agrarian, fiscal and social policy and had no desire to implement a new reformist programme. Its top priority was to engineer a peaceful return to civilian rule under terms acceptable to the military, a task made all the more urgent by the social upheavals in neighbouring El Salvador and Nicaragua. With the Carter administration also exerting pressure for a return to civilian rule, constituent assembly elections were set for April 1980.

The Constituent Assembly elections in 1980 marked the start of a transition to civilian rule and the end of nearly two decades of direct military government. The 1960s were notable for the high level of administrative incompetence (many foreign grants, for example, went undisbursed), the 1970s, for corruption and public scandals. Yet the long period of military rule had witnessed a steady improvement in Honduran social and economic indicators from their abysmally low levels at the beginning of the 1960s.[14] And the second half of the 1970s had coincided with the fastest economic growth ever recorded in the country. The military withdrew from direct rule with its prestige still intact – and on terms acceptable to the high command.

The elections for the Constituent Assembly were expected to produce a conservative majority because the military had worked closely with the Partido Nacional for almost twenty years. An important obstacle, however, to military collaboration with the Liberals was removed when Modesto Rodas Alvarado died at the end of 1979. Although the Rodista faction survived under the leadership of Roberto Suazo Córdova, it lost its anti-militarist character and the new Liberal leadership went out of its way to assuage fears among senior officers of a return to civilian control of the armed forces. The triumvirate no longer had a preference between the two traditional parties and the Liberals, led by Suazo Córdova, scored an impressive electoral victory. The Constituent Assembly determined that the president would be chosen by direct elections for a term of four years. In the November 1981 presidential elections Suazo Córdova for the Liberals won by a clear majority over Ricardo Zúñiga for the Partido

---

[14] Between 1961 and the early 1980s, the illiteracy rate fell from 53 per cent to 40 per cent of the adult population; urbanization jumped from 23 per cent to 37 per cent; and life expectancy rose from forty-four to sixty-two years.

Nacional.[15] In January 1982, therefore, Suazo Córdova became the first civilian president since the ill-fated Dr Cruz.

CIVILIAN RULE SINCE 1982

The transition to civilian rule had been conducted in a manner and on terms acceptable to the military, which was left with a great deal of autonomy and continued to adopt a high profile during the 1980s. The appointment of General Gustavo Alvarez Martínez as head of the armed forces following Suazo Córdova's election brought to power a man with marked authoritarian tendencies and strong anti-communist credentials; Alvarez helped to establish the Asociación para el Progreso de Honduras (APROH), an organization with a corporatist (almost fascist) character. During the first two years of Suazo Córdova's rule, Alvarez steadily gathered the reins of power into his own hands. The civilian government was powerless to resist, but Alvarez's ambitions and his apparent desire to drag Honduras into a war against the Sandinistas in Nicaragua disturbed his fellow officers in CONSUFFAA. In a swift and well-planned move, Alvarez was sent into exile in March 1984, the air force commander, General Walter López, taking his place as head of the armed forces. Soon afterwards, APROH folded and the threat of another period of direct military rule receded. It was, however, significant that, just as in 1956, it was the armed forces which had preserved constitutional rule while the civilian government had been little more than a spectator.

The natural reluctance of the military to retreat to the barracks after the 1980 elections was given additional impetus by the deterioration in the security situation. The civil war in El Salvador drove thousands of Salvadoreans back across the border into Honduras as refugees while the Salvadorean guerrillas used the *bolsones* (demilitarized pockets of disputed territory in the border zones) to regroup their forces. The search for a peace treaty with El Salvador, pursued fruitlessly for most of the 1970s, was given new emphasis by U.S. concerns over guerrilla successes. A peace treaty was signed in December 1980 with unusual haste, leaving the border to be defined at a later date and paving the way for co-operation

---

[15] The small Christian Democratic Party (founded in 1970) and the Honduran Patriotic Front (a broad coalition of left-wing groups) were not allowed to participate in the November 1980 elections. Only the small Partido de Innovación (PINU), founded in 1970 during the national unity dialogue, was allowed to compete against the National and Liberal parties. (It secured a mere 3.5 per cent of the vote.) Both the Christian Democrats and the Patriotic Front were permitted to take part in the November 1981 presidential elections.

between the armed forces of both countries to defeat the guerrilla threat.[16] A mild echo of the Salvadorean guerrilla movement was heard in Honduras itself when three small guerrilla groups attracted publicity with a wave of kidnappings, hijackings and bank robberies. They were, however, no match for the security forces and lacked popular appeal; although Honduran democracy was a far cry from being perfect, it offered sufficient scope for reform and peaceful change to deter all but the most determined from entering the ranks of the guerrilla movement. By 1984, the guerrilla threat had virtually disappeared, resurfacing from time to time in the remote eastern provinces of Mosquitia.

The security threat presented by the Honduran-based opponents of the Sandinista regime in Nicaragua was a much more serious matter because it raised the possibility of a war between the two countries. The border with Nicaragua had been finally settled in 1960, following a ruling by the International Court of Justice, but the rugged terrain and lack of access roads made the frontier virtually impossible to police. After the fall of Somoza in July 1979 the rump of the Nicaraguan National Guard fled across the border to Honduras, contenting themselves at first with cross-border raids motivated by little more than revenge. However, the consolidation of the FSLN (Frente Sandinista de Liberación Nacional) regime and Sandinista blunders in the Atlantic coast provinces of Nicaragua swelled the numbers of these 'contras' during 1980 and 1981 and produced considerable tension between Honduras and Nicaragua over their presence on Honduran territory.

The growth in the number of contras coincided with a sharp deterioration in the relationship between Nicaragua and Washington. A decision was taken by the Reagan administration in November 1981 to authorize CIA covert operations against the Sandinistas with the funds channelled to the contras. The ostensible purpose was to interdict arms supplies from Nicaragua to the Salvadorean rebels through Honduras, but the real aim was destabilization of the Sandinista regime. At the same time, the United States military began a long series of joint manoeuvres with its Honduran counterpart; thousands of U.S. troops were trained to fight in the difficult Honduran terrain and a large number of U.S. military bases were constructed.

The logic of U.S. geopolitical priorities provided little opportunity for

---

[16] The treaty provided for a border commission to determine the frontier throughout its length. If (as happened) the members of the commission could not reach agreement after five years, the dispute was to be submitted to the International Court of Justice for arbitration.

strengthening Honduran civilian rule, especially since Washington's leading local ally was General Alvarez, who shared the Reagan administration's concern over the consolidation of the Sandinista regime. Alvarez's fall in 1984 did not end Honduran military cooperation with the United States, but there was a change of emphasis. The U.S. military base at Puerto Castilla, used for training Salvadorean troops, was closed and the contras were forced to adopt a lower profile. The new Honduran military leadership may have shared Alvarez's distaste for the Sandinistas, but they were not prepared to embark on a war against a Nicaraguan army of far greater strength. Throughout his presidency Suazo Córdova protested feebly that there were no contra bases on Honduran soil. This denial, flatly contradicted by the evidence, earned the Honduran government little respect in international circles, although there was not much else it could do.

As the Reagan administration drew to a close, its Central American policy in disarray, the Honduran government felt able to assert itself more visibly against the contras. President José Azcona Hoyo, who as the Liberal Party candidate had won the presidential elections at the end of 1985,[17] at first limited his demands to a request for an international peace-keeping force to police the border with Nicaragua; by early 1989, however, the Honduran government felt able to join forces with the rest of Central America under the Arias peace plan in calling for the disbanding of the contras and an end to U.S. military support for 'irregular forces'.

U.S. pressure against the Sandinistas and the use of Honduran territory for U.S. military bases left the weak civilian administration with virtually no freedom in foreign policy. Only in domestic policy, therefore, could it establish its identity, and the reform programme, stalled since the late 1970s, received some attention. Land distribution under the agrarian reform law began again, although the main thrust of the programme (financed by the U.S. Agency for International Development, AID) was giving title to peasants with insecure property rights. However, the government's opportunities for carrying out major reforms were sharply cur-

[17] In April 1985 Suazo Córdova triggered a consitutional crisis by attempting in the first place to succeed himself, then to name his successor. The crisis was resolved only after the application of strong pressure by the military. In the November 1985 presidential elections the Liberal party fielded four candidates, the National party three. The Liberals secured a dubious victory because the leading Liberal (José Azcona Hoyo) polled fewer votes than the leading National party candidate (Rafael Leonardo Callejas). Azcona was declared the winner because the combined vote of the four Liberal candidates exceeded that of the three National party candidates. When Azcona succeeded Suazo Córdova as president in January 1986 it was, however, the first time since 1933 that one constitutionally elected president had succeeded another.

tailed by the economic recession, which coincided with the beginning of civilian rule. The deterioration in the external terms of trade and the second oil crisis at the end of the 1970s opened up a huge trade deficit that was financed by borrowing from abroad at high nominal (and real) interest rates. The public external debt, which had been kept within tolerable levels during most of the 1970s, became a serious burden on the economy, and capital flight – a response mainly to the growing regional crisis – aggravated the balance of payments problem. The outgoing military government signed stand-by agreements with the International Monetary Fund in February 1980 and August 1981, but both were suspended when the authorities failed to meet fund targets for the public sector deficit.[18]

The Suazo Córdova government proved much more successful than its predecessor at implementing adjustment and stabilization policies, although this required observance of both IMF guidelines and AID priorities. The authorities, however, insisted on maintaining the parity of the lempira against the dollar despite enormous pressure from U.S. donor institutions; this left non-traditional exports relatively uncompetitive and in a weak position to exploit the opportunities available under the Caribbean Basin Initiative, but it avoided the high rates of inflation which had exacerbated social tensions in neighbouring countries.[19]

The fall in real GDP and real GDP per head during the worst years of the recession (1982–3) was much less severe in Honduras than in the rest of Central America. Indeed, the return to modest rates of growth after 1983 (helped by massive U.S. economic and military assistance) enabled the country to close some of the gap between itself and the rest of the region. By 1990 real GDP per head was comparable to levels in El Salvador and Nicaragua (where civil war had taken an awful toll), but was still far below the average for Latin America. Under IMF prodding, the Suazo Córdova, and later Azcona Hoyo, governments tackled the deteriorating fiscal situation with some courage and raised government revenue's share of GDP to 16.3 per cent by 1987 – a tax effort comparable to that in several major Latin American republics.[20] Yet Honduras was unable to

[18] For further details, see V. Bulmer-Thomas, 'The Balance of Payments Crisis and Adjustment Programmes in Central America', in R. Thorp and L. Whitehead (eds.), *The Debt Crisis in Latin America* (London, 1987).

[19] The Caribbean Basin Initiative, launched by President Reagan in 1982 and formally inaugurated 1 January 1984, offered duty-free access for twelve years on a wide range of non-traditional exports to the U.S. market for most Central American and Caribbean countries.

[20] See Inter-American Development Bank, *Economic and Social Progress Report: Latin America* (Washington, D.C., 1988), table C-1.

generate sufficient resources to service its foreign debt without sacrificing all efforts in favour of reform, and a moratorium was declared at the beginning of 1989.

Thus, Honduras retained during the difficult years of the 1980s the reformist thread which had run through its history since the Gálvez administration. With the possible exception of the populist phase under López Arellano (1972–5), the pace of reform had always been modest and had occasionally ground to a halt, but the direction of change was clear. In matters of labour policy, social legislation, agrarian reform and fiscal effort there was a sharp contrast by the end of the 1970s between Honduras and its immediate neighbours. This contrast provided Honduras with a certain immunity from the subsequent regional crisis, although the country could not escape all the shock-waves emanating from the epicentres in Nicaragua and El Salvador.

The ability of backward Honduras to implement a reform package where more economically advanced countries had failed owed a great deal to its peculiar agro-industrial structure. The absence of a powerful domestic land-owning oligarchy placed foreign capital, particularly the fruit companies, as the key obstacle to reforms. Hondurans of all social classes could unite behind a package of reforms in which the main losers were the fruit companies. (This helps account for the successful introduction of the income tax in 1949 and labour legislation after 1954.) The weak Honduran state had been a poor match for the fruit companies while alternative sources of funds were unavailable and bananas occupied such a key role in the economy, but the post-war period coincided with the emergence of new sources of foreign borrowing (e.g., the World Bank) and the diversification of the economy through the expansion of coffee and cotton.

If Washington had identified with the fruit companies, as happened in Guatemala under Arbenz, the passage of reform measures would have been far more difficult. The State Department, however, had cast a jaundiced eye on the fruit companies in Honduras ever since the disastrous episode in 1910 when dollar diplomacy was thwarted by Sam Zemurray. There were no Cold War reasons to favour the fruit companies under Gálvez and the U.S. Department of Justice filed a civil anti-trust suit against UFCO in 1954. The rapid rise of trade unions with Communist participation, after 1954, presented a major challenge for Cold War strategists in Washington, but successive Honduran governments showed themselves as keen as any U.S. administration to purge the Marxists from positions of influence: both

Honduran and U.S. governments recognized that a 'free and democratic' labour movement could be a source of strength. The post-war rise of an influential agro-export class, symbolized by the formation of FENAGH, posed a potential threat to the reform programme in the mid-1960s, but by then the labour movement was firmly established under anti-communist leadership and the new industrial class competed with FENAGH for government favours. This prevented too close an identification between government and agro-exporters (a major problem in neighbouring countries).

The Honduran reformist experiment failed most obviously in the field of democracy. The political system suffered many weaknesses, not least the overwhelming influence of the military, and lacked credibility as a fully functional democracy. In contrast to El Salvador and Guatemala, the problem could not be identified with the incorporation of an influential Marxist left into the democratic process, because in Honduras the latter remained of marginal importance. Before the 1980s politics in Honduras was dominated by two traditional parties, loose coalitions of warring factions committed to *personalismo* and united only behind the lure of power and access to the spoils of office, which proved incapable of moving with the times and continued to be an obstacle to effective presidential leadership. The cause of democracy in Honduras in the 1980s after the return to civilian rule was not helped by the tension between the United States and Nicaragua. U.S. geopolitical priorities led to a massive build-up in the quantity and quality of the Honduran armed forces as a strategic bulwark against the Sandinistas. The U.S. military presence, semi-permanent from 1983, led to a close collaboration with the Honduran armed forces over counter-insurgency strategy, which largely by-passed civilian members of the government. The emphasis on security increased the importance of the military in internal affairs, at a time when the consolidation of democracy demanded its return to the barracks. Although the armed forces respected the constitution after 1984 and left the civilian government in charge of most aspects of economic and social policy, political progress in Honduras remained fragile.

The basis of democracy in Honduras had, however, become more secure by the beginning of the 1990s. There were two reasons for this: first, with the decline in regional tension following the repatriation of the contras to Nicaragua, the military lost an important justification for their high political profile in the 1980s and the U.S. military presence in Honduras was also rapidly scaled down. Second, the elections in November 1989 were exemplary, with the two leading candidates (from the Liberal and

National Parties) offering the electorate a genuine choice based above all on rival economic programmes. The winner was the National Party's Rafael Leonardo Callejas, who had committed himself to a neoliberal programme; within weeks of taking office, he had floated the lempira — something which all previous governments had said was impossible — and adopted other tough stabilisation measures. Public protest, although loud, was not violent and the military remained squarely on the sidelines. Thus, the consolidation of democracy — that elusive goal in Honduran history — began to look more plausible as regional and international tensions faded into the background.

7

NICARAGUA SINCE 1930

In 1930, more than a century after independence from Spain, the status of Nicaragua as a sovereign nation was in doubt. Occupied by U.S. Marines almost continously since 1912, the country had effectively lost its political independence; indeed, a vocal minority favoured annexation by the United States. With U.S. officials responsible for most aspects of fiscal and monetary policy, Nicaragua had also lost its financial autonomy. The economy was relatively weak. The export sector (based on coffee, bananas, timber and gold) remained the driving force of the economy but lacked the dynamism of neighbouring countries: exports earned a mere $10 million a year. As a result, Nicaragua, with a population of only 680,000, had the lowest income per head in all Central America. Lack of government resources had hindered the spread of public education and the vast majority of the population remained illiterate. Moreover, the task of national integration was not yet complete. The eastern provinces bordering the Caribbean sea remained unconnected by road or rail to the capital, Managua, and the English-speaking inhabitants of the Atlantic coast, whose formal link with Great Britain had only been broken in 1894, continued to regard 'the Spanish' on the western side of Nicaragua as representatives of a foreign country.

THE U.S. MILITARY OCCUPATION

By virtue of its location and unusual geographical features, Nicaragua has excited the interest of outside powers since the earliest days of Spanish colonial rule. During most of the nineteenth century after independence, it was taken for granted by interested parties that a future inter-oceanic canal would be built through Nicaragua, since the easily navigable San Juan River and Lake Nicaragua would limit major construction works to the narrow strip of land separating Lake Nicaragua from the Pacific Ocean. There was intense rivalry between Great Britain and the United States for control of such a canal until the Clayton–Bulwer Treaty of 1850 bound both powers to reject exclusive control over any such project. However, under the Hay–Pauncefote Treaty of 1901, Great Britain acknowledged its reduced influence in Central America and ceded to the United States exclusive control and protection over any canal it should build. President Theodore Roosevelt's recognition of Panamanian independence in 1903 and the construction of a canal across the isthmus (completed in 1914) did not lessen U.S. geopolitical interest in Nicaragua. On the contrary, the stability of countries close to Panama acquired a new significance and it became more important than ever to prevent rival powers from acquiring control of any canal route through Nicaragua. The administrations of the first decades of the twentieth century never renounced the idea of a Nicaraguan canal under U.S. control. Indeed, surveys were carried out at frequent intervals until the early 1930s.

Relations with José Santos Zelaya, the Liberal president of Nicaragua (1893–1909) were, therefore, of special interest to the U.S. State Department. Zelaya granted generous concessions to U.S. entrepreneurs active in Nicaragua's mining, timber and banana industries, but his relationship with the State Department was badly strained by his interventions in the affairs of neighbouring republics (particularly Honduras) and his flirtations with Germany and Japan regarding a possible canal through Nicaragua. Hence, when a Conservative revolt broke out on Nicaragua's eastern seaboard in 1909, the administration of President William Howard Taft was quick to exploit it and force the removal of Zelaya. However, the succession was not smooth and the outbreak of civil war brought U.S. marines to Nicaragua in 1912.

The arrival of the marines put the military seal on a process of U.S. intervention that had begun in October 1910 with the despatch of Thomas C. Dawson, U.S. minister at Panama, to Managua. The 'Dawson agreements', signed in 1911, assumed that a precondition for political stability in Nicaragua was financial stability, and it was taken for granted that this could not be achieved without close U.S. supervision. Thus began the long period of U.S. intervention in Nicaragua's financial affairs, which survived the Good Neighbor Policy of the 1930s and did not finally end until the 1940s. The State Department secured the support of its Nicaraguan political allies for financial intervention by promising a $15 million loan from U.S. banks, the terms and conditions of which were enshrined in the Knox–Castrillo Treaty of 1911. The U.S. Senate, however, rejected the treaty on three occasions, so the Nicaraguan government had to make do with a more modest 'interim' loan of $1.5 million, while financial intervention went ahead despite the absence of the treaty. By the end of the decade, the framework for fiscal and monetary supervision was firmly in place. A U.S. Collector General of Customs was in charge of customs duties, the first claim on which was external public debt service; European bondholders were therefore assured of prompt payment and any possible need for European intervention in defiance of the Monroe Doctrine averted. A National Bank was established with a majority of shares held by U.S. bankers in order to maintain the new currency (the córdoba) at par with the U.S. dollar and keep Nicaragua on a gold exchange standard with reserves held in New York. The bankers also purchased a majority shareholding in the National Railway and, although the Nicaraguan government bought them out in 1924, both the National Bank and the National Railway continued to have a majority of U.S. directors on their boards with the headquarters of both organizations located in the United States.[1]

Following the infamous Bryan–Chamorro Treaty of 1916[2] the State Department pushed through new financial plans in 1917 and 1920 that provided for even closer control of Nicaraguan fiscal affairs. A High Commission was established (with majority U.S. membership) and given control over part of the Nicaraguan government's budget (including public works) and powers to supervise changes in customs duties – a not insignificant function in a country where taxes on external trade accounted for at least 50 per cent of government revenue. The State Department was also instrumental in setting up three commissions, with strong U.S. representation, to adjudicate claims arising out of civil disturbances during the first three decades of the century.

Financial supervision – to the relief of the State Department – was cheap. Neither the bankers nor the U.S. government became major credi-

---

[1] In 1929, the bankers Brown Bros. & Co and J. & V. Seligman & Co resigned. Their place as fiscal agent for the National Bank and the Pacific Railroad was taken by the International Acceptance Bank of New York.

[2] The Bryan–Chamorro Treaty (signed in 1914, but not ratified by the U.S. Senate until 1916) gave the United States, in perpetuity, exclusive proprietary rights for construction, operation and maintenance of an inter-oceanic canal. It also granted the United States a ninety-nine-year lease on the Corn Islands off the Atlantic coast and for a naval base in the Gulf of Fonseca. In return, the United States paid the Nicaraguan government $3 million, most of which was required to be used in settlement of debt arrears. See I. J. Cox, *Nicaragua and the United States (1909–1927)* (Boston, 1927), p. 845.

tors to the Nicaraguan government, whose public external debt continued
to be mainly in the form of bonds owed to Europeans; U.S. foreign
investment – both direct and portfolio – was less important in Nicaragua
than in any other Latin American country except Paraguay.[3] The connections of Philander Knox (Secretary of State in the Taft administration)
with a U.S.-owned mining company in Nicaragua raised some eyebrows,[4]
but the U.S. government could plausibly claim that its motives for intervention in Nicaragua were not economic. Financial supervision was also
effective. The córdoba remained roughly at par with the U.S. dollar
during the difficult years of the First World War and even survived the
worst years of the depression after 1929. The public external debt was not
only serviced promptly, but also declined in nominal terms during the
1920s as repayments exceeded new borrowings. Under the restrictions
imposed by the Collector General of Customs, the High Commission and
the bankers, the government avoided the worst excesses of deficit finance
observed in the Zelaya period, while both the National Bank and the
National Railway became highly profitable.

The assumption in the Dawson agreements, however, that financial
stability would bring political stability, proved quite false. Within a few
months of the withdrawal of U.S. marines in 1925, civil war had broken
out again. Moreover, there was an additional complication in that the
Mexican government was supporting the Liberal opposition led by former
vice-president Juan Bautista Sacasa in its bid to regain power; in addition
to the other reasons advanced in favour of intervention, the U.S. government now had to consider the possible loss of prestige that would result
from a 'Mexican' victory. The U.S. Marines therefore returned again to
Nicaragua in 1926 and in May 1927 a peace treaty between the Liberals
and the Conservatives was signed under the supervision of Henry Stimson,
a former U.S. Secretary of War. This time, as a further precondition for
political stability the State Department demanded the abolition of all
Nicaraguan armed forces (including the police) and their replacement by a
non-partisan National Guard staffed initially by U.S. officers, modelled on
the National Guard in U.S.-occupied Haiti, soon to be adopted in the
Dominican Republic, and designed to overcome the deep divisions in

[3] See E. Kamman, *A Search for Stability: United States Diplomacy Toward Nicaragua, 1925–1933* (Notre
Dame, Ind., 1968), pp. 220–4.

[4] Philander Knox represented at various times the Nicaraguan mining concern La Luz and Los
Angeles Company, owned by the Fletcher family. A clerk from this company, Adolfo Díaz, became
president of Nicaragua on three occasions during the U.S. occupation.

Nicaraguan society between Liberals and Conservatives by convincing the opposition party that it could come to power by electoral means without resorting to force. The peace treaty was not signed by all the Liberal leaders. Augusto César Sandino, who had returned from Mexico in 1926 to join the Liberal revolt and had risen to the rank of general in the army led by José María Moncada, refused to submit to any treaty which left the U.S. Marines in Nicaragua. Sandino took to the hills of Nueva Segovia in northern Nicaragua with a band of thirty men.

The first test of the new order came in the presidential elections of 1928. The electoral contest, like all those since the fall of Zelaya, was supervised by U.S. Marines, but this time the outcome was not a foregone conclusion. The Liberal Party fielded their war hero General Moncada, who secured a narrow victory over his Conservative rival in a hard-fought contest with high voter participation. The Liberal Moncada proved just as anxious to co-operate with U.S. officialdom as his Conservative predecessors, and the 1930 congressional elections, also supervised by U.S. Marines, produced a Liberal majority. In January 1931, Henry Stimson – now Secretary of State in the Hoover administration – announced that U.S. forces would finally withdraw from Nicaragua after the presidential elections of November 1932.

Stimson had become convinced that political stability had finally been achieved in Nicaragua. The U.S. administration had found, somewhat to its surprise, that most of the Liberal leaders were sensitive to U.S. perceptions of the region and willing to accommodate U.S. interests in their policies. The outstanding exception, Sandino, had been denounced by his own Liberal party and Stimson was confident that Sandino could be contained – if not defeated – by the National Guard, which would remain under the command of U.S. officers until the withdrawal of the marines. Domestic opposition in the United States against the presence of marines had increased for both economic and political reasons, while Latin American condemnation of the occupation had grown since discontent had first surfaced at the Sixth Pan-American Conference in Havana in 1928. Last, but not least, the collapse of world trade after 1929 left the Panama Canal with ample spare capacity, so that the need for a second canal through Nicaragua (the right to which had been secured through the Bryan–Chamorro Treaty) was not so pressing. (The last survey of the Nicaraguan canal route was carried out in 1932.)

The legacy of more than two decades of almost unbroken military intervention in Nicaragua was not a happy one. The State Department's supporters could claim some positive gains: financial stability had been achieved; the elections of 1928, 1930 and 1932, conducted under U.S. supervision, were among the freest in Nicaraguan history; the State Department was no longer seen to favour one party (the Conservatives) over the other and could now do business with a new generation of Liberals, making a policy of non-intervention feasible. On the other hand, financial stability had been achieved only by sacrificing Nicaragua's economic development. In modern parlance, growth was sacrificed for the sake of prompt service on the debt. In the decade up to 1926–7 on average more than one-third of government annual expenditure was spent on servicing the debt; following the formation of the National Guard in 1927, military expenditure became a heavy charge on the budget, absorbing nearly 30 per cent in 1929–30; expenditure on public works – a residual under the financial plans after all other expenses had been paid – was so low, a U.S. financial expert commented in 1928:

There is very little to show for such sums, and it is probable that substantial portions, though credited to public works, have been diverted to other purposes, as in the case of public instruction funds. Highways have absorbed the bulk of public works disbursements, yet not a mile of first-class highway exists in the republic outside of certain recently paved streets in the Capital. Other portions of public works funds have been devoted to the construction or repair of public buildings, but here again accomplishments are not in accordance with appropriations.[5]

The U.S. intervention also distorted the perceptions and behavior of the Nicaraguan elite. An entire generation had become accustomed to the idea of U.S. intervention; the vast majority of the Nicaraguan elite – in government and business – not only accepted U.S. intervention as inevitable but welcomed it as desirable. In 1927 the Nicaraguan finance minister proposed that the United States should extend its fiscal control to include internal taxation as well as customs duties, that a board of estimates with a majority of U.S. citizens should prepare the nation's budget and that a U.S. comptroller should supervise all government expenditures. In the same year, President Adolfo Díaz repeated his offer (first made in 1911) to amend the Nicaraguan constitution to allow the United States to intervene almost at will in return for a modest loan. Indeed by the end of the 1920s the U.S. administration was somewhat embarrassed by this obsequious attitude which it had itself engendered.

The Hoover administration's decision to withdraw the marines from

[5] See W. Cumberland, *Nicaragua: an economic and financial survey* (Washington, D.C., 1928), p. 106.

Nicaragua anticipated Roosevelt's Good Neighbor Policy, but a U.S. policy of non-intervention in Nicaraguan affairs was not credible. Fiscal supervision continued as before and the Bryan–Chamorro Treaty giving the United States rights to a canal route together with military and naval bases was still in force. Moreover, it was not believed by the Nicaraguan elite, who for nearly twenty-five years had been mastering the art of interpreting U.S. preferences as a means of political self-advancement. It continued to be assumed that the State Department had its favourites and that the latter would win any contest; political success therefore depended on convincing the public that an individual or faction enjoyed implicit U.S. support.

THE IMPACT OF THE DEPRESSION

By the time the U.S. Marines finally withdrew from Nicaragua – the last left on 2 January 1933 – difficulties had increased considerably as a result of the world economic crisis. The Nicaraguan economy on the eve of the 1929 depression was heavily dependent on exports, which in turn were dominated by coffee; over half these exports went to the United States, while the latter supplied nearly two-thirds of imports. Customs duties and surcharges on these imports accounted for the bulk of government revenue, while external trade also determined to a large extent the level of activity in commerce, transport and services.

Despite the presence of many foreign entrepreneurs, the coffee sector was characterized by inefficiency and low yields; the republic's coffee had not achieved a reputation for high quality – in contrast to Costa Rica, El Salvador and Guatemala – and the price received by growers was lower than in the rest of Central America. These prices peaked as early as 1925, but the precipitate decline did not begin until after 1929. In the first two years (1930 and 1931), the volume of exports was sustained at pre-depression levels, but a poor harvest in the 1931–2 season contributed to a 49 per cent drop in the volume exported and the value of coffee exports in 1932 was only 25 per cent of the level in 1929.

Nicaragua's other exports (mainly bananas, timber and gold) were not as badly affected by the depression as coffee was, but the latter's importance was sufficient to pull down total export earnings from $11.7 million in 1928 to $4.5 million in 1932. At the same time, under the watchful eye of U.S. fiscal intervention, these reduced foreign exchange receipts were still expected to pay for the service charge on the public external debt, which remained the same in nominal terms. This required a cut in imports even more savage than that for exports; imports fell from $13.4 million in 1928 to $3.5 million in 1932. This reduction was achieved without breaking the parity of the córdoba against the U.S. dollar, although Nicaragua did abandon the gold exchange standard and introduced exchange restrictions in November 1931 under a Control Board composed of the U.S. Collector General of Customs, the U.S. manager of the National Bank and the Nicaraguan Minister of Finance.

The public debt (internal and external) was therefore serviced promptly, although amortization of the external debt was partially suspended from 1932 onwards. Nicaragua joined Argentina, Honduras and the Dominican Republic as the only Latin American countries to meet interest payments in full on the foreign debt during the 1930s. Nicaragua's room for manoeuvre, however, was even less than for these other republics, because in addition to the priority given to the public debt, additional expenditure had to be found for training and recruiting the National Guard. The government of President Moncada desperately tried to protect government revenues by introducing customs surcharges,[6] but fiscal receipts still declined from 5.6 million córdobas in 1928–9 to 3.8 million in 1932–3, and the share of receipts committed to the National Guard and debt service rose to 50 per cent by the time the U.S. Marines withdrew.

This critical situation was made even worse by the disastrous earthquake which struck Managua in March 1931, killing a thousand people and destroying virtually all government buildings. The government negotiated a series of emergency loans in 1932, 1933 and 1934 with the National Bank in order to finance the work of reconstruction and the reduction of arrears in public-sector salaries, but expenditures on health, education and road construction virtually ceased and lay-offs among government employees became common. The Banco Hipotecario, set up by the Moncada government in October 1930 to help the farm sector, closed in 1931 before it could start operations and did not reopen until October 1934. Gross domestic product (GDP) per head fell by 32.9 per cent in real terms between 1929 and 1932, the sharpest drop in Central America.[7] Furthermore, the withdrawal of the marines – whose numbers had exceeded 5,000 in January 1929[8] – deprived Nicaragua of a valuable source of purchasing power just as the

---

[6] These surcharges increased the average tariff rate from 34 per cent in 1928 to 50 per cent in 1933.

[7] See V. Bulmer-Thomas, *The Political Economy of Central America since 1920* (Cambridge, 1987), table A3.

[8] They were reduced to 1412 by January 1931 and 910 by the time of the final withdrawal on 2 January 1933.

depression began to have its greatest impact. GDP per head continued to fall and reached its nadir in 1936, by which time it was the lowest in Central America and one of the lowest in all Latin America.

THE SANDINO EPISODE[9]

The withdrawal of the U.S. Marines in January 1933 left Sandino and his army, the Ejército Defensor de la Soberanía Nacional de Nicaragua (EDSN), still at large. In six years of fighting, neither the U.S. Marines nor the U.S.-officered National Guard had been able to destroy the EDSN, despite the use for the first time of aerial bombardment in support of ground troops by the U.S. military. The EDSN, which reached a maximum of 3,000 members (many of whom were part-time), scored some spectacular military successes, including the destruction of the Fletcher family's La Luz y Los Angeles mine, but its base of operations was mainly confined to the remote and thinly populated provinces of Nueva Segovia, Jinotega and Zelaya.[10]

Sandino, who had left Nicaragua in 1920 following a violent incident, had worked for U.S. companies in Honduras, Guatemala and Mexico – an experience which gave him an inside view of the operations of foreign (U.S.) capital in Latin America. He returned to Nicaragua in 1926 inspired, as we have seen, by the Liberal revolt which followed the first withdrawal of U.S. troops. After the return of the marines, Sandino refused to surrender under the terms of the agreement proposed by Stimson in May 1927. Sandino's purpose in launching a Guerra Constitucionalista was ostensibly the restoration of constitutional government in Liberal hands under Juan Sacasa. But Sacasa accepted the Stimson–Moncada pact, and in November 1928, Moncada himself won the presidential elections for the Liberals. Sandino's objective therefore became the defence of national sovereignty, which required at the very least the withdrawal of all U.S. troops. However, the defence of national sovereignty, in a country where two decades of U.S. military occupation had created an extensive network through which U.S. interests were represented, was no simple matter.

The Coolidge and Hoover administration saw Sandino purely in mili-

---

[9] The original meaning of an 'episode' is 'an interval between two choric songs in Greek tragedy'; this seems highly appropiate.

[10] The military aspects of the Sandino episode are competently discussed in Neil Macaulay, *The Sandino Affair* (Chicago, 1967).

tary terms and described him in official communiqués as a bandit, although he was addressed as General Sandino in letters sent to him by representatives of the U.S. military occupation. The U.S. public, meanwhile, received much of its news about Sandino from the Nicaraguan representatives of United Press and Associated Press, the first of whom was the U.S. Collector General of Customs and the second his U.S. assistant.[11] However, when an excess of confidence on the part of U.S. officers resulted in a series of military reversals, North American public opinion began to be affected by the reports of dead or wounded marines. The U.S. administration therefore switched to a policy under which the National Guard rather than the marines would bear the brunt of the fighting, and approval was even given to the formation of a highly partisan group of *auxiliares* to supplement the work of the supposedly non-partisan National Guard.

The consequence of this shift in policy was that the bulk of casualties was borne by Nicaraguans on both sides. Between 1926 and 1933, 136 marines died, but only 47 fatalities were the result of combat action against the EDSN – an average of one every seven weeks.[12] This low figure meant that Sandino's goal of defending national sovereignty had to be achieved by Nicaraguans killing Nicaraguans – a position which underlined the difficulty of prosecuting a nationalist cause in a country where the imperialist power could rely on national agents to defend its interests.

Although Washington saw Sandino as a bandit, public opinion in Latin America regarded him as a hero and symbol of the struggle against the 'Colossus of the North'.[13] Anti-interventionist sentiment in Latin America reached a peak between the Sixth Pan-American Conference in Havana in 1928 and the Seventh in Montevideo in 1933, coinciding with Sandino's campaign, which attracted a wide regional following and found an echo in Europe, Asia and even North America.

Until the end of 1928 Sandino's key representative was the Honduran poet and politician Froylán Turcios, who edited the widely distributed review *Ariel*.[14] However, Turcios broke with Sandino after a dispute that

---

[11] See C. Beals, *Banana Gold* (Philadelphia, 1932), pp. 304–5.

[12] The remaining deaths were due to the following causes: murder (11); accidents (41); suicides (12); disease (24); and shot while resisting arrest (1). See Macaulay, *The Sandino Affair*, p. 239.

[13] Sandino's struggle elicited an extraordinary number of books, articles and pamphlets throughout Latin American from as early as 1927. For an excellent example of these writings, deferential in tone, see Instituto de Estudio del Sandinismo, *El Sandinismo – documentos básicos* (Managua, 1983), pp. 211–31.

[14] *Ariel* was named after a novel by the Uruguayan José Enrique Rodó, written in 1909, which symbolized the struggle between Latin America and the United States. See Hugo Cancino Troncoso, *Las raíces históricas e ideológicas del movimiento Sandinista: antecedentes de la revolución nacional y popular Nicaragüense, 1927–1979* (Odense, 1984), p. 56.

underlined the difficulties found by Sandino in developing a consistent strategy for the defence of national sovereignty. Turcios wrote to Sandino in December 1928, following the election of Moncada as president, to propose a peace treaty under which Moncada would request the immediate withdrawal of U.S. troops and Sandino would then lay down his arms and recognize the Moncada government in return for the latter's commitment to restore the constitution and suppress all unconstitutional edicts and contracts.[15] Sandino rejected this proposal out of hand – hence the resignation of Turcios as his representative – but within two weeks he had written to Rear Admiral Sellers, U.S. Navy Commander, Special Service Squadron, and Brigadier General Logan Feland of the U.S. Marine Corps to say that he would only reach a peace agreement with General Moncada, 'since the latter – being a member of the Liberal Party, which he betrayed – can correct his mistakes through the commitment which he is in a position to make with us, on behalf of the Nicaraguan people and the Liberal Party itself, to respect the proposals which our army will make at a suitable opportunity'.[16]

Sandino was therefore unclear whether his objective of national sovereignty could be achieved by restoring constitutional government under Moncada (or some other representative of the Liberal Party) or whether it required the elimination of all those traditional institutions (including the Liberal Party) which had collaborated with U.S. imperialism. The latter was a much more radical position towards which both the Alianza Popular Revolucionaria Americana (APRA) and the Communist International wished to push Sandino. For APRA, founded by the exiled Peruvian Víctor Raúl Haya de la Torre in Mexico in 1924, Sandino's war symbolized the struggle of the whole Latin American continent for national sovereignty, independence and social equity. Froylán Turcios was named as honorary Aprista and the Peruvian Esteban Pavletich was despatched to Nueva Segovia in 1928 to join the EDSN. Pavletich gained Sandino's confidence and accompanied him on his extended sojourn in Mexico from June 1929 to May 1930, intended to broaden the base of support in Latin America for his struggle. It was from APRA that Sandino borrowed the term 'Indoamericanismo' and his plan to hold a regional conference in Argentina in order to promote an internationally controlled Nicaraguan canal leaned heavily on APRA's scheme to wrest control of the Panama Canal from the United States.

Sandino also borrowed from APRA's social analysis, claiming on one

---

[15] Turcios' letter is printed in full in S. Ramírez (ed.), *El pensamiento vivo de Sandino*, 2d ed. (San José, 1976), pp. 156–8.

[16] See Ramírez, *El pensamiento*, p. 155.

occasion for example, that: 'neither extreme right nor extreme left is our slogan. For that reason, there is nothing illogical in our struggle being based on the co-operation of all social classes without ideological labels'.[17] This analysis appeared consistent with Nicaraguan social reality since the low level of economic development had generated only tiny pockets of proletarians (e.g., in banana plantations and mines) while the bulk of the labour force (more than 80 per cent in the 1920 census) was engaged in agriculture and only a small proportion were landless labourers. Equally, the officers of the EDSN – both Nicaraguans and other Latin Americans – were drawn heavily from the petty bourgeoisie. However, Sandino sometimes spoke in class terms. In a 1930 letter, made famous since the Nicaraguan Revolution of 1979, he wrote that 'with the intensification of the struggle and the growing pressure from the Yankee bankers, the waverers and the timid – because of the form the struggle now takes – are abandoning us; only the workers and peasants will carry on to the end, only their organized strength will achieve victory'.[18] A year later, in a letter written to one of his closest officers, Pedrón Altamirano, he claimed that the Sandinista movement should disassociate itself from all bourgeois elements on the grounds that it was in their interests to favour a humiliating accommodation with the United States.

Such positions reflect the influence on Sandino of the Communist International and the Liga Anti-Imperialista de las Americas, which was founded in 1925, not as a Communist organization but with Communists playing a leading part in its activities. It was through the League that Sandino came into close personal contact with some of the key Latin American Communists of the day, such as the Venezuelan Gustavo Machado, who visited Sandino in Las Segovias, and – more importantly – the Venezuelan Carlos Aponte and the Salvadorean Agustín Farabundo Martí. Both Aponte and Martí joined the EDSN in 1928 and both rose to the rank of colonel, Martí in particular gaining the confidence and close friendship of Sandino.

Sandino was not a Communist and his occasional use of Marxist phraseology and class analysis was more a reflection of his desire to retain the support of the League than a genuine commitment to class struggle. The differences finally surfaced at the end of 1929, during Sandino's ten-month sojourn in Mexico and just before his interview with the Mexican president Portes Gil.

[17] Quoted in R. Cerdas Cruz, *Sandino, el APRA y la Internacional Comunista* (Lima, 1984), pp. 65–6.
[18] See Cerdas Cruz, *Sandino*, p. 106.

By early 1930, the break was complete and the Communist International began to denounce Sandino as a traitor who had become a petit-bourgeois liberal *caudillo*. Abandoned by both Turcios and the Communist International together with its front organizations, Sandino was now more isolated than ever and from mid-1930 had to deal with the confused political situation in Nicaragua surrounded by officers of outstanding courage and military skill but minimal political experience.

Following Sandino's return from Mexico in May 1930, the EDSN's military successes were substantial and clearly enjoyed considerable backing from the population surrounding its bases of operations, although support in the major cities was much less secure. Sandino's call for a boycott of the elections of 1928, 1930 and 1932 together with the EDSN's campaign of disruption were not successful; in every case the turn-out was extraordinarily high.[19] Sandino failed to build a political wing of the EDSN in the main cities: the Partido Laborista (PL), set up in León in 1928 and led by Dr Escolástico Lara, collapsed soon afterwards, while a similar fate greeted the pro-Sandino Partido Liberal Republicano (PLR) set up in Managua. A year before the 1932 elections, Sandino proposed Horacio Portocarrero – a Nicaraguan living in El Salvador – as president of a provisional government, but this initiative also failed to gain support.

These political disappointments contributed to Sandino's uncertainty regarding his relationship with the traditional political parties, particularly the Liberals. At times, he appeared to regard the entire political elite as hopelessly corrupted by U.S. imperialism and incapable of defending national sovereignty. Yet in this, as in so many other areas, he was not consistent, and his dilemma was compounded by the victory of the Liberal candidate, Juan Sacasa, in the presidential elections of November 1932. Sacasa became president on 1 January 1933, the day before the last of the U.S. Marines withdrew, and although he felt betrayed by Sacasa, Sandino could not ignore the change in circumstance which was made even more dramatic by Sacasa's appointment of Sofonías Salvatierra, a Sandinista sympathizer, as Minister of Agriculture.

Salvatierra headed the Grupo Patriótico, formed in 1932 to promote peace between Sandino and the government. Negotiations began in December 1932 and the peace protocol proposed by Sandino on 23 January

[19] In 1928, the voters numbered 133,633 out of an electorate of 148,831 – a turn-out of 88.8 per cent. See Kamman, *Search for Stability*, p. 166, n49. In the 1932 presidential elections the vote dropped to 129,508.

1933 made it clear that the 'defence of national sovereignty' included an end to U.S. fiscal intervention, revision of the Bryan–Chamorro Treaty and reorganization of the National Guard to bring it within the Nicaraguan Constitution.[20] Astonishingly, the final peace treaty – signed in Managua on 2 February – made no mention of these questions. Instead, Sandino settled for a treaty in which the EDSN agreed to surrender its arms in return for access to state lands along the Río Coco, a personal bodyguard for Sandino of a hundred men (subject to review after one year) and a commitment by the government to a public-works programme in the northern departments for a minimum of one year.

Sandino later claimed that he had agreed to this treaty to avoid giving the U.S. authorities an excuse for a third military intervention. The treaty, however, left unresolved all the issues of non-military U.S. intervention in Nicaragua and in particular ignored the unconstitutional character of the National Guard. Within days, there were clashes between the National Guard and former members of the EDSN, Sandino refusing to surrender the rest of his weapons on the grounds that the Guard was not a duly constituted authority and could not therefore receive his arms. This infuriated the Guard's officer corps, and their fury turned to fear, when – in response to a temporary state of siege imposed by Sacasa in August following a series of violent explosions in the main Guard arsenal – Sandino offered to come to the rescue of the government with a force of six hundred armed men. The tension rose sharply at the beginning of 1934, and the senior Guard officers, led by their Jefe Director Anastasio Somoza García secretly agreed to take advantage of a planned trip to Managua by Sandino in February to assassinate both him and many of his supporters. The ruthless destruction of the remnants of the EDSN and their agricultural co-operatives in the northern provinces virtually erased the memory of Sandino for many years. Only two members of his army played an important part in the guerrilla struggles in Nicaragua from the late 1950s onwards and, ironically, Nicaraguans were forced to rely on a book ghost-written by Somoza for any reference to Sandino's writings.[21] The lessons of the Sandino episode were, however, clear for that small group of Nicaraguans – mainly students – determined to keep the memory alive: first, the defence of national sovereignty could not be restricted to ending

---

[20] See G. Selser, *Sandino* (New York, 1981), pp. 161–2.
[21] See A. Somoza, *El verdadero Sandino o el calvario de las Segovias* (Managua, 1936).

U.S. military intervention, and, second, the traditional political elite in the Conservative and Liberal parties could not be trusted to defend the national interest.

THE CONSOLIDATION OF SOMOZA'S RULE (1934–51)

The timetable for withdrawing the marines announced by Stimson in January 1931 accelerated the formation of the Nicaraguan National Guard. It was intended, as we have seen, to be non-partisan. However, given the intense rivalry between Liberal and Conservative families in Nicaragua, this goal was never realistic, especially because political loyalties in Nicaragua had a strong regional dimension.[22] The objective of a non-partisan National Guard was rendered even less realistic by the short time allowed for training the Nicaraguan officers. The military academy set up by the marines had graduated only 39 officers by March 1932 – nine months before withdrawal – when the estimated minimum requirement was 178. The U.S. director of the National Guard, Calvin B. Matthews, felt that these officers were too young and inexperienced to fill the higher ranks, but the determination of the State Department not to delay the evacuation of the marines meant appointing Nicaraguans to the highest posts without proper military training. An agreement was therefore reached at the U.S. legation in Managua on 5 November 1932 (the day before presidential elections) that the Liberal and Conservative presidential candidates would each nominate an equal number of persons from his party who would be acceptable replacements for the U.S. Marine officers. Outgoing President Moncada would then appoint the nominees of the successful candidate after the election and the incoming president would choose the new chief of the National Guard from among their ranks. The 'non-partisan' character of the Nicaraguan constabulary was therefore established on the basis of the political loyalties of its senior officers – a contradiction in terms.

Sacasa's victory in the November 1932 elections guaranteed that Liberal nominees would fill the top posts in the Guard. Moncada's preferred candidate for the post of the Jefe Director was Anastasio Somoza García, who had supported the 1926 Liberal revolt, served as the President's

---

[22] The city of León was the Liberal stronghold, while the Conservative base was Granada. Managua had become the capital in the nineteenth century in response to the bitter rivalry between these two cities.

personal aide and later, after a brief period of disgrace, as his Undersecretary of Foreign Affairs.[23] Moncada's choice of Somoza was undoubtedly influenced by the support Somoza enjoyed in the U.S. camp from the time he attracted Stimson's attention as an interpreter at the 1927 peace conference; by the end of 1932 both the U.S. minister, Matthew Hanna, and the U.S. National Guard chief were convinced that Somoza was the man for the job. Sacasa, however, was unconvinced, his first choice being the Liberal veteran General Carlos Castro Wassmer. Yet because Castro was unacceptable to both Moncada and the U.S. officials, Sacasa was obliged to choose from an approved list of three candidates including Somoza.[24] Under duress he chose Somoza, his niece's husband. From the start, therefore, the relationship between Somoza and Sacasa was strained, with Somoza confident in the knowledge that he enjoyed U.S. support.

The assassination of Sandino by the National Guard in February 1934 temporarily weakened Somoza's position, but Sacasa was unable to capitalize on this, and the young Jefe Director survived his greatest crisis and emerged greatly strengthened. Somoza had personally promised the new U.S. minister, Arthur Bliss Lane, that he would not move against Sandino, and his actions effectively obliged Sacasa to retaliate by replacing several of the officers implicated in the crime with new appointments, many of whom were his relatives, and by temporarily adopting the title commander-in-chief. Somoza, however, was only required to repeat his oath of loyalty in the presence of the diplomatic corps. Despite repeated requests by Minister Lane, Washington refused to make any public declaration discouraging Somoza from undermining the Sacasa government, while the Jefe Director 'leaked' a series of stories suggesting not only that he had ordered the killing of Sandino, but that he had done so in league with U.S. officials. Somoza cultivated the image of himself as Washington's man and the stony silence from the State Department encouraged Nicaraguans to believe the image was true. Sacasa's position was made even weaker when the United States, following its recognition of the Martínez dictatorship in El Salvador in 1934, announced that it was abandoning its non-recognition policy under the Washington treaties of 1923. Moreover, when in 1935 Sacasa's wife informed Lane that her husband was going to ask Somoza to resign as head of the National Guard and that aircraft from El Salvador and Honduras would bomb his headquar-

[23] See B. Diederich, *Somoza and the Legacy of U.S. Involvement in Nicaragua* (London, 1982), pp. 13–14.
[24] See R. Millett, *Guardians of the Dynasty* (Maryknoll, N.Y.), pp. 134–5.

ters if he refused, the State Department intervened quickly to stop the President's plan.

Sacasa's position was further prejudiced by the continued weakness of the economy. World coffee prices remained at one-quarter of their pre-depression peak, while sugar exports suffered from U.S. refusal to allow Nicaragua a sizeable sugar quota under a reciprocal trade treaty.[25] Banana exports, which had challenged coffee in terms of importance at the beginning of the 1930s, started to fall sharply after 1933 under the impact of disease, and by 1943 they had disappeared completely. Within its limited means, the government did what it could: in 1934 the Banco Hipotecario finally began operations favouring coffee growers with a credit policy designed to avoid the need for foreclosures. In the same year the Caja Nacional de Crédito Popular (Monte de Piedad) was established to channel loans to small farmers at very low rates of interest. Two laws were passed (Ley de Habilitaciones and Ley de Usura) to ease the problems of the farm sector, and by the end of 1934 producers were receiving a modest premium over the official rate of exchange for their exports. The value of exports remained deeply depressed, however, throughout Sacasa's term of office (1933–6), pushing down imports and contributing to a permanent crisis in government revenue.

Sacasa's difficulties did not automatically work to Somoza's advantage. A rally held in 1934 while Sacasa was abroad was a failure. And Somoza's control of the National Guard was not yet fully assured. Furthermore, Somoza's presidential ambitions were thwarted by two provisions in the Constitution; the first stated that the head of the National Guard could not be a presidential candidate, while the second demanded a lapse of six months before any relation of the incumbent could himself succeed to the presidency. Somoza explored all manner of ways of circumventing these provisions, including the formation of a special constituent assembly to change the rules, but the lack of trust between himself and Sacasa produced no results.

Somoza was therefore forced to bide his time and concentrate on building a political machine. He formed a gang of thugs, Camisas Azules, consciously modelled on Mussolini's black and Hitler's brown shirts, and used his paper *La Nueva Prensa* to float the idea of his presidential candidacy. Somoza's real breakthrough came in February 1936 when he inter-

[25] The treaty was eventually signed in 1936, after Secretary of State Cordell Hull had applied economic pressure on Nicaragua to lower tariffs on a number of imports.

vened in a taxi driver's strike provoked by petrol shortages. His conciliatory attitude succeeded in ending the dispute, contrasted sharply with
Sacasa's abrasive position, and won him the praise of both labour and
business leaders. The following month, U.S. minister Lane was replaced
by Boaz Long, who proved to be much more warmly disposed towards
Somoza and his presidential ambitions. By May, Somoza felt strong
enough to provoke a confrontation with Sacasa's cousin in charge of the
Acosasco fort at León. The President reacted with unusual speed ordering
his cousin to resist and calling an emergency meeting of Liberal and
Conservative leaders to select Leonardo Argüello as a joint candidate in the
November presidential elections.

Somoza was unperturbed. His National Guard units overpowered Ramón Sacasa in the Acosasco fort, leaving Somoza in complete military
control of the country. Sacasa resigned on 6 June 1936 and three days later
a compliant Congress nominated Dr Carlos Brenes Jarquín as interim
president. The elections were postponed until December and in November
Somoza resigned as Jefe Director of the National Guard so that his ascent
to power could remain within the constitution. The Partido Liberal
Nacionalista (PLN) was formed to launch Somoza's candidacy, which was
also supported by a faction of the Conservative Party. The opposition
called for U.S. supervision of the elections, and withdrew when this was
not forthcoming. However, Argüello's name remained on the ballot paper
and he secured 169 votes to Somoza's 107,201. The president-elect then
resumed control of the 3,000-strong National Guard and combined the
posts of Jefe Director and president from 1 January, 1937.

Support for Somoza was nothing like as strong as the voting figures
suggested. The traditional political elite, which had previously seen in
Somoza a means for pursuing its own ambitions, now began to realize that
his dominant position posed a threat, while some members of the National
Guard were unhappy at the President's handling of military affairs. Somoza, however, possessed an efficient intelligence system, enabling him
rapidly to consolidate his position within the Guard and to divide his
political opponents. He provided huge wage increases for the Guard's
members and began the construction of both an air force and a navy under
National Guard control. The Guard's functions were expanded to include
control of internal revenue and the national railroad, while its grip on
postal, telegraph and internal radio services together with control of immigration and emigration was tightened, providing innumerable opportuni-

ties for members of the force to supplement their salaries as well as to maintain social control.

Somoza's response to the threat from the traditional political elite was more subtle. Although he sometimes resorted to strong-arm tactics, including the arrest at a rally in 1937 of fifty-six members of the Conservative Party, Somoza recognized that these did not offer a long-term solution. He therefore adopted a series of measures to reverse the stagnation of agriculture since the economic interests of the traditional elite – Liberal and Conservative – were bound up with the fortunes of this sector. The most important measure was the series of devaluations, beginning in March 1937, which took the córdoba (¢) from par to five per U.S. dollar by the end of 1939 and gave a huge stimulus to agricultural exports, especially coffee, which was only partially off-set by new taxes on exports and exchange rate transactions designed to boost government revenue. The banking system was encouraged to finance new crops and both cotton and sesame production rose rapidly. Somoza also passed legislation favouring foreign investment; gold exports, in particular, increased sharply as a consequence. He did not, however, neglect his own economic interests; a 5 per cent tax on all public-sector salaries, a 1.5 cents per pound tax on beef exports and a share of foreign mining profits were all assumed to pass through his hands.

These economic measures produced a steep rise in the cost of living. Food retail prices increased by 124 per cent between 1937 and 1939 and those on fixed incomes suffered accordingly. The National Guard, however, was protected by large salary increases and the traditional elite benefited from the higher nominal prices for agricultural products. Elite opposition to Somoza began to crumble and Leonardo Argüello, his erstwhile opponent in the presidential elections, took the lead in unifying the Liberal Party behind the new Nicaraguan *caudillo.* Flushed by his success, Somoza persuaded Congress at the end of 1938 to turn itself into a Constituent Assembly, which extended the presidential term from four to six years without re-election (except for the present incumbent). A few months later, the Assembly reverted to the National Congress, and in one of its first acts declared Somoza president for eight years until May 1947.

His national power base secure, Somoza now turned to the Roosevelt administration, which had invited him for a state visit to Washington in 1939. Somoza secured from Roosevelt most of his demands: assistance in training officers for the National Guard at Nicaragua's Academia Militar, loans from the Export-Import Bank to purchase U.S. goods, and financial and material support to construct a road designed to link the English-speaking Atlantic region with the more densely populated Pacific provinces. The trip was of inestimable value to Somoza since it confirmed the wide-spread public belief that the Jefe Director enjoyed the support of the White House and could therefore not be overthrown without risking Washington's ire. In Nicaragua, non-intervention and the Good Neighbor Policy led to the endorsement of a president whose venality and ruthlessness were well known to U.S. officials.

The outbreak of the Second World War created serious problems for the Nicaraguan economy and temporarily raised the prospect of a revolt against Somoza. Under the inconvertible Aski-mark system, Germany had steadily increased its trade with Nicaragua during the 1930s. The loss of the German and European markets after 1939 was not at first compensated by increased purchases from the United States. At the same time, Somoza's suspension of constitutional guarantees and imposition of a state of siege created wide-spread resentment. The exile community, led by the Conservative Emiliano Chamorro, attempted a challenge but a swift shake-up of the National Guard – including the dismissal of Chief of Staff General Rigoberto Reyes – kept Somoza firmly in control. A lend-lease agreement with the United States in October 1941 provided the National Guard with modern equipment worth $1.3 million, greatly weakening the prospects for any revolt staged by the traditional Nicaraguan method of a poorly equipped volunteer force of exiles invading the country.

The entry of the United States into the war in December 1941 gave Somoza many opportunities to demonstrate his support for the Roosevelt administration at very little cost. Nicaragua immediately declared war on Japan, Germany and Italy, and the United States was invited to build naval and air bases in the republic. The government participated in U.S. schemes to supply the Panama Canal Zone with fruits and vegetables, while work on the Pan-American Highway (two-thirds funded by the Roosevelt administration) proceeded rapidly. Nicaragua promoted rubber production in the Atlantic region as part of the hemispheric effort to provide U.S. access to strategic raw materials formerly obtained from the Far East. Coffee production stabilized under the quota allocated to Nicaragua by the Inter-American Coffee Agreement, while gold exports soared.

Exports almost trebled in value between 1938 and 1944, but imports suffered from shipping and other shortages and only doubled in value. As a result, Nicaragua's gold and foreign-exchange reserves rose steadily during the war, pushing up the money in circulation and contributing to a noteworthy increase in prices. The creation of a Price Control Board headed by the U.S. Collector General of Customs, did little to restrain prices, which rose by 325 per cent between 1939 and 1945. On the other hand, price control coupled with import restrictions created enormous opportunities for graft by the Somoza family, the value of whose fortune rose rapidly during the war. By its end, Somoza was alleged to control fifty-one cattle ranches, forty-six coffee plantations, two sugar plantations, an airline, a gold mine, a milk plant and factories producing textiles, cement and matches. Much of this property had come into his hands as a result of expropriation of enterprises owned by Axis nationals.

The rapid rise in the cost-of-living index created resentment among urban workers, whose numbers had grown during the war. The traditional elite, on the other hand, resented Somoza's use of price and import controls to enrich himself at their expense. Even the Roosevelt administration began to question the wisdom of its support for Somoza when he unveiled his plans for re-election in 1947. All these factors combined to produce a real threat to the Somoza regime from 1944 onwards, but the lack of unity among his opponents, together with the dictator's undoubted tactical skill, enabled the dynasty to survive the greatest challenge to its existence until its overthrow in 1979.

Since the taxi drivers' strike of February 1936, Somoza had enjoyed posing as the friend of organized labour. His inclusion of minor social reforms in the Constitution of 1938 had contributed to the difficulties of the Partido Trabajador Nicaragüense (PTN), founded in 1931 as the party of organized labour. The PTN leadership subsequently divided over the attitude the labour movement should adopt towards Somoza, and the party dissolved itself in 1939. During the war Somoza invited Lombardo Toledano, the Mexican Marxist labour leader, to Nicaragua, and he frequently promised to introduce a Labour Code which became a central demand of both pro-Somoza labour groups and the Partido Socialista Nicaragüense (PSN), formed in 1944 by former leaders of the PTN. The attitude of these groups was not, however, one of confrontation with Somoza, who, for his part, manoeuvred to secure labour endorsement of his plans for re-election.

The attitude of the traditional elite, who felt they had more to lose from the dictator's continuation in power, was more hostile. Somoza's decision early in 1944 to seek re-election split the Liberal Party and led to the formation of the Partido Liberal Independiente (PLI) which made common

cause with the Conservatives to launch a strike designed to bring down
Somoza in mid-1944. The labour movement, still hopeful for the Labour
Code, did not, however, support the strike, which was also undermined
by the announcement of Irving Lindberg, U.S. Collector General of Customs and head of the Price Control Board, that any business participating
in the strike would be expropriated.

Washington, which had not authorized Lindberg's intervention, was
also anxious to prevent Somoza's re-election. His requests for additional
weapons in 1944 and 1945 were refused and strong pressure was brought
to bear. Yet the dictator did not yield until the end of 1945, by which
time the PLI and the Conservatives had agreed on Enoc Aguado as their
joint presidential candidate. Somoza invited the aged Leonardo Argüello,
his opponent in 1936, to represent the Somocista cause and Argüello duly
won a handsome election victory in May 1947. However, the new president demonstrated a surprising degree of independence and immediately
began to attack Somoza's power base in the National Guard by reassigning
officers. The dictator was shaken, but recovered his composure rapidly and
carried out a coup d'état within the month removing Argüello and ensuring that Congress chose Somoza's uncle, Victor Román y Reyes, as interim
president.

This move provoked a major crisis since the Truman administration
refused to recognize the new regime even after it had adopted a new constitution with strong anti-communist provisions. Recognition of the Román y
Reyes government at the end of 1947 by the governments of Costa Rica and
the Dominican Republic marginally reduced the isolation of the regime,
but the Truman administration stood firm until March 1948, when Somoza
played his trump card by invading Costa Rica in support of President
Teodoro Picado, whose government was backed by the Communist Party, in
the Costa Rican civil war. The Truman administration was keen to see the
elimination of Communist influence in the Costa Rican government and
persuaded Somoza to withdraw his troops in return for recognition of the
Román y Reyes regime, a step that was formally taken following the meeting of the Organization of American States (OAS) in April 1948. For the
next thirty years, successive U.S. administrations never again wavered in
their support of the Somoza family.

Meanwhile, Somoza had turned on his erstwhile allies in the labour
movement. The Labour Code of 1945 was ignored, the PSN outlawed,
and organized labour was so effectively crushed that it played no significant role until the 1970s. The student opposition, through which the

memory of Sandino had been kept alive, was undermined by closing universities and selective imprisonment. The traditional elite, however, were treated quite differently. Following a series of tactical agreements a pact was signed in 1950 by Somoza and Emiliano Chamorro under which the Conservative Party would be guaranteed one third of the seats in Congress together with representation in government and the judiciary. Most importantly the elite was guaranteed 'freedom of commerce', which meant that the Somoza family would share the benefits of economic growth with the traditional ruling classes. The 1950 pact paved the way for a presidential contest between Somoza and Chamorro, that duly provided the former with a further six-year term.

By 1951, at the start of his last presidential term, Somoza's rule had been firmly consolidated. He had thwarted all efforts to unseat him by deftly playing off one opponent against the other. Except in 1947–8, when he turned on the labour movement, he did not rely on extensive repression preferring exile and temporary imprisonment to weaken his opponents. He had manoeuvred his way around U.S. opposition to his continuation in power, appealing to the military against the State Department when necessary. Nicaragua remained a backward country with a weak export sector and limited opportunities for capital accumulation, but the 1950 pact finally resolved the division of labour between the Somoza family and the traditional elite and ensured the latter's support for the regime for the next twenty years.

ECONOMIC TRANSFORMATION AND THE FOUNDATION OF THE SOMOZA DYNASTY

The Nicaraguan economy on the eve of the Somoza–Chamorro pact was virtually stagnant; real GDP per head was still below the level of the late 1920s and virtually unchanged since 1941.[26] Real income per head was not only the lowest in Central America but also the lowest in Latin America except Haiti.[27] For almost a century, Nicaragua had followed an export-led model with only the most modest of results; exports in 1949 were a mere $23 per person (compared with $63 per person in Costa Rica) and this figure falls to a derisory $15 if gold exports (a virtual foreign enclave) are excluded. However, from 1949 to 1970, the Nicaraguan economy grew faster than

[26] See V. Bulmer-Thomas, *Political Economy of Central America*, table A3.
[27] See CEPAL, *Series históricas del crecimiento de América Latina* (Santiago, 1978), Cuadro 2.

any other Latin American country's (including Brazil's); by the mid-1960s real GDP per head had overtaken the rest of Central America (except Costa Rica) and climbed to the middle of the Latin American rankings. In the same period (1949–70), Nicaraguan exports grew by 667 per cent – an annual rate of 10.2 per cent – compared with 178 per cent for Latin America as a whole, so that exports had jumped to $98 per person by 1970, the second highest figure in Central America (after Costa Rica) and one of the highest in Latin America.

This transformation of the economy was not a smooth process. It was subject to marked cycles: the first half of both the 1950s and the 1960s were periods of exceptional growth followed in each case by five years of modest economic expansion. Both the rapid expansion and the cycles were dictated by the fortunes of the export sector, which added several new products to the list of traditional exports.

The first such product was cotton, which had made a brief appearance in the export list in the late 1930s. In 1949 cotton accounted for less than 1 per cent of exports; by 1955, this proportion had reached 38.9 per cent, making cotton more important than coffee (34.9% per cent) or gold (10.2 per cent). This was followed by a period of retrenchment, caused by lower world prices and technical difficulties, until a second boom in the first half of the 1960s lifted the volume of cotton exports fourfold in the five years up to 1965. The increase in beef exports after 1958 was almost as spectacular. The cattle industry, a traditional stronghold of the Conservative elite based in Granada, was transformed by the introduction of modern abattoirs and an efficient transport system; the Somozas played a pioneering role in beef exports to the United States, which rocketed from zero in 1958 to nearly $30 million by 1970, equivalent to 15 per cent of total exports. The success of beef as an export product was followed in turn by sugar, which benefited from the re-allocation of Cuba's U.S. sugar quota after 1960. In this case the main beneficiary was the Conservative Pellas group, the principal shareholders in the San Antonio sugar mill, although the Somoza family by the end of the 1960s owned two of the six mills operating in Nicaragua.

The boom in agro-exports was made possible by economic policies which gave absolute priority to this branch of agriculture. Until the córdoba was officially devalued in 1955 (from 5 córdobas to 7 córdobas per U.S. dollar), agro-exporters were able to convert their dollar earnings to local currency at the favourable free-market rate. Following the devaluation (the last until 1979), Nicaraguan farmers enjoyed exceptional price stability, which kept input costs firmly under control. They also benefited from the weakness of rural trade unions, the failure to apply the 1945 Labour Code to agricultural workers and the absence of minimum rural wages (at least until 1962), which, coupled with demographic pressures, guaranteed adequate supplies of labour, even at harvest time, at a fixed real wage. Last, but not least, the allocation of credit was deliberately distorted in favour of agro-exports, which were subject to a maximum charge of 2 per cent (compared with 8 per cent for other commercial bank credits) for much of the period.

Agricultural products were not the only source of Nicaragua's export boom. The creation of the Central American Common Market (CACM) in 1960 provided the basis for a rapid increase in manufactured exports to the rest of the region. Many of these products, such as cooking oil and textiles, were based on the new agricultural exports, but others were the more familiar import-intensive 'finishing-touch' consumer goods that had become immensely profitable as a result of the new tariff structure adopted by CACM. Multinational capital (mainly from the United States) was attracted to Nicaragua by these industrial opportunities, underpinned by exceedingly attractive tax treatment as well as by the opportunities for profit in the commercialization of agricultural exports, the production of which, however, generally remained in national hands.

The cotton boom at the start of the 1950s was so profitable that the beneficiaries soon found themselves in possession of a large financial surplus. This stimulated the creation of two privately owned financial institutions outside the control of the Somoza family. The first, Banco de América (BANAMER), was founded in 1952 by a group of Granada-based businessmen led by Silvio F. Pellas, a member of the Conservative elite. The second, Banco Nicaragüense (BANIC), began operations in 1953 with the main shareholders linked to León and the Liberal Party. The new banks played a key role in the establishment of modern capitalism in Nicaragua. They robbed the Somoza family of its virtual monopoly over the allocation of scarce credit, each bank building up a series of enterprises in different sectors under the full or partial control of shareholders, so that it became possible to identify two dominant groups in the Nicaraguan economy outside the Somoza family. The BANAMER group, the BANIC group and the Somoza family all had major interests in agricultural exports, manufacturing and commerce, while the first two groups enjoyed a privileged position (at least until the early 1970s) in construction.

The Somoza family continued to enjoy a special status in relation to public financial institutions, a position strengthened by the creation in 1953 of the Instituto de Fomento Nacional (INFONAC) and by the establishment in 1966 of the Banco de la Vivienda. Nevertheless, the establishment of BANIC and BANAMER provided an opportunity for the traditional elite and a small group of new entrepreneurs to share in the benefits of economic transformation. As a result, the resistance of the bourgeoisie to the consolidation of Somoza's rule in the 1940s on the grounds of unfair competition was overcome and did not re-emerge until the mid-1970s.

The benefits of the economic transformation after 1950 were nevertheless very narrowly distributed: in the late 1960s 1 per cent of depositors accounted for nearly 50 per cent of savings deposits.[28] At the same time, the rapid transformation of agriculture produced a major social upheaval since the expansion of the new export products occurred not on the frontier (towards the Atlantic coast) but in the settled Pacific coast departments. As a consequence, some of the peasantry were driven towards less fertile lands in the frontier regions, others were reduced to the status of landless agricultural workers, while a third group migrated towards the cities (notably Managua).

This social upheaval was mirrored in other parts of Central America, but its impact in Nicaragua was particularly dramatic because the pace of transformation was more rapid than elsewhere and because the effort to introduce reforms to off-set the impact of social upheaval was particularly feeble. Although a land reform law was passed and a National Agrarian Institute established in 1963 under the influence of the Alliance for Progress, its impact was minimal. Equally, the Instituto Nicaragüense de Comercio Exterior e Interior (INCEI), set up to promote production of agricultural goods for the home market, was rendered incapable of stimulating domestic production and increasing food security because of a lack of resources. A minimum-wage provision was added to the Labour Code in 1962, but the rates were set so low as to have no appreciable effect on wages received, while the social security programme launched in 1957 never extended outside the city of Managua.

The social upheavals accompanying the economic transformation during the 1950s and 1960s never seriously troubled the Somoza dictatorship. On the contrary, the distractions provided by profitable economic opportunities for his traditional opponents in the Conservative and Inde-

---

[28] See John Morris Ryan et al., *Area Handbook for Nicaragua* (Washington, D.C., 1970), p. 312.

pendent Liberal parties enabled Somoza García not only to rule with a minimum of repression but also to found a dynasty – a combination no other Caribbean Basin dictator of those years succeeded in achieving.

Somoza's two legitimate sons, Luis and Anastasio ('Tachito'), had been groomed for the succession for many years. The eldest son, Luis – an agricultural engineer by training – had played a key role in helping to break the international isolation of the dictatorship in the 1947–8 period, while Anastasio had returned in 1946 from military training at West Point to enter the National Guard. A third (illegitimate) son, José, had entered the Guard as early as 1933 as an enlisted man but had been promoted to officer rank by the 1940s. Luis entered Congress in 1950 and by early 1956 had acquired the key position of First Designate, thus ensuring that a Somoza would fill the presidency if anything should happen to his father. Anastasio, meanwhile, had become acting Jefe Director of the National Guard with José promoted to the rank of major.

Somoza's control of the Nicaraguan state apparatus was secure by the mid-1950s. However, he still faced an external threat from the Caribbean Legion, a loosely knit organization of revolutionaries dedicated to the overthrow of regional dictatorships and whose greatest triumph was provided by José Figueres' victory in the Costa Rican civil war. Figueres did not forget his debt to the Legion and in April 1954 was implicated in a plot by Nicaraguan exiles, led by Emiliano Chamorro, to assassinate Somoza. Although this plot was easily foiled, Somoza was temporarily prevented from retaliating against Figueres by his involvement in the overthrow of the left-wing government of Jacobo Arbenz in Guatemala in May 1954. Somoza had long played the anti-communist card with enthusiasm and had been rewarded with substantial U.S. military equipment, an agreement setting up a U.S. Army mission and a U.S. military assistance program. In return, Nicaragua now provided training centres and other logistical support for Guatemalan counter-revolutionaries. The fall of Arbenz left Somoza free to retaliate against Figueres and in January 1955 the National Guard supported an invasion of Costa Rica by an exile force. Figueres countered with the formation of a volunteer army and a diplomatic offensive that prompted the U.S. military in Panama to come to his rescue and the Organization of American States to offer a mild condemnation of Nicaragua's role in the invasion. Somoza, however, had made his point; by September the two leaders had signed a Pact of Amity and Treaty of Conciliation between their countries and the Nicaraguan dictatorship ceased to be troubled from outside.

The assassination of Somoza in September 1956, after he had obtained the Liberal Party's nomination for a further presidential term, occurred, therefore, at a time when the dictatorship was under no serious internal or external threat. The succession was relatively smooth and was made easier by misleading reports from the U.S. military hospital in Panama, where Somoza had been flown at the personal intervention of the U.S. ambassador, that the dictator would recover. Luis became acting president; Anastasio, Jefe Director of the National Guard; and Colonel Gaitán, who had ensured the loyalty of the National Guard during the tense days after the assassination, was exiled for his pains to Argentina as ambassador.

Luis Somoza formalized his grip on the presidency through fraudulent elections in February 1957 which were boycotted by all the opposition except the puppet Partido Nacionalista Conservador (PNC). The Partido Social Cristiano (PSC) was created in reaction to these elections and received support from younger Conservatives dissatisfied with their party's inability to make any political impact on the dictatorship. The run-up to Luis' six-year term was marked by considerable repression – including the imprisonment of Pedro Joaquín Chamorro, editor of *La Prensa,* and Dr Enoc Aguado, defeated presidential candidate in 1947. Yet, once he was in office, Luis Somoza made it clear that he wanted to modernize Nicaragua as well as to maintain the hegemony of the Somoza family. It is significant that, however cosmetic they may have been, all the major socio-economic reforms of the post-war period occured during his six-year term (1957–63). Moreover, the press became relatively free and in 1959 the constitutional ban on re-election was restored.

The treaty with Costa Rica in 1955 may have ended Figueres' challenge to the dictatorship, but the Cuban Revolution brought into existence a potentially more serious threat. At the same time, it gave the dynasty a great opportunity to play the anti-communist card and curry favour with the Eisenhower and Kennedy administrations. As early as the middle of 1959, only six months after Castro's triumph, Luis Somoza was accusing Cuba of aiding efforts to overthrow his regime and Nicaragua played a leading role in the Bay of Pigs fiasco in April 1961, providing bases for the troop-lift and air attacks. This support for the United States was far from disinterested since the Cuban Revolution provided the inspiration for the more radical opponents of the Somoza dynasty: the Frente Sandinista de Liberación Nacional (FSLN) was formed a few months after the Bay of Pigs by a group of Nicaraguan exiles led by Carlos Fonseca Amador.

Despite the numerous plots against the dynasty, Luis Somoza felt sufficiently confident to engineer the victory of an outsider in the February 1963 presidential elections. His candidate, René Schick, was chosen by the Liberal Party at the insistence of the Somoza family in preference to more popular figures, the Conservative candidate, Dr Fernando Agüero, withdrawing as soon as it was clear that electoral fraud would guarantee Schick's victory. Schick was a puppet, but he managed to irritate Anastasio Somoza by subjecting a National Guard officer accused of murder to judicial process and by intervening to ensure the exile rather than imprisonment of Carlos Fonseca Amador. The Jefe Director, who had never found his brother's theory of indirect rule convincing and felt vindicated by Schick's behaviour, resolved to stand for election in February 1967.[29]

The prospect of another Somoza in the presidency provoked the opposition to mount its most serious challenge to the dictatorship since 1944. The Conservatives, the PLI and the PSC united to form the Unión Nacional Opositora (UNO) to fight the election behind the candidacy of Dr Fernando Agüero. The size of UNO's rallies and the certainty of electoral fraud convinced the opposition leadership that a popular movement could be mounted to bring down the dynasty. A rally of between 40,000 and 60,000 people was held in Managua in January 1967, but the National Guard remained loyal to the Somoza family and dispersed the crowd with heavy casualties. Anastasio Somoza duly won the elections the following month and resumed the directorship of the National Guard. Like his father, he now controlled the two key institutions in Nicaragua and a further restraining influence was removed when his brother Luis died in April 1967.

The legal opposition was crushed by the events of 1967, and the FSLN was unable to establish a base in either the urban or the rural populations. With his opponents demoralized, the young Somoza returned to his father's idea of a pact with the opposition to give them minority representation in return for their acceptance of Somoza family hegemony. The agreement, in which the U.S. ambassador played a decisive role, was reached in March 1971 and provided for the formation of a three-man ruling junta composed of Fernando Agüero together with two Somoza appointees. This Junta was to rule the country from May 1972 to December 1974, when new presidential elections would be held. The pact split the opposition

---

[29] Within two days of Anastasio Somoza's endorsement by the Liberal Party, Schick died and was replaced by Lorenzo Guerrero, who served the remaining few months of the presidential term.

but was duly implemented and left Somoza, still Jefe Director of the National Guard, firmly in charge. He enjoyed the full support of the Nixon administration, faced a weak and divided legal opposition and a minuscule threat from the revolutionary left; when he vacated the presidency, he had every reason to believe that he had been just as successful as his father in guaranteeing the survival of the dynasty.

COLLAPSE OF THE DYNASTY

Unlike the Somoza–Chamorro pact of 1950, the Somoza–Agüero agreement did not consolidate the authority of the regime. On the contrary, the reaction to the pact marked the first stage in the disintegration of the dictatorship. The success of Somocismo had rested on several pillars: a strong National Guard, loyal to the Somoza family; unconditional U.S. support; a tacit alliance with the most powerful sections of the bourgeoisie; and a political party system in which the opposition – in return for freedom of the press and radio and a minimum of repression – generally observed strict limits in the challenge it mounted against the regime. The dictatorship also relied upon a Catholic Church that endorsed its political programme and preached only to spiritual needs.

Both the political-party system and the traditional role of the Catholic Church were ruptured by the Somoza–Agüero pact. The Catholic Church, led since 1968 by Archbishop Miguel Obando y Bravo, refused to endorse the accord and signalled its entrance onto the political stage through a series of pastoral letters critical of the dictatorship. Christian base-communities had been springing up in Nicaragua since the late 1960s and the Catholic Church, as elsewhere in Latin America, had become much more conscious of social questions, although this concern was not so apparent among the Protestant churches dominant on the Atlantic coast. The Conservative Party, the traditional focus of legal opposition to Somocismo, was badly shaken by Agüero's decision to collaborate with the regime and split into four groups. Even the Somocista Liberal Party was affected because the pact virtually guaranteed Somoza the presidency for a further seven-year term in the scheduled 1974 elections and deprived outsiders of a chance of high office. Dr Ramiro Sacasa, a relative of Somoza who had served in various government posts, duly resigned from the party to form the Partido Liberal Constitucionalista (PLC).

Somoza might have weathered these difficulties, but the earthquake that destroyed Managua on the night of 23 December 1972 further undermined support for the regime. For three days Somoza was unable to control the National Guard, which went on an orgy of looting; law and order was briefly in the hands of the troops provided by the United States and a group of Central American countries under the 1964 military agreement known as CONDECA (Consejo de Defensa Centroamericana). The notion of the Guard's invincibility and unquestioning loyalty to the Somoza family was badly shaken; some of the regime's opponents were persuaded that a coup from within the Guard was a possibility, while the militants of the FSLN were convinced that their strategy of armed struggle could indeed succeed.

Somoza responded to the crisis by establishing a National Emergency Committee and dropping the hapless Agüero from the now powerless triumvirate. As head of the committee, Somoza was in a position to determine the allocation of the generous relief funds with which the international community had responded to the earthquake disaster. The resources were spent in a manner involving massive corruption (particularly by the National Guard) and favoured existing or new Somoza industries, the family acquiring important new interests in land development, construction and finance. The tacit alliance with the bourgeoisie began to break down under the charge of *competencia desleal* and members of the BANIC and BANAMER groups, together with the private sector umbrella organization Consejo Superior de Empresa Privada (COSEP), complained that Somoza was using his privileged position to expand his family interests at the expense of the rest of the private sector.

The earthquake also revived the labour movement after twenty-five years of quiescence. The cost of living leapt 20 per cent in the year 1972–3 under the impact of imported inflation as well as domestic shortages provoked by the earthquake. Real wages for all Nicaraguan workers inevitably declined, but the construction workers in Managua were in a strong position to demand salary adjustments; their strike in 1973 was largely successful and marked a triumph for the labour confederation (Confederación General de Trabajo Independiente, or CGTI) formed by the illegal Socialist Party in the 1960s.

Since the crushing of the labour movement in 1948, the labour force had expanded rapidly and wage earners formed a growing proportion of the total. The emphasis on agro-exports had produced a marked rise in the size and importance of the rural proletariat while many small farmers felt threatened by the growth of large-scale agro-enterprises. This presented opportunities for the dictatorship's political opponents, but labour organizations (particularly in rural areas) met with stiff resistance from employers backed by the National Guard. The success of the construction workers gave a new lease of life to the organized labour movement, and the FSLN was particularly quick to exploit the new opportunities registering its greatest successes in rural areas.

Somoza's decision in 1974 to seek (and inevitably win) a further seven-year presidential term provided the catalyst for a regrouping of the opposition forces. The result was the Unión Democrática de Liberación (UDEL) which was led by Pedro Joaquín Chamorro, and which brought disgruntled Conservatives and Liberals (notably Sacasa's splinter group) together with the PLI, the PSC, the PSN and the CGTI. This was the broadest opposition group yet formed against Somocismo, involving both pro-Moscow Communists and representatives of the traditional elite, and it marked an important change from the sectarianism and personalism of the past. Nevertheless, UDEL excluded the FSLN, who denounced it on orthodox Marxist lines for class collaboration, and did not receive endorsement from U.S. officials, who remained loyal to Somocismo and disturbed by the presence of Communists in the opposition. Equally, it did not receive support from all sections of the private sector.

The private sector may have resented the *competencia desleal* of the Somoza group after the 1972 earthquake, but complete anti-Somoza solidarity was undermined by the existence of plenty of profitable opportunities. After a period of relative stagnation from 1969 to 1972, the Nicaraguan economy experienced rapid growth again in 1973 and 1974 as a result of post-earthquake reconstruction and a sharp recovery in the fortunes of export agriculture. Standard Fruit re-entered the country in 1972 and banana exports accelerated rapidly, while cotton began its third post-war boom in 1970 with cotton exports reaching a peak in the middle of the decade. The cost of fertilizers, however, had soared as a result of the 1973 oil crisis and the expansion of cotton could take place only through the incorporation of new lands. This put pressure on domestic food production, which declined in per capita terms, and the high levels of inflation after 1972 made the situation facing the rural labour force (40 per cent of whom were landless) more and more intolerable.

The formation of UDEL presented a challenge to both Somoza and the FSLN. UDEL gave prominence to the FSLN's older rival, the PSN, and it advocated a strategy of tactical class alliances which the FSLN had consistently rejected. The Marxist line of the Frente did not rule out the possibility of membership by non-Marxists, particularly radical Catholics, but the FSLN's hostility was still very profound towards the Nicaraguan bourgeoisie and its collaboration with Somoza. The minuscule FSLN therefore undertook a spectacular kidnapping of leading members of the Nicaraguan elite at the end of 1974, which brought it to national (and international) prominence and re-asserted the Frente's strategy of armed struggle as an alternative to UDEL's emphasis on a broad anti-Somoza alliance and dialogue.

The kidnappings obliged Somoza to meet almost all the Frente's demands, including the release from prison of several of its leaders. As a result the humiliated dictator unleashed the most ferocious wave of repression since the foundation of Somocismo. Although the dynasty was prepared to use force where necessary – notably in 1948, 1956–7 and 1967 – indiscriminate repression had not been the hallmark of either Somoza's father or brother, both of whom had tolerated some press and radio criticism of the regime and had usually released their opponents from prison after a discreet period. Anastasio, however, was unsympathetic to such sophistication and responded to the kidnappings by imposing a state of siege, martial law, press censorship and a campaign of terror under the control of the National Guard. The result was international condemnation by human rights groups, which brought Somoza to unwelcome prominence in the Carter administration's foreign policy at the beginning of 1977; at the same time, Nicaragua's private sector – the boom years now ended – began to distance itself from the regime. New tax increases were greeted with a call for a boycott by COSEP, capital flight began in earnest in 1977 and the regime was forced to rely on foreign borrowings, much of it from U.S. banks, in order to finance the government deficit and maintain currency stability.

The wave of repression did succeed in weakening the FSLN, which split into three groups. Significantly, two of these *tendencias* – the Tendencia Proletaria (TP) and Guerra Popular Prolongada (GPP) – assumed that the Nicaraguan revolution would be a long, drawn-out struggle involving patient ideological work among the urban (favoured by TP) and rural (favoured by GPP) masses. The third *tendencia* felt that the internal Nicaraguan situation had disintegrated so rapidly that the FSLN should press for an immediate full-fledged insurrection. This Tendencia Insurreccional (TI), led by Daniel and Humberto Ortega, was therefore obliged to accept the necessity for tactical alliances with non-Marxist opponents of the regime in order to ensure the success of the insurrection. This position prevailed within the leadership of the FSLN, the TI (or 'Terceristas', as they were also labelled) receiving a further boost when it engineered the formation in October 1977 of a group of twelve distinguished Nicaraguans (*los doce*) who insisted on the FSLN's participation in any post-Somoza regime. In the same month, the Terceristas attempted a national insurrection, but it was easily defeated by Somoza and publicly condemned as premature and adventurist by the other two tendencies.

Under pressure from the Carter administration, Somoza – who had barely recovered from two heart attacks – lifted the state of siege in September 1977. This provided the signal for a wave of protests against the regime. Yet Somoza still felt fairly secure. The National Guard was loyal and had shown, against the Terceristas, that it could be effective against a guerrilla attack; U.S. economic and military aid was still flowing, despite the criticisms of the Carter administration; and Somoza's opponents – Marxist and non-Marxist – were still far from united. The situation changed dramatically, however, with the murder in January 1978 of Pedro Joaquín Chamorro – editor of *La Prensa,* charismatic leader of UDEL and a lifelong opponent of the Somozas. The assassination, in which Somoza's son and heir apparent was implicated, produced a wave of strikes and spontaneous uprisings. More significantly, it galvanized the opponents of the regime into dialogue and produced in a few months an anti-Somoza unity which had not been achieved in the previous four decades.

By May 1978 the unification talks had produced a new organization in the Frente Amplio Opositor (FAO), which embraced UDEL together with the remaining factions of the Conservative Party. Private-sector support for the FAO was secured by the participation of the Movimiento Democrático Nicaragüense (MDN), formed in March by Alfonso Robelo, a leading Nicaraguan businessman and critic of Somoza. The FSLN was not a member of the FAO, but *los doce* agreed to join, thereby guaranteeing the Frente at least a minority position in a post-Somoza government if negotiations succeeded in removing the dictator.

The FSLN, still a minuscule and divided organization of fewer than a thousand members, ran the risk of being marginalized by the FAO despite the presence of *los doce.* However, the spontaneous uprisings of January and February had strengthened the position of the TI and opened the way for unification with the other two *tendencias* (that was finally achieved in March 1979). The Frente's answer to the FAO was the formation in July 1978 of the Movimiento Pueblo Unido (MPU), which included student and youth organizations, Communists and socialists (now weaned from UDEL) and the small labour organizations controlled by the Marxist left (including the Asociación de Trabajadores del Campo [ATC] established in 1977 by the Frente). The MPU, however, lacked the broad appeal of the FAO and represented a defensive move by the Frente in response to the success at unification of the non-Marxist anti-Somocistas.

By mid-1978, therefore, there were two clearly defined alternatives to Somoza, the non-Marxist FAO and the Marxist MPU. The FAO united the traditional opponents of the regime with the private sector and the Christian Democrats (PSC). It used strikes by the private sector to weaken the regime, enjoyed some support within the Carter administration (which suspended arms supplies to Somoza in 1978) and was confident that it could provide a transition to a post-Somoza regime through negotiations or mediation. The MPU, by contrast, pinned its hopes on armed struggle and a nation-wide insurrection, relying on a direct appeal by its mainly Marxist organizations to the most disadvantaged groups in society.

The FAO's position was not helped by a certain ambivalence in the Carter administration towards Somoza. Responding to pressure from Somoza's many friends in the U.S. Congress, President Carter wrote to the dictator in mid-1978 congratulating him on an improvement in the human rights situation at the same time as his aides were trying to assemble support for a package which would lead to the resignation of the dictator, retention of the National Guard and exclusion of the FSLN – a package rapidly dubbed 'Somocismo without Somoza'. The FAO's position was further weakened by the Frente's seizure of the National Palace, which housed the Nicaraguan Congress in August. This action badly humiliated Somoza and triggered off a wave of spontaneous uprisings in September, convincing the Insurrecionistas – now dominant in the Frente and the MPU – of the correctness of their strategy. The seizure of the palace and the subsequent uprisings, although defeated by the National Guard, swelled the ranks of the FSLN so that by the end of the year their numbers had reached 3,000 compared with 10,000 for the Guard.

The challenge from the FSLN gave a new urgency to those looking for a negotiated solution, above all the FAO and the Carter administration. The former's policy of strikes and business closures had not succeeded in crippling the dictatorship, which continued to receive substantial foreign loans (including a major loan from the International Monetary Fund in May 1979), while the latter began to take seriously the revolutionary challenge posed by the Frente and MPU. Even Somoza was finally forced to acknowledge the logic of negotiations and agreed to accept a U.S. initiative under which an OAS team (formed by the United States, the

Dominican Republic and Guatemala) would mediate between him and the FAO. The team began work in mid-October and immediately ran into difficulties over both Somoza's insistence on serving out his term until 1981 and Washington's desire to retain a political role for Somoza's Liberal Party and the National Guard. By the end of October, *los doce* – the only link between the FAO and the Frente – had resigned from the FAO. The following month the Frente, which had watched the mediation process with deep suspicion, returned to armed struggle, prompting the FAO to accept Somoza's call for direct negotiations. This provoked further resignations from the FAO, so that by the beginning of 1979 the initiative had shifted dramatically to the insurrectionary strategy advocated by the Terceristas. The mediation effort finally collapsed when Somoza refused to accept the OAS terms for a national plebiscite on his continuing in power.

In February 1979 the FSLN seized the opportunity afforded by the collapse of the negotiations to broaden its base of support by forming the Frente Patriótico Nacional (FPN), which included *los doce,* the PLI and the Partido Popular Social Cristiano (PPSC), which had split from the PSC in the mid-1970s. The programme of the FPN had a much broader appeal than earlier documents associated with the FSLN and MPU, and it provided the basis for political collaboration with the remainder of the FAO, including the private sector. There was no doubt, however, that the failure of negotiations and the drift towards insurrection had raised the FSLN – formally united in March 1979 – to a dominant position within the anti-Somocista coalition.

The final offensive was launched at the end of May. By this time, the Somoza regime was internationally isolated; several Latin American countries had withdrawn recognition and the Sandinistas were receiving arms through Costa Rica from Panama, Venezuela and Cuba. The Carter administration made a final effort to resurrect its 'Somocismo without Somoza' project but was decisively defeated in the OAS, which accepted the guarantees on political pluralism, a mixed economy and non-alignment offered by a five-member junta appointed by the anti-Somoza alliance in June. The dictator resigned and handed over power to the unknown Francisco Urcuyo on 17 July, his departure to Miami prompting the final disintegration of the National Guard. The victors marched into Managua on 19 July ending a war which had cost an estimated 50,000 lives out of a population of some 3 million.

The events leading up to the fall of Somoza demonstrated the importance of unity in the struggle against the dictatorship. The broad coalitions, first UDEL and later the FAO, had shown the depth of opposition to the Somoza dynasty but had failed to mobilize sections of the labour movement and relied too heavily on U.S. support to persuade the dictator to step down. On the other hand, the FSLN and the MPU had made important progress in incorporating the labour movement into the struggle (particularly rural workers) and posed a direct military challenge to the dictatorship by the end of 1978, but their militants were still no match for the heavily armed National Guard. The failure of negotiations and the collapse of the mediation effort left the FAO with no alternative other than co-operation with the Frente or rapprochement with Somoza; that it chose the former is a tribute to the political skills of the FSLN and the contempt in which the Somoza dictatorship was held.

The new alliance which emerged after February 1979 finally brought together all the social and political groups opposed to the dictatorship. The urban youth, students and workers, were attracted to the FSLN by its courage and daring, most accepting its authority and leadership in the armed struggle. By June, the number of militants trained and equipped by the Frente was sufficient to challenge the National Guard on military grounds, while the dictatorship had become completely isolated politically. Although many groups within the broad alliance had reservations over the wisdom of co-operation with the Frente, the strategy was devastatingly effective in undermining both Somoza and Somocismo.

THE RISE AND FALL OF SANDINISTA RULE

The flight of Somoza and the collapse of the National Guard signalled a total military victory for the anti-Somocista coalition, but the price paid was a ravaged economy in which GDP fell by 26.4 per cent in 1979 in addition to the decline of 7.8 per cent in 1978. International reserves had been completely drained out of the country, and Somoza had left a $1.6 billion debt, much of which had never been invested in Nicaragua and could not be serviced. Agricultural exports were badly affected by the civil war – cotton planting was reduced to the levels of the early 1950s – and inflation leapt to 60 per cent as a consequence of severe shortages.

Now that the dictator had fallen the anti-Somocista coalition also began to experience difficulties.[30] The agreement reached in Costa Rica (the

---

[30] Somoza was assassinated in Paraguay in September 1980; circumstantial evidence suggested that his murder was the work of the FSLN.

Puntarenas Pact) called for the five-member Junta to establish political pluralism, a mixed economy and a non-aligned foreign policy. The first goal would be underwritten by a Council of State with minority FSLN membership and free elections to be called at some unspecified date, while a non-partisan national army would be constructed to replace the National Guard. The FSLN, however, had emerged from the insurrection in a much stronger position than the groups with which it had made a tactical alliance and which had failed to obtain any guarantees from them regarding implementation of the programme agreed at Puntarenas. The Sandinistas enjoyed undisputed control of the battle-hardened military forces which had defeated the National Guard, whose rump had fled across the border to Honduras. Thus, the FSLN, which only a year before had still been a very small and divided organization, was in a highly advantageous position to determine the initial stages of the Nicaraguan Revolution through its grip on military power – and its hidden majority on the Junta. Daniel Ortega was the only avowed member of the FSLN on the Junta, but Moises Hassan – a leader of both the MPU and the FPN – was a close sympathizer and Sergio Ramírez had been a secret, non-combatant member of the FSLN since 1975.

The first step taken by the FSLN was the construction of a standing army, the Ejército Popular Sandinista (EPS), and a police force, Policía Sandinista. As their names imply, these organizations were highly partisan; they laid great stress on political education and training was largely in the hands of Cubans and Eastern Europeans. (Offers of help in training from the United States, Panama and Venezuela were politely, but firmly, refused.) Opposition to the construction of a partisan army, a clear breach of the Puntarenas Pact, was muted until the end of 1979, when Bernardino Larios (a former National Guard officer) was replaced as Minister of Defence by Humberto Ortega – a member of the FSLN National Directorate and commander-in-chief of the EPS. By the end of 1980, the EPS exceeded the size of the National Guard at its peak and, following the introduction of conscription in 1983, leapt to more than 60,000 with recruits passing into the reserves after their two years of service.

The cabinet appointed by the Junta in July 1979 gave the key economic portfolios (with the exception of agrarian reform) to representatives of the private sector. These ministers faced the daunting task of renegotiating the foreign debt, co-ordinating foreign aid through the Fondo Internacional de Reconstrucción (FIR) and channeling credit to the private and public sectors. In the initial stages progress in this area was relatively smooth; foreign lending from bilateral, multilateral and commercial sources was substantial and the debt was successfully rescheduled in two stages on generous terms. The government's priorities were laid out in a document known as 'Plan-80'; special emphasis was placed on the recovery of agro-exports, wage increases were held below the rate of inflation and real GDP rose by 11 per cent in 1980 and a further 5.3 per cent in 1981.

In the early stages of the economic recovery programme, the main challenge came not from the private sector but from the ultra-left. These groups felt that the essentially conservative nature of the government's economic policy (even the Somocista Labour Code was not repealed) represented a betrayal of the revolution and they reacted by provoking strikes and demonstrations. The FSLN responded harshly, using the state of emergency to imprison the ultra-left leaders and ban their organizations early in 1980, while making some concessions to land invasions led by the pro-Sandinista ATC. The agrarian-reform programme was accelerated in mid-1981, when a law was passed to permit expropriation of under-utilized or abandoned non-Somocista properties, but efficient agro-exporters were left unaffected and no upper limit was placed on farm size (unlike in El Salvador).

In some respects the reconstruction of the shattered economy was the easiest stage of the revolution for the government because both the FSLN and the private-sector groups in the anti-Somocista coalition were in broad agreement on what was required. The nine-member National Directorate of the FSLN in which the three *tendencias* were equally represented, remained committed to the goal of socialism in Nicaragua, but this was seen as a long-term objective. For both theoretical and practical reasons it was recognized that the private sector had an important part to play in the work of reconstruction. The Directorate argued, however, that the long-term objective could not be postponed altogether and the first step was the creation of a dynamic state sector (Area Propiedad del Pueblo, or APP); this was achieved through the expropriation of all Somocista properties together with the nationalization of financial institutions, foreign trade and national resources (including mining).

These measures, which would have provoked major private sector opposition in other Latin American countries, produced hardly a ripple in Nicaragua. The Somocista properties, which included 20 per cent of the arable land and some of the most efficient farms and factories, were clearly the spoils of war, while the financial institutions – drained by capital flight – were bankrupt. The expropriated agricultural properties, producing many agro-exports, were turned into state farms under the direction of a new Ministry of Agrarian Reform, and by 1980 the APP had control of 34 per cent of GDP.

Despite the moderate nature of economic policy in the first stage of the revolution, the private sector umbrella organization (COSEP) was in open conflict with the government by the end of 1981, with several of its leaders in prison or exile and one killed. The strained relationship was not so much because of the economic policy of the government (although as early as November 1979, COSEP had publicly aired its concern over the future of private enterprise) as of the political programme of the Sandinistas. The flight of Somoza had led to the total collapse of the old political institutions and the National Directorate of the FSLN, all of whom were Marxists with profound respect for the Cuban Revolution, proceeded to reconstruct the Nicaraguan state along the principles of democratic centralism. This left little room for political influence, or even power-sharing, by the private sector.

The repression during the last years of the Somoza regime had made it difficult for the FSLN – or any other party – to develop mass organizations. In 1977, the Frente had set up associations for both rural workers (the Asociación de Trabajadores del Campo, or ATC) and women (the Asociación de Mujeres ante la Problemática Nacional, or AMPRONAC), but they had not yet risen to the status of mass organizations by July 1979. Sandinista control over urban labour, the small peasantry and the urban petit-bourgeoisie was less secure at the time of the revolution, and the Frente faced competition among all these social forces from the other political parties and their trade-union affiliates. By the end of 1981 the position had changed dramatically. The Central Sandinista de Trabajadores (CST) had acquired a dominant position among urban labour, the pro-Sandinista Unión Nacional de Agricultores y Ganaderos (UNAG) was gaining a strong foothold among the small- and medium-size peasantry, the ATC had consolidated its position among the rural landless workers and the women's association (the Asociación de Mujeres Nicaragüenses 'Luisa Amanda Espinoza', or AMNLAE) had made great strides. The neighbourhood Comités de Defensa Sandinista (CDS), modelled on their Cuban equivalents, had acquired major importance as a result of their role in food rationing and the organisation of militias. The non-Sandinista 'mass' organizations had been reduced to a handful of small labour federations linked to various opposition parties.

The success of the Sandinista mass organizations provided the key to the subsequent consolidation of Sandinismo and was made possible by a variety of factors. First and foremost, by thwarting the creation of popular organizations Somocismo had left a *tabula rasa,* allowing the most dynamic forces in the revolution to start from scratch. Second, the Sandinistas thwarted efforts by their left-wing rivals to gain a foothold among the unorganized masses. Third, all efforts by foreign governments (particularly the United States) to help establish non-Sandinista mass organizations were resisted. Last but not least, public recognition that support for Sandinismo could bring positive results (e.g., ration cards issued by the CDS) was a powerful stimulus for membership in one of the mass organizations.

The Frente's grip on political institutions was increased by a number of cabinet changes at the end of 1979 and changed qualitatively in April 1980, when the composition of the Council of State was announced. Instead of the minority Sandinista position agreed in the Puntarenas Pact, the Frente with its mass organizations now enjoyed an absolute majority. Elections, it was also announced, would not be held for five years. Furthermore, by forming an alliance (Frente Patriótico Revolucionario, or FPR) with sympathetic political parties (including the PLI), the Sandinistas weakened still further the opportunities for the private sector and its political representatives to influence policy. Shorn of power, their two members on the Junta (Alfonso Robelo and Violeta Chamorro) resigned to be replaced by two non-Sandinistas, Arturo Cruz and Rafael Córdoba acceptable to the Frente. Robelo's efforts to turn his MDN into a major opposition party were thwarted by the Sandinistas, and he soon left Nicaragua to become a leader of the counter-revolution.

The private sector was visibly shaken by the departure of Robelo, but the FSLN acted quickly to provide reassurances on the future of private enterprise. The Directorate, both publicly and privately, distinguished between the 'patriotic' and the 'treacherous' bourgeoisie, stressing that the former had a role to play in the economic sphere. With some reluctance, COSEP participated in the Council of State until late in 1980. By that time, the relationship between the Frente and COSEP had deteriorated badly as a result of complaints that the private sector had abused its freedom by engaging in decapitalization and capital flight. Tough penalties were introduced for decapitalization, foreign-exchange controls were reinforced and in September 1981 the Junta introduced a state of economic and social emergency, under which several COSEP leaders were imprisoned.

Intervention by the Mexican government led to an improvement in the relations with the private sector in 1982, but by then the Sandinistas faced opposition from a variety of other quarters. Sandinista troops over-reacted to a riot in the Atlantic coast town of Bluefields in September 1980, driving large numbers of Miskitos and other ethnic minorities into the armed counter-revolution. The Atlantic coast population, which had been largely ignored by Somoza and had played virtually no part in the insurrection, objected to the crude efforts by the Sandinistas to incorporate them into the Nicaraguan revolution. The relocation by force of many Miskitos raised questions internationally regarding Sandinista respect for human rights, and it took the Frente several years to adopt a more flexible policy designed to drive a wedge between the Atlantic coast's desire for autonomy and the counter-revolution's efforts to end Sandinista rule.

The Frente's most formidable opponent was always the Reagan administration. The National Directorate assumed that a confrontation with the United States was inevitable but hoped that it could be postponed until after the consolidation of Sandinismo. From the start the Carter administration had grave misgivings about the Frente and looked with disfavour on Nicaragua's abstention in the United Nations vote condemning the Soviet invasion of Afghanistan. The use of Cubans to train the EPS and their presence in large numbers during the 1980 literacy campaign was not well received, and the administration noted with displeasure the close ties established in March 1980 with the Soviet Union. Nevertheless, President Carter was determined to avoid a repeat of the Cuban fiasco twenty years earlier and pushed through a not insubstantial aid programme (to which Congress insisted on adding a series of humiliating amendments which undermined whatever goodwill the aid programme might have generated).

President Reagan had made clear his total opposition to the Sandinistas even before taking office in January 1981. Once in office, however, he proceeded with caution. His first step was to suspend the aid programme, which was severed completely following allegations that the Sandinistas were heavily involved in supplying and training the guerrillas in El Salvador. The economic pressure was increased in 1982, when multilateral organizations with strong U.S. participation ceased lending to Nicaragua, whose U.S. sugar quota was cancelled in 1983. A trade embargo was finally imposed in 1985, but by that time trade between the two countries was already much reduced.

Despite the rhetoric, the Reagan administration was, like its predecessor, uncertain how to handle the Sandinistas, although the President himself never wavered in his desire to remove them. It was clear to all, with the benefit of hindsight, that the few months prior to the fall of Somoza had represented the best chance for a U.S. administration to influence the course of the Nicaraguan revolution. That chance had now passed and the administration was left with the power to weaken the Sandinistas but not overthrow them. Policy wavered between offers of a 'Finnish solution' and military pressure through the use of proxy troops. The latter option gained strength after the President gave approval in November 1981 for covert CIA operations against Nicaragua designed to destabilize the Sandinistas and interdict the supply of arms to the Salvadorean guerrillas.

The CIA set about organizing the undisciplined bands of former National Guardsmen ("contras") who had fled to Honduras in July 1979 and subsequently extracted revenge on the Sandinistas through cross-border raids. By the end of 1981, their numbers had been swollen by volunteers disillusioned with the Sandinista revolution (many from the Atlantic coast), although the military leadership remained firmly in Somocista hands. This control prevented a successful unification of all the anti-Sandinista forces, some of whom – notably Edén Pastora, who abandoned the revolution in July 1981 – refused to collaborate with the Honduran-based contras and established their own guerrilla campaign in Costa Rica. Under CIA influence, the contras became a more serious threat to the Sandinistas, although in open combat they were no match for the EPS (armed with Soviet and Cuban equipment since 1981). The discovery in 1984 that the CIA had mined Nicaraguan harbours, damaging foreign ships, temporarily weakened U.S. congressional support for the contras, but an unprecedented personal campaign by President Reagan had led to an increase in funding by 1986. By then, however, it was clear that the contras lacked the capacity to hold any Nicaraguan territory permanently, let alone overthrow the Sandinistas, while support for the contras had driven the Reagan administration into numerous violations of both international and U.S. domestic law.

The tension between the Reagan administration and the Sandinistas was viewed with increasing concern by other countries. The Nicaraguan revolution enjoyed overwhelming international support in its early days and the FSLN had won the support of the Socialist International (SI) within which the Sandinistas had observer status. The disillusionment of Costa Rican and Venezuelan social democrats over the course of the revolution led to a serious crisis in the SI in 1982, but the official policy remained one of critical support for the revolution and several SI leaders, notably Spain's Felipe González, acted as unofficial intermediaries between the Sandinistas and the Reagan administration. Other Latin American countries viewed with horror the prospect of U.S. military intervention in Central America and the Contadora group (Mexico, Venezuela, Colombia and Panama) was formed in January 1983 to seek a peaceful solution to the regional crisis. This group devised a twenty-one-point programme of demilitarization and democratization that all Central American countries would have been required to sign. However, the Acta de Contadora did not win the support of the Reagan administration, which did not welcome any agreement that might leave the Sandinistas in power, and despite its formal support for Contadora Washington was able to undermine the process of negotiations through its regional allies (Costa Rica, El Salvador and Honduras). Contadora was broadened in late 1985 by the formation of a support group (Argentina, Brazil, Uruguay and Peru), but by then tension between Nicaragua and its neighbours was so great that there was little chance of agreement on a peace treaty even without U.S. misgivings. The Reagan administration, for its part, launched bilateral talks in Mexico with the Sandinistas in mid-1984, but these broke down in early 1985 in an atmosphere of mutual recrimination and distrust.

The impasse between Nicaragua and its neighbours was made somewhat easier following the election of Oscar Arias Sánchez as president of Costa Rica in 1986. After an uncertain start to his presidency, Arias committed himself to a negotiated solution among the five Central American governments with the Contadora group playing only a secondary role. The Arias plan, launched in February 1987, was endorsed by all five Central American presidents in August of the same year and held out the prospect of an end to the regional crisis. It committed each Central American administration to a dialogue with opposition groups through a National Reconciliation Commission, to an amnesty for those who had taken up arms against the government and to an end to outside military support for 'irregular forces'.

As far as Nicaragua was concerned, the Arias plan implicitly acknowledged the legitimacy of the Sandinista government and promised an end to civil war in return for a significant degree of political pluralism and democratization. The plan therefore went against the preferences of President Reagan, but his administration – weakened by the scandals surrounding the sale of arms to Iran and the illegal diversion of funds to the contras – was unable to carry its Central American policy through Congress where the Democratic Speaker Jim Wright was increasingly active in shuttle diplomacy between Washington and Managua. The Reagan administration tried to maintain the contras in existence despite a renewed congressional ban on military aid, but the Arias plan gathered momentum and a cease-fire was signed in March 1988 between the Sandinistas and the contras in Nicaragua. This cease-fire survived with only minor infringements into the Bush administration at the start of 1989, by which time it was clear that the contras – deprived of U.S. military assistance – were close to collapse. In February 1989, at the third meeting of the Central American presidents under the Arias plan, a decision was taken unanimously to adopt measures leading to the disbandment of the contras and the Sandinistas felt sufficiently confident to advance the electoral calendar and hold elections in February rather than November 1990.

The Nicaraguan economy was seriously undermined by U.S. pressure, but economic performance was not helped by many of the policies adopted by the government. Faced with an exchange rate which became progressively overvalued, non-traditional exports steadily declined; agro-exports were protected by policies designed to supply inputs at a price which guaranteed a positive return, but they could not be protected from falling world prices and total export earnings had fallen to $200 million in 1988 compared with $646 million in 1978. The system of food subsidies used to protect the real incomes of the urban poor became unmanageable as inflation widened the gap between producer and consumer prices, so that the fiscal deficit reached intolerable levels. Efforts by the government to phase out the subsidies in 1985 and 1986 pushed inflation into three-digit figures without curbing the fiscal deficit, which by then was determined primarily by defence spending in response to the contra threat. The growth of black markets accelerated in response to high inflation and official controls, encouraging migration to Managua and a boom in unlicensed petty commerce. Official channels of distribution were increasingly by-passed, production declined almost continuously after 1981 and real GDP per head in 1988 (in which year the country was hit by a hurricane) was back to the level of the 1950s and the lowest in Central America.

By the beginning of 1989, inflation was running at over 100 per cent per month and the Sandinistas faced the prospect of a complete collapse of the monetary and financial system. Orthodox measures to halt inflation could no longer be avoided and – gambling on the collapse of the contras – the Sandinistas began to lay off thousands of public-sector workers including members of the armed forces, putting at risk their chances in the 1990 presidential elections. The exchange rates in the official and parallel markets were brought closer together and for the first time in many years relative prices began to acquire a semblance of rationality, although the private sector remained extremely reluctant to invest in view of the continuing economic and political uncertainties.

Nicaragua's economic difficulties did not prevent the further consolidation of Sandinismo. The early years of the revolution had yielded substantial advances in health, education and literacy (a highly successful literacy campaign had been adopted in 1980), which were only partially reversed during the years of economic decline. These achievements and the growth of the mass organizations gave the Frente a solid base among the workers and peasants it regarded as its natural constituency; the EPS, the militias and the reserves gave the government a potential military strength of around 300,000 – a huge proportion of the adult population. The state of emergency reintroduced in March 1982 was regularly extended and gave the authorities considerable powers to control or suppress dissent. The opposition daily *La Prensa* survived in heavily censored form until 1986, when it was closed for eighteen months. With television under state control and independent radio subject to severe restrictions, the FSLN gradually acquired a dominant position over the means of communication.

The Frente did not, however, seek or achieve the total elimination of internal opposition. Just as the Sandinistas believed in a patriotic or democratic bourgeoisie which would collaborate with the economic priorities laid down in state planning, so they also hoped for the emergence of a loyal opposition which would accept Sandinista hegemony in the new political institutions. The decision to bring forward the elections by one year (anticipating by two days the re-election of President Reagan in November 1984) forced the issue and seven parties (including the FSLN) ranging from the ultra-left to the right-of-centre registered. The government's efforts to involve The Coordinadora Democrática, which represented a right-wing coalition formed in the Council of State in 1982, failed, and the Coordinadora withdrew from the elections. The elections gave the FSLN the presidency (Daniel Ortega became the chief executive) and a solid two-thirds majority in the new National Assembly, where the other political parties played the role of official opposition with varying degrees of reluctance. A new constitution drafted by the Assembly went into force in January 1987 with power heavily centralized in the hands of the President.

The elections clearly revealed the limitations of the opposition parties and left the Catholic Church as the major force resisting the consolidation of Sandinismo. The hierarchy had been weakened in the early years of the revolution by the growth of the popular Church and the presence of several radical priests in the government. However, with his promotion to the rank of cardinal Archbishop Miguel Obando y Bravo began to criticize the government with the same doggedness he had used against Somoza and attracted large crowds to his public sermons. In their dealings with the hierarchy the Sandinistas alternated between repression and dialogue, while hoping – perhaps naively – that the Church would respect and uphold national laws (including conscription). Freedom of religion itself, however, was not an issue between the State and the Church.

Another source of opposition to the Sandinistas came from within the mass organizations themselves. In its first five years the agrarian reform programme had been used to build up state farms, develop co-operatives and give title to the small peasantry with insecure property rights. The top priority had been the maintenance of agro-exports, and although the state farm sector began to decline after 1982, the number of landless workers receiving individual title was very small. Pressure from the ATC and UNAG in 1985 forced a change of policy from the government; the agrarian reform law was amended in January 1986 to conform to the new policy, and thousands of landless peasants received titles to land which in many cases had been previously used for agro-exports. The change was dramatic; within a short period, the conservative Nicaraguan reform programme had been radicalized affecting a majority of the rural labour force. At the same time the new programme threatened to undermine the last remaining sources of export earnings and widen still further the trade deficit.

The U.S. embargo did not cripple Nicaraguan trade with Western countries, and exports, in particular, remained diversified. Nonetheless, dependence on the socialist countries for strategic imports (e.g., oil) and balance-of-payments support had steadily increased. The Soviet Union repeatedly made it clear that it would not underwrite the economic and financial costs of the revolution, as it had done in Cuba, but the geopolitical logic of the tension between Nicaragua and the United States obliged the Russians to increase their commitment year after year. By the beginning of 1989 Nicaragua was receiving special terms from the socialist countries for its agro-exports, had became an observer at COMECON meetings and hoped eventually to be a full member. Western European bilateral aid was still flowing to Nicaragua, which was a beneficiary of multilateral EC aid under a co-operation agreement signed in 1985 with Central America, but its relative importance was declining.

The adoption of the Constitution in January 1987 completed the institutionalization of the Sandinista revolution. If judged by the public commitment to political pluralism, non-alignment and a mixed economy, the revolution had failed since these features were present only in a heavily distorted form. Yet Nicaragua had not become a second Cuba and the Frente could claim with some justification that Sandinismo had created a new Nicaragua rather than another Cuba. The Sandinistas had neither the will nor the capacity to administer all branches of production and individual titles to land (which could be inherited but not sold) were firmly established in agriculture; large-scale private producers in agriculture and industry were tolerated, subject to numerous restrictions on prices, credit and foreign exchange, while a handful of multinational companies continued to do business in Nicaragua and the Constitution promised a new foreign investment law. Criticism of the regime was possible within strict limits and the rudiments of a loyal opposition had emerged in the Assembly; foreign relations were maintained with a wide variety of countries and diplomatic ties still existed with the United States, but the relationship was closest with the socialist countries and Nicaragua's voting pattern conformed closely to Cuba's in the United Nations.

The construction of a new Nicaragua did not, however, mean that the Sandinistas had succeeded in resolving the accumulated problems from the past. The FSLN appeared unwilling to cede power through elections; the dream of a non-partisan armed force, first voiced by the United States in the 1920s, remained remote. The Sandinistas had hoped to build an economy less dependent on primary exports and world market conditions, but had been reduced to managing a stagnant economy, swollen foreign debts and massive balance-of-payments deficits. The Frente retained considerable popular support, yet production levels and real wages were far below their peaks before the revolution, while fiscal and monetary orthodoxy had given way to printing money and accelerating inflation. The Atlantic coast population remained distrustful of rule from Managua and their integration into Nicaraguan life was still far from complete.

The dismal economic situation proved to be decisive in the February 1990 elections which ousted the Sandinistas from power. Although the Sandinistas were by far the single most important party contesting the elections, the formation of a broad coalition of opposition parties and the flooding of Nicaragua with international observers for six months beforehand offered the electorate a clear opportunity to demonstrate their opposition to policies which had contributed directly and indirectly to the collapse of the economy.

The new President, Violeta Chamorro,[31] assumed that the fall of the Sandinistas would be sufficient to guarantee the capital inflows needed to restore the economy to health. However, the tensions within the ruling coalition, the end of the Cold War and the statesmanlike behaviour of the Sandinistas in opposition undermined whatever enthusiasm potential donors might have shown for Nicaragua. Even the United States, which appeared as the main beneficiary of the Sandinista defeat, was slow to vote funds and even slower to disburse them so that progress towards lowering inflation and raising output remained painful.

The electoral defeat of the Sandinistas owed little to the campaign fought by the opposition. On the contrary, just as on numerous occasions in the previous decade, the record of the political forces seeking to prevent the consolidation of Sandinismo had been far from distinguished. The Frente's allies in the struggle against Somoza had shown extraordinary naiveté; the contras had indulged in appalling human rights violations without achieving any military success; the legal political parties weakened themselves through internal dissensions. The formation of a bloc of 14 parties to contest the 1990 elections was based on the most fragile unity, although it did at least offer a chance of defeating the FSLN by electoral means. The Carter administration lost a golden opportunity to promote democracy in Nicaragua by failing to force the resignation of Somoza one year earlier, while the Reagan administration stretched the Western alliance to its limit through its unilateral aggression against Nicaragua.

It was not only the Sandinistas' opponents whose judgement was frequently at fault. The National Directorate of the FSLN misjudged the Nicaraguan bourgeoisie by imagining that its 'patriotic' component would continue to produce and invest once deprived of access to political power as well as foreign exchange. The mixed-economy strategy was therefore prejudiced from the start, but the Sandinista state lacked the resources to take over the private sector's role. The leaders of the Frente sometimes exhibited a poor grasp of the subtleties of international diplomacy, depriving Nicaragua of part of its foreign support quite unnecessarily. The Directorate allowed Nicaragua's history to influence unduly its relations with the United States, whose leaders were clearly uninterested in or ignorant of past U.S. interventions in Central America.

The history of Nicaragua since 1930 has been, and remains, a tragic

---

[31] The widow of the murdered Pedro Joaquín Chamorro, she was also the first woman to be elected directly as President in a Latin American state.

one. An accident of geography has given Nicaragua all the costs of super-power attention without any of the benefits. Local difficulties, which in a less sensitively placed country would have been ignored by outside pow-ers, have provided an excuse for U.S. intervention. The Somozas under-stood the limitations on Nicaraguan sovereignty implied by the country's geographical location, and the founder of the dynasty showed himself to be a tactical genius in his manipulation of domestic opponents. His younger son, however, lacked the father's flair and brought into disrepute the country's client status. By the time of the revolution, few Nicaraguans were willing to re-establish the old order even without the Somoza family. The Sandinistas' attempt to create a new order allotted a role to the United States which was inconsistent with its superpower status, while the Rea-gan administration's attempts to humble the Sandinistas took no account of national pride. President Bush's determination to give a lower foreign policy priority to Nicaragua was made easier by the defeat of the Sand-inistas and the end of the Cold War. Yet this was small comfort for Nicaragua. With support from Eastern Europe and the Soviet Union rapidly crumbling, it was by no means clear at the start of the 1990s that the resources could be found from elsewhere to reverse the decline of the shattered economy; that, in turn, undermined the chances that the re-public would move swiftly to a more normal – less confrontational – pattern of domestic politics.

8

COSTA RICA SINCE 1930

In 1930 Costa Rica, with a landmass of 50,000 square kilometers (more than twice the size of El Salvador), had a population of scarcely half a million inhabitants. The capital, San José, had 50,000 inhabitants; no other town had a population of more than 8,000. More than 60 per cent of the economically active population of some 150,000 worked in agriculture. Production revolved around the cultivation of coffee, which was exported principally to the United States and the United Kingdom. The cultivation of bananas, the second most important export product, was controlled by the United Fruit Company. The country also exported cocoa beans, although in smaller quantities, to practically all of Europe. These three crops accounted for 94.3 per cent of Costa Rica's total income.

The traditional coffee economy had produced a social pyramid with the plantation workers at the base and the growers and exporters, the latter primarily of German descent, at the apex. The coffee growers and merchants also controlled credit, directly or indirectly, through the private banking institutions. Between the two extremes of the pyramid was an important group of small and medium-sized producers who maintained a relative social and economic independence, which had great significance in the national political system.

The development of banana production from the end of the nineteenth century on the Atlantic coast, together with the economic impact of the First World War, had produced some social and economic differentiation, but this was still of a secondary order. A new stratum of waged labour clearly began to take shape during this period, although it remained diversified and could not be strictly described in terms like 'working class' or 'proletariat' more appropriate to developed societies. Less noticeable,

This chapter was translated from the Spanish by Elizabeth Ladd.

but potentially more significant, was the emergence of a middle-class business sector during 1930s. The need to find substitutes for imported products which could not be obtained because of the world crisis and the search for new fields of production combined to stimulate intellectual nuclei which questioned the existing order, criticized the coffee oligarchy and foreign capital (especially North American capital) and sought fresh strategies for national development. The first stage in this process was the emergence of a generation of young people that was strongly influenced by Communism and *aprismo,* and evolved from a populist orientation to a Marxist-Leninist radicalism, founding the Costa Rican Communist Party in 1931. This movement was followed almost immediately by another which leaned more towards the reformist and nationalist currents contained in *aprismo.* This group founded the Centro para el Estudio de los Problemas Nacionales (Centre for the Study of National Problems) in 1940 under the intellectual leadership of Rodrigo Facio (1917–61); it later united with the political movement of José Figueres' Partido Acción Demócrata to establish the Partido Liberación Nacional (PLN) in October 1951, following the civil war of 1948.

Both these movements emerged from a tightly controlled social and political system. Except for the short dictatorship of the Tinoco brothers (1917–19), Costa Rican politics was dominated for the first thirty years of the century by two paternalistic and personalist liberal parties led by Cleto González Víquez and Ricardo Jiménez. The former, known in the country as Don Cleto, had already been president in 1906–10, and his second term (1928–32) was one of transition between the undisputed domination of the coffee growers and the rival groups whose emergence was accelerated by the crisis and who questioned the distribution of power in Costa Rica for the next two decades. It was, however, the third and last administration of Jiménez, better known as Don Ricardo (1932–36), which had to bear the brunt of the crisis.

Although the country had already undergone some democratic change, such as the introduction from 1902 of reforms which changed the traditional voting system into a universal, secret and direct ballot, politics remained under the control of the large coffee growers, importers and bankers, who were strongly linked together by financial and family ties. Contrary to the experience of the rest of Central America, the dominant elite in Costa Rica participated directly in the play of power rather than delegating it outright to the military or to outsiders.

The electoral campaign of 1931 was fought along traditional personalist lines. Even though the Costa Rica economy was feeling the first effects of the crisis, the election centred on well-known political figures who belonged to the dominant social group. Of the organizations contesting the poll of February 1932 the Republican Party's Carlos María Jiménez won 22 per cent; the National Republican Party's nominee Ricardo Jiménez won 46.6 per cent; and the remaining 29.1 per cent of the vote went to the Partido Unión Republicano (PUR) candidate Manuel Castro Quesada, who was backed by bankers and land-owners, and financed principally by Fernando Castro Cervantes, a well-known capitalist closely associated with the United Fruit Company. As expected, none of the candidates obtained the absolute majority required, and the final result produced a tense situation which culminated in a desperate attempt by Castro Quesada to seize power by taking over the Bella Vista garrison on the morning of 15 February 1932, the day after the elections. The ensuing armed encounter confirmed Ricardo Jiménez's victory at the ballot box and was consolidated with an amnesty for the rebels. What the country sacrificed in peace and order, the new administration gained in legitimacy and authority.

The Communist Party was not permitted to participate in these elections under its own name and nominated candidates only in the municipal elections, in the name of the Workers' and Peasants' Bloc. The party had been founded on 16 June 1931 by a group of law students who had formed ties with the artisans' and workers' guilds that already existed in Costa Rica. Although the party declared itself part of the Third International, this was not really the case. After the failures sustained in Nicaragua with Sandino, who in 1931 was declared a traitor who had sold out to imperialism, and in El Salvador with Farabundo Martí, who was disowned as a renegade after the massacre of 1932, the Comintern had abandoned the region, leaving the newborn Communist Party of Costa Rica in an orphaned state that would prove to be its salvation. The Communist movement had decisive importance in contemporary Costa Rican history out of all proportion to its size and without rival in the rest of the Caribbean, except Cuba.

The crisis which struck the country at the beginning of the 1930s created favourable conditions for the development of the Communist Party. After the coffee boom of 1924–29, the price of coffee registered a continuous decline. Taking 1929 as a base year with an index of 100, exports declined to 87 in 1930, 83 in 1931 and 43 in 1932. Taking 1925 as a base year with an index of 100, the price of coffee in London fell from

81 in 1930 to 43 in 1933. Banana exports declined from 7,323,481 bunches at a total price of $5,492,611 in 1928 to 2,908,836 bunches at a price of $1,493,512 in 1935. The impact on public finances was immediate. In round figures, revenues dropped from 35 million colones in 1929 to 23 million in 1932, rising to 26 million in 1934. The years 1930, 1931 and 1932 showed the largest fiscal deficit, creating conflict over the use of unbacked money for fiscal purposes. Imports declined from $20 million in 1920, of which $4 million was for raw materials, to, respectively, $11 million and $2.3 million in 1930, and $6 million and $1.7 million in 1932. Obviously such a marked deterioration in imports in general – and imports of raw materials in particular – indicates the general deterioration of the national economy and the grave decline in standard of living. Unemployment became particularly acute; according to official statistics which some considered too low, 27,000 persons were directly or indirectly affected. Of the unemployed, 75.65 per cent were agricultural workers and 19.67 per cent industrial workers.

Free of what Rómulo Betancourt (later president of Venezuela and at that time a member of the Communist Party of Costa Rica), called 'the ukases and incompetence of the International', the Costa Rican Communists brought the demands of the emerging social sectors into a national political system that demonstrated the necessary flexibility to assimilate them, albeit not without tension and violence. In August 1934 the Communist Party led a major banana strike on the Atlantic coast in the midst of social disturbances throughout the country. The final result, in spite of repression and resistance, was a clear improvement in the standard of living and working conditions of the banana-workers and the opening of a political breach in the liberal system in favour of free unionization and the right to strike.

The national political system, which throughout its evolution had demonstrated some significant autonomy from the dominant economic groups, demonstrated a capacity for reform and adaptation to new circumstances. By permitting the new political groups to formulate their demands, and even allowing many of these to be channelled through the Communist Party, the regime effectively legitimized itself and provided space for modernization. While it maintained an internationalist rhetoric with respect to the USSR, Costa Rican Communism observed in its internal policy an advanced reformist and social democratic line, oriented more towards the correction of abuses and excesses than towards a complete change in customs and practices. This opened up a political perspective which was unique in Latin America, excepting Cuba and Chile. On the one hand, the internal conditions of the country encouraged the formation of multi-class alliances for the achievement of urgent reforms and the promotion of a kind of protectionist nationalism, particularly with regard to the United States. On the other hand, from 1936 the Comintern's strategy coincided with the practice of the Costa Rican Communist Party, insofar as it sought to universalize the experience of the popular fronts in Europe. This consolidated both the local tendencies of the party and its subordination on the international front to the anti-fascist and anti-imperialist tasks so important to Comintern.

Contrary to what might be expected of a country as small and isolated as Costa Rica, the international situation enormously complicated internal politics. The German links of many of the principal coffee-growing and exporting families, the presence of pro-Franco and pro-Mussolini sectors in their respective communities and the volume of Costa Rican trade with the Axis countries, especially Germany, created serious difficulties for any internal alliance which sought not only the acceptance of internal reforms but also an anti-fascist foreign policy. Nevertheless, the urgent need for reforms forced the party into various attempts at political alliances. The first of these was with President Ricardo Jiménez, the indisputably brilliant leader of Creole liberalism, during the electoral campaign of 1939. A second, and far more important, alliance was formed in 1941–2 with the government of President Rafael Angel Calderón Guardia and Archbishop Monsignor Víctor M. Sanabria, leader of the Catholic Church. This pact lasted until the end of the government of Teodoro Picado (1944–8).

The rise of fascism had an especially acute impact on local politics in 1936, when the outbreak of the Spanish Civil War provoked strong confrontations and affected the election of 1936, won by León Cortés (1936–40). As the absolutely anti-communist candidate of the Republican National Party, Cortés won 60 per cent of the total vote and easily defeated the National Party's candidate, Octavio Beeche, an old conservative lawyer; the Communist Party, which campaigned as the Workers' and Peasants' Bloc, gained only 5 per cent of the vote.

The political sympathies of important national leaders for the political experience of Italy and Germany strengthened traditional family and financial ties that already existed between those countries and the coffee growers and exporters. Germany had become one of the principal buyers of Costa Rican coffee (18.9 per cent) and cocoa (80 per cent), and had indicated that it would purchase 40 per cent of the 1939 coffee crop.

Germans were not only the principal coffee growers but also owned 80 per cent of the sugar mills; the expatriate community continued to be bolstered by immigration, and some of its members had risen to occupy key positions in León Cortés' administration. Nevertheless, Cortés himself was less a fascist than attracted by German administrative efficiency, the authoritarian tendencies of which was not entirely alien to his centre-right political philosophy.

It is true, that Cortés praised those German elements who were clearly identified with Nazism, and even allowed them to implement anti-semitic policies from their public posts, particularly with regard to immigration and commercial activities of the Jewish minority in the country. However, he never tried seriously to modify the traditional political system, and his practice in the 1939 electoral campaign was no different from that of his predecessors. Cortés used all the power available to him to minimize the electoral results favourable to the Communists, and he undermined the candidacy of Ricardo Jiménez, then allied with the Communists, thus assuring the landslide victory of the official candidate, Dr Rafael A. Calderón Guardia, who obtained 90 per cent of the vote and who would soon become Cortés' strongest adversary and an ally of the Communists.

A variety of social and political sectors were represented in the government of Calderón Guardia: Cortés' own followers, representatives of national capital, elements of Francoist orientation, and a new group of young people who were seeking to promote institutional and political reform. This amalgam was rapidly split apart by the outbreak of the war. Educated in Belgium and inspired by progressive Catholic theology, Calderón Guardia opted firmly for a democratic alliance against the Axis. This placed him in opposition to the principal coffee families, who imposed such a comprehensive isolation or the President – personal, political and social – that he was forced to enter into an alliance with the Communist Party, his only electoral adversary in 1939. This alliance, although not alien to his mode of thinking in its social reform objectives, contradicted the very essence of his traditional Catholic conception of state and society.

The Calderón–Communist alliance placed the government on the side of the Allied powers whose incessant pressure soon produced concrete actions against the German minority in the country. And not only pro-Nazi elements were affected; persecution was generalized against all persons of Italian and German extraction. With external aid, the government drew up so-called blacklists, which were used to send whole families to camps located inside the country and in the United States. Those included in the blacklists had their goods confiscated in an arbitrary manner and were subjected to multiple abuses, giving rise to wide-spread administrative corruption that was predictably encouraged by the growing crisis of subsistence and the shortage of imported goods provoked by the war.

As the government's isolation from the sectors which had supported it in the election became more accentuated, the alliance with the Communist Party was legitimized by the entry of the USSR into the war against the Axis and by the atmosphere of reform in inter-American relations which Roosevelt's New Deal had created. This domestic and foreign situation also coincided with the Holy See's naming of Monsignor Víctor M. Sanabria (1899–1952) as archbishop of San José and head of the Costa Rican Catholic Church. A man of scarcely forty-two years, superior intelligence and sharp wit, well versed in the social doctrine of the Church and in the country's history, and a consummate politician came to the forefront of a church whose following constituted an absolute majority in the country. He naturally identified himself with the anti-Nazi forces, and he followed a coherent doctrine that led him to repudiate Marxism, although without fearing it or seeing it simply as an object for excommunication. When the Communist Party dissolved itself on 13 June 1943 and became the Partido Vanguardia Popular (PVP), its secretary-general, Manuel Mora, sent a public letter to the archbishop, obviously by prior agreement, asking if he believed there was any obstacle to prevent Catholic citizens from supporting, collaborating or allying themselves with the new party. Monsignor Sanabria answered the same day, assuring him that Catholics could subscribe to the programme and join the new group with no twinge of conscience. This did not, however, prevent Sanabria from taking the initiative to dispute the hitherto unchallenged jurisdiction over the unions enjoyed by the Communists. He sponsored the formation of the Confederación de Trabajadores Rerum Novarum under the direction of Father Benjamin Núñez, who would later become its leader, and the leading opposition activist José Figueres. Nevertheless, Sanabria's participation in the government alliance was decisive, both for the triumph of social reform and for Calderón Guardia's decision to participate actively in it to the end.

This alliance of government, Catholic Church and Communist Party in Costa Rica in the 1940s was more complex than it appeared, there being latent conflicts of fundamental nature within and among each of the factions that only came to light much later. The pact marked the beginning of a period that can be called the 'era of the enemy alliances', which lasted until shortly after the victory of the rebels in the civil war of 1948. On one side was the old coffee oligarchy, opposed to Calderón Guardia's anti-German policy, his social reforms and alliance with communism, irritated by the corruption in public administration and indignant over the government's electoral fraud. Allied with the oligarchy were the small business sectors, which possessed a distinct social and political programme but kept it in abeyance during the struggle against Calderón Guardia and the Communist Party.

The social reforms promulgated by Calderón Guardia's administration took a predominantly constitutional form. First, a new chapter was added to the 1871 constitution, whereby the rights of freedom of association, unionization and strikes were guaranteed, the state's obligation to support production and assure a just distribution of wealth was recognized, and workers were insured against illness, old age and death by a social security system that also provided maternity care. This system was financed through tripartite obligatory contributions by the government, employers and the insured, and was managed by a new independent body, the Social Security Fund. The right to be given notice and to collect unemployment benefits in the case of unjust dismissal was established, as were the rights to paid annual vacations, extra pay for overtime, and the like. The inclusion of these rights alongside the classical individual guarantees in the Constitution was opposed by capitalists – and by the U.S. embassy. However, the reforms still lacked a concrete mechanism for implementation, and a variety of specific laws needed to be passed to put the general principles outlined in the Constitution into effect. And the Calderón coalition faced the threat of defeat in the election of 1944.

Within the opposition to the Calderón–Communist government there were sectors, particularly the members of the Centre for the Study of National Problems, which supported social reform but rejected the procedures used to promote it as well as the political uses to which it was being put by the government. In the words of a leading opposition spokesman, the journalist Otilio Ulate, the reform was simply the 'opium of social guarantees', and the opposition candidate in the 1944 poll, ex-president León Cortés, announced his intention to have it repealed if he won. Indeed, this danger was so real that the anti-Communist union leader Benjamín Núñez voted for the government candidate, Teodoro Picado, simply to protect the new legislation.

Picado was unable to muster the sympathy and support enjoyed by

Calderón Guardia. A cultivated man, historian, lawyer and teacher, but of weak character, he was incapable of matching the political prowess of Cortés. Although the alliance with the PVP guaranteed him the support of important groups, his forces were distinctly inferior to those of the opposition. As a result, the government resorted to violence by armed bands and the intervention of the police in favour of the official candidate. The appearance of Communist 'shock troops', justified by the party as self-defense, exacerbated a political climate that was violent and intransigent, and contributed to the growing lack of legitimacy of the electoral institutions.

Some politicians – the PVP leader Mora among them – sought a candidacy of national consensus. But both Picado and Cortés refused to renounce their candidacies despite the fact that in September 1943 Congress approved the new Labour Law, which then ceased to be a major campaign issue. A joint procession led by President Calderón Guardia, Manuel Mora and Archbishop Sanabria in an open car through the streets of San José served only to unite the opposition behind Cortés. Picado, however, won the election of 13 February 1944 with 82,173 votes to Cortés' 44,435. But the evidence of fraud and popular support for the opposition suggested a very much closer result than was formally declared.

The North American perspective on events in Costa Rica during the Second World War and until 1948 was not always coherent or free of contradictions. At first, the U.S. view of the nature of the PVP coincided with that of other sectors, particularly that of Archbishop Sanabria. The small but important Communist Party was seen not to fit precisely into the rigid mould of the other Latin American Communist Parties, and it was perceived as possessing an ideology closer to that of the Congress of Industrial Organizations (CIO) in the United States than to that of the Third International. This view was, however, soon modified by the party's aggressive attitude towards capital, both national and foreign, particularly the United Fruit Company and the Electric Bond and Share Company, where conflict with the unions had become especially acute.

The dissatisfaction of local and U.S. capitalists was the determining factor which finally led the State Department to change its attitude towards the PVP, although less quickly than its embassy in Costa Rica since from the viewpoint of the general struggle against the Axis powers, the internal alliance between Communists and the Calderón Guardia and Picado administrations did not seem particularly strange or alarming. It should be remembered that in the same period a similar alliance was formed in Cuba under the government of Fulgencio Batista. In the case of Costa Rica a distinction must be made between the changes in U.S. attitude that arose from internal pressures, originating above all from local U.S. investors, and those modifications which came about as a result of the Cold War. Although the final consequences were the same, the different sources of similar behaviour permit an explanation of the vacillations that characterized U.S. policy towards Costa Rica, especially during the administration of Dr Calderón Guardia.

The legitimacy that the alliance against the Axis had conferred on the pact with the PVP disappeared definitively with the end of hostilities and beginning of the Cold War. Trips by opposition leaders, especially Otilio Ulate, to the United States and Europe brought the growing conflict between the United States and the Soviet Union to the forefront of Costa Rican public opinion and gave the opponents of the Picado regime a chance to denounce the danger of world communism and the lack of trustworthiness of its pacts and alliances. The development of the Cold War and the increase of U.S. pressure undoubtedly shook the alliance and augmented the misgivings of the Communists, although they still did not clearly understand the full nature of the changing international situation.

Less obvious, but no less important was the fact that the break-up of the wartime global alliance against the Axis powers effectively destroyed the only political project that existed within the Costa Rican regime. The reforms sponsored by the Communists were oriented towards a total restructuring of the state and national society that required the exceptionally favourable conditions provided by the world-wide struggle against fascism. When these conditions ceased to exist, the project collapsed. The Calderonistas lacked their own political project. They vegetated behind the Communist Party's programme, allowing the conflict with the opposition, to develop into the prospect of either the simple restoration desired by the traditional coffee sectors, or the dominion of the small business sector, whose political-military leader was José Figueres.

The expulsion of Figueres from Costa Rica in 1942, which the government accomplished by invoking reasons of national security and his possible connections and sympathies with Nazism, led to a period of exile in the United States, Mexico and Guatemala. His expulsion took place under circumstances about which there were contradictory explanations. According to Figueres' own version it was a simple matter of persecution by President Calderón Guardia, but according to Manuel Mora, it was the result of a direct action by the U.S. embassy. This version has not been corroborated by documents from the Department of State archives in Washington, although it is explicitly recounted in the memoirs of Ivonne Clays Spoelder, then Dr Calderón Guardia's wife. Politically opposed to the Calderón Guardia brothers, Figueres supported the candidacy of León Cortés in 1944 through his own political organization, Democratic Action, and, as a candidate for Congress, was a direct victim of the electoral fraud that gave victory to Picado.

In July 1943, Figueres had participated in the creation of a revolutionary Central American force to overthrow the dictatorships in the region, since Costa Rica was considered the best place to start the crusade. In this spirit, Figueres combined his struggle against the Calderón–Communist government with regional objectives of larger scope. His plans were greatly helped by the overthrow of the dictatorship of Jorge Ubico and the Guatemalan elections of December 1944, which brought Juan José Arévalo to the presidency of that country. It was under Arévalo's aegis that the so-called Caribbean Pact was formally signed on 16 December 1947 in Guatemala City.

In spite of his nationalist and anti-imperialist tendencies, Arévalo kept the same Central American policy as his dictatorial and reactionary predecessor in an effort to secure Guatemalan hegemony in the region. Figueres' plans fitted perfectly into this perspective because the signers of the pact promised to create a Central American Republic after overthrowing the existing military dictatorships. The fact that the government of Costa Rica had a progressive social policy and was allied with the Communists, who in Guatemala supported Arévalo's government, did not deter Guatemalan support of Figueres. The traditional theme of Central American union around the colonial Captaincy General prevailed over new themes of social policy and universal suffrage, which became a means and not an end.

These international alliances produced true political paradoxes. Arévalo's government, democratic, socially advanced and supported by the Guatemalan Communists, was opposed to that of Teodoro Picado, which was similar in character and had suffered in the past at the hands of Ubico, who had supported Cortés in the 1944 elections. Arévalo now supported Figueres, who had become the leader of the armed branch of the Costa Rican opposition movement headed first by Cortés and then, after his death, by Otilio Ulate. Moreover, in his zeal to promote Central American union, Arévalo sought the support of the conservative government of

Canstañeda in El Salvador, provoking understandable apprehension on the part of the governments of Carías in Honduras, Somoza in Nicaragua and Picado himself in Costa Rica. Both Picado and Somoza thus had a double fear: on the one hand, of the prospect of Guatemala's hegemony over the isthmus, and on the other, of the support that Arévalo lent to political groups who were seeking the armed overthrow of the governments of both countries. This forged the conditions for an alliance between Nicaragua and Costa Rica which contradicted those maintained internally by Picado (pro-communist) and Somoza (anti-communist). This paradoxical situation was heightened by the fact that there was no direct or immediate involvement by the United States in the behaviour of the governments concerned.

In Costa Rica, U.S. policy leaned clearly against Picado and in favour of the opposition, and therefore against the Communist Party. Washington's formula for a solution in this case was to see Picado step down through a victory by the opposition, guaranteed by armed pressure on the part of Figueres, but without giving the latter the chance to take power or fulfil his promises under the Caribbean Pact. In this way Arévalo would remain in a state of confrontation with the rest of Central America, the Caribbean Pact would be aborted, Nicaragua's hands would be free and the Costa Rican political situation would be satisfactorily resolved. However, the history of Costa Rica and the other Central American nations had its own dynamic.

Two great political-electoral coalitions came face-to-face in the elections of February 1948. The first consisted of the government and its Communist allies; with ex-president Calderón Guardia the official candidate. The second comprised the conservative Democratic Party, the centrist and liberal National Union, and the social-democratic group that was the fruit of the fusion of the Centre for the Study of National Problems (led by Rodrigo Facio) and José Figueres' Partido Acción Demócrata; Otilio Ulate was the opposition presidential candidate. The nation was deeply divided in a political climate which exacerbated hatred and promoted violence. Ulate used the slogan 'If he's for Calderón, don't talk to him, don't buy from him and don't sell to him'. Government officials used brutal police methods against the opposition, which had the effect of radicalizing rather than intimidating them.

The union movement was also divided between the Confederación General de Trabajadores Costarricenses (CGTC) and the Confederación de

Trabajadores Rerum Novarum. The first was effectively the union branch of the PVP; it supported the government of Picado and Calderón Guardia, mobilized itself around themes of social reform and labour legislation and would be an important factor in the organization and mobilization of the militia in the civil war that followed the elections. The CGTC was led by Rodolfo Guzmán, educated in the Moscow union school in 1933, and Jaime Cerdas Mora, founder of the Communist Party and one of the principal leaders of the banana strike of 1934. The Confederation's principal strength lay among the banana-workers, although it also had important organizations in the city among shoemakers, construction-workers and bakers.

Rerum Novarum, on the other hand, resulted from Archbishop Sanabria's attempts to create an alternative union inspired by the social principles of the Church. Its supposed purpose was neither to divide the labour movement nor to advocate an anti-communist policy, but to offer all workers, Catholic or not, a non-confessional, non-communist avenue for social revindication. Yet Sanabria had sent its leader, Benjamin Núñez, to the United States to study sociology and become acquainted with union organizations, and Núñez soon acquired a strong anti-communist attitude that led him to identify with the opposition and particularly with José Figueres and his group. Another leader of Rerum Novarum (and future president of Costa Rica), Luis Alberto Monge, was even more closely tied to Figueres. Rerum Novarum relied on the financial support of large national capitalists who sought to weaken the Communists, and on U.S. labour organizations, which were then seeking to expand into Latin America. The two confederations were driven into irreconcilable positions by the conflict of 1948. Núñez was a prominent figure in the civil war and became Minister of Labour in the junta government which was established after Figueres' victory. He promptly and predictably ordered the dissolution of the CGTC, but at the same time he was unable to stem the decline and ruin of Rerum Novarum itself, which never recovered from its politicization in the period prior to the civil war.

The economic situation had begun to improve at the end of the world war. The average price per kilo of exported coffee had risen from $0.35 for the crop of 1944–5, to $0.60 in 1947–8; the value of coffee exports increased from $7,488,761 to $14,189,041. Nonetheless, during this period the trade deficit rose from $15 million in 1945 to $25 million in 1947. The principal imports were related to the production of food, beverages and tobacco, with an increase in capital goods for agriculture, industry and commerce in 1946–7. In 1948 agriculture accounted for 43 per cent of the GDP, commerce 14.7 per cent, services 10.9 per cent, and industry 7.6 per cent. The public sector represented 10.9 per cent of GDP while the national debt stood at $56 million, with $30.2 million in foreign debt.

The government coalition had tried to secure popular support by pushing forward social welfare measures such as the construction of low-cost housing. Nevertheless, neither this nor other measures were able to prevent the deterioration of the regime's popularity, obliging the government to rely heavily upon its control of the repressive apparatus and the Congress, where the Calderón–Communist alliance continued to hold the majority.

The experience of the electoral fraud of 1944 remained acute and placed the opposition's demand for guarantees for a clean election at the centre of politics. The Communists had formulated an Election Code which finally came to regulate the electoral process. But this code then proved unsatisfactory to the opposition. It was not until after the strike of 22 July 1947 led by the business sector that the government gave in to opposition pressure and granted electoral guarantees, which some of its own partisans considered to be nothing less than the surrender of the electoral machinery to the opposition.

This produced a situation where the traditional fraud and manipulation of votes and ballot boxes were a subject for complaint not only by the opposition but also by the government itself. The leaders of the PVP, in particular, had detected illegal movement of voters, exclusion of citizens from the list of registered voters, and so on. Yet, when Otilio Ulate defeated Calderón Guardia, the tendency of the Communists was to accept the electoral results since the PVP itself had elected twelve congressmen out of a total of forty-five, not counting those who had been elected from Calderón's camp. This, however, was not the attitude of its Calderonista allies who had been defeated at the polls. And, finally, partisan interests prevailed over sober political analysis and institutional concerns. Thus, both the losing Calderonistas and the PVP, which on its own had won nearly a third of the seats in Congress, dedicated their efforts to getting the elections results annulled.

In conditions of acute tension that required little to trigger off violent conflict, this was the immediate cause of armed confrontation.

This domestic conflict interacted with another of international character which was no less complex. On one side were the promises Figueres had made in the Caribbean Pact to take advantage of the Costa Rican situation – 'the most convenient and easiest to utilize' – to overthrow the government and begin toppling the dictatorships of Nicaragua, Honduras and the Dominican Republic; to unite Central America under the clear hegemony of Guatemala and Juan José Arévalo; and to promote the formation of new national entities and federations in the Caribbean with greater economic, social and political power. Counterposed to this was Somoza's policy, which sought to block both the actions of the Caribbean conspirators and those of the United States itself, which sought to remove him from power and impose a form of democracy in Nicaragua superintended by the trustworthy National Guard. In Costa Rica, by contrast, the United States was seeking not so much Picado's departure and Ulate's victory – the policy they ended up following – as they were the separation of the Communist Party from the government. Thus, on 22 March 1948 Somoza and the U.S. business attaché, Mr Berhaum, proposed a plan to President Picado to eliminate both Figueres and the Communists with the use of Nicaraguan troops. This proposal was not entirely novel: two years earlier Léon Cortés had offered Picado a pact of support to his government as long as it terminated its alliance with the Communist Party and expelled it from the government. The death of Cortés in March 1946 put an end to the first project; Picado's loyalty to his Vanguardista allies aborted the second.

Armed conflict became the only possible solution to the confrontation. Although there existed within the insurrectionary forces some support for a peaceful solution and negotiations which could prevent more bloodshed, especially on the part of Ulate himself and Mario Echandi, the dominant influence was that of José Figueres, who was determined to go forward with the fighting not only on the national level but on the regional one as well, in accordance with the Caribbean Pact. The insurrectionists mobilized their sympathizers on the basis of slogans linked to electoral freedom, universal suffrage, respect for election results and fear of the Communist threat. On the other hand, social reform, the threat of the repeal of the Labour Law and, paradoxically, denunciation of electoral fraud, were the arguments mobilized by the government and its Vanguardista allies.

The elections themselves had taken place on 8 February 1948. Ulate and the PUN received 54,931 votes while Calderón Guardia's National Republican Party won 44,438. The declaration of the winner could not, however, be made unanimously, as required by law; it was declared by majority because the president of the electoral tribunal refused to cast his vote on account of the circumstances in which the count had been held. The other two members of the Tribunal made their declaration on 28 February. Calderón Guardia presented an immediate demand for nullification to the Congress, which according to the constitution had to make the final decision by 1 March. In the legislative session on that day, in the midst of an unruly street demonstration, Congress agreed by majority vote to annul the presidential elections.

On 12 March there was an armed uprising on Figueres' estates south of San José, located in the mountains separating the capital from the Valle del General, which was promptly taken by the rebel forces. There was also an uprising in San Ramón, to the north of the capital, led by Francisco J. Orlich, but the military actions on this front were less important than those in the south, where the main fighting was centered. The insurrectionists needed to control San Isidro del General in order to possess an airport from which to transport arms and men, which were being sent from Guatemala in accordance with the Caribbean Pact. The rebel presence in the mountains enabled them to cut communications between San Isidro and the capital and maintain an open supply line with Arévalo's government. Shortly afterwards, the anti-government forces attacked the city of Cartago and took it. At the same time, with forces formed by Costa Ricans and Dominican, Honduran and Nicaraguan soldiers from the Caribbean Legion, they took Puerto Limón on the Atlantic coast.

While the Communists, who were bearing most of the burden of the fighting (Calderón Guardia did not call out his partisans until 12 April), maintained that they had enough men and a portion of the arms needed to surround Cartago and overthrow Figueres, Picado's government admitted defeat and decided to seek a formula for surrender. On 12 April, the President called a meeting of the diplomatic corps to solicit their co-operation to save San José. Immediately a delegation of diplomats met with Figueres in Cartago when he presented them with certain demands that produced considerable apprehension in the political circles surrounding Ulate, since the rebel leader required that he himself be named president, which of course implied the recognition of the annulment of the elections in which Ulate had been elected. This was the first symptom of the division which was to occur later when the rebel opposition triumphed.

This issue threatened the talks which began the next day, 13 April, at the Mexican embassy under the auspices of the diplomatic corps, with the participation of Picado and, among others, Manuel Mora of the PVP and

Father Benjamin Núñez for the so-called Army of National Liberation (Ejército de Liberación Nacional). The negotiations were proceeding normally when the U.S. ambassador, Nathaniel Davis, announced that Picado's government had asked Somoza to intervene in Costa Rica and that Nicaraguan troops were already in the town of Villa Quesada, at some distance from the Nicaraguan frontier. The National Guard had attacked the positions of some of the rebels, making it clear that the protestations of 'neutrality' in the conflict and claims that the intervention was only to safeguard the Nicaraguan frontiers from revolutionary actions were palpably untrue. The most serious aspect was that the Somoza regime attempted to legalize its intervention with a request and authorization supposedly submitted to him by President Picado – the version given by the Nicaraguan dictator to the other American governments who were then meeting at the Ninth Inter-American Conference in Bogotá. In Costa Rica, Picado denied Somoza's interpretation, although he did not deny that he had sent Dr Calderón Guardia's brother to ask Somoza to secure his own frontiers in order to prevent people passing from one side to another. At the same time, Rómulo Betancourt, representative of Venezuela at the meeting in Bogotá, and an ally of Figueres, had submitted a petition to the Nicaraguan government asking it to refrain from interfering in the internal affairs of Costa Rica and to withdraw its troops from Costa Rican territory.

The forces supporting the government came from three sources: the PVP militia, which were well disciplined, numerous and combative, but less well armed; the forces of the government itself, which were better armed but without the fighting spirit of the PVP militia and suffered the disadvantages of a policy of sabotage from within on the part of President Picado's brother; and the Calderonista groups, disorganized, mainly billeted in the cities, with a leadership that oscillated between the hopes for Nicaraguan intervention and fear of exile. The fact that after hostilities ended, boxes of modern weapons that had never been used were found in the defeated government's headquarters, while the Vanguardista militia was using single-shot rifles, and that many of these weapons had been taken from the country's arsenals and sold or given by the Minister of War to the National Guard of Nicaragua, the country in which he had sought asylum, clearly demonstrates the importance of the internal divisions in the pro-government alliance. For reasons such as these the peace negotiations could not be restricted to the legal government only but had to include the PVP, which was not only independent from the military point of view but also effectively held political control of the government by the end of the conflict.

On 18 April parallel negotiations were held between Father Núñez, Figueres and Manuel Mora for the purpose of offering additional guarantees that would put an end to hostilities. This led to a meeting on the front line of battle between these three plus Carlos Luis Fallas, the PVP military commander, called at the last minute by Mora to confirm his version of what was said there. The meeting gave rise to what was known as the Pact of Ochomogo. Although no document was signed – no facilities existed at the meeting place – general lines of conduct were agreed upon for the victors. These related particularly to the conservation of the social guarantees and the Labour Law and the legality of the unions and of the Popular Vanguard Party itself. All this was formulated in a private letter that Núñez, following Figueres' instructions, gave to Mora, to which express reference is made in point 6 of the Pact of the Mexican Embassy, which, dated 19 April, put an end to the armed struggle. Father Núñez' letter to the Communist leader Mora carries the same date.

The signing of the Mexican Embassy Pact, later denounced by the victors, put an end to the armed struggle. A transitional government was formed under Santos León Herrera, and almost immediately replaced by a junta headed by Figueres that named itself the Junta Fundadora de la Segunda República.

The establishment of the junta led by Figueres (1948–9) marked the beginning of a political schism in the victorious group. The ideological and political homogeneity within the junta was not complete, nor was there total unity among those who were not in the junta. Yet two clearly defined political centres stood out from the very beginning among the winners. On one side was the political sector around the elected president, Otilio Ulate, of conservative and centrist character, with considerable popular support. On the other was the military sector, led by Figueres, of a populist, reformist character, self-defined as social-democrat and yet lacking in popular support.

Figueres' group, organized in the government junta and with a small contingent in the Constitutional Assembly under the banner of the Social Democratic Party, tried to push through a genuine program of social, educational, financial, economic and institutional reform. The idea of a second republic, of a new and modern role for the state in society and the economy, responded to the urgent needs of an ascending middle class with a business vocation, and clashed with the limited horizons of the traditional elite, who believed that the downfall of Calderón-communism meant the re-establishment of its ascendancy.

The project for a new constitution presented by the Social Democrats combined diverse ideological elements: the populist and nationalist thought of Víctor Raúl Haya de la Torre and *aprismo* plus the moderate distributionist currents of English socialism, North American pragmatism, and the social progressive features of Colombian liberalism. The experiences of Chile and Uruguay provided important institutional models for state decentralization and modernization. These currents coincided with the search for new entrepreneurial and productive horizons beyond the traditional agro-export model. Based above all on the work of Rodrigo Facio, Alberto Martén, and the intellectuals of the Centre for the Study of National Problems, a variety of programs in the areas of education, economy, finance and administrative decentralization sought to open a new social and political project for Costa Rica.

Ulate's group was organized around the PUN (Partido Unión Nacional) and its newspaper *Diario de Costa Rica*. The most prominent capitalists were already beginning to express themselves through *La Nación,* founded in 1946, which was not specifically identified with any political party but represented the traditional conservative tendencies of the country and the interests of the large agricultural, commercial and exporting groups, both national and foreign. Ulate, for his part, was not at all opposed to social change. On the contrary, he perceived the importance and significance of the changes which had taken place in the preceding decade and was responsive not only to the demands of the most important capitalist sectors but also to small and middle-sized producers. As a result, there was later acute friction between him and the representatives of large capital, who eventually withdrew their support. On the other hand, the doubts and reservations about Figueres' real intentions were resolved through the so-called Ulate–Figueres Pact, in which Figueres promised to hand out power to Ulate in eighteen months, postponable, eventually, to twenty-four months.

The junta proscribed the Communist Party (the PVP), had the CGTC declared illegal for being an instrument of the Communist Party, and effected the dismissal without compensation of the partisans of the previous regime, in both private business and the government. It also established special tribunals to try supporters of the defeated alliance. In this initial period there was serious strife over the promises Figueres had made in the Caribbean Pact and over the presence in the country of armed foreigners, who were trying to incite revolutionary international ventures. This was the cause of a protest by some military men in the government itself, headed by the Minister of Public Order (responsible for the police), Edgar Cardona, who attempted a coup d'état against the junta known as 'El Cardonazo' on 2 and 3 April 1949.

During Figueres' government some of the ideas which later would play a central role in national politics were clearly outlined, such as nationalization and development of the electricity industry, and the revision of the country's economic and fiscal relations with the United Fruit Company. From the political and social point of view, however, the most important measure was the nationalization of the banks decreed on 21 June 1948, along with a 10 per cent tax on capital over $50,000. This was the central instrument which permitted the development of the new business sector, politically united in what would later become the Partido Liberación Nacional (PLN) since the growth of this business sector had hitherto been stalled by the financial control that the agro-export and commercial-import groups exercised over private banking and credit.

The coffee oligarchy did not have time to savour its illusory triumph of 1948. Its young Social Democrat allies asserted their independence almost immediately. As early as the battle for Cartago, in the middle of the war, Figueres had rejected attempts by some capitalists to get him to repeal the Labour Law and the social guarantees. A few weeks after Figueres had triumphed, he proceeded to break up the financial monopoly and the social and political influence of the great coffee growers and traders, who were tightly linked by family relationships and most heavily affected by these nationalizing measures of the de facto government. A key factor of their social and political power thus passed to the state, not as a neutral entity but as an effective instrument of development for the emerging political-entrepreneurs.

The reaction of those affected by this policy was to see it as 'communist', not last because of its supposed links with the Caribbean Pact. This distrust grew as illusions about repealing such measures evaporated and the new arrivals in power broadened their base of social support, and stood out as a group who sought hegemony, through a nationalist strategy, over Costa Rican society and politics. The profound nature of the changes was not understood at the time, either by the conservative allies of the previous era, who saw only communism in Figueres and his international allies, or by the Communists, who felt only the repression and anti-communism that surrounded the junta.

One of the most questionable aspects of the governmental actions of the junta revolved around the management of public funds. The lack of proper legal ordinances, the decision to indemnify Figueres for damages to his property during the war, and the issuing of the so-called Decree 80, which empowered Daniel Oduber to dispose of public funds without control or regulation, soon surrounded Figueres' administration with the suspicion of corruption. This was naturally magnified by those who opposed the junta, both those defeated in the civil war and also the junta's own temporary allies, who were beginning to distrust Figueres and the Junta and were readying their weapons for the next political fight.

Another aspect which should be stressed is the conflict that broke out between the junta and the Church, especially when the government attempted to sign an agreement which would create seven bishoprics and two archbishoprics. This was a clear attack on the ecclesiastical leadership of Monsignor Sanabria because of his ties with the previous regime. Furthermore, the leader of the Catholic Church continued to intervene to oppose the abuses being committed against the losers in the civil war; he was decisive in halting an attempt to shoot the leaders of the Communist Party, who were imprisoned in the central penitentiary, which was due to take place at the same time as a group of Communist union leaders on the Atlantic coast were being shot at El Codo del Diablo on the railway to Puerto Limón.

In December 1948, the junta was confronted by a bold attack organized by Calderón Guardia from Nicaragua and sponsored by Anastasio Somoza. Foreseeing the threat posed to him by Figueres and his allies in the Caribbean Pact, Somoza took advantage of the desire for revenge prevalent among the Costa Rican exiles to launch them on an invasion and create a border conflict between the two countries. Somoza sought both to alarm the U.S. Department of State and to warn Figueres against any aggression against him. As soon as the Nicaraguan dictator had secured his own interests and distracted Figueres, he abandoned Calderón Guardia and withdrew from the calculated alliance he had promoted exclusively for his own interests. The defeated Calderón Guardia chose to go into exile in Mexico and wait for another opportunity for a military coup, which occurred fruitlessly, in 1955. Meanwhile, he asked his followers to abstain from participating in the 1949 elections for the National Constituent Assembly. This made it particularly difficult for sectors of his own party, some independents and the Communists, to participate in and influence the Assembly.

The National Constituent Assembly was installed on 15 January 1949 and dominated by Ulate's PUN, which had obtained thirty-four delegates while Figueres' Social Democrats managed to elect only four. In spite of the abstention of the Calderonistas, the Constitutional Party, reputed to be of Calderonista tendency, obtained six seats.

Although Calderón Guardia decided to boycott the election and place his hopes in insurrectionary activity, his former Communist allies were opposed to this line and reached certain understandings with individuals who participated under the banner of the Constitutional Party. These elections, then, marked the beginning of the underlying schism within each of the enemy coalitions of the civil war. On the victorious side there was evidence of profound ideological divergence. The political initiative lay with Ulate and his followers, and not with Figueres and his supporters, in spite of their prestigious military triumph. On the losing side, the Communists emphasized social programmes and internal democratization, which in its current form excluded them from operating legally in the political system and forced them to struggle for legal recognition; their Calderonista allies sought new alliances with Caribbean tyrannies, alarmed by the Caribbean Pact, which was aimed against them and which had converted Figueres' regime into a destabilizing factor for Nicaragua, the Dominican Republic and, more recently, Venezuela, under the control of Marcos Pérez Jiménez.

The basis of discussion in the Constituent Assembly was not the plan for a new constitution presented by the Social Democratic Party, which proposed a much more modernizing, regulationist and innovating document, but rather amendments to the charter of 1871. To this were added various corrections and reforms that attempted to synthesize the dramatic social innovations and institutional experiments of the previous ten years. The new constitution introduced a system of autonomous and semi-autonomous institutions, opening the doors to an inexorable process of administrative decentralization and state intervention that began almost immediately. It also limited the presidentialist regime which had hitherto prevailed, and it introduced guarantees for the secure tenure of public employees. In a decisive departure from the rest of Central America, a Superior Electoral Tribunal was established as the fourth power of the state to manage all electoral matters in an exclusive manner. Efforts were made to eliminate corruption in the re-election of presidents and deputies, and civil rights were strengthened, both in reference to the protection of individual and social rights and specifically with regard to the administrative relations between the individual and the state. The equality of the sexes was recognized and women were granted the right to vote. Nevertheless, the Constitution reaffirmed the Junta's previous ban on the organization of parties which could be identified with the activities, programmes or international links of the Communist Party; this prohibition remained in force until 1974.

The constitution abolished the army as a permanent institution. Although Figueres had already disbanded the military, constitutional confirmation of this act was decisive for the democratic future of Costa Rica and distinguished it sharply from its neighbours. While the army as such had begun its decline during the first term of Cleto González before the First World War, and by 1948 had been reduced to a small mobile unit that was dissolved in the middle of the civil war by the Minister of War, its abolition by constitutional law prevented the victorious group from installing itself in power with its own army at the end of the war. At the same time, the old liberal tradition of division of powers was fortified with the recognition of the independence of the judicial power. Both measures were the culmination of a complex historical process which made the existence of the army unnecessary and existence of an autonomous judicial power unavoidable. Like the abolition of the army, both were decisive for the democratic development of Costa Rican society, in sharp contrast with the rest of Latin America and Central America in particular.

The new constitution also ratified the activity of the state in production and in the distribution of national wealth, by strengthening the mechanisms for its intervention in areas of public interest. Without being cemented into any law, the conviction existed, both in the Constitutional Assembly and in the society at large, that it was necessary somehow to link economic and social development to political democracy.

The old coffee oligarchy and its allies failed to adjust to the new situation and simply followed the initiatives of others. Except for the figure of Ulate, with whom they soon broke, they found no leader who could supply them with unity and a sense of purpose. Equally, Calderón Guardia's group sought little more than political restoration and economic compensation for the persecution of which they had been victims. The Communists were crushed both by the harsh internal repression that ensued after the civil war and by the rapid advance of the Cold War, which was already making its mark on the political climate in Latin America. This left the future to the young political entrepreneurs who created the PLN in 1951 with José Figueres at its head. In founding the new party,

Figueres relied on his recent military victory, the absence of a strong opponent in the electoral field and a team of enterprising men who had their own political plans for the country. Figueres and Ulate had agreed to accept the results of the presidential elections of February 1948 in which Ulate had been elected. However, they annulled the election of congressmen, which had given the Calderón-communists the majority of seats. This was a political arrangement among winners, in which Figueres, albeit reluctantly, handed power to Ulate in spite of his feeling that the latter represented forces and interests contrary to his real political and social programme.

The Ulate administration (1949–53) encountered a climate favourable to economic recovery. Internationally, European reconstruction had favourable repercussions on world trade, and the Korean War contributed to the improvement in the price of coffee. Agricultural exports continued to be the mainstay of national economic activity, with coffee and bananas together representing 89.2 per cent of the total value of exports in 1951. Industry employed a little more than 10 per cent of the economically active population, while agriculture accounted for more than 50 per cent of the work force. Mechanization in agriculture was minimal, and the weight of the international market was highly significant in the national economy and public finance. In 1949, 16,603,580 kilos of coffee had yielded $11,087,136, at an average price per kilo of $.0667; by 1952 the average price per kilo stood at $1.147 and the quantity exported at 21,194,786 kilos, producing a total value of $24,323,613.

Although it had had a precarious and dependent agro-export base, the national economy showed dynamism and growth, facilitating the political and institutional process generated after the civil war and the constitutional assembly. In patronizing this incipient modernization the Ulate administration possessed two advantages: it had no real political opposition, since this oscillated between the illegal Communist Party and a tarnished and exiled Calderonism; and the financial and economic situation permitted a healthy reordering of the state and of public finances. The administration had the means to promote key institutions like the Costa Rican Institute of Electricity, the Central Bank and the National Council of Production – key mechanisms in the new interventionist state – as well as the Costa Rican Social Security Fund, while maintaining the value of the colón and a fiscal surplus, which would never recur after 1953. Ulate also managed to reduce the public debt – internal and external – of the central government from $403 million in 1950 to $328 million in 1953.

The Ulate administration carefully preserved its neutrality in the face of the electoral challenge that gained strength with the foundation of the PLN on 12 October 1951 under the undisputed leadership of José Figueres. Thus began a project conceived a year earlier in Rome, by three persons who would later be presidents under the new party's banner: Figueres, Francisco J. Orlich and Daniel Oduber. Besides the PLN, two other new political formations emerged: the Partido Unión Nacional (PUN) and the Partido Demócrata (PD). The first, whose blue flag had flown over the united opposition headed by Otilio Ulate in 1948, was reorganized in 1952 by Mario Echandi, Minister of Foreign Affairs in the Ulate administration and the principal aspirant to the party's nomination. The second, which brought the most powerful capitalists together, finally selected Fernando Castro Cervantes as its presidential candidate. Owner of substantial assets, Castro Cervantes was trusted by the United Fruit Company and could rely on the support of the moneyed group which increasingly gravitated towards *La Nación,* a paper which was careful, however, to avoid letting electoral bias colour its steadfast defence of more permanent interests. A fourth party attempted to enter the contest under the name Partido Progresista Independiente, nominating Joaquín García Monge, a distinguished educator and intellectual who had studied in Chile and was founder and director of the *Revista Repertorio Americano,* an important cultural magazine. The PVP supported his candidacy in an effort to evade its outlaw status but in spite of the respect in which García Monge was held, the party was declared illegal and excluded under Article 98 of the Constitution.

Much of the electoral debate revolved around the PLN and the controversial figure of Figueres, who was increasingly accused of being a Communist, of having secret pacts with international soldiers of fortune, and of having indulged in administrative corruption in the exercise of power. It soon became evident that capital supported Castro Cervantes, forcing Echandi to join forces with the PD and run only as an independent candidate for congressman in San José. Eventually both the PVP and Calderonism backed Castro Cervantes, motivated more by resentment against Figueres than by the ideological and social content of the contending factions. The elections in which women voted for the first time, were held on 26 July 1953. The result clearly favoured Figueres, who captured 123,444 votes, 65 per cent of the total cast.

Ulate held a non-binding referendum at the same time as the general elections, in order to change from eight to four years the period a president had to wait before running for office again. This referendum was approved by a large majority, but the outcome was not respected by Figueres and his group. The legislative assembly, where the matter had to be ratified closed the door to the constitutional amendment and thus to the eventual return of Ulate to power. This precipitated a confrontation between Ulate and Figueres, after which they were irreconcilably opposed to each other.

With the rejection of this constitutional amendment the PLN clearly revealed its intentions to control national politics in opposition to both its adversaries and its former allies in the civil war. This provoked the formation of diverse and contradictory electoral alliances against the party in power. For the conservative sector, Figueres was a Communist because of his ties with Rómulo Betancourt and his statist policies, which was only possible 'in Russia and Costa Rica'. When Ulate broke definitively with Figueres he dusted off old documents from Betancourt's first exile in Costa Rica, during which he was a militant in the Communist Party, and used them to attack Betancourt's friendship with Figueres. Even to the Calderonistas, Figueres' nationalizing tendencies looked suspicious and seemed to bring him closer to their old Communist allies. Thus the PVP's isolation was doubly intensified. All this in turn confirmed the PLN's independent identity and forced an alliance between the wealthy conservative groups and the Calderonistas, who lacked any political program of their own other than the defeat of Figueres.

The economic conditions in which the new government came to office were favourable. The average price per kilo of exported coffee rose from $1.193 in 1953 to $1.483 in 1956 although a fall in quantum exports in that year meant that revenue from coffee sales was only marginally above that for 1953. Nonetheless, during the first PLN administration movement in the volume and prices of coffee exports usually compensated each other. The PLN administration addressed itself to demanding fair prices for export products from the consumer countries and denounced those aspects of commerce that were unfavourable to Latin American development in general. This policy led to friction with Washington, which also distrusted Figueres' efforts to modify the terms of the economic relations between the Costa Rican state and the United Fruit Company at a time when the company was in confrontation with the Guatemalan government of Jacobo Arbenz. In negotiations with the banana company, Figueres managed to raise the government's share of United Fruit's profits from 15 per cent to 30 per cent. He also obtained an increase in wages as part of his policy of strengthening consumption and developing the internal market for the new business sector.

The Figueres administration used its congressional majority to modernize and stabilize the state apparatus through administrative specialization and expansion of the autonomous institutions. The state began to offer all kinds of services, developing the communications network, undertaking important energy projects, and extending education throughout the country. The state thus became a large employer of the electoral constituency of the new party, and a mechanism for social and economic advancement for the rising middle sectors of society. Between 1950 and 1958 the economically active population grew by 2.77 per cent per annum while employment in the public sector grew by 7.44 per cent. The state also became a large market for goods and services, highly conditioned by political and electoral considerations. Between 1950 and 1953 public investment had an 18 per cent share of the GDP, but in the period between 1954 and 1958 it passed the 22 per cent mark, the share of autonomous institutions and the Ministry of Public Works being particularly pronounced.

This strategy had been elaborated by the Centre for the Study of National Problems as well as by Figueres himself, and it was now strengthened by the explicit adoption of the Keynesian economic thought. The nation's wealthy were considered 'timid and cowardly, incapable of boldly undertaking new economic enterprises', in the words of Rodrigo Facio, the government seeking to compensate for their organizational and psychological weakness with state intervention. The financial lever for this was the nationalization of the banks, which was to supplement the economic resources available for the emergence of a new business sector oriented to internal consumption in industry, agriculture and services through the policy of higher salaries and the increasing consumption of goods and services by the state apparatus.

The financing of the modernization effort was based principally on the imposition of indirect taxes, which contributed 48 per cent of the government's revenues, as opposed to direct taxes, which accounted for 12.6 per cent in the period between 1946 and 1958. The other major factor in finance was the internal and external debt: in 1953 the public sector owed $380,980,000, and in 1956, $452,384,000, of which over a quarter was external debt.

The growth of the state was not entirely Figueres' work. The phenome-

non of state expansion and institutional diversification had been present in
Costa Rica since the 1920s, became more accentuated in the 1930s, and
was evident in the process which took place from 1941 to 1948. What
distinguishes Figueres' project is that both he and his group linked the
process directly to the emergence of a new sector of entrepreneurs who
sought to use the State to modernize the nation and form an internal
market. They tried to consolidate their political and social hegemony
through a populism which, with the state as employer, would supply
them with a permanent social and electoral constituency. They already had
influence with the peasantry. The new measures created a rising middle
sector, both private and bureaucratic, which needed the power of the state
for its own development.

The Figueres administration encountered political conflict on two
fronts. Internationally, its head-on collision with the dictatorships of the
Caribbean led it in 1954 to abstain from participating in the Tenth Inter-
American Conference in Caracas, where the Guatemalan regime of Arbenz
was condemned, and to refuse to fraternize with Somoza and other dictators at the Presidents' Conference in Panama. In addition, its constant
demands for better prices in the world market, and its friendliness towards
exiled politicians, including Rómulo Betancourt of Venezuela and Juan
Bosch of the Dominican Republic as well as numerous Nicaraguan exiles,
brought it into opposition with their respective tyrannies and with certain
sectors in the United States. Nevertheless, on the advice of a few liberal
North American friends like Adolf E. Berle and others, Figueres made
important efforts to improve his image in the United States, especially
among the Democrats. He even paid large sums to a public relations
agency to promote his image as a champion of democracy, which proved to
be particularly useful at the time of the armed invasion against his government in 1955. Until that time only Somoza among the heads of state in
Central America had bothered to cultivate an image and try to influence
U.S. public opinion.

On the national level, the overwhelming PLN majority in Congress
clashed with an especially capable opposition, in which the agility and
aggressiveness of Mario Echandi played a critical note. Echandi earned the
hatred of his adversaries and the sympathies of the Calderonista masses,
who saw the true expression of their own sentiments in his attacks against
the government. They forgot that the fiery legislator had been a highly
placed leader in Ulate's camp in the 1948 election, an active opponent in
the civil war and Minister of Foreign Affairs in Ulate's government. The

weakness of the Figueres administration before this implacable opponent grew day by day while Echandi, without a programme but with great technical skill, exploited the government's errors. Perhaps his lack of a programme helped Echandi to knit together those political forces whose common denominator was opposition to Figueres and his party. In all events, a somewhat oligarchic but simple and witty political style helped him to capture widespread popular sympathy and would later give his own administration a traditionalist republican flavour.

In the judgement of the Calderonistas both external and internal conditions were propitious for the removal of Figueres from power through armed action. They were encouraged in this view by growing support from the the public, who frequently booed ministers in the stadiums and protested openly against government measures. Externally, a recalcitrant anti-communism was spreading through Latin America and legitimizing the tyrannies of Trujillo, Pérez Jiménez and Somoza. The conspirators believed that Washington would support the new alliance of populist Calderonism and conservative capital. The Calderonistas explicitly rejected the former alliance with the PVP and their clandestine rebel radio constantly attacked Figueres for his supposed alliance with Communism. The return of Calderón Guardia was considered virtually a fait accompli.

Somoza exploited this situation no less astutely, as he had done that in December 1948. Now he had the support of the other dictators in the Caribbean, and was again ready to test his relations with the U.S. government as far as he could in order to stay in power, if necessary by securing the overthrow of the decidedly threatening government in San José. Nevertheless, Somoza had a clear conception of his purposes, and once the challenge to his own regime was suppressed, he was quite prepared to coexist with the Figueres government. This was not the case with Calderón Guardia, who wanted above all else to overthrow Figueres and was prepared to go to extremes in search of this objective.

The *coyotepes* – as the calderonista insurrectionists were called from the town in Nicaragua where they were trained – entered Costa Rica in January 1955, but their military actions did not meet with the success the rebel leaders and their allies had hoped for. The people remained passive in the face of aggression that did not respond to their needs or their spirit. Moreover, the operation had a strong foreign association which the government stressed, appealing to the inter-American organizations to intervene to pacify the frontier, if not to condemn Nicaragua. The invasion proved to be a fruitless venture from the beginning and only served to help the government recover its lost prestige. The United States took the side of Figueres' constitutional government and demonstrated its repudiation of Somoza's actions through the symbolic sale of three fighter planes at a dollar apiece. The Organization of American States sent forces to seal the frontier and disarm the rebels, who returned to Nicaragua defeated once more and betrayed by Somoza. (When he saw the firm attitude of the United States and the imminent failure of the invasion, Somoza suspended the shipment of arms and logistic support he had promised.) Calderón Guardia, who lost an eye in the fighting, decided to go into exile in Mexico again, burdened by the military failure and the humiliation of an alliance with the tyrants.

The PLN tried to take advantage of the moment to subordinate congressional opposition, especially that of Echandi. The government accused him and another Calderonista congressman of being in collusion with the invaders, stripped them of their parliamentary immunity and had them indicted for treason. Scandalous acts of disrespect and violence occurred during and after this session, and when Echandi decided not to offer any defence against baseless charges, he won a complete pardon from the highest court in the country. His opposition colleagues in Congress decided not to attend the legislative sessions until both congressmen's rights were restored, a situation which lasted for eight months. The victory was thus a shared one: militarily and politically, the government was the victor, but Echandi had also second a political and personal triumph, which enabled him to defeat the two other contestants for the opposition candidacy. He then entered the 1958 election as the sole, and highly popular, opponent to the PLN.

Liberationism, by contrast, presented a divided front. Jorge Rossi, a conservative ex-Minister of Finance and aspirant to the PLN nomination, withdrew from the party denouncing acts of fraud against him and founded the Partido Independiente, which nominated him as its presidential candidate. Another sector, more clearly linked with what was beginning to be called the party machine, nominated Francisco J. Orlich. Figueres, in open defiance of the election laws, lent his support to Orlich, an old comrade-in-arms on whose estate the party had been founded.

The national political system was still very weak. One sector of the populace felt excluded from the political contest and had to support candidates who were not strictly speaking their own although the Calderonistas, many of whose leaders remained in exile, registered their congressmen with the Republican Party. The Communists, who tried to participate under the name Partido Unión Popular, were once again declared illegal and had to limit themselves to choosing among the candidates that the system allowed to participate. Appreciable progress had been made towards cleaner and more democratic electoral processes, but to make further advances it was necessary to remove one giant obstacle: the national divisions and political intolerance that derived from the military confrontations of 1948 and 1955.

The elections were held on 2 February 1958 and 229,543 voted. Echandi obtained 46 per cent of the vote, Orlich, 43 per cent, and Rossi 11 per cent. The president-elect took office on 8 May. However, he lacked a majority in the Legislative Assembly since the anti-PLN vote remained divided between congressmen of Echandi's PUN and Calderón Guardia's Republicans. The independents and Liberationists responded by forming a powerful parliamentary bloc made up of the most able men of both parties, who had been divided more by purely electoral considerations than by profound ideological differences.

Contrary to expectations, Echandi's term was characterized by moderation, a spirit of dialogue and respect for the law. The new president's clear purpose was to complete the consolidation of the rule of law, respect public opinion and give substance and stability to the institutions that had emerged from the new constitution.

Echandi's most difficult task, however, was to heal the divisions caused by the military struggles of 1948–9 and 1955. Surprising some by his lack of vengeance and angering others who did not want to see his administration commit a dangerous act of Calderonista restoration, the President took a major step in this direction by permitting the return to Costa Rica of Calderón Guardia. The return of the 'Doctor' was the cause of one of the largest popular demonstrations seen in the country. The event showed that Costa Rican democracy needed to include that third of the Costa Rican population who identified with 'the eight-year regime', as the administrations of Calderón Guardia and Teodoro Picado were pejoratively called. Special courts ordered the return to the Calderonistas of property which had been seized after the civil war, and those prisoners who had been sentenced at the same time by the so-called Tribunal of Immediate Sanctions were released.

Echandi's failure to obtain a parliamentary majority was compounded by the quality and belligerence of the opposition congressmen, and it was only the President's skill and experience that enabled him to exclude the PLN from the presidency of the Legislative Assembly which was a key post because it controlled the composition of the parliamentary committees. The government was also severely taxed by the banana strike of 1959 on the Pacific coast, where the workers demanded pay for a thirteenth month from the banana company. An agreement was eventually reached whereby the government paid the wages for that year, but the strike demonstrated the recovery of the unions in the banana zone and opened a new phase of tough collective bargaining by labour with foreign companies. At the same time, the situation on the Nicaraguan frontier remained unstable, not least because Figueres continued to instigate and participate in conspiracies against Somoza. The Nicaraguan government captured an arms cache in Punta Llorona, and produced evidence that PLN leaders had participated in their transfer. A few exiled Nicaraguans tried to carry out military actions against Somoza, and he retaliated by detaining a Costa Rican Airlines plane. Echandi, who was maintaining cautiously cordial relations with the dictator, took a firm stand against Somoza's action and forced him to return the airplane. When a Costa Rican officer who was a close friend of the President was killed in a frontier incident, Echandi further hardened his stance towards this kind of activity.

In his relations with communism, which were aggravated by the victory of Castro in Cuba, Echandi took care not to apply the administrative procedures which were provided for in the constitutional prohibition against the Communist Party and which seriously limited individual guarantees. The President began the practice of having the Department of the Interior return publications which were confiscated by the customs service; he allowed the radio broadcast of a speech by Manuel Mora, banned under the Figueres administration, and increasingly left it to the courts to decide the precise meaning of the prohibition against Communists participating under their own party name in elections. In the meantime, he permitted the opening of the PVP party headquarters, the holding of assemblies and meetings, and the publication and circulation of the party paper. Even after Costa Rica broke off relations with the revolutionary regime in Cuba (over the execution of supporters of Batista) Echandi tried to prevent illegal anti-Cuban military activities.

The Cuban Revolution activated the agrarian question in Costa Rica although there was relatively little real grass-roots pressure, as opposed to party propaganda, over the issue. The concentration of property was undeniable – estates of more than 2,400 hectares accounted for only 0.11

per cent of all farms yet occupied 26.56 per cent of the arable land – but the problem still did not produce serious social conflict.

The general elections of 1962 saw the old rivals from the civil war era return to the fray with their own parties. Otilio Ulate, candidate of the National Union, obtained 14 per cent, Calderón Guardia of the National Republican Party won 35 per cent, and Francisco J. Orlich, candidate of the PLN, triumphed with 50 per cent of the vote. The left-wing Popular Democratic Action also ran, although its aim was primarily to secure a radical presence in Congress after so many years of political ostracism.

In the early 1960s the urgent task was no longer democratic consolidation – this had been secured by Echandi – but economic development. The country was suffering from adverse international economic conditions. The prices of coffee, bananas and cocoa were in decline. Exports, which had grown by 6.6 per cent per annum between 1951 and 1957, grew by only 2 per cent in 1962. To this was added the eruptions of the Irazú Volcano during 1963, 1964 and 1965, which affected the coffee crop and disturbed all agricultural production in the central meseta. The gross internal product had seen an average rate of growth of less than 4 per cent between the last year of Figueres' government and the end of the Echandi administration.

The Orlich administration (1962–6) adopted the goals of the Alliance for Progress, which led to a significant inflow of capital from multilateral organizations and initiated a policy of external indebtedness, which was tied during this initial stage to the creation of favourable conditions for production and investment. Industrialization was seriously promoted, first by implementing a law for industrial protection and development passed in 1959, and later through the entrance of Costa Rica into the Central American Common Market (CACM).

The negotiations and studies for the creation of the Central American Common Market had been started by the United Nations Economic Commission for Latin America (CEPAL) in 1951 and lasted until 1958. However, U.S. pressure ensured that the project, which was cemented in 1960 with the signing of the General Treaty of Economic Integration and the creation of the Central American Bank of Economic Integration, finally took shape without CEPAL's most nationalist proposals. This created the dilemma for Costa Rica of whether to accept a project practically imposed by El Salvador and Guatemala, and motivated by North American interests, or to remain outside the common market. The Echandi administration had attempted bilateral negotiation and a gradual entry which would avoid a sudden inrush of competing foreign capital free of the social charges that burdened Costa Rican investment, and preserve an internal market for national capital. In the prevailing international economic situation, and under pressure from an expanding labour market — the result of a demographic explosion which was a reflection of improvements in health and other living conditions in the country — a pure and simple objection to integration was insufficient.

The PLN by contrast, was impatient to join the process of economic integration in Central America, and on 23 July 1962, as soon as the elections were over, President Orlich expressed the willingness of Costa Rica to become part of the Central American Common Market. From the economic point of view, entry into the CACM meant the adoption of import substitution, based on the use of a technology which, although outmoded in its countries of origin, was sufficiently advanced in the underdeveloped Costa Rican economy to undermine the utilization of the abundant labour force, whose employment was supposedly one of the principal objectives of the integrationist policy. Investments were not regionalized and ended up competing between the member countries. The sum total of the five feeble markets of the participating countries excused them, for the moment, from having to develop a true internal market through reforms in agriculture. The blow to public finances was no less destructive. In the zeal to compete for foreign investment with the other countries of the CACM, the principal weapon used was tax exemption through the application of the incentives built into the Law of Industry. This gave rise to a chronic fiscal crisis which culminated a few years later in general economic crisis.

The CACM produced significant social differentiation within national society. There was an increase in local entrepreneurs who participated in the Market under fiscal protection and those who established ties with foreign capital. In the wake of this limited industrial expansion a new working class developed, with working conditions and social relations that were different from those that had traditionally prevailed. The special characteristics of this stratum made the organization of strong unions in the private sector very difficult, and union activity continued to be concentrated in the areas of banana production and the public sector.

Although a certain symbiosis was subsequently to be established with the traditional coffee-growing and agro-export group, the new entrepreneurs tied to the CACM initially encountered a climate of confrontation originating in the costly policy of industrial protectionism. The new entrepreneurs and managers were unable to consolidate an independent political identity and therefore began to enter the existing political parties. Through this route and from the areas of the state which they managed to control, they subsequently exerted considerable influence over economic policy.

The Orlich government, besides pursuing international policies in the interests of the coffee sector, attempted to pursue a policy of development from within by fostering the national production of bananas in the Atlantic zone while simultaneously negotiating with multinational banana corporations interested in investing in Costa Rica. The monopoly the United Fruit Company had held in the national production of bananas was thereby broken. By 1975, 41 per cent of a much-increased banana production was controlled by national enterprises. Nevertheless, commercialization remained in foreign hands: COBAL, first controlled by German capital and later by United Brands, brought 95 per cent of its export crop from national producers; BANDECO, first owned by the West Indies Company and later by Del Monte Corporation, 55.5 per cent and the Standard Fruit Company, a subsidiary of Castle and Cook, 44.1 per cent. United Fruit Company, by contrast, only acquired 3 per cent, producing 97 per cent of its exports on its own plantations. While this generated an important new entrepreneurial sector, its principal social effect was the development of a belligerent agricultural proletariat which, when added to that of the Pacific coast, would strengthen Communist unionism until the crisis of 1984.

The diversification of production embraced other activities, such as sugar exports, favoured by the redistribution of the Cuban quota among Latin American countries producing sugar cane, and the export of meat and cattle. This generated new and larger revenues in foreign currencies, a certain level of industrialization – sugar mills, meat-processing plants, and the like – and, in the case of livestock, which was extensive, the development of large properties and systematic deforestation. There were also ventures into cotton and pineapples, which together with livestock consumed the greater part of external credit aimed at promoting agricultural production.

Following a clear policy of expansion of public spending and state intervention, the Orlich administration created a series of new autonomous institutions, which were financed in part by increasing the foreign debt. This had serious repercussions on the independence of the government, particularly in relations with the United States, and was probably one of the reasons why Costa Rica sent civil guards to the Dominican Republic to support the North American intervention in 1965. The implementation of these policies also led the Orlich government to increase tax rates, to stop paying the state's quota to the Social Security Fund, and to begin the practice of financing public works with government bonds – which would be out of control by the end of Oduber's administration (1978) and create a crisis during Carazo's term in office (1978–82).

The elections for Orlich's successor were held on 6 February 1966. The PLN was unified electorally but manifested growing differences between its most prominent leaders. Its candidate was Daniel Oduber, a brilliant politician who had been a founder of the Centre for the Study of National Problems, Secretary of the government junta of 1948 and the administrator of Decree 80, which had been central to the management of public funds. Oduber had also been president of the Legislative Assembly and Minister of Foreign Affairs in the Orlich administration. A lawyer who had studied in France and Canada, he occupied the third-ranking position, after Figueres and Orlich, in the party hierarchy. The opposition, on the other hand, was obliged to undergo a political transition in order to control the elections as a united force. This meant dispensing with the historical candidates of the main parties and selecting a compromise candidate in Professor José J. Trejos Fernández, a liberal economist and academic by profession and a man of great equanimity and tolerance.

The opposition attempted to organize the campaign around the issues of Communism and corruption, accusing Oduber of symbolizing both. The PLN laid great stress upon the experience of 1948 and championed its own record in government. This gave the opposition the opportunity to denounce PLN continuism, Trejos openly challenging the post-1948 model by supporting private banking and affirming the principle that the state should only intervene where private persons could not or would not do so. The Communists tried to participate in league with the Partido Alianza Popular Socialista, whose proposed candidate was the former Liberationist military leader Marcial Aguiluz, who had left his former party and allied himself with the PVP. However, in October 1967 the party was again declared illegal following a motion of the PLN and a nearly unanimous vote in the Legislative Assembly.

This was perhaps the closest election in national history: Trejos Fernández obtained 222,810 votes (50.5 per cent) and Oduber 218,590 (49.5

percent). In spite of this, the Legislative Assembly, which was elected together with the local governments on the same date as the presidential election, remained under the control of the PLN, which secured twenty-nine seats. Unificación Nacional, as the opposing alliance was called, elected twenty-six congressmen; a paramilitary rightist group, which soon disappeared, electing the remaining two.

The new administration inherited a public debt, excluding the debt owed to the Costa Rican Social Security Fund, of more than $870 million; the external debt stood at $100 million. Trejos Fernández responded by imposing a policy of austerity and containment of public spending. Employment was directed towards the private sector, producing friction with both Ulate and Calderón, who were under pressure from their respective electoral constituencies to provide jobs in the public domain. In accordance with his idea of the state as complementary to private enterprise, Trejos tried to repeal the state monopoly of banking. This initiative opened a particularly heated debate, which culminated on 23 July 1967 when the project was rejected.

The administration provoked further controversy when, in April 1970, it approved a contract with the multinational aluminum company ALCOA. The agreement was denounced in student circles and by the left in general as being unfairly one-sided and contrary to the national interest. Among those in the National Assembly who opposed it was Rodrigo Carazo, who exploited this issue to the full in developing his own political platform and ambitions. When congressmen from both parties approved the contract by a majority, the Legislative Assembly building was stoned and almost burned down by students on 24 April. Although there were riots in the capital and clashes with the police, the contract was immediately ratified by the executive. Nevertheless, having undertaken no work in the area in question, ALCOA soon withdrew and terminated the contract.

The political consequences of this event were significant. In the first place, it effectively suppressed the practice, inherited from the era of banana contracts, of granting concessions to foreign companies, guaranteeing them special privileges and compromising the sovereignty of the state. Second, it encouraged the student movement as well as other popular sectors to look for political alternatives to Communism and Castroism, encouraging the formation of a variety of leftist organizations from 1970 onwards.

The Trejos admininstration's economic policy was at first greatly complicated by a significant fall in coffee prices. Between 1966 and 1968 the average price per kilo of coffee exported fell from $0.959 to $0.806, although a modest increase in the volume of exports avoided a major fall in revenue. The price improved slightly from 1969, and by 1970 stood at $1,057 per kilo, further increases in volume exported producing an income from coffee sales that was, at $73 million, some 50 per cent higher at the end of the Trejos government than at its start. In 1969 total investment stood at $173.3 million, with $36.7 million, or 21.1 per cent, directed to the manufacturing sector. Thus, despite the generally unfavourable situation in coffee prices, the economy exhibited some dynamism as a result of the Trejos administration's policy of containing public spending, stabilizing government finances and slowing the growth of the state sector. Nevertheless, by 1970 the crisis of the Central American Common Market was already manifest.

In the elections of 1 February 1970 two ex-presidents, José Figueres and Mario Echandi, faced each other although neither of them had won their nominations easily. Figueres had succeeded in persuading Daniel Oduber to postpone his aspirations to stand for a second time, but Rodrigo Carazo, hitherto a political protégé of Figueres, had the impertinence to put up his own name at the convention and ran against the old *caudillo*. Carazo obtained a third of the votes, which intensified the conflict to such a point that he was practically expelled from the PLN. A little later he founded the Partido Renovación Democrática around his charismatic figure.

In Echandi's case, there were two great difficulties to overcome: the support pledged to Ulate's candidacy, and the attempts by a few Calderonistas to nominate their own candidate. Although Echandi managed to isolate Ulate from the capital, from his Executive Committee, and even from the National Assembly of his own National Union Party, the invectives launched by the veteran of 1948 succeeded in sharply impairing the credibility of Echandi's candidacy. At the same time a schism within the Calderonista ranks gave birth to the Partido Frente Nacional, and although the strength of the new party diminished as the campaign progressed, its mere existence, added to Ulate's efforts, irreparably weakened Echandi's chances against Figueres. Even Calderón Guardia himself was unable to overcome the effects of the division through a vigorous campaign in support of Echandi. By then Calderón's health was failing, and at the end of 1970 his rich and adventurous life came to an end.

The 1970 election was notable for the fact that the Christian Democrats participated as a party for the first time, and that the Communist Party,

Partido Acción Socialista, was able to compete. This was because although the Supreme Electoral Tribunal considered that it fell under the prohibition of Article 98 in the constitution, the Legislative Assembly did not become aware of the situation in time and did not decree its proscription by the two-thirds vote required by the law. Figueres, who had been closely linked with proscription in 1948, now requested that the Communists be completely legalized. (In fact, Figueres had not been in agreement with the legal prohibition of the Communist Party after the civil war although he accepted the majority decision of the rest of the members of the government junta, which was radically anti-communist.) It is noteworthy that thanks to the intervention of Luis Burstin, Figueres' physician, who had been a militant member of the Communist Party and very close to Manuel Mora, a close relationship had been established between Mora and Figueres. The two agreed that Mora would see to it that the Soviet Union purchase Costa Rica's coffee surplus, which was saleable only in new markets, in exchange for which the price and commissions would be distributed among the new coffee exporters, and the excess profits used to finance the cost of Figueres' campaign. Figueres, for his part, promised to legalize the Communist Party and establish diplomatic relations with the Soviet Union. The election results gave Figueres victory with 54.78 per cent of the vote while Echandi obtained 41.17 per cent and the other three candidates received less than 2 per cent.

Between 1961 and 1971 there had been a significant degree of concentration of income in the intermediate strata of society, and it was evident that the middle and upper sectors had become concentrated in secondary and tertiary activities. There was an increase in the number of professional employees, many of whom now worked for the state or in large private companies. Likewise, there was an increase in the relative percentage of waged workers in the secondary sector, reducing the corresponding number of workers employed in agriculture which had itself undergone appreciable differentiation with the appearance of important nuclei of national entrepreneurs in livestock, sugar cane, bananas and, later, rice, bolstering the growth of management groups in industry, both national and multinational.

Thus, during nearly ten years of the Central American Common Market the middle sectors had strengthened their presence in society and the state. Furthermore, the process of industrialization and modernization in agriculture had augmented the numbers of the proletariat, from 48.1 per cent of the economically active population in 1960 to 55.1 per cent in 1970. In his electoral campaign Figueres championed not only the democratic system, and especially the independence of the judiciary, but a fairer distribution of wealth and the struggle against extreme poverty, which, in his judgment, threatened the outbreak of violence within Costa Rican society. In addition to winning the presidency, Figueres had an overwhelming majority in the Legislative Assembly that comprised the thirty-two PLN congressmen, two Communist deputies (one of whom was Manuel Mora) and the Christian Democrats, who were in many aspects an extension of the government party. The government also controlled nearly all the municipalities. Moreover, as a result of a confidential arrangement with the Calderonista leader Francisco Calderón Guardia, the administration was able to control the autonomous institutions by introducing Law 4646, which guaranteed four seats for the government and three for the major opposition party on the boards of directors.

With such resources at his disposal, Figueres was able to create the Instituto Mixto de Ayuda Social (IMAS), whose mission was to eliminate extreme poverty in Costa Rica over a ten-year period. He introduced family allowances, expanded the coverage of social security (which rose from 46 per cent of the population to 85 per cent in 1978) and promoted higher education, increasing the number of universities to four, with a student body of 48,000, which represented 2.16 per cent of the country's population. Figueres also acquiesced in the proposal by a sector of the PLN to establish the Corporación Costarricense de Desarrollo (CODESA), and he ensured that the economic independence of the judiciary was constitutionally consolidated by allotting it a fixed percentage of the national budget. Figueres fulfilled his agreement with Manuel Mora; he established relations with the Soviet Union to the opposition of the right and the applause of the left, and legalized the Communist Party, repealing paragraph 2 of Article 98 of the Constitution.

On the other hand, the government soon found itself involved in several scandals, the most important of which was caused by the government's protection of the international fugitive Robert Vesco, for whom President Figueres himself wrote a defence speech. The financier, who had been charged in the United States for laundering money, financed part of the PLN election campaigns in 1970 and 1974, and set up a newspaper of social democratic leanings, *Excelsior,* to compete with *La Nación.* Yet the Vesco affair was only the most infamous of the series of financial and political scandals connected with the expansion of the state and welfare services that created a constant deficit in the state budget and an increase in public debt.

The rise in the price of petroleum struck home in 1973, but no preventive measures were taken. The resources of the Costa Rican Oil Refinery (RECOPE) were committed to financing the construction of stadiums and playing fields and recreational facilities in the ports. The government resorted to deficit and debt, in the thousands of millions, first in colones, and later in dollars.

In spite of his control over the executive power, the Legislative Assembly, the municipalities and the autonomous institutions, Figueres felt that he had not been able to govern as freely as he wanted. He declared that the Costa Rican state had grown too large, and was impossible to control. In his judgement, a de facto government like that of 1948 ought to be established for a period of two or three years in order to introduce reforms without legal or bureaucratic impediments, the normal system of elections every four years being reestablished thereafter.

In the elections of February 1974, the opposition to the PLN again failed to unite behind a single candidate. In addition to Daniel Oduber for the PLN and Fernando Trejos Escalante for Unificación Nacional, there were six other candidates including a Christian Democrat; Rodrigo Carazo for the new Renovación Democrática party; Jorge González Martén for the Partido Nacional Independiente (PNI) which sought to champion the interests of integrationist managerial sector; and Manuel Mora for the Partido Acción Socialista.

Opposition to the PLN was not the only source of division. The Communist Party for the first time had to face the emergence of other political groups whose convictions were more or less close to their own. To their left stood the Movimiento Revolucionario Auténtico with a Castroist orientation, and the Costa Rican Socialist Party; and to their right, the Partido Frente Popular, which only presented candidates for Congress.

The divisions within the opposition assured Daniel Oduber victory with 43.44 per cent of the vote (just under 300,000 votes); the Unificación Nacional candidate received 30.39 per cent, Carazo won 9.1 per cent, and González Martén 10.9 per cent. On the left, Mora obtained 2.4 per cent, the Socialist Party 0.5 per cent – the same as the Christian Democrats.

Upon taking office, the new president, much to Figueres' annoyance, made a speech around the theme 'Down with corruption', thereafter introducing a series of policies with remarkable speed. Oduber completed the universalization of social security, established his own programme of family assistance, and extended state services and the network of public roads. He increased the purchase of land to be distributed among the peasants, and stimulated the modernization of communications and the production of electric power. By 1978 health services, which in 1970 covered barely 46 per cent of the population, had expanded to cover 86 per cent, infant mortality dropped to 21 per thousand in 1978 while life expectancy passed the seventy-year mark.

Politically, the Oduber administration (1974–8) broke the alternation of power and was effectively the second part of a Liberationist administration of eight years (1970–8). At the same time, the PLN lacked a clear congressional majority, and although it was often able to reach agreement with Unificación Nacional, the other emerging parties subjected the government to sharp criticism. The government relied heavily on a significant rise in the price of coffee, from $1.384 per kilo in 1974 to $4.721 in 1977, which was unprecedented in the country's history and propelled total sales from $124.8 million to $319.2 million over the same period. The government also utilized internal and external credit for expansion during the international crisis of 1974–5. This, in turn, contributed towards the exhaustion of the programme of the PLN despite the singular efforts to promote an entrepreneurial state. This policy was linked to the appearance of a second generation of party leaders composed not of entrepreneurs who needed political power for their own modernization projects ('political entrepreneurs'), but of politicians and bureaucrats who wanted to enter the productive sphere in order to broaden their jurisdiction and private capital. This group may be termed 'entrepreneur-politicians' or a 'bureaucratic bourgeoisie'.

It soon became clear that the principal representative of the first generation of PNL political-entrepreneurs continued to be ex-president Figueres, while the second generation was represented in political and ideological terms by Daniel Oduber and in social terms by Luis A. Monge, whose successful electoral slogan in 1982 was that his only business had been the PLN.

The continuous exercise of political power by the PLN between 1970 and 1978 allowed this new social segment to launch the political programme of the entrepreneurial state, one of whose principal manifestations was CODESA. This corporation was created from the perspective that the state would develop projects in a number of economic areas where the private sector might have an interest but lacked the necessary resources. In order to avoid foreign control over these areas, the state would make the initial investment and, once the business was making a profit, would pass it back to the private sector. Those sectors of the economy that were considered vital would remain directly in the hands of the state. Nevertheless, in practice the postulates of the law establishing CODESA were very rarely followed. In addition to undertaking infrastructural activity, such as the production of hydrocarbon alcohol and cement, CODESA engaged in others where private enterprise had failed and still others in which its errors, losses and poor standards caused political and financial scandals. Thus, the nationalist ethic behind certain aspects of the entrepreneurial state and CODESA was profoundly compromised by economic confusion and suspicions of corruption.

With this transformation to the entrepreneurial state, the public sector was expanded once again, assuring for the new bureaucratic bourgeoisie, the income – from high salaries, tax exemptions, expense accounts, cars, house, credit and so on – and prestige that had previously been reserved for successful private businessmen. The financial sources for this political project included an increased public deficit and increases in tax rates on producers and citizens, an exaggerated and excessive external debt, bond issues and a rise in the internal debt. Thus the size of the investment, the concentration of capital, the privileges deriving from the essential nature of public enterprises, converted an entrepreneurial politician sector, unfamiliar with the real and substantive notions of profitability, efficiency, waste-trimming and satisfactory performance standards, into a dangerous competitor for the traditional private business sectors and, eventually, into an incontrovertible adversary.

Public sector entrepreneurialism deepened the segmented nature of the state. Each bureaucracy sought to protect itself though the feudalization of its institution. Institutional particularism was the dominant theme in matters of policy, pensions, salaries, commissions, permits, vacations, and so on. Differentiation arose not only between the institutions but also within them, reproducing the general social differentiation between the poor, the middle-income and the rich. At the same time, there was a manifest lack of coordination, and chains of command dissolved into hierarchical formalities incapable of changing policy. The state thus grew at an accelerated and a disorganized pace; it covered every facet of the social life of the country, reinforcing the image of a government with a giant body and a weak head.

At the end of the Oduber administration, Figueres announced that the country did not know where public affairs ended and private affairs began, thus legitimizing the suspicions of corruption against the government. Furthermore, he expressed his belief that Monge, the Liberationist candidate in the elections of 1978, would be defeated by the opposition. Since the constitutional reform of July 1969 expressly prohibited the re-election of a president, Figueres was able to make such provocative statements without prejudicing his own political ambitions. He therefore broke free from the traditions of his party to declare that the Costa Rican state was not only corrupt but also bureaucratic and indeed ungovernable.

Oduber's term ended not only in a fiscal crisis but also one of parties, ideologies and the nature of the State. The outgoing president's entrepreneurial state was a stillborn experiment. Symbolically, this took on a tone true to magic realism when his successor opened and closed, on the very same day, the installations of CATSA, the largest sugar center for the production of anhydrate alcohol in the country, property of CODESA.

Despite the participation of eight candidates, the 1978 poll centred on two principal groups: the Partido Unidad, whose candidate was Rodrigo Carazo, and the PLN, led by Luis A. Monge. Both the PNI and Unificación Nacional were abandoned by their supporters because of their supposed collaboration or complicity with Oduber; neither was able to elect a congressman to office. The PVP joined several small leftist groups under the name Pueblo Unido. The election was a clear victory for Carazo, who obtained 50.5 per cent of the vote against 43.8 per cent for Monge. The PVP obtained 2.7 per cent, and Unificación Nacional, which claimed to represent authentic Calderonism and counted Francisco Calderón Guardia among its leadership, only 1.7 per cent. The name of Calderón Guardia and his electoral heritage, however, were preserved by the opportune shift of several family members and important leaders, especially the son and widow of Dr Calderón Guardia, to the Partido Unidad, which they themselves had helped to create.

President Carazo had been a leader of the PLN, and his economic policies were influenced by those of his original party, although they also contained neo-liberal tendencies and a very marked personalist manner in decision-making. Carazo also presided over an incoherent alliance which tended to side with the Partido Liberación Nacional on certain issues, and as soon as he took office he found himself without a parliamentary faction of his own. The congressmen elected by the new Partido Unidad had different loyalties to those the leadership of the alliance, and the administration soon found itself isolated in the face of severe internal and external problems that it could not control.

Through the alternation between the principal parties every four years, the Costa Rican state had found a corrective factor for the excesses in spending and public investment by the governments of the PLN. Prudent rectifications in fiscal and monetary matters, and more sober utilization of governmental spending and external resources, brought equilibrium to public finance and the national economy. This process was interrupted by the election of the succeeding PLN administrations of Presidents Figueres and Oduber and then that of President Carazo, who had the same political and ideological origins as his predecessors. The Carazo administration thus failed to introduce the kind of corrective measures that might have rescued the financial situation of the country. The President did not put the currency on sound basis, failed to advance vigorous new policies, cut public spending or consolidate a consensus around the government that might have put an end to the abuse of internal and external credit.

Such failure was all the more marked in view of the gravity of the economic crisis the country suffered in this period. The GDP growth rate fell from 6.4 per cent in 1979 to 0.8 per cent in 1980, −2.3 per cent in 1981 and −7.3 per cent in 1982. The external public debt rose from $1 billion in 1979 to $3.7 billion in 1982. Exports, however, followed a different rhythm: in 1978 they stood at $1 billion as against $1.3 billion in imports; and in 1980 exports were $1.2 billion and imports $1.65 billion. Inflation advanced at an accelerated pace from 7.8 per cent in 1979 to 81.8 per cent in 1982. The colón lost its value in a similar pattern; in 1981 the real devaluation of 51 per cent was the largest in the country's economic history. In the first two years of the subsequent administration, the currency was devalued by 23 per cent, the figure for 1984 and 1985 being 9.6 per cent and 12.7 per cent respectively.

This economic crisis led to a series of open clashes between Carazo and the IMF and other international organizations, creating a climate of tension in foreign affairs that was greatly aggravated by the war in Nicaragua, which impinged directly on Costa Rica. Despite heading an avowedly conservative coalition, Carazo decided to give outspoken support to the insurrection against Somoza's regime. Combining the personal inclinations of the President with the legitimate policies of the state on the international level, and protected by the traditional anti-Somoza sentiments of the Costa Rican people, the Carazo regime became directly involved in the conflict. The prospect of a generalized instability that the fall of the Somoza regime implied was ignored, as was the impact that the illegal shipment of arms and personnel implied in a society like Costa Rica, which lacked adequate resources and mechanisms to manage and control the situation.

The crisis, however, was even more profound, and one of its clearest manifestations was the absence of political leadership. The older generation had lost its most outstanding leaders: Calderón and Ulate had already died; Figueres was now old and neutralized by Daniel Oduber; Mora not only carried the burden of his age, but his leadership was seriously questioned within his party, leading, in December 1984, to a major split in the PVP and a weakening of its union organizations. The conflict which occurred that year with the removal of Manuel Mora from the Party's general secretariat was encouraged by the Soviet embassy, which considered Mora to be weak and reformist at a time when Moscow was advocating a radical policy in Central America and total support for the Nicaraguan revolution. The party divided into two factions, one of which, led by Humberto Vargas and Arnoldo Ferreto, relied on the approval of the Soviet Union. With the take-over of the Central Committee by Vargas and Ferreto, Mora immediately founded a new organization, the Costa Rican National People's Party, with the political support of the Cuban government, and with the advantage that he maintained control over the finances of the old party. The group led by Vargas and Ferreto continued to use the name and flag of the PVP and organized a strike on the banana plantations of the southern Pacific coast, with a view to proving its national strength and dominance over the unions. This occurred at the same time as the United Fruit Company decided to cease banana cultivation in Costa Rica. The strike only encouraged the company in its plans, and was a complete disaster. The closure of the banana industry dissolved a long-standing concentration of workers, and the union movement lost its strength in the country. The blame for these events fell on the PVP, but the popular sectors punished the left as a whole, which failed to achieve even 5 per cent of the vote in the election of 1986.

Thus the general crisis of the Costa Rican state and the Costa Rican economy was exacerbated by a crisis of the Costa Rican political system, marked by both an absence of leadership and a neutralization of the different factions into which society had become divided. The problems were so profound and varied that they required a national consensus, or at least a consensus among key social forces, in order to overcome the exhaustion of post-war political strategies. As the regional conflict in Central America deepened and the role of the United States within it grew, what came to be questioned was the very viability of Costa Rica as a sovereign, independent nation with its own cultural and historical profile.

In 1982 the political pendulum swung back towards the PLN, which once again presented Luis A. Monge as its presidential candidate. Monge was a former union leader with Benjamín Núñez, and had been a Social-Democrat delegate to the constitutional convention in 1949. He possessed long-standing ties with the United States and now found support among the electorate for a close alliance with the U.S. embassy, which was strongly opposed to Carazo.

The Partido Unidad, oppressed by the weight of the Carazo administration and by the crisis for which the government was blamed, nominated as its candidate Rafael Angel Calderón, the son of Dr Calderón Guardia and ex-Minister of Foreign Affairs under Carazo. Also participating were the Movimiento Nacional, with ex-President Echandi as candidate (he had been exempted when the constitutional prohibition against presidential re-election had been written), the PVP and its allies under the United People's Coalition, and two parties, the Democratic Party and the Independent Party, which lacked a clear political and ideological profile. The PLN won 58 per cent of the votes; the Partido Unidad received 33.6 per cent; Echandi's Movimiento Nacional only 3.8 per cent; and Pueblo Unido 3.3 per cent.

The problems inherited by the new Monge administration were serious, but the PLN victory was great enough to allow it to attempt profound and radical changes in society, the economy and the state. This, though, was not the new president's calling, and he governed in a listless fashion, which by the end of his administration produced a multitude of very serious political scandals. Perhaps the greatest of these was on the international front, when Monge declared a policy of neutrality, yet allowed the anti-Sandinista activities of the Reagan administration to take place on Costa Rican soil with the full knowledge of the government.

The Monge government enjoyed the apparent good fortune of being able to exploit the exceptional regional situation, which attracted an uncommon involvement of foreign agencies and governments channeling important financial resources to Central America that, under other conditions, would perhaps have been directed to different places. Thus the total amount of new resources from external financing received by the public sector alone rose from $469.4 million in 1981, to $494.2 million in 1985. When these figures are added to the overdue amounts in debt service and its scheduling, they came to a grand total of $4,132 million between 1981 and 1985. This foreign aid permitted and even encouraged the continuation of the paralysis and stagnation of the previous period. The privileges derived from state employment continued, although, under pressure from the international lending agencies, Costa Rica would have to abandon momentarily some of the most sordid and critical aspects of the entrepreneurial state model and make room for the impetuous and disorderly emergence of a private finance sector, closely linked to these same agencies.

The absence of significant rectifications and the artificial climate which produced this generous U.S. aid did nothing to impede the transfer of the cost of the crisis to the weakest economic sectors and the middle classes, which were directly affected by the stagnation of production, the fall of real income, high taxes and debt service. Between 1979 and 1982 real income declined by between 30 and 40 per cent. In 1982, income reached its lowest level and inflation reached 9 per cent, its highest level, while production fell 7 per cent. It is estimated that even if production had not declined, the national gross income would have been 12 per cent less as a result of unfavorable exchange rates and payments to meet the external debt.

External economic aid was attached to clearly neo-liberal policies which sought the denationalization of the economy and its reorientation on the basis of simple fiscal equilibrium, geared towards the production and export of non-traditional goods. In other words, the objectives of these policies did not lie in resolving the crisis of the country and re-establishing a healthy direction for its development, but rather in ensuring at any cost that it would meet its obligations to the international banking system, in accordance with the bias characteristic of the agreements with the International Monetary Fund.

For the international agencies this responded to a clear logic which saw everything (loans, structural adjustments, letters of intent, etc.) from the perspective of liberalizing the economy, reducing the sphere of public investment and facilitating the fulfilment of servicing the public debt. While the external public debt showed, in millions of U.S. dollars, capital gains of $207.0 in 1982, $609.1 in 1983, $454.5 in 1984 and $491.7 in 1985, the debt service actually realized was, for the respective years, $169.0, $637.7, $315.4, and $563.1, leaving the balance of net external resources at $38 million for 1982, −$28 million for 1983, $139 for 1984 and −$71.4 for 1985.

From the national point of view, the problem was much more complex than the heavy burden of debt service. The criteria of comparative international costs used to evaluate the profitability of a productive sector led to the eventual liquidation of entire branches of the economy. Dependency on the flow of external resources made the slightest regression critical in its effects, and the national economy became chronically dependent on the goodwill and distribution of aid from the international agencies and friendly countries.

Such a state of affairs postponed the solution of structural problems, but it did re-establish confidence and preserve social peace. This was less the result of the government's own initiative than of U.S. policy to make financial concessions and grant aid so as to secure a degree of tranquillity and non-military influence within Central America. At the same time, the emphasis of foreign aid on the private sector raised the possibility that its principal beneficiaries might accumulate sufficient economic and political authority to break the existing impasse and establish a new hegemony. The weakening of the state monopoly on banking in 1984 strongly suggested that the balance of forces was moving in this direction.

However the private financial sector lacked autonomous economic power. Basically speculative in character, its activities were heavily dependent on the flow of external economic aid after 1982. Since very little of this aid was directed to the public sector the new financiers certainly had access to unusual resources. Yet the dependence on external aid and the favouritism that went with it were naturally conditioned by fluctuations in the aid itself and by the international economic situation. Thus, when the favourable character of these changed for the worse, the impact on the local financial sector was immediate. This began to happen quite quickly. Second, the objective limits on the opportunities for productive investment, beyond transactions in foreign money and state securities, played a negative role. Much speculative activity involved foreign currency transactions, in many cases skirting the restrictions established by the Central Bank. These and other activities provoked financial scandals and numerous bankruptcies, which eroded public confidence in the new financial groups and indirectly strengthened the national banking system.

Although the economic crisis, regional conflict, and expansion of foreign influence produced an unprecedented challenge during the 1980s, they also helped to promote the values of the Costa Rican democratic way of life. The country's indices of health and education remained among the highest in Latin America; the regime of political parties, free elections and respect for human rights constituted true accomplishments on the part of a people which had learned, in the midst of scarce resources and the inherent problems of its underdevelopment and dependency, how to preserve its profile as sovereign, democratic and independent.

The 1986 election victory of the PLN candidate Dr Oscar Arias brought into relief the national, democratic and pacifist nature of Costa Rica. The new president diligently sought to resolve the ambiguities of the Monge government, most particularly in the field of foreign relations. In February 1987, Arias presented a plan to secure the cessation of the civil wars and foreign armed intervention in the region. For this he was awarded the Nobel Peace Prize, and the peace plan was formally adopted by Central America's presidents in August 1987. This initiative by no means succeeded in immediately quelling the fighting and only modestly reduced Costa Rica's vulnerability to destabilization from abroad. Nevertheless, it produced a palpable shift in the regional balance of forces and political atmosphere, introducing a modicum of Costa Rican equanimity into the violent affairs of its neighbours. In the wake of this celebrated enterprise in foreign policy, the overriding challenge that remained was to secure a strategy that would resist the decay of the considerable accomplishments of Costa Rican society, overcome the adverse conditions that had prevailed for the previous decade, and provide a dynamic basis for economic welfare and political democracy in the last years of the century.

BIBLIOGRAPHICAL ESSAYS

LIST OF ABBREVIATIONS

ESC	*Estudios Sociales Centroamericanos*
HAHR	*Hispanic American Historical Review*
JGSWGL	*Jahrbuch für Geschichte von Staat, Wirtschaft und Gesellschaft Lateinamerikas*
JIAS	*Journal of Inter-American Studies and World Affairs*
LARR	*Latin American Research Review*
TA	*The Americas*

1. THE AFTERMATH OF INDEPENDENCE, *c.* 1821 – 1870

A comparison of Lázaro Lamadrid, 'A survey of the historiography of Guatemala since 1821. Part 1 – The nineteenth century', *TA*, 8/2 (1951), 189–202; W. J. Griffith, 'The historiography of Central America since 1830', *HAHR*, 40/4 (1960), 548–69; and Griffith, 'Central America', in C. C. Griffin (ed.), *Latin America, a guide to the historical literature* (Austin, 1971), 403–21, reflects the rapid growth of historical publications in the mid-twentieth century. The following essay is concerned principally with works published since Griffin and will be most useful when employed together with the guides mentioned above and the extensive bibliographical essay in R. L. Woodward, Jr, *Central America, a nation divided* (2nd edn, New York, 1985), 278–312, as well as with appropriate sections of the *Handbook of Latin American Studies*.

While earlier general works continue to have utility, Woodward, *Central America*, and Ciro Cardoso and Héctor Pérez, *Centroamérica y la economía occidental (1520–1930)* (San José, 1977) incorporate much of the recent scholarship on the first half-century of independence, especially for the economic and social history. Edelberto Torres Rivas, *Interpretación del desarrollo social centroamericano* (San José, 1971) has provided much of the inspiration for serious recent historical research in the social sciences in Central America. Histories of individual states that reflect recent scholarship have been few, but exceptions are Alastair White, *El Salvador* (New York, 1973); Narda Dobson, *A history of Belize* (London, 1973); O. N. Bolland, *The formation of a colonial society: Belize from conquest to crown colony* (Baltimore, 1977); and David Luna, *Manual de historia económica* (San Salvador, 1971). For reference, although uneven in quality, the *Historical Dictionary* series published in Metuchen, N.J., are useful: Philip Flemion, *El Salvador* (1972); H. K. Meyer, *Nicaragua* (1972) and *Honduras* (1976); R. E. Moore, *Guatemala*, rev. edn (1973); and Theodore Creedman, *Costa Rica* (1977). Also useful are the first volumes in the World Bibliographical Series (Oxford: Clio Press): R. L. Woodward, *Belize* (1980) and *Nicaragua* (1983), and Woodman Franklin, *Guatemala* (1981).

Several recent studies deal with specific aspects of the post-independence period: D. R. Radell, *Historical geography of Western Nicaragua: the spheres of influence in León, Granada and Managua, 1519–1965* (Berkeley, 1969); David Browning, *El Salvador, landscape and society* (Oxford, 1971); Alberto Sáenz M., *Historia agrícola de Costa Rica* (San José, 1970); Carolyn

Hall, *El café y el desarrollo histórico-geográfico de Costa Rica* (San José, 1976); Constantino Láscaris, *Historia de las ideas en Centroamérica* (San José, 1970); Carlos González, *Historia de la educación en Guatemala*, 2nd edn (Guatemala, 1970); Otto Olivera, *La literatura en publicaciones periódicas de Guatemala: siglo XIX* (New Orleans, 1974); Arturo Castillo, *Historia de la moneda de Honduras* (Tegucigalpa, 1974); Samuel Stone, *La dinastía de los conquistadores* (San José, 1975); Cleto González Víquez, *Capítulos de un libro sobre historia financiera de Costa Rica*, 2nd edn (San José, 1977); and R. L. Woodward, Jr, *Privilegio de clases y el desarrollo económico: el consulado de comercio de Guatemala, 1793–1871* (San José, 1981), which contains extensive documentary appendices not included in the 1966 English edition. Among the most noteworthy articles based on new research and new methodologies recently published in Central American journals are: Ciro Cardoso, 'La formación de la hacienda cafetalera en Costa Rica (siglo XIX)' *ESC*, 2/6 (1973), 22–50; Carlos Araya, 'La minería y sus relaciones con la acumulación de capital y la clase dirigente de Costa Rica, 1821–1841', *ESC*, 2/5 (1973), 31–64, and 'La minería en Costa Rica, 1821–1843', *Revista Historia* (Costa Rica), 1/2 (1976), 83–125; Héctor Pérez, 'Economía y sociedad en Honduras durante el siglo XIX. Las estructuras demográficas', *ESC*, 2/6 (1973), 51–82; Guillermo Molina, 'Estructura productiva e historia demográfica (Economía y desarrollo en Honduras)', *Anuario de Estudios Centroamericanos*, 3 (1977), 161–73; and Alberto Lanuza, 'Nicaragua: territorio y población (1821–1875)', *Revista del Pensamiento Centroamericano*, 31/151 (1976), 1–22, 'Comercio exterior de Nicaragua (1821–1875)', *ESC*, 5/14 (1976), 109–36, and 'La minería en Nicaragua (1821–1875)', *Anuario de Estudios Centroamericanos*, 3 (1977), 215–24. R. L. Woodward, Jr has reviewed the literature on the demographic history of the period in 'Crecimiento de población en Centroamérica durante la primera mitad del siglo de la independencia nacional', *Mesoamérica* 1/1 (1980), 219–31. Although he overlooks some of the work already done, Thomas Schoonover, 'Central American commerce and maritime activity in the nineteenth century: sources for a quantitative approach', *LARR*, 13/2 (1978), 157–69, provides some guidance in this area.

Among recent works dealing with the establishment of Central American independence, clearly the most important is Mario Rodríguez, *The Cádiz Experiment in Central America, 1808–1826* (Berkeley, 1978). While Louis Bumgartner, *José del Valle of Central America* (Durham, N.C., 1963) remains the definitive work on that important political figure, Ramón López, *José Cecilio del Valle, Fouché de Centro América* (Guatemala, 1968) offers some new insights, and Rafael H. Valle, *Pensamiento vivo de José Cecilio del Valle*, 2nd edn (San José, 1971), is an excellent anthology of his writings and synthesis of his ideas. The role of the first Central American Constituent Assembly is dealt with in detail by Andrés Townsend, *Las Provincias Unidas de Centroamérica: fundación de la República* (San José, 1973) in a substantial amplification of his 1958 book of the same title. Two revisionist articles on the Federation period are Philip Flemion, 'States' rights and partisan politics: Manuel José Arce and the struggle for Central American Union', *HAHR*, 53/4 (1973), 600–18, and Mauricio Domínguez, 'El Obispado de San Salvador: foco de desavenencia político-religiosa', *Anuario de Estudios Centroamericanos*, 1 (1974), 87–133. Francisco Morazán's *Memorias*, written following his defeat in 1840 and published in Paris in 1870, were reprinted in Tegucigalpa in 1971, and a collection of his personal papers have appeared in W. J. Griffith, 'The personal archive of Francisco Morazán', *Philological and Documentary Studies*, II (Publication 12, Middle American Research Institute, Tulane University, New Orleans, 1977), 197–286. For the post-independence period, T. L. Karnes, *The failure of union: Central America, 1824–1975*, rev. edn (Center for Latin American Studies, Arizona State University, Tempe, 1976), is identical to his earlier work, and Alberto Herrarte, *El federalismo en Centroamérica* (San José, 1972), is a condensation of his *Unión de Centroamérica* (Guatemala, 1964). F. D. Parker, *Travels in Central America, 1821–1840* (Gainesville, Fla., 1970), deals with a number of the perceptive travel accounts of this period. Reflecting substantial new research are the articles on Guatemala by Mario Rodríguez, Miriam Williford, R. L. Woodward, Jr and W. J. Griffith, in *Applied Enlightenment: 19th-century liberalism* (Publication 23, Middle American Research Institute, Tulane University, New Orleans, 1972). Griffith's article in that volume, 'Attitudes toward foreign colonization: the evolution of nineteenth-century Guatemalan immigration', expands upon the ideas earlier presented in his *Empires in the wilderness* (Chapel Hill, N.C., 1966). See also Williford's 'The educational reforms of Dr. Mariano Galvez', *JIAS*, 10/3 (1968), 461–73. For the diplomatic history of the period, in addition to Mario Rodriguez's excellent *Palmerstonian diplomat in Central America: Frederick Chatfield, Esq.* (Tucson, Arizona, 1964), see R. A. Humphreys, 'Anglo-American rivalries in Central America', in *Tradition and revolt in Latin America* (London, 1969), 154–55; David Waddell, 'Great Britain and the Bay Islands, 1821–

61', *The Historical Journal*, 2/1 (1959), 59–77; C. L. Stansifer, 'Ephraim George Squier: diversos aspectos de su carrera en Centroamérica', *Revista Conservadora del Pensamiento Centroamericano*, 20/98 (1968); Cyril Allen, *France in Central America* (New York, 1966), which concentrates on canal agent Felix Belly; and Andrés Vega Bolaños, *Los atentados del superintendente de Belice* (Managua, 1971), which focuses on British activities of 1840–2. José Ramírez describes the career of an early Nicaraguan diplomat in his *José de Marcoleta: padre de la diplomacia nicaragüense* (2 vols., Managua, 1975). Chester Zelaya and L. F. Sibaja treat Costa Rican acquisition of Guanacaste in *La anexión del partido de Nicoya* (San José, 1974). Zelaya has also elucidated the career of J. F. Osejo in *El Bachiller Osejo* (2 vols., San José, 1971). Traditional liberal condemnations of Rafael Carrera have been challenged by Luis Beltranena, *Fundación de la República de Guatemala* (Guatemala, 1971), and Keith Miceli, 'Rafael Carrera: defender and promoter of peasant interests in Guatemala, 1837–1848', *TA*, 31/1 (1974), 72–95, as well as by R. L. Woodward, 'Liberalism, conservatism and the response of the peasants of La Montaña to the government of Guatemala, 1821–1850', in *Plantation Society in the Americas*, 1/1 (1979), 109–30. See also Pedro Tobar Cruz, *Los montañeses: la facción de los Lucíos y otros acontecimientos históricos de 1846 a 1851* (Guatemala, 1971). An important memoir of the period has been republished in Francisco Ortega, *Cuarenta años (1838–1878) de historia de Nicaragua*, 2nd edn (Managua, 1974).

The Anglo-American rivalry for a transoceanic route and the William Walker episode continue to attract historical writings at all levels. Enrique Guier, *William Walker* (San José, 1971), offers nothing new but is a competent work, while Frederic Rosengarten, *Freebooters Must Die!* (Wayne, Penn., 1976) combines a lively account with many contemporary illustrations and maps. More scholarly are the works of David Folkman, *The Nicaragua route* (Salt Lake City, 1972); R. E. May, *The southern dream of a Caribbean empire, 1854–1861* (Baton Rouge, 1973); and Germán Tjarks *et al.*, 'La epidemia del cólera de 1856 en el Valle Central: análisis y consecuencias demográficas', *Revista de Historia* (Costa Rica), 2/3 (1976), 81–129. Alejandro Bolaños has begun to publish a series of works on the Walker period based on the enormous volume of materials he has been accumulating. Of the first volumes to appear, perhaps the most interesting is his *El filibustero Clinton Rollins* (Masaya, Nic., 1976), in which he exposes Rollins, supposedly an associate of Walker, as the pseudonym of H. C. Parkhurst and his accounts of Walker as fiction.

For the close of the period, Wayne Clegern, author of *British Honduras: colonial dead end* (Baton Rouge, 1967), suggests a transitional role for the Vicente Cerna administration in 'Transition from conservatism to liberalism in Guatemala, 1865–1981', in William S. Coker (ed.), *Hispanic-American essays in honor of Max Leon Moorhead* (Pensacola, Florida, 1979), also published in Spanish in *Revista del Pensamiento Centroamericano*, 31/151 (1976), 60–5. There are studies of major figures in Costa Rica and El Salvador during this period: Carlos Meléndez, *Dr. José María Montealegre* (San José, 1968), and Italo López, *Gerardo Barrios y su tiempo* (2 vols., San Salvador, 1965). Finally, valuable contemporary impressions of the period have been reprinted: Francisco Lainfiesta, *Apuntamientos para la historia de Guatemala, período de 20 años corridos del 14 de abril de 1865 al 6 de abril de 1885* (Guatemala, 1975), and Pablo Levy, *Notas geográficas y económicas sobre la República de Nicaragua*, 2nd edn (Managua, 1976).

2. THE LIBERAL ERA, *c.* 1870 – 1930

There is an extensive bibliographical essay in R. L. Woodward Jr, *Central America. A nation divided* (New York, 1976), 278–321.

Three books provide a general view of the period 1870–1930: Mario Rodríguez, *Central America* (Englewood Cliffs, NJ, 1965), which is rather favourable to United States policies in the isthmus; Woodward, *Central America*; and Ciro Cardoso and Héctor Pérez Brignoli, *Centroamérica y la economía occidental (1520–1930)* (San José, 1977). The best general book on an individual Central American state is David Browning, *El Salvador. Landscape and society* (Oxford, 1971).

On the Central American coffee economies, see C. Cardoso, 'Historia económica del café en Centroamérica (siglo XIX): estudio comparativo', *Estudios Sociales Centroamericanos*, 4/10 (1975), 9–55. On the banana plantations, general works are Stacy May and Galo Plaza, *The United Fruit Company in Latin America* (Washington, DC, 1958), which is favourable to the company; Charles Kepner, *Social aspects of the banana industry* (New York, 1936), and Kepner and Jay Soothill, *The banana empire* (New York, 1935), which are far more critical.

By far the best publications on economic history are for Guatemala and Costa Rica. For Guatemala, see Alfredo Guerra Borges, *Geografía económica de Guatemala* (2 vols., Guatemala, 1973); Valentín Solórzano, *Evolución económica de Guatemala* (Guatemala, 1970); Sanford A. Mosk *et al.*, *Economía de Guatemala* (Guatemala, 1958); Mauricio Domínguez T., 'The development of the technological and scientific coffee industry in Guatemala 1830–1930' (unpublished PhD thesis, University of Tulane, 1970); Julio C. Cambranes, *Aspectos del desarrollo económico y social de Guatemala a la luz de fuentes históricas alemanas 1868–1885* (Instituto de Investigaciones Económicas y Sociales de la Universidad de San Carlos de Guatemala, Guatemala, 1975); Julio C. Cambranes, *El imperialismo alemán en Guatemala. El tratado de comercio de 1887* (Guatemala, 1977); Roberto Quintana, *Apuntes sobre el desarrollo monetario de Guatemala* (Guatemala, 1971). For Costa Rica, see Rodrigo Facio, *Estudio sobre economía costarricense* (2nd.edn, San José, 1972), still useful after more than 30 years; Alain Vieillard-Baron, *La production agricole et la vie rurale au Costa Rica* (Mexico, 1974); C. Cardoso, 'The formation of the coffee estate in nineteenth-century Costa Rica', in Kenneth Duncan and Ian Rutledge (eds.), *Land and labour in Latin America* (Cambridge, 1975), 165–202; Carolyn Hall, *El café y el desarrollo histórico-geográfico de Costa Rica* (San José, 1976) and *Formación de una hacienda cafetalera 1889–1911* (San José, 1978), the best texts available on the coffee economy of Costa Rica; Ana Cecilia Román Trigo, 'El comercio exterior de Costa Rica (1883–1930)' (unpublished thesis, Universidad de Costa Rica, San José, 1978); Thomas Schoonover, 'Costa Rican trade and navigation ties with the United States, Germany and Europe, 1840 to 1885', *JGSWGL*, 14 (1977) 269–308, which argues for an earlier American pre-eminence in commercial matters than is usually recognized; Carlos Araya Pochet, 'El segundo ciclo minero en Costa Rica (1890–1930)' (Universidad de Costa Rica, San José, 1976, mimeo); Rufino Gil Pacheco, *Ciento cinco años de vida bancaria en Costa Rica* (3rd edn, San José, 1975).

On the economic history of Honduras, see Charles A. Brand, 'The background of capitalistic underdevelopment: Honduras to 1913' (unpublished PhD thesis, University of Pittsburgh, 1972); Vilma Laínez and Victor Meza, 'El enclave bananero en la historia de Honduras', *Estudios Sociales Centroamericanos*, 2/5 (1973), 115–56; Jorge Morales, 'El Ferrocarril Nacional de Honduras: su historia e incidencia sobre el desarrollo económico', *Estudios Sociales Centroamericanos*, 1/2 (1972), 7–20; Kenneth V. Finney, 'Precious metal mining and the modernization of Honduras. Inquest of "El Dorado"' (unpublished PhD thesis, Tulane University, 1973); *Historia financiera de Honduras* (Tegucigalpa, 1957). On El Salvador, see in particular Browning, *El Salvador*, and David A. Luna, *Manual de historia económica de El Salvador* (San Salvador, 1971); also

Legislación salvadoreña del café, 1846–1955 (San Salvador, 1956). And, on Nicaragua see Pedro Belli, 'Prolegómenos para una historia económica de Nicaragua de 1905 a 1966', *Revista del Pensamiento Centroamericano*, 30/146 (1975), 2–30.

The social history of central America has been studied more by anthropologists and sociologists (see Woodward, *Central America*, 313–14) than by historians. Nevertheless see José L. Vega Carballo, 'El nacimiento de un régimen de burguesía dependiente: el caso de Costa Rica', *Estudios Sociales Centroamericanos*, 2/5 and 6 (1973); James Backer, *La Iglesia y el sindicalismo en Costa Rica* (2nd edn, San José, 1975); Mario Posas, *Las sociedades artesanales y los orígenes del movimiento obrero hondureño* (Tegucigalpa, 1978); Roque Dalton, *Miguel Mármol. Los sucesos de 1932 en El Salvador* (San José, 1972); Thomas F. Anderson, *Matanza* (Lincoln, 1971) and *El Salvador 1932* (San José, 1976). Edelberto Torres Rivas, *Interpretación del desarrollo social centroamericano* (San José, 1971), which is somewhat outdated by recent research on economic and political history, still offers an interesting general interpretation of the history of this period.

On political history, a general overview is offered by Edelberto Torres Rivas, 'Poder nacional y sociedad dependiente: las clases y el estado en Centroamérica', *Estudios Sociales Centroamericanos*, 3/8 (1974), 27–63; Reynaldo Salinas López, 'La unión de Centroamérica, 1895–1922' (unpublished dissertation, Mexico, 1978), discusses US pressures against Central American union.

There are a number of recent works on the Guatemalan Liberal reforms: Jorge M. García L., *La reforma liberal en Guatemala* (Guatemala and San José, 1972); Thomas R. Herrick, *Desarrollo económico y político de Guatemala durante el período de Justo Rufino Barrios (1871–1885)* (San José, 1974); Paul Burgess, *Justo Rufino Barrios* (San José, 1972); Roberto Díaz Castillo, *Legislación económica de Guatemala durante la reforma liberal. Catálogo* (Guatemala and San José, 1973). On Costa Rican political history, Samuel Stone, *La dinastía de los conquistadores* (San José, 1975) is outstanding. See also, José L. Vega C., 'Etapas y procesos de la evolución sociopolítica de Costa Rica', *Estudios Sociales Centroamericanos*, 1/1 (1972), 45–72. About the Honduran Liberal reforms there are two opposing views: Héctor Pérez Brignoli, 'La reforma liberal en Honduras', *Cuaderno de Ciencias Sociales* 1/2 (1973), 2–86, and Guillermo Molina Chocano, *Estado liberal y desarrollo capitalista en Honduras* (Tegucigalpa, 1976).

3. CRISIS AND CONFLICT SINCE 1930

There is abundant literature on Central America since 1930. See Edelberto Torres Rivas and Maria Eugenia Gallardo, *Para entender Centroámerica: resumen bibliográfico* (San José, 1985), and Kenneth Grieb, *Central America in the Nineteenth and Twentieth Centuries: An Annotated Bibliography* (Boston, 1988). An analysis of what has been written in the last twenty-five years, however, reveals that 80 per cent of all Spanish texts about Central America in general or any of the countries in particular have been written since 1979. Similarly what has been written in English consists, in essence, of a literature of 'the crisis'. Nevertheless, both before and after 1979, important works were published which are fundamental to an understanding of Central American history.

There are few works which treat the Central American region as a whole and which at the same time respect national features and local peculiarities. Franklin Parker, *The Central American Republics* (London, 1964), contains an analysis of and useful information about the economy, society and institutions of each country, covering the period up to 1960. More comprehensive and underlining regional homogeneity is Ralph L. Woodward, *Central America: A Nation Divided* (2d ed., New York, 1985), which also contains an exhaustive Selective Guide to the Literature on Central America. The two-volume text by Mario Monteforte Toledo, *Centro América: subdesarrollo y dependencia* (Mexico, 1972) is important for the quantitative information it contains. Also important because they contain interpretive propositions for the entire region are Edelberto Torres-Rivas, *Interpretación del desarrollo social centroamericano* (San José, 1971), one of the first works to treat the region as a whole; and Héctor Pérez Brignoli, *Breve historia de Centroamérica* (Madrid, 1986). The most detailed and comprehensive political history of Central America in the twentieth century is James Dunkerley, *Power in the Isthmus: A Political History of Modern Central America* (London, 1988).

Several other works also address themselves to Central America as a whole but concentrate on specific aspects or specific periods. Rodolfo Cerdas Cruz, *La hoz e el machete* (San José, 1986) examines the role of the Third International in Central America. For the period of the Second World War and its immediate aftermath, see Thomas M. Leonard, *The United States and Central America 1944–1949* (University, Ala., 1984); Andres Opazo, *Estructura agraria, dinámico de población y desarrollo capitalista en Centroamérica* (San José, 1978), is a detailed analysis of changes in agriculture and population movements. In *The Religious Roots of Rebellion: Christians in Central American Revolution* (New York, 1984), Phillip Berryman explains the changes experienced by the Central American Church and the role of the clergy in political struggle. Of the many works written on the political crisis that developed at the end of the 1970s, three contain particularly well-articulated analytical propositions: Donald E. Schulz and Douglas H. Graham (eds.), *Revolution and Counterrevolution in Central America and the Caribbean* (Boulder, Colo., 1984), a collection of historical and theoretical essays; Walter LaFeber, *Inevitable Revolution: The United States in Central America* (New York, 1984), an examination of U.S. policy in the region; and Morris Blachman et al., *Confronting Revolution: Security Through Diplomacy in Central America* (New York, 1986), a collection of essays on international relations in the Central American crisis.

On the Central American economy several books are indispensable. First is the result of an ambitious research project carried out by SIECA (Secretaria de Integración Económica Centroamericana), also called the Rosenthal report, after the economist who headed the project: *El desarrollo integrado de Centroamérica en la presente década: bases y propuestas para el perfeccionamiento y la reestructuración del Mercado Común* (Buenos Aires, 1973) comprises thirteen volumes of the most complete review of the regional economy ever undertaken. Two recent studies with a regional perspective by North American economists are John Weeks, *The Economies of Central America* (New York, 1985), a general analysis concentrating on the period since 1950; and Robert C. Williams, *Export Agriculture and the Crisis in Central America* (Chapel Hill, N.C., 1986), an extraordinary and well-documented look at the effects of the regional economic 'boom' of the sixties and seventies and, in particular, the social – and ecological – impact of the introduction into Central America of the export production of cotton and cattle. W. A. Durham, *Scarcity and Survival in Central America: Ecological Origins of the Soccer War* (Stanford, 1979), contains a rigorous quantitative analysis of population problems in El Salvador and an interpretation of the so-called 'useless war' of 1969. Also important is Richard Fagen (ed.), *Transition and Development: Problems of Third World Socialism* (New York, 1986), which brings together various analyses of economic policy in revolutionary Nicaragua and offers a theoretical discussion on the viability of socialist change in the Central American 'periphery'.

Finally, mention should be made of Victor Bulmer-Thomas, *The Political Economy of Central America Since 1920* (Cambridge, 1987) which is without any doubt the best work published to date on Central America. It contains not only an economic history of the last sixty years but also an outstanding analysis of the region's political and social life.

4. GUATEMALA SINCE 1930

Despite its age and limited attention to historical developments, Richard N. Adams, *Crucifixion by Power: Essays on Guatemalan Social Structure, 1944–1966* (Austin, Tex., 1970) continues to occupy a central place in the literature on Guatemala in the twentieth century. A more recent narrative account of republican history is Jim Handy, *Gift of the Devil: A History of Guatemala* (Toronto, 1984), popular in style but with a full scholarly apparatus. The period up to the mid-1930s is covered in the engaging study by Chester Lloyd Jones, *Guatemala Past and Present* (Minneapolis, 1940). Providing full statistical material supported by a rather uneven text on the following two decades is Mario Monteforte Toledo, *Guatemala: monografía sociológica* (Mexico, 1959), while Carlos Guzmán-Böckler and Jean-Loup Herbert, *Guatemala: una interpretación histórico-social* (Mexico, 1970) is overwhelmingly analytical in perspective. Alfonso Bauer Paiz, *Como opera el capital Yanqui en Centroamérica: el caso de Guatemala* (Mexico, 1956), and Thomas and Marjorie Melville, *Guatemala: The Politics of Land Ownership* (New York, 1971), are both polemical in style and secondary studies but do give cogent overviews of two important factors in twentieth-century society and economy.

General economic developments in the post-war period are treated in more technical fashion in World Bank, *The Economic Development of Guatemala* (Baltimore, 1951), and Lehman B. Fletcher et al., *Guatemala's Economic Development: the Role of Agriculture* (Ames, Iowa 1970). The complexities of peasant agriculture are treated in many studies, among the most suggestive of which are Lester Schmid, 'The Role of Migratory Labor in the Economic Development of Guatemala', Research Paper, Land Tenure Center, University of Wisconsin (Madison, 1967); Manuel Gollas, 'Surplus Labor and Economic Efficiency in the Traditional Sector of a Dual Economy: the Guatemalan Case', *Journal of Development Studies* 8, no. 4 (1972); Ivon Lebot, 'Tenencia de la Tierra en el Altiplano Occidental de Guatemala', *Estudios Sociales Centroamericanos,* no. 13 (1976); Thomas J. Maloney, 'El Impacto Social del Esquema de Desarrollo de la Franja Transversal del Norte sobre los Maya-Kekchi en Guatemala', *Estudios Sociales Centroamericanos,* no. 29 (1981), and Carol A. Smith, 'Local History in

Global Context: Social and Economic Transition in Western Guatemala',
Comparative Studies in Society and History 26, no. 2, (1984). Smith's long
article on the urban sector, 'El Desarrollo de la primacia urbana', *Mesoamérica,* no. 8 (1984), is one of the very few studies to follow the pioneering
work in this field by Bryan Roberts, *Organizing Strangers* (Austin, Tex.,
1973), although it takes a more structural and historical perspective.

Much of the extensive work undertaken in the field of anthropology
subordinates historical approaches, but some studies in this discipline
have greatly advanced historical knowledge and thrown light on contempo-
rary socio-political developments: Eric Wolf, *Sons of the Shaking Earth*
(Chicago, 1959); Ruth Bunzel, *Chichicastenango. A Guatemalan Village*
(Seattle, 1952); Ricardo Falla, *Quiché Rebelde* (Guatemala, 1979); John D.
Early, 'The Changing Proportion of Maya Indian and Ladino in the Popula-
tion of Guatemala, in 1954–1969', *American Ethnologist,* 2, no. 2 (1975);
Paul Diener, 'The Tears of St Anthony: Ritual and Revolution in Eastern
Guatemala', *Latin American Perspectives* 5, no. 3 (1978); Robert M.
Carmack, 'Spanish-Indian Relations in Highland Guatemala, 1800–
1944', in Murdo J. Macleod and Robert Wasserstrom (eds.), *Spaniards and
Indians in South Eastern Mesoamerica: Essays in the History of Ethnic Relations*
(Lincoln, Neb., 1983); 'Death and Disorder in Guatemala', *Cultural Survival Quarterly* 7, no. 1, Special issue (1983); and *Panzós: testimonio* (Guatemala, 1979). A magisterial but highly controversial survey of the history
of the 'Indian question' is given in Severo Martínez Peláez, *La patria del
criollo* (Guatemala, 1973), to which a vivid and powerful autobiographical
counterpoint may be found in Elizabeth Burgos Debray (ed.), *I . . .
Rigoberta Menchú* (London, 1983). Both works are placed in a general
contemporary context in Carol A. Smith, 'Indian Class and Class Consciousness in Pre-revolutionary Guatemala', Working Paper no. 162, Latin American Program Woodrow Wilson Center (Washington, D.C.,
1984).

Consolidated studies of developments in the formal and national circles
of power and politics are much thinner on the ground. Other than the
contemporary hagiographies, Kenneth J. Grieb, *Guatemalan Caudillo: The
Regime of Jorge Ubico* (Athens, Ohio, 1979), is a solitary study and remains
the principal consolidated source on politics during the 1930s. The final
section of David McCreery, 'Debt Servitude in Rural Guatemala, 1876–
1936', *Hispanic American Historical Review* 63, no. 4 (1983), provides a
somewhat more sober view of the impact of Ubico's policies in one important area. The relevant chapters of Handy's *Gift of the Devil* are the best

substitute for the startling lack of a comprehensive survey of the reform between 1944 and 1954. However, certain aspects of this period are covered in Ronald M. Schneider, *Communism in Guatemala, 1944–1954* (New York, 1958); Leo A. Suslow, *Aspects of Social Reform in Guatemala, 1944–1949* (New York, 1950); Neale J. Pearson, 'Guatemala: The Peasant Union Movement, 1944–1954', in Henry A. Landsberger (ed.), *Latin American Peasant Movements* (Ithaca, N.Y., 1969); and Robert Wasserstrom, 'Revolution in Guatemala: Peasants and Politics under the Arbenz Government', *Comparative Studies in Society and History* 17, no. 4 (1975); Luis Cardoza y Aragón, *La Revolución Guatemaltica* (Guatemala City, 1955); Manuel Galich, *Por Que Lucha Guatemala. Arévalo y Arbenz. Dos hombres contra un Imperio* (Bueno Aires, 1956). Far greater attention has been paid to the intervention and counter-revolution of 1954, but the leading studies of that crisis do consider its local background to varying degree: Stephen Schlesinger and Stephen Kinzer, *Bitter Fruit. The Untold Story of the American Coup in Guatemala* (New York, 1982); Richard H. Immerman, *The CIA in Guatemala: The Foreign Policy of Intervention* (Austin, Tex., 1982); José M. Aybar de Soto, *Dependency and Intervention: The Case of Guatemala in 1954* (Boulder, Colo., 1978). A wider range of Guatemalan and U.S. literature on the intervention and its background is noted in Julio Adolfo Rey, 'Revolution and Liberation: A Review of Recent Literature on the Guatemalan Situation', *Hispanic American Historical Review* 38, no. 2 (1958).

From 1954 the government of Guatemala rested largely with the military and proved resistant to detailed monographic treatment. Differing views on the electoral process can be found in Kenneth F. Johnson, 'The Guatemalan Presidential Election of March 16, 1966: An Analysis' (Institute for the Comparative Study of Politics, Washington, D.C., 1967), and John W. Sloan, 'Electoral Frauds and Social Change: The Guatemalan Example', *Science and Society* 34, no. 3 (1970). A polemical, pro-guerrilla perspective is taken in Eduardo Galeano, *Guatemala: Occupied Country* (New York, 1969), and views from within the guerrilla provided in Ricardo Ramírez, *Lettres du Front Guatemaltèque* (Paris, 1970), and Orlando Fernández, *Turcios Lima* (Havana, 1968), themselves subjected to unsympathetic analysis in David A. Crain, 'Guatemalan Revolutionaries and Havana's Ideological Offensive of 1966–1968', *Journal of Inter-American Studies* 17, no. 2 (1975). Mario Payeras, *Days of the Jungle: The Testimony of a Guatemalan Guerrillero, 1972–76* (New York, 1983), is an insider's account of the emergence of the second generation of rebels against a military order described in great detail and with minimal sympathy in Michael McClintock, *The American Connection: State Terror and Popular Resistance in Guatemala* (London, 1985). Both sides are depicted in the polemical study of contemporary politics by George Black, *Garrison Guatemala* (London, 1984), which is more up-to-date but less sober and interested in socio-economic developments than Roger Plant, *Guatemala: Unnatural Disaster* (London, 1978), while a wider variety of sources is provided in Jonathan Fried et al. (eds.), *Guatemala in Rebellion: Unfinished History* (New York, 1983), which shares the radical tone of the other two texts.

5. EL SALVADOR SINCE 1930

Despite a significant increase in the number of studies – largely of a secondary character – since 1980, the scholarly literature on El Salvador in the twentieth century remains thin. Although they were written before the political developments that prompted the 'new wave' of books, two English language texts remain indispensable as general surveys: David Browning, *El Salvador: Landscape and Society* (Oxford, 1971), which adopts a predominantly geographical approach to socio-economic development, and Alastair White, *El Salvador* (London, 1973), which devotes more space to history and politics. Mario Flores Macal, *Origen, desarrollo y crisis de las formas de dominación en El Salvador* (San José, 1983), and Rafael Guidos Vejar, *Ascenso del militarismo en El Salvador* (San José, 1982) provide general overviews of political history, while the work of Rafael Menjivar links politics more closely to developments in political economy: see *Crisis del desarrollismo: caso El Salvador* (San José, 1977); *El Salvador: el eslabón mas pequeño* (San José, 1981); and *Formación y lucha del proletariado* (San José, 1982). Menjivar also contributes a chapter to *Centroamérica hoy* (Mexico, 1976), an important collection of comparative essays that situates the country within a regional framework. W. H. Durham, *Scarcity and Survival in Central America: ecological origins of the Soccer Wars* (Stanford, 1979) also takes a comparative approach, contrasting the rural subsistence economy of the country with that in Honduras, a counterpoint being given by Eduardo Colindres, *Fundamentos económicos de la burgesía salvadoreña* (San José, 1977), which was the basis for the author's many articles on the landlord class and direction of the modern coffee and cotton sectors. Other useful economic surveys include T. J. Downing, 'Agricultural Modernization in El Salvador' (Occasional Paper, Centre for Latin American Studies,

University of Cambridge, 1978), and Hector Dada, *La economía de El Salvador y la integración social, 1954–1960* (San José, 1983).

Segundo Montes, *El compadrazgo: una estructura de poder en El Salvador* (San Salvador, 1979), and Carlos Cabarrús, *Génesis de una revolución* (Mexico, 1983), are rare studies of social structure, the first concentrating on aspects of Indian society and the second focussed on the north of the country and the origins of the contemporary peasant rebellion. There is still no adequate study of the 1932 revolt from the perspective of the peasantry, but the general origins and political course of the uprising are covered in some detail by Thomas P. Anderson, *Matanza: El Salvador's Communist Revolt of 1932* (Lincoln, Nebr., 1971). Roque Dalton, *Miguel Marmol* (New York, 1987) is an outstanding biographical account of a radical activist that covers the first four decades of the twentieth century. A modest biography of the Communist leader of the 1932 rising is provided by Jorge Arias Gómez, *Farabundo Martí* (San José, 1972), but none yet exists for General Martínez. Aspects of Martínez's government are, however, covered in Kenneth J. Grieb, 'The United States and the Rise of General Maximiliano Hernández Martínez', *Journal of Latin American Studies*, 3, no. 2 (1970); Everett Wilson, 'The Crisis of National Integration in El Salvador, 1919–1935', unpublished Ph.D. thesis, Stanford, 1970, and Robert E. Elam, 'Appeal to Arms: The Army and Politics in El Salvador, 1931–1964, unpublished Ph.D. thesis, University of New Mexico, 1968), which remains the best resource on modern military history. The 1969 war with Honduras is treated in general terms by Thomas P. Anderson, *The War of the Dispossessed: Honduras and El Salvador, 1969* (Lincoln, Neb., 1981), and within a socio-economic framework in Marco Carías and Daniel Slutsky (eds.), *La guerra inutil* (San José, 1971), and Vincent Cable, 'The "Football War" and the Central American Common Market', *International Affairs* 45 (1969). Material on modern political parties is scarce, the only monograph being Stephen Webre, *José Napoleón Duarte and the Christian Democratic Party in Salvadoran Politics, 1960–1978* (Baton Rouge, 1979), written before Duarte became president but valuable for its treatment of political life in the 1960s. A good example of orthodox political science that reflects the expectations of some democratic progress during that decade is Ronald H. McDonald, 'Electoral Behaviour and Political Development in Salvador', *Journal of Politics*, 31, no. 2 (1969).

Material on the 1970s and 1980s is much more extensive and frequently contains useful and original treatment of the previous period even though many contemporary books adopt a generally polemical tone. Latin America Bureau, *El Salvador Under General Romero* (London, 1979), contains a detailed analysis of the military regime of 1977 to 1979, and James Brockman, *The Word Remains: A Life of Oscar Romero* (New York, 1982), provides an interesting survey of local ecclesiastical life as well as a biography of the archbishop who opposed his namesake in the presidential palace. Jenny Pearce, *Promised Land: Peasant Rebellion in Chalatenango, El Salvador* (London, 1985) develops some of the themes of Cabarrús's text and is one of a growing caucus of books containing oral testimonies. Michael McClintock, *The American Connection: State Terror and Popular Resistance in El Salvador* (London, 1985) is no less unsympathetic to U.S. policies but provides considerable detailed information on the military and paramilitary forces, while Morton Halperin (ed.), *Report on Human Rights in El Salvador* (Washington, D.C., 1982) is one of the most lucid examples of the burgeoning oeuvre that itemizes the results of their activity. General studies of political developments since the early 1970s include: Enrique Baloyra, *El Salvador in Transition* (Chapel Hill, N.C., 1982); Robert Armstrong and Janet Shenk, *El Salvador: The Face of Revolution* (London, 1982); James Dunkerley, *The Long War: Dictatorship and Revolution in El Salvador,* 2d. ed. (London, 1985); Tommy Sue Montgomery, *Revolution in El Salvador: Origins and Evolution* (Boulder, Colo., 1982). Tomás Guerra (ed.), *Octubre Sangriento* (San José, 1980), and Dermot Keogh, 'The Myth of the Liberal Coup: The United States and the 15th October 1979 Coup in El Salvador', *Millennium* 13, no. 2 (1984) concentrate on the important final months of 1979. Mario Menéndez, *El Salvador: una auténtica guerra civil* (San José, 1980) is a highly partisan but vivid account of the guerrilla war. Adolfo Gilly, *Guerra y política en El Salvador* (Mexico, 1981), contains suggestive political essays from the left on the first phase on the conflict. And Raymond Bonner, *Weakness and Deceit: U.S. Policy and El Salvador* (New York, 1985), is a detailed account of the following years from a journalist's perspective as well as a strong attack on U.S. policy.

6. HONDURAS SINCE 1930

The social and economic backwardness of Honduras in the period since 1930 is reflected in the shortage of good general works and specialized monographs. Only in the last few years, as Honduras has become a focus of international attention, has the situation begun to change, although few works on Honduras in this recent period can be regarded as scholarly.

One of the more satisfactory general studies of Honduras is Mario Posas and Rafael Del Cid, *La construción del sector público y del estado nacional en Honduras 1870–1979* (Tegucigalpa, 1981), which is broader in coverage than its title implies and particularly strong in its interpretation of the period up to 1972. The standard text on Honduras in English is William S. Stokes, *Honduras: An Area Study of Government* (Madison, Wisc., 1950), a remarkably detailed picture of Honduras up to the close of the Cariato, but weak on economics. James Morris, *Honduras; Caudillo Politics and Military Rulers* (Boulder, Colo., 1984), tries to pick up the story where Stokes left it but lacks Stokes' insights and is rather descriptive. As a solid introduction to Honduras, although very heavy on factual information, Howard Blutstein et al., *Area Handbook for Honduras* (Washington, D.C., 1970) still has value.

No history of Honduras in the twentieth century can ignore the fruit companies. On the earlier period, there is a wealth of information in Charles Kepner and Jay Soothill, *The Banana Empire: A Case Study in Economic Imperialism* (New York, 1935). The Standard Fruit and Steamship Company has found a competent biographer in Thomas Karnes, *Tropical Enterprise* (Baton Rouge, 1978), but the United Fruit Company has still not spawned a satisfactory monograph; Stacy May and Galo Plazo, *The United Fruit Company in Latin America* (New York, 1958) is a eulogistic account. There is, however, a good study of the Honduran banana industry from its origins in V. Lainez and V. Meza, 'El enclave bananero en la historia de Honduras' in *Estudios Sociales Centroamericanos* (May, 1973). A similar, slightly more detailed study is Daniel Slutzky and Esther Alonso, *Empresas transnacionales y agricultura: el caso del enclave bananero en Honduras* (Tegucigalpa, 1982). The dispute between rival banana companies, which nearly provoked a war between Honduras and Guatemala, is described in Virgilio Rodríguez Beteta, *No es guerra de hermanos sino de bananos* (Guatemala, 1980).

The Cariato (1933–48) remains one of the most barren periods in Honduran historiography. There is a most unflattering portrait of the dictator in Filánder Díaz Chávez, *Carias – el ultimo caudillo frutero* (Tegucigalpa, 1982), and an interesting study of the problems facing the Liberal Party at this time in Carlos A. Contreras, *Entre el marasmo: analisis de la crisis del Partido Liberal de Honduras 1933–1970* (Tegucigalpa, 1970).

There is also an account of Honduras in this and later periods in Guillermo Molina Chocano, 'Honduras: de la Guerra Civil al Reformismo Militar', in Pablo Gonzalez Casanova (ed.), *América Latina: historia de medio siglo,* vol 2 (Mexico, 1978). The last years of the Cariato and the relationship between Honduras and the United States during that period are covered in Thomas Leonard, *The United States and Central America, 1944–49* (Birmingham, Ala., 1984). For the economic history of Honduras in these years there is much of interest in the Comisión Económica para América Latina (CEPAL), *El desarrollo económico de Honduras* (Santiago, 1960).

The banana strike of 1954 deserves a monograph in its own right but has not yet received one. One of the best discussions of the strike is to be found in Mario Posas, *El Movimiento Campesino Hondureño* (Tegucigalpa, 1981). A study that compares the strike with the peasant uprising in El Salvador in 1932 is Vinicio González, 'La Insurrección Salvadoreña de 1932 y la Gran Huelga Hondureña de 1954', *Revista Mexicana de Sociología* (April 1978). Other competent works on the Honduran labour movement are Victor Meza, *Historia del Movimiento Obrero Hondureño* (Tegucigalpa, 1980), and Mario Posas, *Lucha ideológica y organización sindical en Honduras* (Tegucigalpa, 1980). There is also an interesting anthology for the 1970s by Victor Meza, *Antología del Movimiento Obrero Hondureño* (Tegucigalpa, 1980).

The social reforms begun under President Ramón Villeda Morales are studied in several works. There is a good biography of Villeda Morales, which discusses his social programme in detail, by Stefania Natalini de Castro, María de los Angeles Mendoza Saborio and Joaquín Pagan Solorzano, *Significado histórico del gobierno del Dr. Ramón Villeda Morales* (Tegucigalpa, 1985). The agrarian reform is usefully discussed in R. Robleda, 'Latifundio, Reforma Agraria y Modernización', *Economía Política* (January 1982). This journal, published by the Instituto de Investigaciones Económicas y Sociales at the Universidad Nacional Autónoma de Honduras, has done much to stimulate research and writing on twentieth century Honduran social science. A good study of agrarian reform, bringing the story up to the mid-1980s, is Charles Brockett, 'Public Policy, Peasants and Rural Development in Honduras', *Journal of Latin American Studies* 19/1 (1987).

The war with El Salvador in 1969 is discussed thoroughly in Thomas Anderson, *The War of the Dispossessed* (Lincoln, Neb., 1981). Another study, which concentrates much more on the international law aspects of the dispute, is James Rowles, *El conflicto Honduras–El Salvador* (San José,

1980). However, William Durham's study of the ecological origins of the war remains by far the most satisfactory; *Scarcity and Survival in Central America* (Stanford, 1979). This was the first work to draw proper attention to the land shortage created by Honduran geography on the one hand and demographic pressure on the other. It finally dispelled the notion that Honduras was a land-surplus country. There is also an interesting series of essays in Marco Carías and Daniel Slutzky (eds.), *La Guerra Inutil: Análisis socioeconómico del conflicto entre Honduras y El Salvador* (San José, 1971).

Several works cover Honduran economic development in recent decades. In INFORPRESS, *El Futuro del Mercado Comun Centroamericano* (Guatemala, 1983), there is an illuminating discussion of the reasons for Honduras' departure from the Central American Common Market. A fine, detailed study of the emergence of the beef industry is Daniel Slutzky, 'La agroindustria de la carne en Honduras', *Economía Política* (July 1977). On Honduran industrialization see Rafael Del Cid, 'Honduras: industrialización, empleo y explotación de la fuerza de trabajo', *Economía Política,* no. 13 (1977). An overview of Honduran economic development can be found in Benjamín Villanueva, 'Institutional Innovation and Economic Development, Honduras: A Case Study', unpublished Ph.D. thesis, University of Wisconsin, 1968. Surprisingly, there is still no major work on the Honduran coffee sector.

There have been remarkably few studies on the military as an institution in Honduras. An early effort is Steve Ropp, 'The Honduran Army in the Sociopolitical Evolution of the Honduran State', *The Americas* 30 (April 1974). Ropp, with James Morris, has attempted to build a corporate model to explain Honduran development, but the result is not wholly convincing: 'Corporatism and Dependent Development: A Honduran Case Study', *Latin American Research Review* 12 (Summer 1977). There are also few works on the Catholic Church as an institution in Honduras, although several books describe the growing political involvement of individuals within the Church. See, for example, Father James Guadalupe Carney, *To Be a Revolutionary* (San Francisco, 1987), the posthumously published autobiography of a Catholic priest killed in eastern Honduras.

The growing U.S. involvement in Honduras in the 1980s and the repercussions of the regional crisis on Honduras have produced a huge literature of uneven quality. One of the better efforts is Mark Rosenberg and Philip Shepherd (eds.), *Honduras Confronts Its Future* (Boulder, Colo., 1986), which presents a series of essays by leading Hondurans on the political economy of the 1980s. A perceptive account of the recent period can be found in Guillermo Molina Chocano, 'Honduras: la situación política y económica reciente', in Donaldo Castillo Rivas, *Centroamérica – más allá de la crisis* (Mexico, 1983). Finally, mention should be made of a book by Gautama Fonseca, a Honduran journalist who has written a number of reflective essays on the Honduran political system: *Cuatro ensayos sobre la realidad política de Honduras* (Tegucigalpa, 1982).

7. NICARAGUA SINCE 1930

Nicaraguan historiography is extremely uneven in both quality and quantity. Although there is still no satisfactory general work on the years since independence, certain events in Nicaraguan history have attracted enormous attention, notably the proposed inter-oceanic canal in the nineteenth century; the U.S. occupation in the first third of the twentieth century; the Sandino episode; and, more recently, the Sandinista revolution.

The international attention devoted to Nicaragua since the collapse of the Somoza dynasty in 1979 has created a demand for comprehensive bibliographies, previously a neglected area. The most impressive is the three-volume *Nicaraguan National Bibliography, 1800–1978,* produced by the Latin American Bibliographic Foundation (Redlands, Calif., 1986–7), with more than twenty thousand entries. A more modest, but useful, bibliography is in the Clio Press series: Ralph Lee Woodward, Jr., *Nicaragua* (Oxford and Santa Barbara, 1983). For the post-1979 period, there is such a rapid increase in publications every year that any bibliography runs the risk of being out-of-date as soon as it is published. Hans Aalborg, however, has compiled a helpful work for the first five years of the revolution: *The Nicaraguan Development Process* (Centre for Development Research, Copenhagen, 1984).

Of several good works on the U.S. occupation of Nicaragua, which ended in 1933, the best is William Kamman, *A Search for Stability: United States Diplomacy Towards Nicaragua, 1925–1933* (Notre Dame, Ind., 1968), although this focusses almost exclusively on the period after the marines returned to Nicaragua in 1926. Roscoe Hill, *Fiscal Intervention in Nicaragua* (New York, 1933), is an excellent study dealing with the non-military side of U.S. intervention. For a dry, but very thorough, account of the intervention years, see Department of State, *The United States and Nicaragua: A Survey of the Relations from 1909 to 1932* (Washington, D.C., 1932). A more interesting account, written by a U.S. journalist, is Harold Denny, *Dollars for Bullets: The Story of American Rule in Nicaragua* (New

York, 1929). This book was deservedly reprinted by Greenwood Press in 1980.

The Sandino episode has generated two waves of publications. The first, written by contemporaries, ended with the publication of Anastasio Somoza, *El verdadero Sandino, o el Calvario de las Segovias* (Managua, 1936). The second wave began with the Nicaraguan revolution and has been spearheaded by the Instituto de Estudio del Sandinismo in Managua. During both these periods, writings on Sandino and Sandinismo have suffered from a lack of scholarly detachment. Fortunately, a small number of works were produced on Sandino between the two waves, which are exemplary in their attention to detail; these include Neill Macaulay, *The Sandino Affair* (Chicago, 1967), and Gregorio Selser, *Sandino: General de Hombres Libres*, 2 vols. (Buenos Aires, 1959), although the latter is at times somewhat uncritical. Mention should also be made of Donald Hodges, *Intellectual Foundations of the Nicaraguan Revolution* (Austin, Tex., 1986); although Hodges does not succeed in his ambition to establish Sandino as a consistent and original political thinker, he does provide a wealth of new material and gives due attention to the intellectual climate in which the Sandino episode evolved. Another excellent book, drawing attention to the international and regional situation at the start of the 1930s, is Rodolfo Cerdas Cruz, *La hoz y el Machete* (San José, 1986), which, while focussing on the role of the Communist International throughout Central America, devotes a great deal of research to Nicaragua during the Sandino episode.

A number of general works on the history of Nicaragua during the years of the Somoza dynasty include Richard Millett, *Guardians of the Dynasty* (New York, 1977), concerned mainly with the National Guard from its formation at the end of the 1920s but with much of interest on other aspects of Nicaraguan society. Both Bernard Diederich, *Somoza* (London, 1982), and Eduardo Crawley, *Dictators Never Die* (London, 1979), are primarily concerned with the Somoza family but also furnish useful accounts of the general political background. Claribel Alegría and D. J. Flakoll, *Nicaragua: la revolución Sandinista: una crónica política 1855–1979* (Mexico, 1982), is a good account of the rebirth of the Sandinista movement after the assassination of Sandino in 1934; despite the title, however, it has little to say on the period before Sandino's death. Another useful book focussing on the revival of Sandinismo is Hugo Cancino Troncoso, *Las raíces históricas e ideológicas del movimiento Sandinista: antecedentes de la revolución nacional y popular Nicaragüense, 1927–1979* (Odense University

Press, 1984). Finally, mention should be made of Humberto Ortega's *50 años de lucha Sandinista*, which, published in 1976 in 'algún lugar de Nicaragua', provides the Frente Sandinista de Liberación Nacional account of how the Sandinista struggles of the 1960s and 1970s were linked to the much earlier Sandino episode.

The economic history of Nicaragua has attracted growing interest since the publication of Jaime Wheelock's influential *Imperialismo y dictadura: crisis de una formación social* (Mexico, 1975). Jaime Biderman, 'Class Structure, The State and Capitalist Development in Nicaraguan Agriculture' (unpublished Ph.D. dissertation, University of California, 1982), is an excellent study highlighting the rise of the cotton industry after the 1940s. Earlier works which still have much to offer include International Bank for Reconstruction and Development, *The Economic Development of Nicaragua* (Washington, D.C., 1953); Comisión Económica para América Latina, *El desarrollo económico de Nicaragua,* (New York, 1966), and Luis Cantarero, 'The Economic Development of Nicaragua, 1920–47' (unpublished Ph.D. dissertation, University of Iowa, 1948).

The labour movement under the Somoza dynasty, neglected for years, has recently received some attention. A good study of the 1940s is Jeffrey Gould, ' "For an Organised Nicaragua": Somoza and the Labour Movement, 1944–1948', *Journal of Latin American Studies* 19, no. 2 (1987). A more general work is Carlos Pérez Bermúdez and Onofre Guevara, *El Movimiento Obrero en Nicaragua* (Managua, 1985). This controversial work seeks to justify the role played by the Partido Socialista Nicaragüense under Somoza but nevertheless is an unrivalled source of information on many aspects of the labour movement's history.

The Nicaraguan revolution leading to the overthrow of Somoza has produced many books and articles, of which the best are John Booth, *The End and the Beginning: the Nicaraguan Revolution* (Boulder, Colo., 1982), and George Black, *Triumph of the People: The Sandinista Revolution in Nicaragua* (London, 1981). Anastasio Somoza's own version of the events leading to his overthrow, *Nicaragua Betrayed* (Boston, 1980), gives a very partial, but fascinating, description of his relationship with the Carter administration. This same question is taken up by Robert Pastor in *Condemned to Repetition: the United States and Nicaragua* (Princeton, 1987), where the author makes a courageous effort to explore what went wrong in a relationship in which he himself played a minor part as President Carter's Latin American specialist on the National Security Council.

The period since the revolution has seen an explosion in writings on

Nicaragua. The best of these tend to be sympathetic to the revolution, but fall short of the highest standards of scholarship; examples are Thomas Walker (ed.), *Nicaragua: The First Five Years* (New York, 1985); Carlos Vilas, *The Sandinista Revolution* (New York, 1986); and Richard Harris and Carlos Vilas (eds.), *Nicaragua: A Revolution Under Siege* (London, 1985). A less committed but still sympathetic treatment of the revolutionary period can be found in David Close, *Nicaragua: Politics, Economics and Society* (London, 1988). Works critical of the revolutionary period tend to be written by exiles or foreigners without access to primary sources; among the better examples is Xavier Zavala et al., *1984 Nicaragua* (San José, 1985).

Economic development, including agrarian reform, under the Sandinista regime has begun to receive the attention it deserves. A good example, bringing together many of the best scholars in the field, is Rose Spalding (ed.), *The Political Economy of Revolutionary Nicaragua* (Boston, 1987). Specialist works on agriculture include Forrest Colburn, *Post-Revolutionary Nicaragua: State Class and the Dilemmas of Agrarian Policy* (Berkeley, 1986), although this study was subsequently overtaken by changes in Nicaraguan agrarian reform. The latter is studied in a large number of articles, including I. Luciak, 'National Unity and Popular Hegemony: The Dialectics of Sandinista Agrarian Reform Policies, 1979–86', *Journal of Latin American Studies* 19 (1987), and Carmen Diana Deere, Peter Marchetti and Nola Reinhardt, 'The Peasantry and the Development of Sandinista Agrarian Policy, 1979–84', *Latin American Research Review* 20 (1985).

Sandinista foreign policy, a major source of friction in U.S.–Nicaraguan relations, is discussed in Mary Vanderlaan, *Revolution and Foreign Policy in Nicaragua* (Boulder, Colo., 1986). The Catholic Church in Nicaragua has received a great deal of attention in recent years, both because of the friction between the hierarchy and the Sandinista government and because of the growth of a 'popular' church. A thoughtful study which reflects both sides of the question is Laura O'Shaugnessy and Luis Serra, *The Church and Revolution in Nicaragua* (Athens, Ohio, 1986). Another work along similar lines is Rosa Maria Pochet and Abelino Martinez, *Iglesia: manipulación o profecía?* (San José, 1987).

The Atlantic coast region and its ethnic minorities have not yet received proper attention. Craig Dozier, *Nicaragua's Mosquito Shore: The Years of British and American Experience* (Birmingham, Ala., 1986), gives an excellent account of the coast in the nineteenth century, but offers only a sketchy treatment of the more recent period. It is to be hoped, however, that the new Centro de Investigación y Documentación de la Costa Atlántica, which has begun the difficult task of assembling in Nicaragua the relevant documents, will stimulate research in this area. A special issue of the Nicaraguan journal *Encuentro* was devoted to the Atlantic coast in 1985 and deals with both the past and present; see 'La Costa Atlántica: Pasado y Presente', *Encuentro* (April-September, 1985).

8. COSTA RICA SINCE 1930

A pioneering general interpretation of Costa Rica that considers the country's development from a variety of perspectives is Samuel Stone, *La dinastía de los Conquistadores* (San José, 1975). The same broad approach is also adopted in the excellent studies written by Carolyn Hall: *El café y el desarrollo histórico-geográfico de Costa Rica* (San José, 1976) and *Costa Rica: una interpretación geográfica con perspectiva histórica* (San José, 1984). Other general interpretative surveys include José L. Vega, *Poder político y democracia en Costa Rica* (San José, 1982), and *Orden y progreso: la formación del estado nacional en Costa Rica* (San José, 1975); Carlos Meléndez's more dated *Costa Rica: evolución de sus problemas más destacados* (San José, 1953); Wilburg Jiménez, *Génesis del gobierno de Costa Rica, 1821–1981* (San José, 1986), which concentrates upon administrative issues; and the collection of provocative essays edited by Chester Zelaya, *Costa Rica contemporánea* (San José, 1979). The perspective of the Partido Liberación Nacional (PLN) is reflected in Carlos Monge, *Historia de Costa Rica* (San José, 1962); Eugenio Rodríguez, *Apuntes para una sociología costarricense* (San José, 1953) and Hugo Navarro, *La generación del 48. Juicio histórico sobre la democracia costarricense* (Mexico, 1957). For a rigorously Marxist interpretation, see Reinaldo Carcanholo, *Desarrollo del capitalismo en Costa Rica* (San José, 1981).

Studies of social groups and the development of the labour force include: Lowell Gudmundson, *Hacendados políticos y precaristas: la ganadería y el latifundismo guanacasteco, 1800–1950* (San José, 1983); Mitchell Seligson, *Peasants of Costa Rica and the Development of Agrarian Capitalism* (Madison, Wisc., 1980); Roger Churnside, *Formación de la Fuerza Laboral Costarricense* (San José, 1985). Raimundo Santos and Liliana Herrera, *Del artesano al obrero fabril* (San José, 1979) is strongly syndicalist in its approach but contains useful information. Important studies of other sectors include: Víctor H. Acuña, 'La ideología de los pequeños y medianos productores cafetaleros costarricenses', and Alfonso González, 'El discurso oficial de los pequeños y medianos cafetaleros (1920–1940; 1950–1961)' in *Revista de Historia,* Universidad Nacional, Heredia, no. 16 (1987); and Manuel Rojas, 'El Movimiento Obrero en Costa Rica', in P. González Casanova (ed.), *Historia del movimiento obrero en América Latina* (Mexico, 1984). The debate over the nature of social and political power in the country is engaged from an entirely different perspective in the two volumes written by Oscar Arias: *Grupos de presión en Costa Rica* (San José, 1971), and *Quién gobierna en Costa Rica?* (San José, 1977). A number of studies analyse the role of elites from different sectors of the economy. For the cattle ranchers, see Irene Aguilar and Manuel Solís, *La elite ganadera en Costa Rica* (San José, 1988). For sugar, see Mayra Achio and Ana C. Escalante, *Azúcar y política en Costa Rica* (San José, 1985). For the banana industry, Chester Lloyd Jones, *Costa Rica and Civilization in the Caribbean* (Madison, Wisc., 1935) remains useful for the background; Frank Ellis, *Las transnacionales del banano en Centroamerica* (San José, 1983), covers the more modern period from an economist's perspective; and Jeffrey Casey Gaspar, *Limón: 1880–1940. Un estudio de la industria bananera en Costa Rica* (San José, 1979), provides an excellent case study.

The question of land tenure, which acquired particular importance in the post-war era, is treated in CEPAL, *Costa Rica: características de uso y distribución de la tierra* (San José, 1972), and critically analysed in two suggestive essays: Mario Fernández, 'Dinámica de capital, evolución de la estructura de la tenencia de la tierra y paisaje rural en Costa Rica', *Revista de Estudios Centroamericanos,* no. 36 (1983), and Edelberto Torres Rivas, 'Elementos para la caracterización de la estructura agraria de Costa Rica', *Avances de Investigación,* Instituto de Investigaciones Sociales, Universidad de Costa Rica (San José, 1978). The role of the state in economic development became the subject of increasing debate with the onset of economic crisis at the end of the 1970s. Rodolfo Cerdas provided an early contibution in 'Del estado intervencionista al estado empresario. Notas para el estudio del estado en Costa Rica', *Anuario de Estudios Centroamericanos,* no. 5 (1979), and 'La crisis política nacional: origen y perspectivas', in Armando Vargas (ed.), *La crisis de democracia en Costa Rica* (San José, 1981). Other works that consider this subject in the light of modern developments in the country's political economy include: Ana Sojo, *Estado empresario y lucha política en Costa Rica* (San José, 1984); Mylena Vega, *El estado costarricense de 1974 a 1978. CODESA y la fracción industrial* (San José, 1982); Helio Fallas, *Crisis económica en Costa Rica* (San José, 1980); and Juan M. Villasuso (ed.), *El sector productivo: crisis y perspectivas* (San José 1984). The liberal approach to this issue is represented in Víctor H. Cespedes, Alberto Dimare and Ronulfo Jiménez, *Costa Rica: recuperación sin reactivación* (San José, 1985), and in the publications of the Academia de Centroamérica, such as *Problemas Económicos de la Década de los 80* (San José 1982) and *Costa Rica: estabilidad sin crecimiento* (San José, 1984).

Among general surveys of the evolution of political thought, two in particular stand out: Constantino Láscaris, *Desarrollo de las ideas filosóficas en Costa Rica* (San José, 1983), and Luis Barahona, *Las ideas políticas en Costa Rica* (San José, 1977). Those who are particularly interested in the philosophical influences on the 'Generation of '48' who dominated the country's politics after the civil war of that year should also consult Roberto Brenes, *El político* (San José, 1942).

The literature on modern history is notably uneven in terms of its concentration on certain periods, particular attention being paid to the late 1940s. However, a number of valuable studies consider the social and political background to the crisis of the 1930s that decisively influenced subsequent developments. For an excellent appraisal of a leading political figure of the 'Olympian' epoch, see Eugenio Rodríquez, *Ricardo Jiménez Oreamuno: su pensamiento* (San José, 1980), which is usefully complemented by Joaquín Vargas Coto, *Crónicas de la epoca y vida de Don Ricardo* (San José, 1986). Marina Volio, *Jorge Volio y el Partido Reformista* (San José, 1972), and Miguel Acuña, *Jorge Volio, el Tribuno de la Plebe* (San José, 1972) give good accounts of the career and ideas of the leading oppositionist of the 1920s, whose influence is discernable in later decades. More general surveys of this period include Cleto González, *El sufragio en Costa Rica ante la historia y la legislación* (San José, 1978), and Tomás Soley, *Historia Económica de Costa Rica* (San José, 1949). International relations are treated in Richard Salisbury, *Costa Rica y el Istmo, 1900–1934* (San José, 1984). The development of the labour movement, which exercised growing influence from the early 1930s, is presented in Vladimir de la Cruz, *Las luchas sociales en Costa Rica (1870–1930)* (San José, 1983).

The birth of the Communist Party is set in its socio-economic context in Ana María Botey and Rodolfo Cisneros, *La crisis de 1929 y la fundación del Partido Comunista de Costa Rica* (San José, 1984), and analysed in terms of external influences in Rodolfo Cerdas, *La Hoz y el Machete. La Internacional Comunista en América Latina y la Revolución en Centro América* (San

José, 1986). The speeches and activities of its principal leaders provide a vital source for understanding the party's subsequent development: Gilberto Calvo and Francisco Zúñiga (eds.), *Manuel Mora: discursos (1934–1979)* (San José, 1980); Arnoldo Ferreto, *Vida militante* (San José, 1984); and Marielos Aguilar, *Carlos Luis Fallas: su época y sus luchas* (San José, 1983).

One of the very few studies of the administration of León Cortés (1936–40) is Theodore A. Creedman, 'León Cortés y su tiempo', *Anales de la Academia de Geografía e Historia de Costa Rica*, (1967–9). Carlos Calvo, *Costa Rica en la Segunda Guerra Mundial (1939–45)* (San José, 1985), provides an extensive analysis of the war years, and relations with the United States up to the Cold War are treated in some detail in Jacobo Schifter, *Las alianzas conflictivas: las relaciones de Estados Unidos y Costa Rica desde la segunda guerra mundial a la guerra fría* (San José, 1986). Another work by this author, *La fase oculta de la guerra civil en Costa Rica* (San José, 1981), provides a complementary analysis of developments within the country during the civil conflict of 1948.

The civil war and its origins are the subjects of an extensive literature. Oscar Aguilar, *Costa Rica y sus hechos políticos de 1948: problemática de una década* (San José, 1969), contains a very useful selection of documents and interviews, as does Guillermo Villegas, *Testimonios del 48* (San José, 1977). The same author's *El otro Calderón Guardia* (San José, 1985) provides important insights on the leader of the defeated forces, and another text, *El Cardonazo* (San José, 1986), considers an important event in the immediate aftermath of the fighting. From the point of view of the victorious rebels, Alberto Cañas, *Los ocho años* (San José, 1955), continues to be a classic text, as is *El espíritu del 48* (San José, 1987), by their leader, José Figueres. Roberto Fernández, *La huelga de Brazos Caidos* (San José, 1953), gives a good depiction of the political atmosphere on the eve of the conflict. The perspective of the Communist Party is presented in Partido Vanguardia Popular, *Como y por qué cayó la democracia en Costa Rica* (Guatemala, 1948), and Manuel Mora, *Dos discursos en defensa de Vanguardia Popular* (San José, 1959). Later, and more sophisticated, interpretations made from the same political perspective include Manuel Rojas, *Lucha social y guerra civil en Costa Rica* (San José, 1980), and Gerardo Contreras and José Manuel Cerdas, *Los años 40: historia de una política de alianzas* (San José, 1988). The record of the defeated Picado regime is defended in Enrique Guier, *Defensa de los Señores Licenciados Teodoro Picado y Vicente Urcuyo* (San José, 1950), and by Picado himself in *El pacto de la embajada de*

Mexico; su incumplimiento (Managua, n.d.). Another attack on Figueres, this time for his failure to honour pledges to the Caribbean Legion, is made in Rosendo Argüello, *Quienes y como nos traicionaron* (Mexico, 1954). John Patrick Bell, *Crisis in Costa Rica: The 1948 Revolution* (Austin, Tex., 1971) remains one of the best sources on the civil war and its immediate background.

For studies of Archbishop Victor Sanabria, who played a major role in the political events of the 1940s, see Ricardo Blanco, *Monseñor Sanabria* (San José, 1962); Santiago Arrieta, *El pensamiento político-social de Monseñor Sanabria* (San José, 1977); and James Baker, *La iglesia y el sindicalismo en Costa Rica* (San José, 1978). Rafael Calderón Guardia is the subject of a number of studies in addition to that by Villegas just noted. Among the most useful are: Carlos Fernández, *Calderón Guardia: líder y caudillo* (San José, 1939); the compilation edited by Mario Hidalgo, *Dr Calderón Guardia: reformador social de Costa Rica* (San José, 1983); and Jorge M. Salazar, *Calderón Guardia* (San José, 1985). The literature on Figueres is more extensive and includes a number of eulogistic or uncritical works, such as Hugo Navarro, *José Figueres en la evolución de Costa Rica* (Mexico, 1953); Arturo Castro, *José Figueres: el hombre y su obra. Ensayo de una biografía* (San José, 1955); and Charles Ameringer, *Don Pepe: A Political Biography of José Figueres of Costa Rica* (Albuquerque, 1978). A useful bibliography is Harry Kantor, *Bibliography of José Figueres* (Tempe, Ariz., 1972); the same author's *The Costa Rican Election of 1953: A Case Study* (Gainesville, Fla., 1958) is also valuable to students of Figueres' role in national politics. The Constituent Assembly of 1949 is described from a journalistic perspective in Rubén Hernández, *Desde la barra: como se discutió la Constitución de 1949* (San José, 1953) while the Charter itself is analysed in the excellent work by Oscar Aguilar, *La Contitución Política de 1949: Antecedentes y Proyecciones* (San José, 1975). For broader consideration of constitutional issues, see Hernán G. Peralta, *Las Constituciones de Costa Rica* (Madrid, 1962), and Jorge Saénz, *El despertar constitucional de Costa Rica* (San José, 1985). The fullest survey of the nationalization of the banks undertaken during this period is Rufino Gil, *La nacionalización bancaria* (San José, 1962), which complements the same author's *Ciento cinco años de vida bancaria en Costa Rica* (San José, 1974). For the post-civil war administration of Otilio Ulate, José Luis Torres, *Otilio Ulate: su partido y sus luchas* (San José, 1986), stands alone in its field. It is usefully supplemented by Ulate's own writings, collected in *A la luz de la moral política* (San José, 1976). Further information on this period may be gleaned from the relevant chapters of two general studies: Joaquín Garro, *Veinte años de historia chica: notas para una historia costarricense* (San José, 1967), and Jorge Rovira, *Estado y política económica en Costa Rica, 1948–1970* (San José, 1983).

The presidency of Mario Echandi still awaits a detailed historical assessment. However, some interesting material is available in María Gamboa (ed.), *Los vetos del Presidente Echandi: sus razones y justificación: 1958–1962* (San José, 1962), and Mark Rosenberg, *Las luchas por el seguro social en Costa Rica* (San José, 1980). The literature on the Trejos Fernández administration is similarly thin, but important documentation is given in José J. Trejos Fernández, *Ocho años en la política costarricense* (San José, 1973), and a number of useful insights may be derived from Oscar Aguilar, *Democracia y partidos políticos en Costa Rica (1950–60)* (San José, 1977), and Jorge E. Romero, *Partidos, poder y derecho* (San José, 1979).

By contrast, the history of the PLN is covered by numerous works. For the party's background, see Carlos Araya, *Historia de los partidos políticos de Costa Rica: liberación nacional* (San José, 1968), which provides a most useful analysis despite the partisan position of the author. A key programmatic statement from the early years is *Ideario costarricense: resultado de una encuesta nacional* (San José, 1943), important documentation of subsequent developments being contained in two anthologies: Alfonso Carro (ed.), *El Pensamiento Socialdemócrata. Antología* (San José, 1986), and Carlos José Gutiérrez (ed.), *El pensamiento político costarricense: la socialdemocracia* (San José, 1986), which is more extensive and systematic in its coverage. The leaders of the PLN have themselves produced a number of important works. Daniel Oduber, *Raíces del Partido Liberación Nacional: Notas para una evaluación histórica* (San José, 1985), is extremely useful on the origins of the party, and Figueres' writings provide abundant material on the development of the PLN's ideology and outlook. *Cartas a un ciudadano* (San José, 1956); *Los deberes de mi destino* (San José, 1957); *Estos diez años* (San José, 1958); and *La pobreza de las naciones* (San José, 1973), are broadly representative of the ex-president's output, although it should be noted that his views did not always enjoy a consensus within the party. Moreover, an understanding of the early approach adopted by currents which were later to form the PLN cannot be gained without reference to the work of Rodrigo Facio, particularly *Estudio sobre economía costarricense* (San José, 1942); *El centro ante las garantías sociales* (San José, 1943); and *La moneda y la Banca Central en Costa Rica* (Mexico, 1947). For independent treatments of the party, see Burt H. English, *Liberación nacional in Costa Rica: The*

Development of a Political Party in a Transitional Society (Gainesville, Fla., 1971), and James L. Busey, *Notes on Costa Rican Democracy* (Boulder, Colo., 1962). A critical analysis is given in Susanne Jonas Bodenheimer, *La ideología socialdemócrata en Costa Rica* (San José, 1984). Analysis of elections constitutes an important feature of the literature on Costa Rican politics. Among the best work containing both data and interpretation, see Eduardo Oconitrillo, *Un siglo de política costarricense* (San José, 1981), and Wilburg Jiménez, *Análisis electoral de una democracia* (San José, 1977). Other studies in this area include Olda M. Acuña and Carlos F. Denton, *La elección de un presidente: Costa Rica 1982* (San José, 1984); Mario Sánchez, *Las bases sociales del voto en Costa Rica (1974–78)* (San José, 1985); and C. Granados and A. Ohlsson, 'Organización del Territorio y Resultados Electorales en Costa Rica, 1953–1982', *Estudios Sociales Centroamericanos,* no. 36 (1983).

The general survey of the post-war economy provided in Carlos Araya's *Historia económica de Costa Rica, 1950–1970* (San José, 1975) is complemented for the more recent period by Jorge Rovira, *Costa Rica en los años 80* (San José, 1987). The nature of industrialization in the post-war epoch is considered in Leonardo Garnier and Fernando Herrero, *El desarrollo de la industria en Costa Rica* (Heredia, 1982), and Garnier's 'Industria, Estado y Desarrollo en Costa Rica: Perspectivas y Propuestas', *Revista de Estudios Centroamericanos,* no. 37 (1984). The Escuela de Ciencias Económicas y Sociales of the Universidad de Costa Rica produced a number of publications concerning important economic developments from the late 1950s under the general title of *El desarrollo económico de Costa Rica: estudio del sector externo de la economía costarricense* (San José, 1958); *Estudio del sector industrial* (San José, 1959); and *Estudio del sector público* (San José, 1962). For an analysis of the country's economy in the immediate postwar period from a North American perspective, see Stacey May (ed.), *Costa Rica. A Study in Economic Development* (New York, 1952). Two quite different interpretations of developments in the modern era may be found in Rodolfo Cerdas, *Crisis de la democracia liberal en Costa Rica* (San José, 1972), and Sergio Reuben, *Capitalismo y crisis económica en Costa Rica* (San José, 1982).

INDEX